This book is due for return on or before the last date shown below.

Don Gresswell Ltd., London, N21   Cat. No. 1207   DG 02242/71

**BOLLETTIERI'S TENNIS
HANDBOOK by
BOLLETTIERI, NICK**

North Lincs College

Human Kinetics

NORTH LINCOLNSHIRE COLLEGE
LIBRARY

Library of Congress Cataloging-in-Publication Data

Bollettieri, Nick.
  Bollettieri's tennis handbook / Nick Bollettieri.
      p. cm.
  Rev. ed. of: Bollettieri. 1st ed. c1999.
  Includes bibliographical references and index.
  ISBN 0-7360-4036-6
    1. Tennis--Handbooks, manuals, etc. I. Bollettieri, Nick. Bollettieri. II. Title.

  GV995 .B68347 2001
  796 342--dc21   2001024449

ISBN: 0-7360-4036-6

This book is a revised edition of *Bollettieri Classic Tennis Handbook,* published in 1999 by Tennis Week.

Acquisitions Editor: Martin Barnard
Developmental Editor: Leigh LaHood
Copyeditor: Robert Replinger
Proofreader: Sarah Wiseman
Indexer: Betty Frizzéll
Graphic Designer: Nancy Rasmus
Graphic Artist: Judy Henderson
Cover Designer: Keith Blomberg
Photographer (covers and page 433): James Bollettieri © 2000
Photographers (interior): photos in chapter 11 by Tom Roberts; all other photos by Peter D. McCraw
Illustrator: Peter D. McCraw
Printer: Bang Printing

796·342

Purple

1001516

PUBLISHED PRICE
NET

£17.95

Human Kinetics books are available at special discounts for bulk purchase. Special editions or book excerpts can also be created to specification. For details, contact the Special Sales Manager at Human Kinetics.

Printed in the United States of America   10 9 8 7 6 5 4 3 2 1

Human Kinetics
Web site: www.humankinetics.com

United States: Human Kinetics
P.O. Box 5076
Champaign, IL 61825-5076
800-747-4457
e-mail: humank@hkusa.com

Canada: Human Kinetics
475 Devonshire Road Unit 100
Windsor, ON N8Y 2L5
800-465-7301 (in Canada only)
e-mail: orders@hkcanada.com

Europe: Human Kinetics
Units C2/C3 Wira Business Park
West Park Ring Road
Leeds LS16 6EB, United Kingdom
+44 (0) 113 278 1708
e-mail: hk@hkeurope.com

Australia: Human Kinetics
57A Price Avenue
Lower Mitcham, South Australia 5062
08 8277 1555
e-mail: liahka@senet.com.au

New Zealand: Human Kinetics
P.O. Box 105-231, Auckland Central
09-523-3462
e-mail: hkp@ihug.co.nz

There is an old adage that says, "Any life can be damaged by the wrong words from the right person's lips." Conversely, any life can be healed by the right words from the right person's lips. Each of our lives has been touched by the presence of one individual who made a tremendous difference. That individual may have trusted in you when others doubted, backed you up when others backed away, saw deeper into your soul than you ever imagined possible. That person provided a kind word at a critical moment, an encouraging smile, or an arm around the shoulder.

In my life, that individual was my dad, James T. Bollettieri. He loved me more than I realized at the time. He provided unconditional support and love and throughout my life remained nonjudgmental. He was a quiet man who never said much but saw everything. He never chose sides in my disputes, but with the wisdom of a scholar, reminded me of the price I would pay for my actions. I can still remember going to him after deciding not to finish law school. "That's okay," he said, putting his arm around me. "I'll back you no matter what you decide to do."

My dad passed away and it is some consolation that his name lives on in my son, James. I never took the time to say "thank you," and I will always regret that we never became close friends. But life is about healing, honesty, and closure. Thanks, Dad! This book, a compilation of my life's work, is dedicated to you, and to Willa Bay Breunich, my first grandchild.

With love,
Nick

Praise for Nick Bollettieri

"Nick, I've spent time with Vince Lombardi, Bob Knight, Tony Larussa, Tommy La Sorda, Joe Torre, Larry Brown, Casey Stengel, and Gus D'Amato—just to name a few—and they're all successful and they're all different.

"The key thing for a coach and for a human being is to be yourself, and Nick, this is the characteristic you share with all those Hall of Fame coaches (whose league you are in). You are yourself. You're the consummate coach. You care desperately about the game, about the way it is played, and about the person who is playing it. You don't quite demand perfection, but you damn well want it.

"You coached me through the book we wrote together. Of all the people I've worked with on books—Joe Namath, Joe Montana, Billy Crystal, Bo Jackson, Tom Seaver, Dave Debusschere, and Jerry Kramer—nobody drove me as hard as you did, nobody cared more about the final product, nobody tried harder to give and share. You called me at any hour from any place to make suggestions, to offer information, even after the book had gone to press, and I think I found out what it was like to be a tennis player coached by Nick Bollettieri. All you asked was everything, and that's you, and that's terrific.

"Nick, you remind me of the first time I met George Allen. I walked into his Redskins' training camp in Carlisle, Pennsylvania, and before I could ask him anything about football, he pointed to the cooler of bottled water and launched into a lecture on the unmatchable virtues of that particular kind of bottled water. George Allen wanted everything to be the best—down to the bottled water. You include dark tans and bright teeth in your repertoire.

"And one more thing: Larry Brown's ultimate term of respect is to call someone 'Coach'—as in 'Coach Holzman' or 'Coach Smith.' You are Coach Bollettieri."

—Dick Schaap
Author and host of ESPN's
The Sports Reporter

"What is my definition of coaching? Very simply, it is the ability of an individual to get maximum efficiency out of each one of the athletes that come under his or her guidance. Developing a positive attitude and maximizing the performance of each athlete is a key component of all successful coaches. Coaching is the ability to communicate your concepts and your beliefs into making that athlete the best possible performer he or she can become. Once you develop the individual talents so they can excel in their own area of expertise, the next factor is to blend the individuals into working with others in formulating a winning team. It is vital that coaches convey to their athletes the necessity of having a sense of pride in themselves, as that plays a big role in forming a winning attitude. Pride to me can be broken down as follows: P for perseverance, R for respect, I for intelligence, D for the four D's of life—desire, dedication, determination, and discipline of body and mind—and E for enthusiasm. If a coach can successfully develop players with P.R.I.D.E. and get each athlete to perform to the best of his or her ability, then that coach has succeeded and has earned the right to feel like a championship coach.

"Nick Bollettieri has always been a man with great vision and a charismatic personality that energizes everyone in his presence. I have watched Nick coach athletes of all abilities, from professional status such as Monica Seles, Andre Agassi, and Jim Courier to junior high school beginners. His enthusiasm and ability to communicate to players of all levels is outstanding. His positive teachings, with his energetic approach, usually lead to the development of a successful tennis player."

—Dick Vitale
ABC/ESPN
basketball analyst

"Having moved in with Nick at the age of 13, he became a surrogate father to me. Nick stressed discipline and self control, but most of all he believed in me. Nick has the uncanny ability to know what each individual player needs to be motivated. For me, it was praise. The most lasting impression that I have about Nick is simply the feeling that came over you whenever he was on the court with you. Even to this day, if I'm playing tennis and Nick is there, the adrenaline starts to flow and I leave the court sure that I can conquer the world."

—Jimmy Arias

Following Jim Courier's five-set victory over Greg Rusedski in the fifth and final match of the Davis Cup tie versus Great Britain, Nick sent this fax:

Dear Jim,
Your success is not an accident. You work. You fight. You do anything you have to in order to win. I'm proud of you.

Your friend,
Nick Bollettieri

The following fax was sent in response:

Dear Nick,

Thanks for your kind fax. The qualities you pointed out in your fax—the hard work, the fighting—are qualities that were molded in your backyard.

Thank you for giving the opportunity to hundreds of dreamers like myself. There are a lot of us out here doing this for a living who would be working elsewhere if it weren't for you.

All my very best,
Jim Courier

"Nick has not only been a great help to our tennis, but he has also been a close friend of the family for years. His friendship and instruction have been invaluable to us."

—Venus Williams

"I really think that Nick is not just a coach but a friend, and someone that you can talk to. As a coach he really knows what to tell the player—so the player will be able to take the next step to be on the top. He has personally helped me to realize that I need the small things more than the large things. In the end, Nick is a great person and my friend."

—Serena Williams

"Nick is not only a terrific coach but a great motivator. He makes you feel good on the court no matter what. Also, knowing him for the past 7 years, he's not only a coach to me but a great friend with a big heart. He'll always be special."

—Tommy Haas

"I think Nick is a great motivator. He is always looking forward to helping you even in bad times. He does a great job coaching. He loves it and he puts a lot of effort into what he does."

—Marcelo Rios

In March 1999, Martina Hingis was interviewed by Associated Press sports writer Steven Wine. The headline of the resulting newspaper article read, "Hingis rolls into semis, will face Serena." "Last year," Wine wrote, "Hingis lost in the semi-finals of the French Open, Wimbledon, and the U.S. Open, then lost the No. 1 ranking to Davenport. Chastened, she prepared for 1999 by training with Nick Bollettieri in Bradenton." He continued, "Fit and trim again, Hingis has regained her remarkable sense of anticipation. Her serve and forehand, meanwhile, are more powerful than before."

"That was the first time after a long time I really worked for two weeks, day after day, three or four hours of tennis. You can see it, I mean, I'm back to No. 1. The scores tell it."

—Martina Hingis

"As usual, Nick has shown his comprehensive knowledge of tennis and the industry in the *Classic Handbook*. If anyone has seen it all and done it all—and has the right to say it all—it's my friend and respected colleague, Nick Bollettieri."

—Tim Heckler
USPTA CEO

"Nick has made his mark in the tennis world. He pioneered the concept of a full-time tennis academy, has nurtured the tennis careers of many players, and is the consummate salesman of his profession."

—Dennis Van der Meer
President of Van der Meer
Tennis University and
President of the USPTR

"Bollettieri is a coach's coach. His instincts are legendary. His head for success uncanny. The *Classic Handbook* lets us all in on Nick's secrets. Most important, this book shares one of the most compelling life lessons—bypass the big serve, the flashy footwork, the killer backhand. Those are merely surface. Laser in on what's under the surface—in the heart and mind—that's where the real stuff of winners, their full potential for greatness lives. This book is a coaching classic. Ad-out to the reader!"

—Harvey Mackay
Author of *Swim With the Sharks*
and *Pushing the Envelope*

CONTENTS

PREFACE

I have created this volume of work with one purpose—to share the experiences of my 44-year career. It will describe my concepts on teaching players of all levels, from beginner to no. 1 in the world. I will relate stories about many of the players I've worked with. I'll describe their strengths, idiosyncrasies, fears, and paranoid behaviors. One look at the table of contents will show the range of topics the book covers, from physical conditioning to parenting to the composition and tension of your racquet strings. I hope that we have included something for everyone. If the players, coaches, administrators, and parents who read this book feel that a light went on, that they learned something new, I will consider the thousands of hours of production time to have been worthwhile. The book is the product of curious people who diligently attempt to remain on the cutting edge of the tennis industry.

At the outset, I want to be clear that the opinions expressed in this handbook are born of the experience acquired over more than four decades of instructing. I don't profess to be right, and I don't accuse anyone whose methods are different of being wrong.

In numerous instances I have shown a variety of techniques for comparison. The handbook contains far more than the fundamentals of hitting a tennis ball. It includes advanced, world-class techniques and the nuances that can make a good player a great player.

I have attempted to share how the game has changed over the past four decades. The book is organized in such a way that you can seek specific information—when and how to start your children in tennis, how best to prepare for college, how to secure a college scholarship or play for the college of your choice, how to select a tennis academy or summer camp, how to distinguish a coach from an instructor, and how to choose between them. I have recounted the growth experiences of some of the greatest players of the generation—Agassi, Krickstein, Courier, Horvath, Bassett, Sampras, Seles, Pierce, Majoli, Rios, Hingis, Haas, Philippoussis, Becker, Venus and Serena Williams, and others. I hope you enjoy reading about these players as much as I enjoyed compiling the material. In any case, visit my Web site at **www.imgacademies.com** and send me an e-mail.

Throughout more than four decades of coaching, I have interacted with people from all walks of life. I continue to be disappointed with myself for not having kept a daily diary, something to bolster my memory and prevent the inevitable loss of detail that accompanies the passage of time. So before you end up with the same regrets, start keeping a diary today. Diaries become treasures that recall the minutia of an event, those details that make it worth remembering in the first place.

I have had the pleasure of witnessing the complete metamorphosis of tennis. As a coach, I've had to adjust to new styles of play. If I had not adjusted, my students would have been victimized by developments in equipment, strategy, and tactics. At the end of the day, however, hard work, dedication, and the willingness to accept responsibility for failure have always been the underpinnings of a champion. Practicing with purpose and performing drills repeatedly is what allows an athlete to achieve absolute confidence. Repetition translates into championship performance. The player has hit that shot a thousand times before and knows that he or she can hit it this time and the next as well.

All a coach can hope to achieve is to enable students to reach the maximum level of their ability. Trust me, this is not easy! Coaches who understand their students—their moods, fears, and needs—can gain their respect. These coaches have a chance of lifting their students to their potential. Indeed, the ability to understand the student may be the defining characteristic of a coach, the quality that differentiates a coach from a teacher or instructor.

A coach develops an understanding of the true personality and hidden nuances of the student. This description is not intended to diminish the value of an instructor, who plays a vital role. But the road to exceptional, outstanding, or world-class performances is littered with the casualties of talented individuals who took to the road without a coach.

My Perfect Athlete

My perfect athlete would win far more often than lose. No one wins all the time—not Michael Jordan, not Muhammad Ali, not Roger Clemens. But my perfect athlete does not lose often. He or she plays to win.

When my perfect athlete wins, he or she would win fairly and graciously, abiding by the written rules and the unwritten ones, neither antagonizing nor demeaning the opponent. When my player loses, he or she would lose with equal grace, would lose by being outplayed, not by failing to give total effort. My athlete would congratulate the opponent and not look for excuses. He or she would make a personal vow to work harder to change the result the next time.

My perfect athlete would be eager to work hard to improve, to approach perfection. He or she would be an observer and a listener, learning by watching and by listening to advice.

My perfect athlete would love the game, its history, its intricacies, and would be a credit to the sport and to his or her family and friends, not an embarrassment. My player would be its spokesperson, by actions even more than by words. He or she would be its eternal advertisement, yet my player's interests and persona would transcend the game.

My perfect athlete would remember how to be a true champion and would act as a champion on and off the playing field. My player would be self-confident, but not arrogant. He or she would share knowledge, techniques, and insights with others. My player would inspire and tutor the next generation and be, automatically, a role model.

My perfect athlete could be male or female, tall or short, black or white. He or she would have a lot of Arthur Ashe inside, a lot of Wayne Gretzky, a lot of Bart Starr, a lot of Bill Bradley, a lot of Martina Navratilova.

I would love to coach the perfect athlete. Just once.

Although the perfect athlete I describe may exist only in fantasy, there are a few individuals who stand out from the crowd, a few masters who during their time captured our attention and consumed our imagination.

Who can forget the fire, the passion, and the mastery of John McEnroe? His gifts come along only once in a while.

When I think of a competitor, a fighter, someone who refused to quit, someone who even today thinks he can beat everybody, I think of Jimmy Connors. I love watching him fight, and I can't imagine tennis without him.

I will never forget the perpetual youth, the constant bouncing up and down, the enthusiasm of Tracy Austin, two-time U.S. Open Champion and still hitting winners as a television commentator.

The term *pioneer* is exemplified by Billie Jean King, the driving force in elevating the women's game to prominence. Even today, she continues to give, promote, and elevate.

Wayne Gretzky's recent retirement solidified his position as one of the most respected athletes of all time. I'll never forget a comment he made at a recent interview, a comment that explains his immense popularity. He said that in every game, every exhibition, every charity performance, every practice session, he did exactly the same thing—he gave his very best. We could all learn from his attitude.

Chris Evert left her mark on tennis. She exemplifies the word *R-E-S-P-E-C-T.*

Who can forget Bjorn Borg? His focus and concentration allowed him to win Wimbledon six times as a baseliner. Unbelievable!

I could not end my list of almost perfect athletes without the name of Arnold Palmer. He is a standout performer, the quintessential gentleman, and a fine model for all of us.

ACKNOWLEDGMENTS

My sincere thanks to Mark McCormack and Bob Kain of International Management Group for allowing me to remain "Nick Bollettieri" after the purchase of my academy. They, like myself, have worked tirelessly towards helping the game of tennis. To Betsey Nagelsen McCormack, you are an unbelievable person inside and out. Thank you.

I would like to thank and acknowledge Human Kinetics for their patience and professional approach to producing this edition of my book.

In addition to my family, I would like to acknowledge and express my sincere appreciation to my team. These people have spent hundreds of hours editing this edition of my book: Pat Dougherty, Geoff Lance, Louise Luscombe, and Peter McCraw. A sincere thank you must also go to the many others who provided valuable input that led to the completion of this work.

The continuing support of the following people and organizations have also contributed immensely:

Fila	Swiss Army Brands	Oakley
Volkl	Penn	Bill & Catharina Birchall
Bob Davis	Mr. & Mrs. Oscar De La Renta	Mr. Bill Dennis
Don Engel and family	Barry Gimelstob	Mr. Leland Hardy
Monte Hurowitz and family	Bob Jellen and family	Terry Kennedy and family
Andy Krieger and family	Dr. Murf Klauber*	Ryszard Krauze and family
Nate Landow and family	Dan Lufkin	Louis Marx Jr. and family
Louis Marx III	Marty Mulligan	Dr. Glen & Marilyn Nelson and family
Steve Owens	Samuel Reid	Charlie Reed
Gary Scheck and family	Bernie & Margot Schmidt	Richard Schutzman and family
Jack Schneider and family	Tom Seavey and family	Lenny Solomon
Allen Wheat and family	Richard Williams and family	Marylou Whitney and John Hendrickson

Mike Callans	Jerry Glauser and family	Murray Evans and family
Terry Havens	Fulton Liss	Mark Fisher and family
Dr. Lawrence Lieberman	Judge Robert Farrance	Steve Jonsson
Ivano Panetti	Dr. Terry Alford	Norbert Peters

and to Barry Gibb and family: Keep playing that Saturday Night Fever

*My initial success in the tennis business was due, in large part, to Dr. Klauber's support and confidence in me. From my beginnings at the Colony Tennis and Beach Resort until today, Dr. Klauber has maintained his resort as one of the finest in the world. Thanks, Doc!

The following individuals have given of themselves selflessly to me for 20 years or more. It is only through their devotion and dedication that we have succeeded beyond all expectations and have been dubbed by *The New York Times* as "The Mothership of All Academies."

Greg Breunich	Chip Brooks
Chip Hart	Gabriel Jaramillo
Ted Meekma	Julio Moros
Carolina Murphy	Steve Shulla

Special thanks to an old friend, confidante, and collaborator, Mike DePalmer Sr. Mike is the individual who guided my footsteps to the Bradenton area. After several months, Mike had a dream and prodded me into developing the very first Bollettieri Academy. Thanks, Mike!

I would be remiss if I didn't acknowledge and thank my five children—Jimmy, Danielle, Angel, Nicole, and Alex—who have offered their love, support, and understanding throughout my career. And thanks to Kristen who puts up with all my crazy ideas. For many who have dedicated their lives to their work, family life suffers at times.

And to the fans, media, and players of our wonderful game, you have continued to support me, seek my advice, attend my academy, and otherwise provide motivation to me for more than four decades. Over the years, you have become a source of strength and an extended group of family and friends.

I also want to recognize many of the pioneers of the teaching profession, upon whose shoulders I stood to develop my own skills: Harry Hopman, Dennis Van der Meer, Vic Braden, and John Wilkerson, and for those coaches whose names this senior moment has permitted me to overlook. A special thanks to Eugene Scott, editor of *Tennis Week* magazine, who always has the courage to stand up for the truth, to hold inequities up to the sunlight for all to see. Thanks to the USPTA and the USPTR for doing their part striving for excellence and to all the other tennis academies that, like mine, recognize the difficulties, accept the challenges, grit their teeth, and make a difference in the lives of hundreds and thousands of players.

I am also very excited about the changes the USTA is making to its programs. I am looking forward to working more closely with them on some very exciting projects in the years to come.

Alumni

Nick has worked with the following Pro Tour players on a personal basis, or they have trained at the Nick Bollettieri Tennis Academy:

WTA Tour Players

Nicole Arendt

Carling Bassett

Daja Bedanova

Elena Bovina

Sandra Cacic

Pam Casale

Catalina Cristea

Erika de Lone

Mariaan de Swardt

Ruxandra Dragomir

Mary Joe Fernandez

Andrea Glass

Julie Halard-Decugis

Daniela Hantuchova

Martina Hingis

Kathleen Horvath

Anke Huber

Jelena Jankovic

Sonya Jeyaseelan

Anna Kournikova

Mirjana Lucic

Iva Majoli

Amelie Mauresmo

Rachel McQuillan

Karin Miller

Terry Phelps

Mary Pierce

Rafaella Reggi

Brie Rippner

Chanda Rubin

Patty Schnyder

Monica Seles

Anne-Gaelle Sidot

Alexandra Stevenson

Helena Sukova

Andrea Temesvari

Caroline Vis

Marlene Weingartner

Serena Williams

Venus Williams

ATP Tour Players

Andre Agassi

Julian Alonso

Paul Annacone

Hicham Arazi

Jimmy Arias

Hugo Armando

Boris Becker

Jim Courier

Martin Damm

Mike DePalmer Jr.

Slava Dosedel

Younes El Aynaoui

Thomas Enqvist

Brad Gilbert

Justin Gimelstob

Marc-Kevin Goellner

Brian Gottfried

Jim Grabb

Oliver Gross

Tommy Haas

Rodney Harmon

Chip Hooper

Yevgeny Kafelnikov

Cedric Kauffman

Mark Knowles

Petr Korda

Aaron Krickstein

Karol Kucera

Giovanni Lapentti

Magnus Larson

Jean Rene Lisnard

David MacPherson

Xavier Malisse

Cecil Mamiit

Nicolas Massu

Paul-Henri Mathieu

Andrei Medvedev

Max Mirnyi

Francisco Montana

Diego Nargiso

Yannick Noah

Magnus Norman

Jiri Novak

Marcus Ondruska

Mark Philippoussis

David Rikl

Marcelo Rios

Christian Ruud

Andrea Sa

Marat Safin

Pete Sampras

Cyril Suk

Jeff Tarango

Laurence Tieleman

Daniel Vacek

Glenn Weiner

David Wheaton

Todd Witskin

CHAPTER 1

The Bollettieri Development System

Our philosophy is to coach people, not just skills. It is not only about producing better players, but also about helping students develop in all walks of life.

In the early stages of my career, I realized that if I worked longer and harder than anyone else and surrounded myself with loyal, committed people, I could be somebody. I realized that if I learned from my defeats and had the support of my friends, I could make an impact. In the 1950s and early 1960s, you only needed to pick up a can of tennis balls, go to the park, and occupy one of the many vacant courts to play tennis. The tennis boom began in that era. Things have changed dramatically over the last four decades. Today, tennis clubs are often part of a family recreation complex that might include aerobics centers, physical fitness clubs, racquetball courts, squash courts, pro shops, and salons. Today's tennis pro needs an understanding of business to survive. Just as important, today's pro needs to understand that many club owners must diversify to make their clubs financially profitable.

Our system integrates all aspects of training: physical, technical, tactical, mental, nutritional, regenerative, and social. During our sessions, students will work on and off court on techniques, the strategies of playing the game, constructive practice sessions, movement, the mental necessities you must accept and deal with, and finally, physical development of your body and how to use it no matter what happens.

History

The Nick Bollettieri Tennis Academy (NBTA) began in 1977 at the Colony Beach and Tennis Resort on Longboat Key, Florida. The idea for the academy came from Mike DePalmer Sr., a close friend of Nick's. The academy began training junior tennis players on the weekend for $35 per session. At first, the academy drew students only from Sarasota-Bradenton. Word soon spread throughout the state, however, and Nick began to attract players from Jacksonville to Miami. Soon, 30 to 40 youngsters were taking part in the program. To accommodate as many students as possible, six to eight juniors would share a room at the Colony.

During the summer of 1978 Nick told students at his summer camp in Beaver Dam, Wisconsin, that he was opening a school in Sarasota. The school would offer tennis instruction and room and board. That summer, he lined up 20 students to start in September, even though boarding facilities were not yet available. During the first few years, half the students lived in Nick's house and the others were scattered among the homes of the teaching staff. His pros were not only tennis instructors but cooks, maids, tutors, and drivers.

One of the earliest and more prominent boarding students was a young girl from West Virginia named Anne White. Anne is best known for the shocking form-fitting white bodysuit she wore in her first-round match at Wimbledon in 1985. Her challenge to traditional etiquette put her photo on the cover of every tennis magazine in the world. The publicity drew much attention to Nick's new academy.

Later that year NBTA had the first of its many growth spurts. By now the academy was overflowing with students. Court space and housing capacity were inadequate. To solve the court problem, Nick teamed up with Mike DePalmer Sr. to purchase a tennis club located on 75th Street NW in Bradenton. The facility, christened the DePalmer-Bollettieri Tennis Club, still operates today as the Nick Bollettieri Tennis Center.

The housing situation was solved by purchasing the Manatee Court West Motel, located at 6300 Manatee Avenue West. The motel was converted into the world's first boarding tennis academy. From this central location, students could walk to the academic school, Bradenton Academy. From there, they were later bused to either the colony or the club.

This was the beginning of the Nick Bollettieri Tennis Academy. The tuition for one year was $12,000. These were the glory years. Students included Jimmy Arias, Kathleen Horvath, and Carling Basset, all of whom became ranked in the top 10 in the world.

But this was not enough. Nick felt he needed a new facility for the kids. He imagined a larger, self-contained facility complete with courts, dormitories, a kitchen, and a dining hall. The dream had begun!

Early Years

In 1980 Bollettieri decided it was time for another move. With his partners he bought a 10½-acre tomato field on 34th Street West. There he built 22 courts, 32 condominiums, a dining hall with kitchen facilities, and a swimming pool. Initial enrollment at the academy was 100 students overseen by 22 staff members. The rooms were designed to accommodate four students per room, but by the time construction was completed, the academy's enrollment required Nick to cram eight students into a room.

Even with the expansion Nick was not content to sit back and enjoy his success. It was time to dream again.

In 1982 Nick purchased 13 acres adjacent to the academy, on which he built 22 more courts and the first indoor tennis complex south of Atlanta. Many said that Nick had lost his mind because he built indoor courts in Florida, but Nick knew he needed a more complete facility to attract more and better players.

Then, in 1983, Jimmy Arias, ranked top five in the world, reached the semifinals of the U.S. Open. Jimmy's success and Nick's vision for the future began to attract players with higher rankings and greater potential.

Later that year Nick added two more buildings to the academy. With the addition of 16 more dormitories, the academy was able to increase its enrollment to 160 students.

In 1986 the academy added an adult program to increase enrollment. This meant adding more courts, bringing the total to 54 (14 clay, 4 indoor, and 36 stadium hard courts). By this time, NBTA was recognized as the premier tennis academy in the world. Nick coached and trained many of the top-ranked players. Before 1990 NBTA would produce three world no. 1 players on the professional tour (Andre Agassi, Jim Courier, and Monica Seles). The academy was featured on such television shows as *20/20* (ABC), *60 Minutes* (CBS), and the *NBC Evening News* (NBC).

The publicity attracted the attention of International Management Group (IMG), the largest sports-management company in the world. In 1987 Nick sold NBTA to IMG. He felt that if the academy were to continue to grow and expand, it needed the exposure and financial backing of IMG. Nick agreed to stay on with the academy as president and founder.

With the addition of IMG the academy was again able to expand and update its facility. The dining area was expanded to accommodate adults. Another pool, recreational facilities, and a performance training center for off-court training were built.

With the success of NBTA, Nick, Ted Meekma, and CEO Greg Breunich decided it was time to dream again. In 1990 they duplicated in other sports what Nick had accomplished with his teaching and training methods in tennis. Thus the Bollettieri Sports Academy was created. The philosophies that Nick used in tennis would now be offered in other sports programs. This idea would mark the first attempt to train multiple sports at one facility. Critics said it couldn't be done.

Present

By 1994 another Bollettieri vision became reality. With the introduction of three new sports, NBTA became the Bollettieri Sports Academy (BSA). With the addition of the David Leadbetter Golf Academy, the Soccer Academy, and the Baseball Academy, BSA is now the largest sports academy in the world. The 45-acre facility, still located at 34th Street West in Bradenton, offers the most complete state-of-the-art sports complex for athletic training anywhere.

In 1996 BSA completed the International Performance Institute (IPI) indoor complex. In essence, this building is a 30,000-square-foot indoor football field with synthetic grass turf. The IPI dome, as it is called, is used for multisports training, regardless of weather, and is equipped to accommodate virtually every sport that uses a ball.

In the same year BSA opened its Sports Medicine Therapy Center. Open to the public, the center employs fully licensed sports therapists. Throughout the year, top pro athletes from various sports frequent the therapy center.

In 1997 BSA became home to the Eddie Herr Junior Invitational, one of the world's most prestigious events in amateur athletics. This year was the most successful in the international tournament's 11-year history, with 1,100 players from 87 different countries participating. Among the competitors were 130 ranked no. 1 nationally and 88 ranked no. 2 nationally in various age divisions.

BSA now has more than 400 full-time students from over 40 countries. Summer camps and vacation weeks see more than 500 at a time. With the completion of the first 10 buildings of the Bollettieri Villas, the academy can now meet this increasing demand. Current cost for a sports program for the academic year (September to May) is approximately $28,000, plus school. BSA also has a limited number of scholarships available for those who need financial assistance or those with exceptional talent.

BSA has come a long way from having a tennis staff of 22 doing all the work. The academy currently employs 250 people in 25 departments, including tennis professionals (adult and junior); golf, baseball, soccer, basketball, and hockey personnel; guest services; sales and marketing; reservations; housekeeping; a full kitchen; sports psychology; fitness; research and development programs; and more.

The Manatee County Chamber of Commerce estimates that the academy puts more than $20 million into the local economy each year. BSA has had tremendous local support. Local residents agree that the academy is a modern success story and are proud that it has remained in Bradenton. Nick has had many opportunities to relocate to sites that are more accessible, but he likes the community and feels at home there.

Future

The Bollettieri Sports Academy, now known as the IMG Academies, has a lot in store for the future. The Bollettieri Resort Villas have proven to be a tremendous success and now also include a clubhouse/conference center and pool. The owned and leased land controlled by IMG Academies totals 190 acres. In 2001 over 100 of these acres will be developed to include a new golf training facility, two baseball fields, five soccer fields, up to 15 more tennis courts, and 60 more villa units. New sports introduced will include basketball and cycling camp academy programs.

Nick Bollettieri, IMG, and the IMG Academies team look forward to continuing to set the standard by which all others in the multi-sport training business are measured, well into the 21st century.

Coaching

We make a big distinction between teachers and coaches. We are coaches and educators. Coaching involves setting challenging tasks to improve players' knowledge, skills, and attitudes. The secrets of our coaches are the following:

- Organizing and planning
- Directing, guiding, and challenging
- Monitoring and evaluating
- Communicating and motivating
- Setting clear goals and objectives
- Sacrificing and working hard
- Putting students first
- Continuing our education
- Being team players and having respect for our colleagues
- Enjoying our work

Coaching Skills by Steps

Coaching is a process. Our system moves from one step to the next so that practice has structure and a logical progression. There are no quick fixes. The best way to approach a student is with the intention of improving his or her performance permanently. Our system is an educational process.

Some coaches teach one stroke at time. For example, forehand is the first lesson, backhand the second, and so on. But the player will not encounter this sequence of situations in a game, and the student will not learn motor skills. Our coaches are knowledgeable about the principles and steps by which people learn motor skills.

The Bollettieri method teaches the students a variety of skills in a single session. As we teach strokes, we teach the student what to do with the ball according to where they are on the court, and we train them how to identify the type of ball they are receiving. Students also set goals and know the purpose of each exercise.

Continuing Education

All members of the NBTA coaching staff go through a rigorous training process. Subsequently, we emphasize continuing education. Our coaches meet daily to study topics such as

- stroke production,
- video analysis of a particular student,
- mental conditioning,
- physical conditioning,
- results and comments from our coaches when they return from tournaments, and
- presentations by guest speakers.

We meet each Saturday for two hours to discuss coaching styles, new trends, and so on. Every six weeks we conduct an eight-hour periodization class and plan for the next phase of the program.

Organization and Planning

NBTA has been producing top players for the last 20 years. Our record of accomplishment speaks for itself. Our success has not come by accident. Years of hard work, planning, monitoring, evaluating, and goal setting are required to develop every player. To develop players in the most effective way, coaches need to know a great deal about them:

- Goals and ambitions (reviewed periodically with the students)
- Personality—how players handle the pressure of everyday life, including athletics
- Stages of development; strengths and weaknesses; technical, tactical, strategic, physical, and mental skills; nutritional habits; maturity
- Social background—parents, friends, and so on

All these factors determine a coach's course of action. Each student is different.

Farm System

NBTA was the leader in teaching an individual sport in a group setting. This was contrary to the conventional wisdom of the day that one-on-one teaching was the only way to go. Coaching in groups has many advantages. Students learn from each other, and they push each other to higher levels through motivation and competition.

At the academy we have been very successful in using the farm-system approach. We place students in groups according to match results. Students play challenge matches and move to higher or lower groups based on match results. We emphasize competition and learning how to win. Playing singles and doubles every day is essential. In special cases we consider gender, age, years of playing experience, and so forth when forming groups.

The development of a player is a long-range program that includes different schedules, smaller groups, and one-on-one help. Throughout the history of the academy, our system has been flexible enough to adjust to the developmental needs of many players. Not surprisingly, players' needs are individual and require independent solutions. Our system allows us to pinpoint parts of players' games that will allow them to move to another level of play.

Students become sparring partners for the dozens of pros that live or train here. For example, in December 1997 Xavier Malisse won the prestigious Eddie Herr International Junior Tournament. He bypassed the Orange Bowl to spend three weeks practicing with Marcelo Rios, Tommy Haas, Mark Philippoussis, Jimmy Arias, Petr Korda, and Thomas Enqvist. Shortly after this experience, Xavier turned pro, and *Tennis Magazine* predicted big things for him. It is unlikely that Xavier could have obtained this level of practice elsewhere. In 1997 and 1998, while still a junior, Tommy Haas practiced with Boris Becker. Haas and Becker continue to work out together. Martina Hingis trained at the academy in November 1998 in preparation for the WTA Tour Chase Championships. While here, she spent two hours a day practicing with my best young students, who couldn't believe they had the opportunity to hit with her. Venus and Serena Williams, along with Jimmy Arias, beat up everyone in the academy when they train here.

You can't put a price tag on this type of experience!

Groups

When the full-time students arrive in September, we play matches the entire first week. We record the results of all matches and place students in groups according to match results. It is interesting to note that Andre Agassi was ranked 32nd while a junior at NBTA. Tommy Haas was ranked 7th. These statistics give you an idea of the competition level at the academy.

Today, we have a group of girls at the academy who are training under Nick's supervision and who have the potential to become top-ranked WTA tour players. For example, Jelena Jankovic won the 2001 Australian Junior Open at age 15. She is curently ranked no. 2 junior in the world. Jamea Jackson was ranked no. 1 in the 16 and unders in the United States at age 13. Maria Sharapova at age 13 won the prestigious Eddie Herr 16 and unders. Tatiana Golovin won the 14 and under French National Championships at age 12 and the 12s Orange Bowl. Stephanie Herz was ranked no. 1 in the 12 and unders in the Netherlands at age 9. Nick feels that there are many similarities between this group of girls and the group of boys he had back in the late 1980s (Agassi, Courier, Wheaton, etc.).

In the boys, we have Todd Reid and Adam Kennedy who are the no. 1 and 2 ranked boys in Australia. Horia Tecau was the semifinalist in the 1999 boys 14 and under Orange Bowl and is ranked no. 1 in Romania in the 16 and unders. Dong Choi, who won the 12 and under Orange Bowl in the boys 12s is the highest ranked 14 year old in the ITF 18 and under rankings. Jarrett Chirico is ranked no. 2 in the United States boys 14s and his brother Christopher is ranked no. 1 in the 12 and unders in the United States.

Each group has a coach who is responsible for the student's program, specific to the level of the group. The coach helps plan and organize the student's program for the entire school year (nine months). The coach directs, guides, and challenges the student and helps the student set goals. We frequently monitor and evaluate these goals. The coach is also responsible for communication with parents.

Parents

Parents play a vital supportive role in any athlete's career. Most great players have had the support of their mother or father. Parents know their children well. They understand their mood swings, what makes them tick, their fears, and so forth. Parents, coaches, and students must learn to work together and must maintain good relationships. Parents can be a powerful force not only during the junior career but also during a pro career.

One of the most difficult parts of coaching is dealing with parents. Through the years we have had the opportunity to work with many parents. As coaches, we believe that one of our main jobs is to educate parents on the importance of their involvement in a supportive role. Parents can become involved in both positive and negative ways. For instance, many parents have lost their child through their actions on or off the court. Parents can become dictators who try to control every second of the student's life. They talk about tennis on and off the court and may set unrealistically high goals for their children. Parents often try to live their unrealized dreams of success through their sons and daughters. Tennis becomes a nightmare for the child, and the parent becomes the enemy. It is nearly impossible to live every second under such pressure. A coach will find it difficult to communicate with a child whose parents have imparted continual criticism. Players often want their parents to be mom and dad, not coaches.

Andrea Tamisvary and Mary Pierce are just two examples of players whose parents agonized over their kids. In retrospect it seems that these parents couldn't decide when to let go. As a result their relationships with their daughters suffered. Tamisvary and Pierce experienced difficult times with their parents, and each eventually went her own way. Both players broke into the top 10 and won many championships, including Grand Slam titles. Imagine trophies and money driving a wedge between parents and children! Is this the way to go? Not in my book!

Other parents, like Krickstein's, Agassi's, and Courier's, although deeply involved, seemed to have a sense of when to back off. They understood the game well but used the coaches to impart instructions, corrections, and motivation. We worked closely with these players by constantly reviewing goals, monitoring, evaluating, and motivating. The key was communication among all parties. The player was the captain of the ship, and all members of the crew needed to understand that. An example that illustrates this relationship occurred during a U.S. Open. Aaron Krickstein played poorly and lost a match. Aaron's father, Dr. Krickstein, was going crazy in the stands, saying that Aaron couldn't serve or hit a forehand and was slow. After the match Dr. Krickstein presented a much different side of himself to his son on the way to the locker room. He congratulated Aaron and gave him a hug to express how proud he was. He told his son that his opponent had outplayed him and that Aaron could have done nothing more. Dr. Krickstein was able to break away from being a coach and focus on being a father. He left the coaching work to the coaches. Aaron and his father still have a close relationship.

Mr. Seles was a little different. He and I were the coaches. Mr. Seles was involved in every aspect of Monica's training. From the beginning I suggested that Mr. Seles talk about tennis only on court. Once they left academy grounds they should not discuss tennis again. Mr. Seles was able to follow my advice, and Monica and her father built an unbelievable relationship. Many parents are unable to separate on-court and off-court life. The families go home, and the parents keep talking about the forehand volley that lost the point. Students need to have lives with their families separate from their tennis lives.

When we meet with parents, especially those here every day throughout the year, we try to coach them to understand several points:

- The best way to help their son or daughter is to communicate through the coaches and trust the coaches to do what is best for the student.
- Their role in the support system is extremely important.

- They should give their children positive feedback and lots of love.
- Topics related to tennis are addressed through the coaches.
- All parties (parent, student, and coach) must understand the player's goals and the system that will be used to reach them.

Bollettieri Athlete Training and Development*

We approach athlete training and development very seriously. Our programs today are fully integrated to ensure that each student's development is maximized. The forthcoming training year starts long before the first ball is hit, with staff planning every aspect of the students' year. The technical, tactical, mental, and physical components are planned and monitored. In addition, growth and development, cultural and social aspects are integrated to ensure we are developing both a complete player and person.

Periodization

NBTA was first in the use of periodization to train tennis players. Periodization is the means of planning short- and long-term training and competition by optimizing content, volume, intensity, and frequency of preparation to achieve maximum performance. Periodization simply means to work in cycles or time segments. Each cycle has a specific proportion of time, and each cycle is proportional to the others.

Periodization offers several advantages:

- The athlete reaches peak performance at the crucial time.
- Work is more efficient.
- Goals are clear and defined.
- The work-rest plan is specific for short and long term.
- Variety in practice prevents boredom.
- The risk of overtraining, overuse injuries, and burnout is reduced.

Rotations

To maximize training effects, students go through three rotations every day. The following is an example of a typical day at NBTA:

- Drilling courts (1½ hours)—14 courts available
- Match-play area (1½ hours)—33 courts available including the indoor and clay courts

---

*This section by Peter D. McCraw.

- International Performance Institute—conditioning everyday at 4:30 for one hour; Performax mental conditioning

Each group meets with the mental conditioning department on Monday, and the coach reinforces the theme for the entire week.

The program is divided into three parts: macrocycle, mezocycle, and microcycle.

Macrocycle

The annual plan for tennis forms the foundation of the training year. The macrocycle is a specific period that outlines personal training, focusing on work versus rest periods. Our macrocycle is nine months long, beginning when students arrive in September and ending when they depart in June. During this macrocycle we use multiple periodization. To accommodate the tournament schedule, the annual cycle requires high intensity and a relatively high volume of training all year round. During multiple periodization we frequently introduce breaks to prevent overtraining, overuse injuries, and burnout.

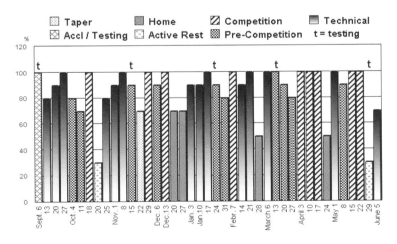

Mezocycle

The seven-week cycle is divided into one testing and acclimation week, three technical weeks, two precompetition weeks, two days of competition, and five days of active rest. Further monitoring takes place by dividing the phase into *microcycles*, which are one week long. Our mezocycle is divided into four different microcycles: technical, precompetition, competition, and rest.

Phase 1 - General Squad
September 6 - October 24

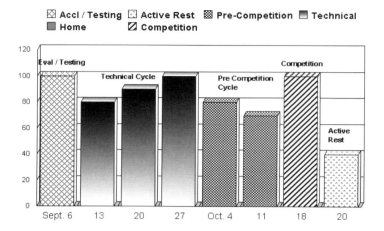

Microcycles

We divide the mezocycles into microcycles, which are minicycles or weekly workouts. Microcycles are instruments for controlling and optimizing short-term adaptation, or how the students are reacting to the daily training loads. Each coach identifies the training load for the group during a microcycle, taking into consideration volume, intensity, specificity, frequency, and recovery. The big picture must be clear before implementing short-term planning.

Micro Cycle 6 - Pre-Competition Cycle

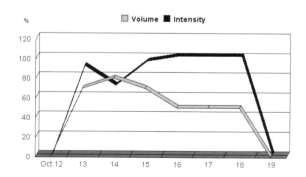

Dividing Up the Week

Each microcycle forms the blueprint for the week's training. All that is left are the daily details—the minute by minute plan of how each group is to spend their time. Given the size and layout of the academy, our daily drill sheet is very detailed indeed.

Below is an overview of the microcycle variables we use:

• **Weekly volume.** The weekly volume determines the length of both the drilling and matchplay rotations. In technical microcycles the volume is high—90 to 100 percent. Length of rotations are 90 minutes long. As we move into precompetition microcycles the volume decreases to 70 to 90 percent. Rotation times are also decreased to 75 minutes to offset the increased intensity of training. In a competition microcycle volume is typically 60 to 75 percent, with rotation times varying from 60 to 75 minutes.

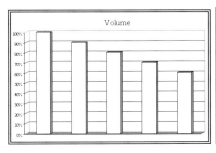

VOLUME	ROTATION
100%	90 min
90%	90 min
80%	75 min
70%	60 / 75 min
60%	60 min

• **Weekly intensity.** The weekly intensity determines the heart rate range of both the drilling and matchplay rotations. As the weekly volume decreases, the intensity (heart rate) of the week increases. Intensities of 100 percent are trained in competition microcycles to replicate the actual matchplay environment. Intensities of 80 to 90 percent are trained in precompetition microcycles, and intensities of 70 to 80 percent are trained in technical microcycles. The 60 percent intensity is used for recovery, flushing, and active rest microcycles.

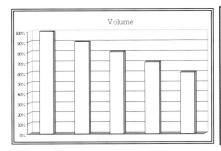

INTENSITY	HEART RATE
100%	160-180 bpm
90%	140-160 bpm
80%	130-150 bpm
70%	120-140 bpm
60%	100-120 bpm

• **Daily loading.** The daily loading determines the percent of time spent training and the length of each drill in the drilling and matchplay rotations. Based on a 90 minute rotation (drilling or matchplay) on a heavy day, groups spend 80 percent of the 90 minutes actually drilling. The rest of the time is spent resting, hydrating, receiving instruction, and picking up balls. Like-wise the progression follows on medium days, 70 percent, and light days, 60 percent.

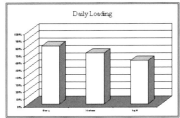

LOADING	%	DRILLING	MATCH PLAY
		* Based on 90 minute rotation	
Heavy	80%	10 min*	20 min*
Medium	70%	8 min*	16 min*
Light	60%	6 min*	12 min*

Putting It All Together

Integrating the weekly volume, intensity, and daily loading provides the means by which we vary the training load on the students over the nine-month training year. This ensures optimum adaptation to all students and avoids burnout, overtraining, and injuries.

Technical

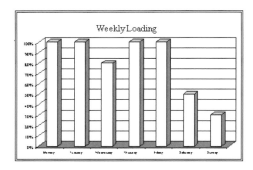

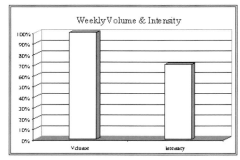

Precompetition

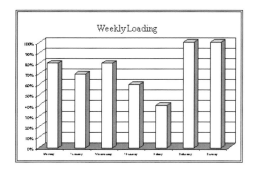

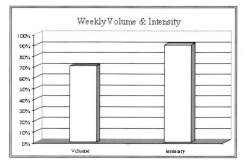

Competition

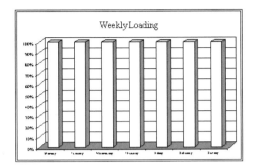
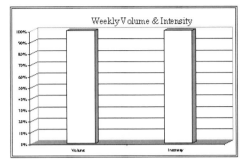

Active rest

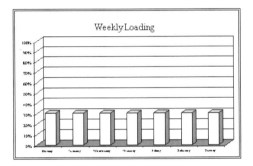
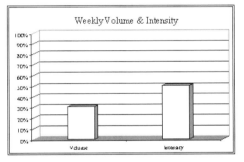

The accumulation of similar training loads contributes to excessive fatigue and slows the restoration process. By changing the workloads (level of adaptation) we allow our players to begin the next workout fully recovered. In other words, by adding variety in daily workouts, our students are more excited about practice. They will improve more, recover faster, and feel less fatigue. It is important to have a different sequence in training loads when the volume and intensity of workouts are not uniform. One day can be a hard day of practice, the next can be medium, another can be light, and still another day can be very hard to shock the system. These several days of loading are followed by one or two days of rest.

Adaptation is how students assimilate the training. If students can't adapt to the training load and intensity, we introduce a new training load to enhance adaptation. Microcycles are the most easily controlled units of training during the annual process. Coaches can make quick adjustments when required. Microcycles provide flexibility.

We emphasize quality in a workout, but at times we train in quantity. Coaches and players must monitor training and performance to ensure optimum short- and long-term adaptation to training. We believe that nothing promotes more improvement than sport-specific training.

When designing, sequencing, and implementing our weekly microcycles, we observe these principles: skill before speed, speed before power and strength, power before strength (anaerobic alactic before anaerobic lactic), and strength before endurance.

Technical Phase

- Practices are done with one objective—to improve the biomechanics of stroke production.
- Drills are slow (low intensity).
- Students hit many balls, and practices are long (high volume) with lots of repetition.
- Students develop muscular endurance and cardiovascular capacity.
- Players work on lower-body strength.
- We do lots of videotaping of the students' strokes.
- We recommend that students not play tournaments and only a few matches in this phase. Students are becoming accustomed to corrections and will be heavy and slow during this time.

Sample weekly technical overview

Tennis—on-court
- Long slow and steady week. Volume (90 percent) at an easy pace (70 percent).
- Week of technical fundamentals and foundation work. Heart rate range 120 to 140 bpm.
- Rest intervals—3 minute max, or when heart rate is less than 100 bpm.

Drilling focus—fed ball
- Serve and return
- Groundstrokes
- Approach/volley/ overhead

Match play focus—live ball
- Groundstroke fundamentals—CC/DTL
- Depth/accuracy and rally speed
- Combinations—2 on 1 patterns

Precompetition Phase—Training to Compete

- The objective of this second phase of training is to fine-tune the student for competitive performance.
- This is the final stage of technical, tactical, physical, and mental preparation before competition.
- During this period emphasis is placed on tactics and strategy.

- The student should identify and understand his or her style of play.
- Students should improve shot selection and combinations and learn to play the points according to the score.
- Matches become important in evaluating the strengths and weaknesses of performance. Evaluation helps us optimize the student's on-going preparation.
- It is important to work with the student's style of play. The exercises must be specific. Students should hit every ball with a purpose.
- Our program is designed to replicate the conditions in competition to maximize specific adaptations and performance.
- In this phase students learn to perform under pressure because they are exposed to all competitive conditions during training. During match play, students are given different situations. For example, they play matches starting at 3-3, love-15, they play three-out-of-five-set tiebreakers only with the results counting for ranking, they play with someone else's racquet, they stop for 15 or 30 minutes to simulate a rain delay, and so forth.
- In this phase students improve the explosive movement of the first step with exercises mixing power and speed.
- Every Tuesday and Thursday we work on tennis-specific plyometrics. These drills make students stronger and faster.

Sample weekly precompetition overview

Tennis—on-court
- Faster tempo week 80 percent volume—75 minute rotations.
- Week of precompetition drills/point play and sets. Emphasis on change of direction, style of play.
- Overall heart rate range = 130 to 150 bpm.
- Serving and recovery jog 5:00-5:30 P.M. each day.

Drilling focus—live and fed ball
- 2 on 1 combinations
- Approach/volley/passing shots/overhead
- Serve and return

Match play focus
- Set play—Monday and Thursday
- Points—serve and volley/style of play
- 11-point games—specific task

Daily rotations—75/60 minutes
- 1:30–2:45 P.M.
- 2:45–4:00 P.M.
- 4:00–5:00 P.M. (60 minutes)

Daily task

- 5:00–5:30 P.M.—All groups either jogging or serving
- 20 minute recovery jog—70 percent max HR (130 to 140 bpm)

Competition Phase—Training to Win

- The objective of this phase is to reach the maximum level of play.
- During the "Training to Win" phase using multiple periodization, about 80 to 85 percent of training is sport or event specific.
- Although the student may still improve in technique and fitness, most of the progress will come from experience, modeling from other players, tactical improvements, and improvements in mental capacity.
- During this phase players will expand their knowledge of what works for them. Examples include warm-up, cool-down, strategies, hydration and nutrition, and recovery and regeneration for the next match.
- In the "Training to Win" phase the main components of training and performance include maintenance of the existing physical capacity, taper and peak, mental focus, and recovery and regeneration.
- The psychological component of training and performance is also a priority.
- As students approach their fitness and technical limits, psychological skills and capacity play a dominant role in performance. But if the student has not fully developed fitness, technical ability, and tactical competence, psychological skills cannot make a champion.
- During this phase, students play matches and tournaments. The player should focus on strategy, tactics, and mental discipline.
- During conditioning, we work on speed, agility, and recovery and regeneration.
- Students and coaches should evaluate performance to help design short- and long-term goals.
- To maximize training and performance, players and coaches must be able to see the big picture.

Sample weekly competition overview

Tennis—on-court

- 5 days of competition—Grand Prix #1.
- Round Robin Day 1 and 2 to decide seedings for single elimination tournament.

- Doubles to replace singles consolation. Sign in Wednesday, first round Thursday.
- 3 out of 5—No ad scoring, tiebreaker at 4-4.
- Style of play.
- Game plan—Strategy and tactics as per style of play.
- Emphasis—Warming up, being organized, on time, and prepared.
- Play to win.

Rest Phase

- To avoid sluggish training and reduced performance levels, or when overtraining and stress are present, the rest period can be scheduled to counteract unwanted fatigue levels. The player's individual needs will determine the length and sequencing of this cycle.
- The rest cycle allows students to recover from the physical and mental stress of the workouts.
- Rest can be of two types—total rest and active rest. Both are important in achieving maximum levels of performance.
- The level of work to rest should be determined by the body's natural rhythms and by the patterns evident when the student is improving or has become stagnant at the same plateau.
- During active rest the student works easily for 30 to 90 minutes with no sets. We also recommend cross-training with other sports in which we promote competition in a more relaxed atmosphere. During cross-training the body works but the mind rests.
- During total rest the student does not practice. Here we recommend that the student take long walks.
- Before competition we gradually reduce the intensity of practice sessions, allowing the body time to recover and regenerate. This routine, called tapering, allows the student to give total effort during competition.

Sample weekly competition overview

Tennis—on-court

- Active rest week—Light training very low intensity and volume.
- Non-tennis-specific training.
- Rest and regeneration activities.
- Watch Eddie Herr Invitational Tournament at academy.

Full-Time Admissions at the Bollettieri Tennis Academy

Students who are fortunate enough to visit the Academy on a full-time basis are required to send an application to the Admissions office. We also encourage a personal visit to the academy and the three academic schools available to our participants. If a personal visit is not possible, the director of admissions conducts a phone interview with the applicant to determine if he or she is a candidate who will fit into the program.

Once all the necessary forms have been completed and everything is in order, we send a letter of acceptance to the applicant and obtain a deposit. Our full-time semester generally begins in late August; however, we accept students at any time during the school year.

Life at the Academy

Upon arrival at the academy, all students check in with our reservations department. We arrange an orientation. They tour the academy and meet the sports directors, nurse, and director of student services, all of whom will be involved with their training and life at the academy.

The majority of our players attend academic school in the morning and participate in one of our six sports programs in the afternoon and on Saturday morning. School is from 8:00 A.M. to 12:30 P.M. Students then return to the academy for lunch.

The sports programs are from 1:30 P.M. to 5:30 P.M. Students who do not attend academic school can attend a sports program in the morning. Rates are based on which programs the student enters as well as whether the student is boarding or nonboarding. Tuition may be paid in one or two installments; however, the price is lower if the fee is paid all at once.

After dinner all players attending academic school attend a study hall. We have a coordinator who works with the schools to ensure that our players are doing well academically. Students who need extra help can remain at school until 2:30 P.M., when a bus picks them up. Tutors are available at additional cost for students requiring extra help with their studies.

Many of our nonboarding players attend school in the morning, come to the academy for lunch and the afternoon sports program, and then return home for dinner and to sleep. They are also welcome to participate in our extracurricular activities. Although we make some exceptions, we generally require players who have finished high school and are over 18 years of age to live off campus.

In the evening, students must clean their rooms before bedtime, keeping their areas tidy, beds made, and so on. A housekeeping staff does the major cleaning. We furnish an evening snack in the cafeteria for all our boarding students. Laundry is collected at specified times each week for our boarding students and returned at a specified time.

Each dorm has a supervisor who looks after the boarding participants. These staff members are available to assist our participants should a need arise. They may help younger boarders in getting their laundry together and overcoming homesickness. They deal with roommate issues and manage everything about living on campus. The dorm staff also make certain that students observe all rules, and they report to the director of student services when a problem arises.

We assign our boarding players a room according to age, school, and sport. If a roommate situation is not working, we are open to changing rooms to accommodate the player's personality. It is possible for returning players to request a particular roommate.

We plan extra activities for our participants, such as trips to the beach, local malls, theme parks, movies, and various other activities. Dances are periodically held at the academy, and we offer other activities as well (i.e., deep-sea fishing, jet skiing). Our transportation department is available to take our players to and from planned activities, doctor appointments, and so forth.

Although we do not allow our participants to leave the academy grounds unattended by a staff member or a person designated by a parent or guardian, students can arrange to be dropped with a group at a restaurant for dinner. They must remain there for pick up at a designated time. Although we are open 365 days a year, the breaks for our students coincide with those of the academic schools. No one is required to leave during the holidays, spring break, or winter break, and we provide a sports program for an extra fee for those remaining at the academy.

Each student has a bank account held and maintained by the academy. The parent or guardian can replenish the account with a check, credit card, or international wire transfer. Our bank is open each day at specified times. We furnish a copy of a child's personal account at any time to the parent or guardian upon request.

Language barriers sometimes cause difficulty because we enroll students from all over the world. Because the director of admissions speaks English, Spanish, and some French, we can overcome some of those barriers. Through experience, we have learned to deal with other languages as well. Sometimes we need an interpreter, and we seek out players' parents who are staying locally.

Because the majority of players attend academic schools, we work to maintain a good working relationship with the Pendleton School, Bradenton Academy, and St. Stephen's School. The director of admissions acts as a liaison between NBTA and the schools. To keep our relationships amicable, we act promptly should a problem arise.

International players attending our all-day tennis program must attend under a visitor's visa. International players attending academic schools must apply separately to the academic school of their choice. Bradenton Academy offers an ESOL (English for Speakers of Other Languages) program that makes it possible for international players to study in an American school. Once a student is accepted to school and the first semester is paid, the school will issue an I-20 visa. The student must present this document at the American embassy in the home country so that the passport can be stamped with a study visa. Once the student arrives at NBTA, all passports and airline tickets are filed at Guest Services to ensure their safekeeping. Our in-house travel agency is available to assist in travel bookings for our students.

We have families in need of financial aid apply to send their talented children to the academy. Although we do not normally have scholarships available, we look at each case individually. We answer each request for financial aid but normally suggest that families seek a local sponsor. We furnish all prospective students with an application to our program and encourage them to complete it and return it for our files should their situation change. IMG prepares a scholarship list each year for players they wish to sponsor. NBTA maintains a list of scholarship recipients as well. Discounts are distributed to our returning students according to number of years attending (i.e., one year, 5 percent; two years, 10 percent; three years, 15 percent; and four years, 20 percent).

The director of admission sits in on all disciplinary action taken on our full-time participants. This discussion includes the director of students, the dorm staff, and the sports director or coach if necessary. A student handbook, provided to all players attending our full-time program, outlines rules and regulations.

All parents and participants must sign and return our drug and alcohol policy form, which is part of our registration packet. We will not condone use of any controlled substances. Use of controlled substances will result in immediate dismissal from the academy.

Special Help

Any student having problems with his or her stroke or needing a little extra time on tennis receives special help for the specific need. The player or the coach of the player can request assistance. The academy offers weekly special help on Saturday mornings from 7:00 A.M. until 8:30 A.M. In addition, students who are making major changes to their technique are offered special help during the week. The student receives one-on-one training for 30 minutes, with emphasis on improving only one aspect of his or her game, for example, the forehand ground stroke or how to play points. After the session the student writes in a personal notebook the main points of the lesson.

Once again after reviewing the 2000-2001 program, Nick and Gabriel Jaramillo (Program Director) will add a complete new program for the fall of 2001.

Three of the academy's coaches of long standing and experience will be stationed on courts 1, 2, and 3. They will see on a daily basis individual groups and their coaches working on technique and drills. All of their activities will be videotaped throughout the year with each student getting a copy at the end of the year.

At the same time these three courts are in progress, the director coach of each court will select students experiencing difficulty and send them to the stadium court to receive help from Gabriel and Nick.

Note: This court will also be videotaped and then reviewed by the three directors of the three courts and the student's daily coach. This system allows the entire team, including coach and student, to know exactly what has taken place.

Injured Students

Any student who feels injured or sick is responsible for going to the nurse. The nurse will evaluate the student and recommend a course of action. No student is allowed to return to his or her room during practice sessions. If the student has suffered a minor injury, he or she may return to practice immediately. For a more severe injury or illness, the student may be instructed to watch practice or remain in the nurse's station. A trip to the doctor's office will occur if the nurse feels it is necessary or if the parent requests it. Each student's recovery is reevaluated each day, and a new course of action is determined based on the recovery process.

Homesickness

A student may experience homesickness at any point in the training. When we recognize homesickness, we provide one-on-one counseling to identify the issues the student is dealing with. If necessary, we contact a parent to help the student through this trying time.

Tournaments

Tournaments are spaced throughout the year in different parts of the state, country, or world. A tournament may include both genders of all age groups or may be more limited. We post sign-up sheets for local tournaments and include information about the date and cost of the trip (entry fee, transportation, food, and hotels if necessary). Tournaments located outside the local area will cost more and take more planning. At least one coach accompanies the students to each tournament. Each tournament offers a different level of competition, so students can attend tournaments appropriate to their level of play.

Video Lessons

Any student may request a video lesson. For an extra fee the student has a one-hour lesson with a private coach. The lesson can focus on the student's needs or cover all strokes. The coach and the student will review the tape to discuss strengths and weaknesses. The video is for the student to keep and review.

The academy has introduced an addition to our teaching system. Individual private lessons with video at the same time (this is often done by the coach who works with that student on a daily basis). Note: Short tennis, summer campers can also request this type of lesson.

Lessons With Nick Bollettieri

Any student may request a lesson with Nick for an extra fee. Nick will either work with the student on general aspects of the student's game or focus on specifics. The lesson with Nick will provide an evaluation of the student's game, offer insight on where the student can improve, and indicate where the student ranks compared with other players. Nick's court has a complete video analysis setup to record every aspect of the lesson. He uses this system to provide a review medium for the student. Each recording is duplicated. We keep one copy on file and send the other home to the parents.

Holidays and Summer Camps*

What do Walt Disney World and the Bollettieri Tennis Academy have in common? A mouse with big ears? A duck that can talk? Cinderella waiting for the stroke of midnight? None of the above. WDW and NBTA have made their philosophy simple and direct: "Let the guest enjoy the experience of fantasy and real life in one stop."

NBTA is an experience for any young or young-at-heart athlete. It is an athletic training facility that allows each guest to grow as an athlete and as a person. At NBTA we have gone through some growing pains and have learned from each of them.

Years ago we sent the majority of our 30 tennis coaches to run satellite summer camps around the world. Although these 8 to 12 summer camps provided a healthy saturation of the marketplace, the "mother ship" aspect of the NBTA experience suffered. Now we are committed to keeping the people, places, and things consistent for our short-time or weekly guests so that they can experience the life of a professional athlete while visiting NBTA.

---

*This section by Chip Hart and Ken Merritt.

Fun Versus Work

We have some real characters who work as coaches of the NBTA tennis program. These professional coaches can make or break the visit of the short-time guest. The coaches at NBTA are hard edged, but they provide an atmosphere conducive to learning and training. NBTA coaches treat every student, young or old, like a potential professional athlete. Much small talk occurs between the coaches and the customer-students. But all the talking and yelling is healthy and fun loving, done to provide an atmosphere dedicated to education and fun.

This hard-edged style of coaching, combined with tenderness and compassion, can be seen and felt on a daily basis. Typically, when the guests start their programs on Monday morning, they are nervous and sometimes scared, so the coaches spend a great deal of time getting to know them. But by Wednesday morning, look out. It is the toughest morning of the week. After NBTA coaches "bust them up" on Wednesday morning, we offer an optional beach trip that afternoon.

I Want to Be Discovered

The experience at NBTA would not be complete without the figurehead himself, Nick Bollettieri. When in residence, Nick is on court everyday working his magic, with one eye on his students and one eye on everything else.

Sometimes he has a top professional player on his court, like one of the Williams sisters, Tommy Haas, or Max Mirnyi. Other times he is sneaking up behind the courts to watch an 11-year-old, visiting for only a week, play a match. He has the ability to make anyone play better just by being around. I really feel that every guest at NBTA wants to be discovered to become Nick Bollettieri's next great player. Each wants to hear Nick say, "Let me be your coach. I'll take you to another level of excellence."

Typical Week

The typical summer student or weekly guest arrives on Sunday, somewhat nervous and anxious. The student checks in, opens up a bank account, has a picture ID taken, and meets all of his or her roommates. Most of the guests then explore the 190 acres of our athletic training facility.

An orientation meeting is mandatory for every new arrival at 7 P.M. every Sunday evening. This gathering gives the guests a chance to learn what to expect that week, from campus rules to the "Don't forget your sunscreen and waterbottle" speech.

Monday morning: Did anyone really sleep last night? Nerves can be cut with a knife. The evaluation is about to begin. Everyone is quiet and attentive. This is the last time the coaches will see them like this all week. The coaches move players around the courts until all are pretty well matched up with players of equal ability. Sometimes it seems a little confusing or even frustrating to see a player start at the top court only to be sent from one court to another until the player finds his or her peers.

Before evaluation starts, there is an edge of anxiety between the coaches on one side of the fence and the players on the other. Finally, one of the coaches breaks the tension with a welcome "Good morning." It still amazes me, after all the years, how the coaches at NBTA can tell the real players from the wannabes just by looking at them, before they even hit a ball. After the evaluation, the weekly guests get a chance to meet their head coach in a group orientation meeting. They exchange names, hometowns, and lengths of stay. Then the work begins.

When the bell rings at 8:00 A.M. every coach starts the daily chore of turning the guests into the best players they can become by Friday. Monday mornings are committed to the techniques of the Bollettieri Killer Forehand. At the same time the students are becoming accustomed to the way our coaches feed the balls and what their expressions mean, phrases like "Low to high catch the racquet at the top" and "Accelerate the racquet head."

Monday afternoon: Guests put their newfound knowledge to the test with matches against group peers. From an intensity point of view, Mondays are what we call medium-heavy days.

Tuesday: Tuesday morning is spent covering the techniques of the Bollistic Backhand one-handed, two-handed, and two-handed with a one-handed follow-through. The intensity declines a bit from Monday simply because we know our guests are tired and a little sore from the previous day's work.

Wednesday morning: Wednesday morning is dedicated to developing a Sonic Serve and a Right-back-atcha Return.

Wednesday afternoon: NBTA offers a beach trip for those who want to go. It is an optional trip, but over 80 percent of the student-campers end up going.

Thursday morning: This time is spent improving volleying skills, overheads, and general transition games. Wait a minute. Everyone says that Bollettieri doesn't work on the volleys. But the fact is that Nick and the coaches spend hours improving the guests' net games.

Thursday afternoon: This is where guests have the opportunity to play matches. Players go head-to-head with the group either directly above or below their own. The team spirit and camaraderie is exhilarating. The pressure is unbearable, but the atmosphere is fantastic. And they say tennis is not a team sport.

Friday: All our guests participate in the precompetition games and drills, a weekly tradition that started years ago. Music is blasting and players are diving, all in match-specific games that allow everyone the chance to be a star.

Saturday morning: Now it is time to review. Each student gets one final chance to clean up a particular stroke before heading home to win his or her club championship.

The high point of the week is having Nick in residence. He sees the group twice, with the first session being motivational and the second is answering students' questions. Nick does the same with the adult program.

Off Court

The tennis court is why guests come to NBTA in the first place. They all want to become as good as possible in a short time. But I believe the off-court time is why they continue to come back.

Keeping the holiday or summer break in mind and making it a major part of the experience is what brings and holds memories. Once their sport programs are finished for the day, they can act like kids at summer camp. Let me set the scene for you: approximately 400 boys and girls, from over 40 countries, milling around the swimming pool and patio area during dinner trying to decide what they are going to do that evening and with whom they are going to do it. They have tons of choices with between seven and nine buses going to the movies, mall, arcade, go-cart track, stores, museums, and so on. Or they can stay on campus and be involved in activities like a pool party, talent show, music jams, art classes, Ping-Pong tournaments, or pool tournaments.

A Balanced Life

To achieve the maximum result from your effort, no matter what task you are undertaking, you have to be focused. You cannot step between the lines and hope to give your best when your thoughts and concerns are elsewhere. No one understands this better than Nick does. He can watch a student walk up to the court from 20 yards away and know immediately if the student is focused and ready to give his or her best. He can tell by body language, by the way the athlete carries himself or herself, whether the student is focused and ready to go or whether the student has something standing in the way of total commitment. Because he understands this so well, Nick emphasizes what we call our Student Life program. The clear understanding is that students have to be happy and not distracted to perform to the best of their ability. If they are not happy they will not be focused or committed on court. It is up to the staff working with students off court to help them reach the point where they can be ready to play. The life of our young athlete must have balance—the right amount of recreation and social interaction. And, of course, student academics must be under control. Without proper balance no student can perform at the top of his or her game. No balance means no happiness and no success! Attitude is the key word to success or failure.

Student Life Program

The activities coordinator is an essential part of the development of the mind and spirit of the student body at the Bollettieri Tennis Academy. We have six sports and over 400 students from 45 countries living in a focused and structured community. Trying to make all the students feel like they are part of a family, the Bollettieri family, is the underlying philosophy of the night shift. The difference between our program and similar programs on a college or university campus is that we have children as young as 12 years old and as old as 19. We all know growing up that there is a fine line between being best friends with your little brother or sister and having him or her become your worst enemy. The activities coordinator is the one who has to juggle these chronological and biological age differences.

This area of student-athlete development is really the only opportunity for the student to make a choice with the daily schedule. Students are told what to do from the time they wake up until the time they go to bed, but these activities give them a chance to say no or a chance to choose what they want to do.

Without our activity program, students would have no life other than their sport. Below is a list of activities and a sample calendar of events for students at the academy.

Intramural leagues and tournaments

We offer and encourage participation from each student or staff member on campus in several sports activities.

- Five-on-five flag football league
- Soccer tournament for nonsoccer players
- Three-on-three basketball
- Ultimate Frisbee
- Tennis tournament for nontennis players
- Nongolfer golf outing

Cultural development

Because of our relationship with the community, we are able to offer educational and enjoyable activities for the more culturally minded students.

- Theatre
- Concerts
- Museums
- Aquariums
- Study groups

- Nutrition meetings
- Religious meetings
- Learn-to-dance classes
- Modeling, beauty, and make-up seminars

Music and arts

We provide one or more professional instructors to teach music and art classes for creative students attending NBTA.

- Music appreciation
- Learn to play music
- Piano lessons
- Painting and ceramics
- Drama and play club

Entertainment

On-campus entertainment builds spirit, passion, and camaraderie among the student body. Holding special entertainment functions on a monthly basis livens up the place at night.

- Lip-sync competitions
- Talent show
- Poetry night by the pool
- Pay-per-view night in the video room
- Hall versus hall themes
- Lock-ins
- Guest speakers or group sessions
- "Nick at Night" parties
- Pool parties

Special events

Using the special-events bulletin board allows us to have direct communication with every student on campus, thus creating themes and campuswide activities throughout the normal day of training and living.

- Chat sessions with a coach
- Home country nights
- Staff versus students events
- Olympic competition
- Special dining menus
- Holiday celebrations

Trips

We schedule trips to meet the everyday needs of the student.

- Mall
- Movie
- Bowling
- Salon

Extended Family

The family system is crucial to the life of our boarding students. The first principle of systems is wholeness. The whole is greater than the sum of its parts. The system results not from the elements added together but from the interaction of the elements. The elements in this case are the student, his or her direct family, and the NBTA support staff. Without interaction there is no system. The main function of the dorm staff is to recognize these elements and guide our students to the best of their abilities. The main goal of a healthy extended family system is to have key staff members in place so that all students feel safe and free to communicate on all levels.

What will our students take away from NBTA when their stay ends? More than anything, it will be relationships—relationships with support staff, with coaches, and, more directly, with fellow students, friendships that may last a lifetime. During a stay at NBTA a student may interact with people from over 40 countries. This alone can provide one of life's greatest learning experiences. Any family system is composed of connecting relationships. Students from diverse backgrounds come together at NBTA chasing individual dreams. This factor links our students in a common goal—the love of their game and where they want to take it. Family systems, like all systems, relate through a process called feedback, the loop that keeps the system functioning. Staff who listen and talk to students understand what the students are going through mentally—the joy of winning, the agony of defeat, the struggle of dealing with injury and recovery. When the boy or girl is away from the support of Mom or Dad, it is up to the night staff to be someone to listen to, relate to, and talk to. The night staff are the key if NBTA is going to produce the great players for which Nick and the coaches have become world famous. Night supervisors have an important job as the extended family that offers a healthy and safe place for students to achieve their dreams and goals in life.

Family Rules

All families have rules, some more, some less. Nevertheless, parents understand that all kids need guidance! There is no way around this. When applying to NBTA, parents are always happy to hear about our firm policies and procedures to protect and guide their children. The kids aren't quite as enthusiastic. We understand that parents have entrusted their children to us, and we take this as our most serious responsibility. Parents are asking us to assist them in raising, shaping, and molding the future of their most prized possession. Wow! Tell me that is not some serious responsibility. The common thread that links the home family structure with the NBTA extended family structure is the existence of family rules and the consequences associated with breaking them. The reason for rules in both instances is to help keep the child pointed in the right direction on the trek to adulthood. Although most families are concerned about the common good of a family of four or five, we are concerned with providing a common ground for about 200 students who live with us full time.

To do this, we needed to develop a system that was workable for this number of students. The system had to provide clear direction to students while not appearing to be unbearable. A natural tie-in with the student's existing family structure was required. We researched many boarding schools that had been in existence since the 19th century. We saw no need to reinvent the wheel when these schools had been perfecting systems for over 100 years. All the schools had systems in which students earned either merits or demerits based on their actions or ability to follow rules. We just needed to adapt that philosophy to our unique setup. Because the idea of achieving at high levels has always been synonymous with NBTA, we decided that students would earn or achieve points based on their own choices. We call our version of this simply the point system. The system requires that each student achieve a certain standard each week to participate in extracurricular social activities. A family might use a similar system, requiring the child to maintain a certain level of behavior each week in order to go out to a dance on the weekend or to a movie with friends. If the behavior does not meet a certain acceptable level, the parent isn't going to allow the child to participate. When the child demonstrates a proper level of responsibility, he or she gains more freedom. It is up to the child to determine if the activities are important or not. This system sets up the need for young adults to make choices and abide by the consequences. It also helps the student make the transition from young adult to adult. Consequences of not abiding by the rules may include restriction to campus, work details, and, in extreme cases, suspension from sport or school. All of this means nothing if the people who oversee the family rules are not firm and fair.

Melting Pot

Full-time dorm life at NBTA is a melting pot of cultures, personalities, skills, and interests. Although students choose to attend NBTA because of its sports programs, those who live on campus face unique challenges away from their chosen fields. Students, perhaps for the first time, are away from home, living on their own and interacting in close proximity with others who may not share the same values, language, customs, or even diets. The dorm supervisor's job is to establish a common set of rules that combine all aspects of students' wants, needs, and wishes. This is not an easy task, nor is it always possible. But by using a mixture of frankness, consistency, reasoning, and sometimes humor, it is possible to set standards students will follow. We always encourage an open sharing of opinions, suggestions, and conversation among roommates and dorm staff. This openness gives the students the feeling of being heard and included, inevitably leading to the development of leadership abilities among the students. As with any group, not all students will get along with each other, nor even accept differences. What we can encourage and demonstrate through our policies and attitudes are tolerance and understanding of these differences.

Some examples of the blending of differences can be seen when students are asked to cook a meal from their country or share some of their country's customs. Students also have an opportunity to intermingle in events that present room versus room or dorm versus dorm situations. Differences tend to fade to the background when members of a group must rely on each other to reach a goal. The more common goals we can set, the more students tend to rely on each other in spite of their differences.

NBTA is also concerned about our student's needs after they leave our academy. To this end we offer and encourage students to participate in a variety of outside activities; everything from sporting events to opera, from driving courses to SAT preparation courses, from lectures on personal hygiene to taking a student to church.

Overall, NBTA staff act as surrogate parents, handling everything from discipline to understanding. From life skills to sports skills, from social graces to academic success, NBTA staff are ready to help guide and mold tomorrow's winners, on or off court.

Academics

One of the most difficult tasks we face when working with full-time students is the same one that millions of parents of teenagers face each year. How do I get my child to focus on academics and teach him or her that academic performance now will count in the future? This battle rages each day at NBTA. The task can be especially difficult with some of our more gifted athletes. Some of these students are under the mistaken impression that school doesn't matter because they will make millions on the athletic field and be set for life. In all the years of the existence of this academy, just one student failed to heed our academic advice. He needed remedial work to be accepted into college. He simply didn't realize that every day he didn't spend making academics a priority was another day spent later digging out of a hole.

We understand and reorganize erratic thought processes and take extra precautions to provide our students with a first-class academic support team. We take the academic portion of the student's life so seriously that we hired one staff member specifically to oversee and coordinate all academic activity. These duties include interviewing and hiring the best and brightest tutors for our students and organizing compulsory evening study halls based on specific course needs, grouping students who need help in, for example, history or math. This supervisor attends weekly meetings with representatives of both academic schools to monitor the progress of specific students. The supervisor sets up private tutoring for students who need extra help and organizes Scholastic Aptitude Test (SAT) preparation classes. These are the main points of support we provide in conjunction with the schooling at The Pendleton School, Bradenton Academy, and St. Stephen's. College preparation for seniors is another major undertaking by our staff. Besides being offered SAT preparation courses, seniors are educated on how to write college essays, fill out applications, write letters of interest to specific colleges, and make athletic videos to send to colleges. In 1998 NBTA senior students were collectively offered approximately one million dollars of athletic and academic scholarships. That's serious money!

Here is a partial list of colleges that granted early acceptance to our students for the 1999–2000 school year:

Harvard University	Duke University
Princeton University	University of Pennsylvania
University of Oxford	London School of Finance
Vanderbilt University	Boston University
Worcester Polytechnic Institute	Adelphi University
Wake Forest University	University of Notre Dame
St. Lawrence University	Florida Institute of Technology
Fairfield University	Colgate University

Chasing the Dream

Each September as the doors open on a new school year at the academy, several hundred children and young adults pass through the gates of an institution that for the last 20 years has produced tennis champions and, more important, champions in life. They come from all points of the globe and represent a variety of cultures and religions. They have upbringings as varied as one can imagine. Some come from well-to-do families. Others from families that have scraped their pennies together by selling or remortgaging homes, by changing jobs, or even by uprooting households—all to give their child a chance to chase a dream.

College Tennis in Perspective

By Scott Treibly, Tennis Coach, Texas A&M University

Deciding the right time for a player to become a professional is a continual topic at tennis events around the world. To be a tennis "pro" today you must be mentally tough, physically fit, spiritually sound, and financially stable. For some of the top juniors it could mean right now. For others developing their minds and bodies through the college tennis system should be an absolute consideration. Young players should carefully and truthfully evaluate their ability before making the jump in either direction. "The top Americans today should use college tennis as a springboard into the pros. It buys players time to work on weaknesses and allows youth to prosper," Texas A&M University coach Tim Cass says. "Unless a player is guaranteed one million dollars he or she should make the college step."

John McEnroe, Jimmy Connors, Arthur Ashe, Stan Smith, and Tim Mayotte: All these great players used college tennis as a stepping stone to the pros. If this step is good enough for them, it's good enough for juniors today.

The greatest benefit of college tennis today is that it allows you to play both college matches and pro tournaments. Other sports don't allow you to play 20 professional competitions while wearing your school colors. With the increase in pro tournaments around the United States, student athletes can use the summer, holidays, and parts of the season to play future, challenger, and grand prix events. If you're good enough to make the tour on a regular basis then you can make the jump.

Consider Arthur Ashe, John McEnroe, and Stan Smith as players that have utilized the collegiate ranks. Ashe performed consistently in tour events throughout his college career but chose to remain in school for the education and a chance to win a national team and individual championship. In 1966, after he had won the team and individual championships, Ashe began playing full-time on the tour. In 1968, he won his first of three grand slam crowns at the U.S. Open. Ashe, one of tennis' all-time greats, was the first African-American to distinguish himself in both the collegiate and professional tennis ranks. McEnroe made massive waves prior to his freshman year in college as he advanced to the semifinals of Wimbledon. In 1978 he won the NCAA team and individual championship for Stanford before declaring himself pro. Stan Smith played at USC from 1966-1968 and won the NCAA singles championship in 1968. After school Smith also prospered on the pro tour, winning the U.S. Open singles championship in 1971 and the Wimbledon championship singles in 1972. In more recent tennis history, Stanford standout Marissa Irving played college tennis while being ranked 81 in the world. She lost in the second round of the Australian Open before starting the spring season. Matt Anger had similar results at USC. He made the third round of the Australian Open before returning to school. These players from the past and present are examples of why college tennis can enhance a professional career.

There are many benefits to taking the road of college tennis. One such benefit is the coaching. "College, much like the AAA league in baseball, provides a valuable training ground and important guidance," University of Florida coach Ian Duvenhage says. This type of guidance helps develop the fundamentals of the game. Another benefit of college tennis is that it helps a player step up the ladder and teaches the value of team. Within the team student-athletes learn the values of time management and discipline. Other benefits include nice facilities, travel, scholarships, and national newspaper and television coverage. On top of these benefits to your tennis game, you also gain a college education.

However, there are some young players who should go directly onto the pro circuit. Rare talent like Andre Agassi, Jim Courier, and Pete Sampras should turn pro after high school. They were born great. Andy Roddick, Vince Spadea, and Jan-Michael Gambill were also successful straightaway on the professional circuit. Choosing to turn professional for these players was the right move given their progress and results as juniors. In contrast, David Wheaton, who grew up in the same generation, chose to attend college. Only after two years of collegiate competition and physical development did he turned pro and achieve a career high ranking as no. 12.

Timing is of the essence because players grow and mature at different stages. The range of a professional tennis career spans from ages 15 to 35. Competing at the highest level on the ATP and WTA tour requires perfection. Pros on the highest level can exploit your weaknesses and not allow you to play with your strengths. "I do not believe a tennis player should turn professional unless they are All-World," says Coach Duvenhage. You can not have holes in your game if you want to compete with the world's best. American upstart Andy Roddick, a former top junior in the world, turned professional after winning the Eddie Herr International, the Orange Bowl, and the Australian Open junior championships. Two years before, it had looked as if Andy could benefit from college tennis. However, he managed to improve many facets of his game and began dominating all of his peers. This type of success encouraged his decision to turn pro.

The tour is glamorous, and for players wanting to perform in the elusive tennis arena it might be more beneficial to skip the college tennis step on their way to the top. Bypassing the collegiate setup can create extreme situations. Do you want to play the beginning level pro tournaments on court #28 in Indonesia for one ATP point or travel to Spain weeding your way through the plethora of up and coming players on red clay?

Thousands of great athletes have passed through the doors of college tennis. After preparing themselves physically and emotionally during college many have gone on to become successful tennis professionals,

(continued)

College Tennis in Perspective *(continued)*

doctors, teachers, and businessmen. The college atmosphere challenges athletes daily and forces them to make decisions to maintain discipline and character. The making of a champion on this level takes a unique combination of talent, heart, commitment, and sacrifice.

Doubles

Why is college doubles so great? Doubles is one of college tennis' greatest assets. There are not many competitive venues in the world that spend so much time on fundamental doubles. There are many doubles strategies that can be taught, learned, and executed. In practice, college coaches emphasize ball placement, the importance of the first serve, using variety on the return (lobs, slice, down the line, and cross court), playing the first volley deep off the serve, how to communicate in between points, and how to poach the middle effectively. Strategy in doubles becomes scientific because there is less court space. Less space creates fewer variables and increases the importance of your opponents' strengths and weaknesses.

Fact: 37 collegiate players have won grand slam doubles titles in the last 20 years. There are a number of reasons to consider. Players often start and finish team workouts with doubles. There is on-court coaching for singles and doubles matches. Doubles is a major momentum swing putting pressure on players to win their pro set. College drills practicing the finer points are normally not exercised in Europe and South America. These continents often do not even host doubles events. Finally, college matches are played on hard courts where the aggressive style necessary in doubles is common.

Doubles has always been a game that is enjoyable. College tennis has increased the quality and allowed many players to go on and have successful careers on the tour.

Chasing the dream takes on different forms depending on which student you speak to. The dream usually ranges from "I want to be no. 1 in the world" or "I want to be a pro player" to "I'd like to play in college." When we interview potential students for acceptance to NBTA, the most important part of the process is not the child's ability level but whether he or she has a dream and is willing to make the sacrifices necessary to chase it. Many people who are not familiar with the academy believe that we are only about creating tennis champions. Those familiar with the academy and its goals understand clearly that world champions, those who can make a career out of playing the sport, are rare. What really takes place on a day-to-day basis is preparing our students to be future champions in life. Most students will be affected as much by what happens off the field of play as by what happens on it. Our real goal is to produce successful, well-rounded people!

CHAPTER 2

Stroke Fundamentals

"There is no sub-
stitute for hard
work. There will
be disappoint-
ments, but the
harder you work,
the luckier you
will get. Never be
satisfied with less
than your best
effort. If you strive
for the top and
miss, you'll still
'beat the pack.' "

Former President Gerald R. Ford made this comment that applies as much to sports and coaching as it does to any other human endeavor.

These words apply to athletics, coaching, raising children, going to school, or just getting out of bed on a cold, dreary morning. The dreams attached to any athletic contest cannot be manifested without the application of an uncommon work ethic. The single greatest component of success in sports is discipline.

Past

I have heard about strokes and grips for many years. At the early stages of my career (the late 1950s and 1960s) there were only a few types of grips and swings. The following was the conventional wisdom about ground-stroke grips at the time.

1. For the forehand, players used the eastern forehand grip.
2. For the backhand, players used the eastern backhand grip. The majority of players were one-handed.

3. The strokes were very quiet. For the most part players did little running around when choosing to hit a forehand or backhand. (Today, players tend to hit as many forehands as possible.)

4. Players assumed ready position at the center hash mark. The only time there was a choice of which stroke to use was when the ball came down the middle of the court.

5. At contact and recovery, players had to finish the stroke, avoid jumping, keep the back foot behind them, and so on. They were then to recover and return to the center-court position.

6. Players were expected to meet the ball in front of the lead foot.

Exceptions

Harold Solomon and Eddie Dibbs were hitting two-handed backhands at the time. Harold had a funny grip (full semiwestern to western). In hindsight it is now clear that the grips of Solomon and Dibbs were ahead of their time. At the same time Jimmy Evert was teaching his daughter, Chris, a two-handed backhand.

Forty years later there is an entirely new view. This chapter will give you a look at what is going on today. Even though the look has changed, some basic principles seem to be eternal. When I first started teaching the game, my knowledge was limited. Today, I realize that the lack of technical knowledge contributed to both my successes and my failures. I looked at students and let them do what was natural. I knew almost nothing about the volley, but somehow Brian Gottfried, one of my students in the early 1960s, became one of the best volleyers in the game. Accidents happen.

In 1996 Bjorn Borg visited the academy to get ready for the Senior 35 Tour. In talking to Bjorn, I realized that his style of play was not taught. He did it naturally. I came to understand that his fantastic career was a result of working with natural talent and instinct, especially his western grip. He would run for every ball (his trademark). He hit with heavy spin, looped backhands with two hands, and at times would hit with two hands and follow through with one. He was unique. Those who said that he couldn't win on grass were silenced by his six Wimbledon titles. Borg knew how to win. I thought the same thing when I saw Martina Hingis at age 11. Her strokes were

Life is built on strengths and weaknesses; you must blend them for success!

somewhat iffy, but she knew what to do with the ball! Her mom deserves a Golden Ball award for not letting someone else teach her.

During Borg's few months' stay at the academy, he told me he liked to play rather than just hit; he simply liked doing what felt natural to him. Bjorn would also run down anything that wasn't nailed on the court. This is the philosophy that I try to implant in all my students. Two students that come to mind are Jimmy Arias and Andre Agassi. Both of their dads told them simply to "hit the hell out of the ball."

Basic rules are necessary no matter what type of player you work with. But you must remember that all players are different. Even with the fundamentals, there might be slight differences. I often repeat myself by saying that hitting a ball is not enough to reach one's potential. Every player has assets and liabilities. Life is built on strengths and weaknesses; you must blend them for success. Few fundamentals can be put aside if a player is to reach higher levels.

In the end, people will usually play in a fashion that is consistent with their personalities. Take Aaron Krickstein for example. He is a quiet and introspective player. During matches he would play exactly like that, although he was extraordinarily competitive.

Another example is Monica Seles. She is extremely quiet in practice (except for that incredible squeak). This quiet demeanor belied her aggressive nature. She is almost Jekyll and Hyde in contrast.

Carling Basset was always the same, both on and off the court. She was aggressive but used a style that won people over to become fans.

Jimmy Arias has an unwavering personality. He will bet on anything and is always coming at others, both on and off the court.

Andre Agassi is an extremely competitive player, but not as loud as Arias in his words and actions. On court, however, he was relentless and often enjoyed punishing players by keeping them on the court much longer than he had to.

Martina Hingis has an engaging smile and is quiet, but don't let that fool you. She is the most dangerous kind of player, a professional assassin with a smile.

Helping the Student's Game

I have always had a simple, uncomplicated approach to tennis and life. On and off court, in good times and bad, the art of reducing problems to their simplest form has served me well. As with life, teaching well can be simplified by reducing it to its basic elements. My experience has shown that at its simplest level, tennis can be divided into three sections: technique, mental ability, and physical conditioning.

Note that we now try to identify and include in the equation inherited athletic traits, athletic background of the family, statistical analysis of playing characteristics, and testing to determine size, nutrition, and so on.

Before we get into grips, swings, and other intricate parts of the game, let's discuss key expressions used by coaches when teaching, by commentators when calling a match, and even by parents as they speak to their children.

• **Keep the ball in play (consistency)**—The player should always have the goal of hitting the ball over the net one more time than the opponent does. Impatient players may want to go for a big shot early. Coaches can allow this, but they should make sure that the player earns it by putting a specific number of balls in play before going for a winner. This idea is important to instill in players who seek to take their game to another level. Examples of instructions to players are the following:

1. Keep the ball in play but don't push.
2. Keep the ball in play for a certain number of strokes, then go for the winner without waiting for margin of error.
3. Keep the ball in play until the opponent misses.

• **Hit to a certain spot or location (placement)**—The first priority is keeping the ball in play. The next challenge is to place the ball to selected areas.

• **Keep the opponent deep**—Depth prevents a player from gaining control. The player must achieve depth early in the development of a point. Adding more height clearance over the net will produce deeper balls.

• **Action on balls (variations of spin)**—Hitting the ball the same way all the time may not be enough to beat a good opponent, especially if the opponent tunes in to the player's single style of play. Adding spins to the ball can create a major weapon!

• **Power, or better, "controlled power"**—Players must understand that power does not come about by sheer physical energy. Marcelo Rios is only five-foot-nine, yet he generates great power on serves and ground strokes. This power comes from lots of practice, with timing and increased racquet-head speed being the primary ingredients.

Athletic Skill Development

In sports we all dream of being the best. But no one dreams about the hard work, dedication, knowledge, and sacrifices it takes to excel in a sport. Life is not much different, and most people you meet would like to be successful in life. As in sports, being successful is a matter of dedication, sacrifice, and application. If you want to be the world's best salesperson, you had better know more than how to knock on doors. Before you can sell anything you must understand the art of selling. To succeed, you must understand that knowledge, dedication, and hard work go into it.

The same understanding applies to tennis players, who basically want to hit the ball over the net one more time than their opponents do. The more the player learns about the ball before making contact, the more success he or she will have in controlling the return.

Players need to be familiar with the elements of their sport. I start young children in any sport by first allowing them to have fun while they develop their motor skills, their confidence, and an understanding of how and why balls bounce. In some fun way I would teach them the feel and flow of the object of the sport, be it a ball, a puck, the water, or even a horse. This rhythm, this idea of becoming one with the ball, teaches the discipline needed to succeed at a game, a project, or a career. Children are sponges and acquire most of the knowledge of their lives in the first three years of existence.

It's my judgment that in sports in general and in tennis in particular, beginners and even accomplished players experimenting with new shots should not concern themselves initially that their balls are spraying all over the court. Rather, they should learn how the ball feels, how it bounces, and what it can do.

The level of understanding is simple:

1. Knowing something about the ball

2. Knowing how to get ready for the ball and how to move toward it

3. Knowing what happens at contact

4. Coordinating the racquet and the body

This simplicity is evident in beginners and advanced players. The beginner should focus on contact rather than the construction of the shot. Consider the example of an advanced student being taught how to hit a slice. Before the student can perfect the shot, he or she must first know its bounce, its changing direction, about moving forward or backward, and the rationale behind hitting a slice.

Only when the student understands all these concepts can a coach devise a practice session that will spill over effectively into matches. My most profound advice is to get to know the ball. It's impossible to have success with any sport, car, computer, mathematical problem, whatever, until one is completely at ease with the fundamentals. For instance, Dale Earnhardt, one of the best race-car drivers in the world, had a staff possessing the best mechanical expertise money can buy. Still, Earnhardt could tell you the amount of air in his tires and how the engine worked. It's the same story with Microsoft chairman Bill Gates. He can discuss every aspect of his business, from invention to sales.

With tennis I play simple games with my students. I ask them to see the ball as soon as they can and react to it.

1. A lower intermediate player reacts to the ball after it bounces on his or her side.

2. A solid intermediate player reacts to the ball as it crosses the net.

3. An advanced player reacts to the ball when it leaves the opponent's racquet.

4. Top players—by looking at the racquet face, level of contact, and the opponent's body position—can anticipate with accuracy what type of ball will cross the net and where it is likely to go.

Racing experts say that Michael Schumacher knows his automobile so well and is so in tune with the feel and sounds that he knows how fast he's going within two miles per hour without looking at the speedometer. This quality makes him among the best in the world.

Note the following:

1. Players should know what type of ball they will be receiving and where in the court they will receive it.

2. Players should note mentally the trends of opponents—where they usually play their shots and what their patterns of play are.

Every player has a certain style. Sampras hits the forehand relatively flat. On the backhand he can hit flat down the line and crosscourt with some spin. Seles hits the ball early and has spin on both sides. Marcelo Rios hits the ball early and relatively flat on both sides. If the experts are largely predictable, at any lesser level it should be a snap to anticipate ball direction.

Players should note these tips for picking up the ball early:

1. Check the book on the opponent's preferences before the match.

2. Observe the opponent's position, stance, and preparation.

3. Note the angle of the racquet.

4. Notice whether the swing is low to high or high to low.

5. Note the speed of the swing.

Several indications can help the player anticipate early on the return of the serve:

1. Height of the toss. Does it vary with certain serves?

2. Direction of the toss.

3. Variety of leg use.

4. Amount of hip and shoulder rotation.

By looking for these clues, the player will be able to pick up the ball earlier. Baseball scouts are ahead of the field in this art. In an effort to anticipate what type of ball the pitcher will throw, they videotape pitchers and look for small differences on each pitch.

It's the same for quarterbacks or backfield men in football. Running backs may set up in a different way if they are to block rather than carry the ball. By observing multiple repetitions, opponents or scouts can detect the little moves one makes without the ball.

In a 1997 playoff game, the New England Patriots picked up on the signals of Dan Marino. They sacked him repeatedly or intercepted him. Result: Miami lost.

Through my years of teaching one obvious standard has emerged. Students who give 100 percent have a better chance to reap the benefits. We tell all our students—full time, short time, adults, juniors, and professionals—that the two important tips to improving without taking a lesson are the following:

1. Never think you can't reach a ball. If you try for every ball, even the impossible ones, you'll reach balls you never thought possible.
2. Never let the ball bounce twice in practice. If you train yourself in this manner, you will learn to pick up the ball earlier.

Movement

The ready position, the first step to the ball, adjustment steps, the first recovery step, shuffle steps, the split step, speed, balance, and power are all key elements to movement.

1. Ready position—intense and focused but still relaxed, using a balanced position to move from and control the effectiveness of the first step to the ball
2. First step to the ball—usually a step out in the direction of the ball that is fast, strong, and balanced, leading the player to the shortest distance to contact
3. Adjustment steps—small steps that allow the player to be in the strongest hitting position possible
4. Recovery—must be part of the swing so that at the end the player ends up in a balanced position for the first step back to the center
5. First-step recovery—usually a crossover step to cover the open court faster, which leads to several shuffle steps to cover the court behind the player
6. Shuffle steps—steps that put the player into good position to move in any direction and usually end in a split step just as the opponent makes contact

Obviously, conditioning, speed, strength, and anticipation are more natural for some players. Good movement techniques, however, can benefit all players. Intensity, focus, and anticipation all improve if the player sees the ball early off the opponent's racquet.

Along with picking up the ball sooner, the player must learn to move the feet. There is no alternative. Countless simple routines can improve physical conditioning. When considering on-court movement, the thrust is always how to get to the ball quickly without wasted motion. How does the player arrive at the ball so that he or she can make contact in good balance? How does the player recover? The process is move, balance, contact, and recover.

Recovery

During my early years of teaching, including hearing and watching players and other coaches, I learned that the recovery could not be overemphasized. Hitting the ball is only part of the stroke production. The player must get back to position for the return of the next ball.

Think of a shortstop making full extension to field a ground ball. The fielder must not only glove the ball but also throw it to one of the bases. With the body in full motion it's impossible to stop when fielding the ball, so the shortstop takes a few steps, executes the throw to first base, and then recovers to second base if needed. I think of a tennis player performing the same kind of movement. I have my players on the run take an earlier step or two after contact and use the extra step for a push back to position for the next ball. Look at Andre Agassi, Michael Chang, Jim Courier, and Venus Williams and you'll see that they not only take an extra step but also leave their feet during the contact point and finish in the direction of recovery.

A player will hit some outright winners, but the majority of balls will come back to the player. It is infinitely more important to learn how to hit and recover, not just back to the center of the court but to where the next ball might be coming. Some of today's top players (Jim Courier, Tommy Haas, Steffi Graf, Andre Agassi, Martina Hingis, Marcelo Rios, and the Williams sisters) embrace this rule whenever possible.

For many years the center of the court was the only place to go to, but stronger and faster athletes using advanced racquet technology have developed powerful new weapons. With this in mind, players should find a recovery point that favors their style of play.

Making Changes

In almost every area of human endeavor, people are reluctant to change and may even fight it. The mere suggestion of change indicates that something is wrong with the status quo, a concept that most people have difficulty accepting. Changing the status quo may be unacceptable, especially for people who have had some success. More important, almost everyone is comfortable with the status quo.

If you ask someone to change, you must first be aware of the fear that change engenders. From a coach's point of view, allow us to share our experiences.

A change in the grip, for example, will definitely be uncomfortable. No one knows if the change will be successful. As in all changes, much depends on the eagerness and determination of the one making the changes. But, as a coach, if you believe you are doing what is best for the student, you must take the challenge and face the risk. With most students, you must be prepared to deal with the student and their parents.

In making changes, consider the approach of making small adjustments so that the student isn't even aware that changes are being made. A good model is the dentist who distracts the patient when administering an uncomfortable shot. That is, you can prevent your student from thinking about the big changes by making small but gradual changes.

Some students are fearful of any change. With these students, you can accomplish major changes only if you are willing to do some ancillary work. In particular, you must first discuss with the student and the parents what the changes involve and what will likely happen to the student's game. Consider what happens when changing an extreme western grip to an eastern grip.

- A loss of power will occur. The extreme western grip offers the feeling of strength, great racquet speed, and lots of spin with the face of the racquet closing very quickly.
- With the new grip the racquet face will not close as quickly, and the ball will probably go high and out. The eastern grip may be too much change to effect in one step because strength issues, lack of racquet speed, face on contact, spin, and so on will result in all sorts of hits, including balls going high, deep, and far out of play.
- Physical discomfort (blisters) and mental anxiety (loss of confidence) will occur.
- The process may take a long time. You as a coach must realize the change could require changing the student's practice sets and tournament play. The two options are making the change all at once or making the change in small segments to limit the trauma to the student.

Before making any changes, it is necessary to consider many factors:

- Age of the student
- Athletic ability of the student
- Goals of the student
- Rest of the student's game
- Type of game the student plays
- Present results as a player
- Mental attitude of the student
- Parents' ability to accept change

For instance, Pete Sampras accepted the wisdom of Dr. Fischer, a far older coach. Fischer advised Sampras that to compete at the top of the world some day, he needed to augment his God-given talents. Primarily, he had to change from a two-handed backhand to a one-handed backhand. This decision was difficult because Sampras had done reasonably well with his two-handed backhand. The discussion has been much talked about because Pete was only 14 at the time. It took two years of losses and the loss of his junior standing for Sampras to achieve his goal. You decide if it was worth it.

After considering all these factors, you as coach must be patient and positive, working as much with your student's mental attitude as with the technicalities of change. You might need help from an outside source.

More on Making Changes

As someone who has changed many players, I find the method of making changes a little at a time the most interesting and most challenging. Trying to get your student to the next level by effecting some small change, particularly when the student fears change or is satisfied with success, is one of the most challenging obstacles any coach can confront. Our way is to accept their intransigence as a fact and to work indirectly.

For example, a student comes to us with a high circular backswing. We notice that on the run he has difficulty hitting a forehand crosscourt. The first thing we do is get the student to admit he has "some" difficulty hitting crosscourt. We use the word "some" because it's important not to destroy confidence or challenge the ego. The next step should be a discussion that contains the following elements:

- Define the situation.
- Be sure that both player and coach agree that a problem exists.
- Determine the recommended solution.

Difficulty in hitting on-the-run crosscourt shots is usually caused by

- using too big a backswing,
- preparing too late, often caused by using a circular backswing that is too high or a double backswing, or
- allowing movement to upset timing.

We then place the racquet in a complete backswing before the running begins. In doing this, the student needs only to swing forward to hit crosscourt. This invariably increases the chance of making the shot.

Having All the Information

My teaching career began in the late 1950s. Techniques were the main part of the lesson.

- Grip—eastern forehand and eastern backhand
- Swing—straight back
- Contact—slightly in front of the hitting foot or out in front of the body
- Follow-through—a swing through the ball with a long follow-through to the target, no extra motion with the body, and no extra step with the back foot

As the game increased in popularity in the 1960s and 1970s, we made additions to our teaching techniques. One of the reasons for the academy's continued success is our ability to evolve with the sport. New thinking, new options, and new facilities keep the academy at the cutting edge of teaching.

Since my rather humble beginnings, sweeping changes have occurred in the game's techniques and tactics. The building of points in long rallies has given way to taking the ball early and pounding winners from anywhere on court. Athleticism and movement are now fundamentally different. In the 1950s we took tennis players and attempted to make them athletes. We now take superb athletes and make tennis players of them. Along with this change have come sports psychologists and scouts, mental training, nutrition, statistical video reports, longer and more powerful racquets, and so on.

Scouting reports come in many forms: computer reports that show statistics and patterns of play, complete video of matches, or prematch information such as player profiles and previous results.

Keep in mind that too much talk or pregame strategy can hurt because it takes away from natural playing instincts. The player may come to rely too heavily on advice instead of using his or her own mentality.

If you treat your players like champions, they'll perform like champions!

Scouts play an important part in winning. Selected because of specialized knowledge, the scout can turn losses into wins. Following most sporting events coaches and players can use videotape sessions to see together what was successful, what needs to be trashed, and where improvements can be made. In many cases, players don't believe a coach's account of what they've just done.

Taking the Racquet Back

I have worked with Marcelo Rios on and off for the past three years. Three weeks before the start of the 1998 Grand Slam Cup, Marcelo felt that his forehand was not quite right. He had the same feeling at the U.S. Open a few months earlier. It's important to understand that players will give signals that they are not comfortable with something. Marcelo does not say much to begin with, and most people find it difficult to communicate with him. But I believe that if you treat your players like champions, they'll perform like champions. I advised him to make a few simple adjustments on his backswing to correct the problems he was experiencing.

Marcelo has gifted hands along with the ability to pick up the ball early, move in, and make early contact. I noticed the following:

1. From his ready position, which is quite low, he dropped the racquet head even lower when starting his backswing.

2. He led the backswing with his elbow.

3. He held the throat of the racquet with his nonhitting hand to such an extent that he completed nearly 75 percent of the backswing before taking his hand off the racquet.

Marcelo is a gifted young man, so he can compensate when late. But that continual compensation can lead to other problems. I told him not to drop the head on the first part of the backswing, to release the opposite hand a little sooner, and to let the racquet head lead the backswing.

A few weeks later, Marcelo beat Andre Agassi in the Grand Slam Cup and won $1.4 million. As a coach you must take a stand and risk telling your student what you feel is right, even though the student may be unwilling to accept it. How you tell the student is key, so know your student's personality!

At the same time, I was also working with Venus Williams, who is totally different on her backswing. She immediately separates her hands, and the racquet goes back very high and as quick as the backswing of anyone in the game.

"Take the racquet back early" is probably one of the most common expressions used by teaching pros. I still use it, and it's worth examining in detail. The phrase became a little more involved, and slowly a new saying emerged: "Turn your hip and shoulder" or "Turn your shoulders."

With some players the racquet went back at the initial turn of the hips and shoulders. Other players turned, and the racquet and arms did nothing but stay in the ready position. I have gone back to the old saying "Get your racquet back," but my eyes are focused to see whether the hips and shoulders are rotating.

It's not who hits the first ball in, it's about who hits the last ball in!

If they are not, I find it much easier to stay with the words "racquet back" and then talk about the hips and shoulders.

Today, I'm once again saying to students who appear to have trouble meeting the fast ball out front, "Take your racquet back early." Iva Majoli and the Williams sisters have extremely quick backswings, which I feel allows them to hit any variation on the forehand.

I don't demand that my students prepare as early as Iva Majoli does, but with students beyond the beginner level, I pay close attention to the backswing. In most cases I'm back to my old expression "Get the racquet back early." But I am also watching and hoping for shoulder and hip rotation.

Stroke Selection

Shot selection is as important as shot execution. Players should stay with the high-percentage shots that they are confident of making. They should vary their shots in a given situation so that their opponents cannot anticipate the shot and gain advantage. Low-percentage shots should be avoided, especially at crucial points. For example, a player should not try to force a winner from 10 feet behind the baseline.

Players should select shots that move their opponents around and force them into unforced errors or weak defensive shots.

Stroke Consistency

Players should be determined to hit the ball over the net one more time than their opponents do. The approach is to be patient, ready to stay on the court as long as it takes to win. This is especially true for play on slow courts.

Stroke Accuracy

Accuracy in tennis means hitting for a certain area with enough margin of safety. The player who has the ability to place the ball will cause many unforced errors.

The player should strive for accuracy that allows a shot to be off a little yet still in the target area. Having this sort of accuracy will reduce unforced errors and allow the player to remain in points without making errors. No one was better at this than Chris Evert and Bjorn Borg were.

Racquet-Head Speed

Pow! Bang! Bam! Does this sound like the balloons in a Batman cartoon? It's really the sound of today's professional tennis. Everyone knows that tennis is changing to a more powerful, faster game. One needs to look only at players like Boris Becker, Andre Agassi, Goran Ivanisevic, and Mark Philippoussis—each big but not much bigger than the average recreational player.

What separates the pros from the recreational players? The critical difference is the ability to generate power. The most commonly asked question at Bollettieri Tennis Academy, famous for producing world-class forehands, is "How can I hit the ball harder?"

How do the pros do it, and how can the student do it better? Let's explore the answers both scientifically and practically. We will suggest some ways to add power by measuring racquet-head speed without losing control. We will also make some comparisons between the student player and some of the world's best players.

What Is Racquet-Head Speed?

Much has been written about the pace of today's game—some of it positive, some of it negative.

- Is power an unfair advantage for some players?
- Should big servers be limited to one serve?
- Should balls be made heavier to sustain longer rallies?
- Should new technologies be outlawed?
- Is the speed of the ball changing the complexion of the game?
- What are the factors contributing to increased power?

It has been well established that power, or the lack of it, is determined by the player's ability to generate racquet-head speed. Racquet-head speed, incoming ball speed, and the spot on the racquet where the ball makes contact all contribute to the speed of the ball leaving the racquet.

Swing Tip

Racquet-head speed is the speed the racquet is moving at the point of ball contact. Generating this speed consistently is the solution to a more powerful game.

Many of us are able to generate racquet-head speed but may be using too much wrist or body in the shot. A sloppy wrist or excessive body movement, caused by throwing the body into the shot before or during the hitting motion, can be easily detected.

Swing Tip

Top players use their wrists efficiently and effectively by educating their wrists to coordinate all action with the movement of their bodies.

How do we develop power for our players without sacrificing control? We gradually increase a player's ability to develop consistent racquet-head speed to the ball while maintaining the same or better control.

Increase Racquet-Head Speed Without Sacrificing Control

As fully demonstrated in my video *Killer Forehand*, several factors are involved in maximizing the forehand weapon. First, you can't fire a cannon from a canoe. The player must create a strong foundation to provide power and control for high swing speeds.

Hitting stance has a major bearing on the amount of racquet-head speed that can be developed. I recommended hitting from both an open and neutral stance to improve racquet-head speed on forehand and backhand. What about hitting while in the air, having jumped off the ground? Endless hours of practice are required to control a ball as the pros do when jumping into the air. Determine the capabilities of your student.

Besides a strong foundation, the student must consider how the butt cap of the racquet is aligned in relation to the oncoming ball at the beginning of the forward swing. If the butt of the racquet is aligned to the path of the oncoming ball, the player will be able to apply the greatest amount of power to the ball through leverage, thus increasing racquet-head speed.

The grip and hitting arm or arms should be relaxed at all times. Gripping too hard and trying to muscle the ball causes a loss of power because of a lack of flexibility in the arm or arms. Working with a solid foundation and flexible arms is like having a whip handle and a loose whip rope. The two work together to create acceleration and a crack of the whip.

Swing Tip

Quick racquet-head acceleration along a swing line across the body applies the greatest speed and leverage to the ball. The action is similar to jerking a towel from someone's hands.

All these factors contribute to learning how to produce maximum racquet speed while maintaining control and consistency. Note that the student will lose control of the stroke if he or she snaps the wrist into the point of contact and finishes with the palm of the hand facing himself or herself in the follow-through.

The student should grip the racquet with a semiwestern grip, strike the ball on a vertical plane, and turn the wrist over on completion of the stroke. Refer to my *Killer Forehand* video for more insight into increasing racquet-head speed with all sort of spins, chops, slices, and so on.

Swing Tip

The correct wrist action for a topspin forehand has the palm facing away from the player with an eastern grip and the palm facing toward the ground for the player with a semiwestern or western grip.

Scientific Opinion

Dr. Howard Brody of the University of Pennsylvania physics department, who chairs the USTA's research and development on matters of physical explanation, says:

"It does not matter what your body is doing. It does not matter what your head, arms, or legs are doing. It does not matter whether you are holding the racquet head loosely or in a death grip. The racquet-head velocity at the point of contact is all that matters. By using a racquet that has a hinge between the head and the handle we have demonstrated that the racquet gives full power. What the hinge does is demonstrate that the racquet head has no way of knowing what the head, arms, shoulders, hips, etc., are doing at the point of contact. The hinge essentially disconnects (the racquet head and the arms from each other). It is only the racquet-head velocity that determines the ball's path and speed."

Bruce Wright, director of Bio-Tennis Sports Science, owner of the world's only device for determining proper string type, gauge, and tension based on individual swing speed and the pace of the incoming ball, agrees: "Racquet head speed is essential in developing the ball's speed. However, a player's physical ability will determine the capacity of the most efficient racquet-head speed. It is important to remember that regardless of physical strength, at some point any player will begin to lose control."

Several products on the market can help players determine their racquet-head speed and the approximate pace of their shots. Most pro players grip the racquet with a semiwestern grip, strike the ball on a vertical plane, and turn the wrist over on completion of the stroke. It's important to remember that the world's best players keep the wrist free to move on a vertical plane. The player who allows the wrist to move horizontally will develop a sloppy wrist before you can say, "Pow! Bang! Bam!"

Oh Yes, and Finally Power

Power must be the final product, once the previously discussed technique is mastered. I often find that students who have mastered the other basics will automatically hit with more power because of sound technique and confidence. Additional power will also come about through normal physical development and a directed physical fitness program.

Finally, the majority of players feel they get more power by using more body. This is not so! They should swing in a normal fashion using the legs, racquet acceleration, and the power of the opponent's ball.

Tell Me About the Game!

Not a day goes by that a student or adult doesn't ask me how to get more power. My answer is simple. Power is not useful unless the player controls it as a part of the entire process of hitting a ball.

Step by step

    Keep the ball in play—No matter what it takes, the student must keep the ball in play and try to maintain correct stroke techniques.

    Hit to targets—The player must keep the ball in play, maintain techniques, and practice hitting to the same place.

    Height and depth—Hitting balls deep to the opponent's court and repeating these first three steps will control rallies.

    Variations—The student should apply different spins.

Speed

A player's attitude can be positive or negative when moving to the ball. He or she should start racquet preparation early, have a quick first step, and fire the body into action to respond with lightning speed.

As the player gets closer to the ball, the steps should become shorter so that he or she can set up and maintain balance at contact. Having a poor foundation and weak posture limits the ability to execute shots with consistency.

Players should work on improving agility while maintaining balance. Skipping rope, on-court foot drills, quick-reaction drills, court sprints, and interval training can all improve agility. Players should move smoothly without jerky motions and think "fast feet" at all times.

Michael Chang and Martina Hingis have excellent speed and agility. They get to almost every ball. The key to movement is simply to believe that you can reach every ball! We often see players scramble to reach a ball. All players can do the same thing if they work at it.

Footwork

Footwork is the foundation upon which one builds strokes. Without proper footwork the player will not get to the ball or, upon reaching it, will be unbalanced and out of position

Having great footwork gives the player options and creates openings that other players don't have. Notice I say great footwork—not good footwork. The student must make a point of working to develop impeccable footwork and foot speed in every practice session.

Refer to chapter 11 for exercises to develop speed, agility, and footwork.

Racquet Preparation

When the feet set up in a stance, they are trying to support the effort of the stroke. In the process of racquet preparation, the brain sends a message from the hands to the feet about how to set up. If racquet preparation gets behind the body with the butt of the racquet pointing to the side instead of toward the net, the feet get the message to set up in a stance that directs the power to the side instead of toward the net. This is known as the closed stance.

If the player prepares the racquet in the backswing, whether straight back or circular, and the racquet stays ahead of the body as the player moves to the ball, the natural process will be to set up in the open stance, with the option of driving into a neutral stance.

If the butt of the racquet were a flashlight, in preparation the beam of light should never get behind the player or point to the side of the court. The beam of light should stay ahead of the body as the player moves.

Preparing early allows the feet enough time to adjust into the desired hitting stance. Preparing late often leads to hitting late, rushing the stroke, and having the feet set up incorrectly or too late.

Recovery

The recovery should be a natural progression of the follow-through that moves the player back into a ready position. The student must develop the habit of recovering after every shot to be prepared to continue the point. The footwork patterns used on recovery vary from shuffle steps to crossover steps, in which the shoulders remain facing forward, allowing the player to go back in the direction from which he or she came. Once the ball has been hit, the player can turn and run.

Keep It Simple!*

Almost everything about today's game is faster and more powerful. Players are faster, fitter, and get back into position sooner. Racquet and string technology speed up the game. The ball reaches the player quicker than ever before. To handle the pace, the student must simplify the strokes. He or she must prepare earlier and keep the swing compact. The Bollettieri Tennis Academy hosts players, both juniors and adults, of all skill levels. The most common stroke adjustment we make, at every level of play, is reducing the backswing.

In sports like golf, baseball, and, of course, tennis, the farther the club or bat or racquet is from the player, the more difficult it is to control. When the circular motion on the backswing is too big or the straight-back backswing goes too far back, we find that the racquet head tends to get too far from the body. The foundation begins to wobble, and balance falters. The player can end up reaching or stretching for the ball, often hitting the ball with a straight arm. Then what happens? Technique breaks down, and the player loses control of the racquet head, cutting down the options.

The player should reach the ball with the feet, not the racquet, moving the feet close enough to make a compact swing.

---

*This section originally appeared in *Tennis Magazine*. Reprinted with permission.

Let me repeat: to handle today's power, the player must consolidate the ground strokes—they have to be shorter and simpler. And with today's increased power and spin on the ground strokes, the player must also adjust volley technique. With simpler strokes, less can go wrong.

Shorter strokes are the key to success in today's power game.

Forehand

As I said 40 years ago, get the racquet back!

Before doing anything to make the forehand swing more compact, the student must find out if he or she is seeing the ball soon enough. The player should react the instant the ball leaves the opponent's racquet. If the player waits for the ball to cross the net and bounce before beginning to prepare, as 90 percent of players do, it makes no difference what the swing is like—the player is going to have a problem. Starting today, as soon as the ball leaves the opponent's racquet, the student should say "Ball." This will improve focus and promote earlier preparation.

In terms of making the swing simpler, what I'm saying to my students today is exactly what I said in 1958: get the racquet back!

The player should turn those hips and shoulders. Moving the racquet from the ready position isn't necessary—the player should just coil the upper body immediately. During the last few months, I've been spending time with Venus and Serena Williams. I'm impressed by their strong hip and shoulder rotation and the way they get the racquet head back quicker than anybody I've worked with. They are good models to copy.

The other element to consolidating the swing is to keep the elbow and racquet a little closer to the body on the backswing. A loss of control occurs when the player swings with the arm straight and the elbow away from the body.

Now let me give you a few simple drills to help your student develop a shorter, consolidated swing.

1. The player stands inside the baseline and hits all ground strokes from there. The player will naturally make a quicker turn and shorter swing to hit the ball well.

2. Have a practice partner serve from the service line as the player stands a couple of feet inside the baseline to receive. The player has no choice but to pick up the ball early and shorten the backswing. After doing it on the return to get the idea, the player can apply it to backcourt play on all ground strokes.

3. Have the player tuck a ball under the armpit. That's what I asked Anna Kournikova to do at the academy. She had her arm much too far away from her body on the backswing and at impact. When we tucked a ball beneath her armpit, the ball dropped when her arm got

too far away. To keep it from falling, she had to learn to keep her elbow closer to her body. At the Lipton Championships I saw a major improvement in Anna's forehand from a year earlier when I had talked to her about trying to keep that arm closer to the body.

Backhand

The student should make a full-turn backswing.

The way to simplify the backhand is to take the racquet all the way back in one motion. Most players, even the very best, have a tendency initially to make only half a backswing on the backhand. Then, from that half backswing, either they will try to swing forward and not get enough on the ball or at the last second they will draw the racquet back farther and contact the ball too late. The ball gets behind them, they slap at it, and they can't get under it for spin. They also cannot hit crosscourt when pressured. A two-handed player can get away with a two-segment swing a bit more because the extra hand can sometimes make up for the late contact. The two-hander can also make an abbreviated motion work because the two hands generate more power than one hand from a half backswing.

Whether using two hands or one, however, the player should make a full-turn total backswing. Watch the two-handed backhands of Andre Agassi, Michael Chang, Venus Williams, and Serena Williams. The racquet shoots back like a cannon. Watch the one-handed backhands of Pete Sampras and Tommy Haas. The second the ball comes toward the backhand, the player should make a total hip and shoulder turn and get the racquet all the way back. All he or she has to do from there is swing forward. A player who has spent some time training at my academy, Mark Philippoussis has significantly improved his backhand. At the tournament he won in Memphis, it was out of sight. Why? He had a tremendous, quick turn. He was able to angle the shot crosscourt when hitting a running backhand, whereas most players can only hit down the line.

Volley

Everything starts with the ready position.

On the volley, the ready position is even more important than it is at the baseline because the ball gets to the player twice as fast. The ready position should be similar to that used by athletes in other sports requiring quick reaction, such as the baseball shortstop and the football tackle. A catlike position provides the best opportunity for success. For the volley that means feet planted, weight slightly forward, racquet out in front to permit movement in any direction or to be in position with good balance for the ball that comes right at the player.

When the ball is away from the player, he or she moves to it with the feet. Instead of reaching or feeling for the ball way out in front, the player should move into a good position and then wait for the ball. Most players will be surprised at the control they have on the volley using this method.

With a solid foundation, the racquet can accommodate any type of ball. The player can use the opponent's power by simply directing the racquet head to the ball. If the oncoming ball is very difficult, a shorter swing should be used. For an easy ball, a bigger swing can be taken.

Stefan Edberg and Boris Becker are great volleyers for one reason above all others: both have superb foundation and balance. They move into good position, they establish good balance—they do not reach or fall when they hit the ball—and they use a short stroking motion. As a result they are in control of the racquet head, which displays little variation on contact. They also love volleying and go to the net all the time. If the player wants to learn to volley, he or she can read all about it, but it comes down to trying it. The player has to go up there. If the player tries 50 times and hits just 2 volleys, that may be 2 more than he or she has ever hit before. Next time, it may be 3, and confidence will build from there.

Serve

The player should keep the racquet head higher on the backswing.

The serve is one of the basic strokes, a major part of the game. If a player is having difficulty coordinating the toss and the racquet, or dealing with sun and wind, it's time to consider the simplification used on the other strokes.

No single service motion is best for everyone. In the classical serves of Pete Sampras or Boris Becker, the racquet and tossing hand start down together, and then the racquet head goes past the leg and back toward the fence while the tossing hand starts coming up. The player who is doing well with this complicated, complete swing should keep it.

But if the player is having trouble, let's make the serve simpler. Look at the pros who use a shorter motion with little or no downswing at the start—Patrick Rafter, Marcelo Rios, Iva Majoli, to name three. Many players, including beginners, weekend warriors, and perhaps your student, should consider a more compact motion.

Mary Joe Fernandez came to the academy about a year and a half ago and said, "Nick, I'm not satisfied with my serve. My racquet and toss don't seem to work together." She said that her toss drifted and she couldn't generate enough power.

To help solve the problem, I started by having her just drop the racquet over her shoulder and serve from there. Then I asked her to take a half backswing. When she asked what I meant by that, I said, "Just turn your shoulders and keep your racquet head about waist high on the backswing."

She said it felt great, but asked, "What does it look like?" Some players hesitate to do something different. I said, "I don't care what it looks like. The important thing is what happens—the result." This little adjustment to a consolidated motion gave Fernandez confidence that the ball toss was going to the same place each time. She didn't have to worry about deviations. She said that it made a tremendous difference.

If a player has difficulty with timing the toss and the swing or with toss consistency, he or she should consider adjusting to a simpler serve motion.

Grips*

Once again, I refer back to my early days of teaching. I went to the books. The experts described the grips, and that was it. I'm happy I don't read or follow instructions too well because I quickly realized that each person's style and grip would be his or her brand. Many factors come into play when selecting grips:

1. Dealing with bounces off different court surfaces
2. Handling balls of varying height
3. Adding spins to the ball
4. Having weapons with minor grip changes
5. Hitting on the rise
6. Using one hand versus two hands

We can keep talking, but for a fact, certain grips just seem to perform better on certain shots.

The original few grips for holding a racquet have expanded to include cousins, aunts, and uncles of the first styles. In the 1960s and 1970s coaches were far too rigid about what grips they instructed their students to use. Not today. Grips now range in dimension from a quarter to almost a half of a turn (i.e., continental to semiwestern or eastern forehand to full western). No matter what grip a player uses, he or she must accept that different shots, surfaces, and conditions will require small variations in the standard grips.

A player's grip often evolves from the environment in which the player learned the game. For example, players from South America who grow up on clay (red dirt) generally use a semiwestern to western grip because they had to deal with high bouncing balls.

Note that the illustrations in this chapter are for right-handed players. We have included a grip reference table at the back of the grip section (table 2.1 on page 78) outlining the grip positions for left-handed players. The double-handed player will also find this section useful because the grip reference table profiles grips for both double-handed forehands and backhands.

Finding a Grip

To locate each grip, the player places the base knuckle of the index finger and the heel pad of the palm on the numbered bevel shown in figure 2.1. This will

*This section by Nick Bollettieri and Peter D. McCraw.

ensure that the hand is correctly aligned on the grip. For example, the continental grip is located by placing the base knuckle on bevels 1-2 (top bevel–top right bevel) and the heel pad of the palm on bevel 2.

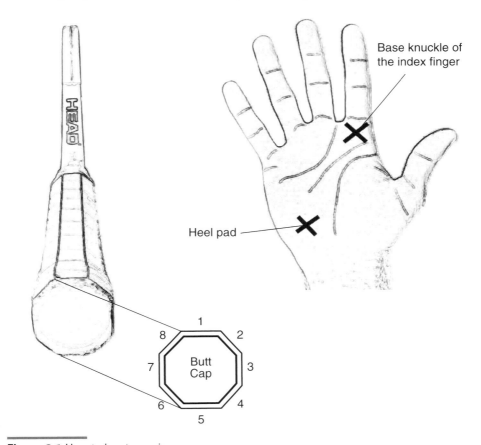

Figure 2.1 How to locate a grip.

Single-Handed Grips

Players use four basic single-handed grips:

- Continental
- Eastern
- Semiwestern
- Western

Each of these grips has advantages and disadvantages. Ultimately, the player needs to use a grip that provides a blend of consistency, control, and power for his or her style of play.

Continental Grip

The continental grip was once the universal grip used to hit forehands, backhands, specialty shots, volleys, overheads, and the serve. It originated on the soft, low-bouncing clay courts of Europe. Although it has been superseded in today's game, it still serves as the foundation grip for the volley, serve, and overhead for most players. See figure 2.2.

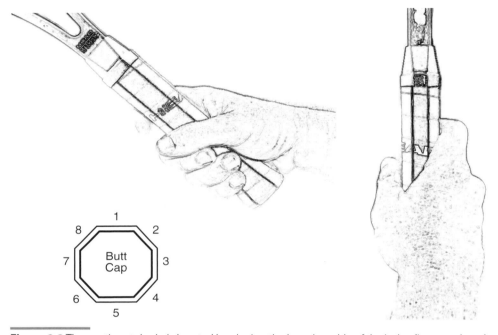

Figure 2.2 The continental grip is located by placing the base knuckle of the index finger on bevels 1-2 and the heel pad of the palm on bevel 2.

Advantages

- Low balls and stretch balls
- Control
- Transition to the net
- Drop shot
- Spin on serve
- Underspin on volleys
- Serve and volley

Disadvantages

- High balls
- Cannot generate a lot of topspin
- Difficult to generate power
- Specialty shots—topspin angles and lobs
- Weak forearm
- Requires impeccable timing

Forehand

As tennis has evolved, the continental forehand grip has become the least favorite grip. I generally don't recommend it as a forehand grip because it requires an exceptionally strong forearm and impeccable timing.

Backhand

This grip is used less often today to hit the power backhand. Though effective for producing a slice backhand, the continental grip does not provide the strength or stability in the racquet head to handle powerful ground strokes from an opponent. It is difficult to produce topspin, and I recommend it only to players who are learning to slice.

Volley

The continental grip is my preferred grip for teaching the volley to advanced players. The continental grip does not require a grip change, and it offers the most support to the wrist when hitting forehand and backhand volleys. In today's game, it is the preferred grip for most top professionals. This grip allows the net player to execute the serve, overhead, and forehand and backhand volleys without changing grips.

Eastern Forehand

The eastern grip originated on the medium-bouncing courts in the eastern United States. It is the classic forehand grip. The eastern grip offers flexibility for individual styles, comfort for beginners, and versatility for all surfaces. This is the simplest grip to learn and use. See figure 2.3.

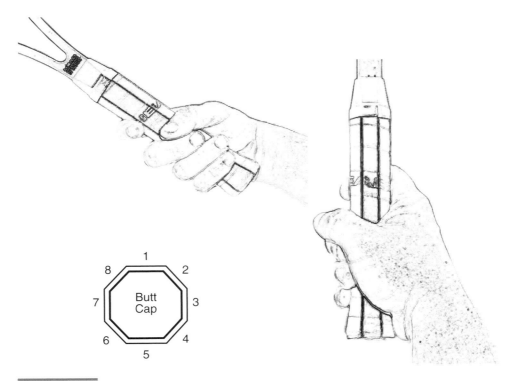

Figure 2.3 The eastern forehand grip is located by positioning the base knuckle of the index finger on bevel 3 and the heel pad of the palm on bevels 2-3.

Grip Tip

Some players naturally adopt the "hammer grip" on the forehand with all the fingers together and the thumb touching the index finger. When using that grip most players experience a loss of feel and control. I instruct my students to spread the index finger out to improve both feel and racquet-head stability at contact.

Eastern Backhand

The eastern backhand, the classic backhand grip, offers maximum stability and allows the player to drive the ball and hit with topspin. Pete Sampras and Petr Korda are among the professionals who employ this grip. I recommend to most players that they adopt a strong eastern grip on topspin backhands. See figure 2.4.

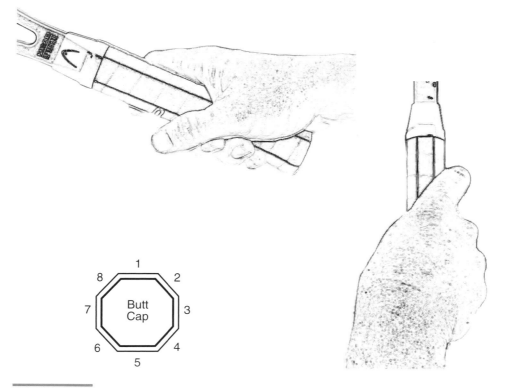

Figure 2.4 The eastern backhand grip is located by positioning the base knuckle of the index finger on bevel 1 and the heel pad of the palm on bevels 1-8.

Grip Tip

From the eastern forehand grip, a quarter turn to the left yields the eastern backhand. The base knuckle of the index finger should move from bevel 3 to bevel 1. The heel pad should move from bevels 2-3 to bevels 1-8.

Advantages

- Easy for beginners
- Easy to generate power
- Waist-high balls
- Adaptable for different surfaces
- Variety—topspin, underspin, flat drive

Disadvantage

- Difficult for very high balls

Semiwestern Forehand

This grip offers both strength and control to the forehand. Beginners feel comfortable with it because the palm of the hand supports the racquet and provides additional racquet-head stability at contact. It is especially suited for hitting powerful topspin and loop forehands. See figure 2.5.

Grip Tip

I recommend that beginners start and stay with a strong eastern to semiwestern grip on the forehand.

Advantages

- Shoulder-high balls
- Heavy topspin ground strokes
- Hitting the big, heavy spin power ball
- Swinging volleys with power and spin
- Disguise on shots

Disadvantages

- Low balls
- Difficult to apply slice on drop shots
- Difficult to volley very low balls
- Major grip change required

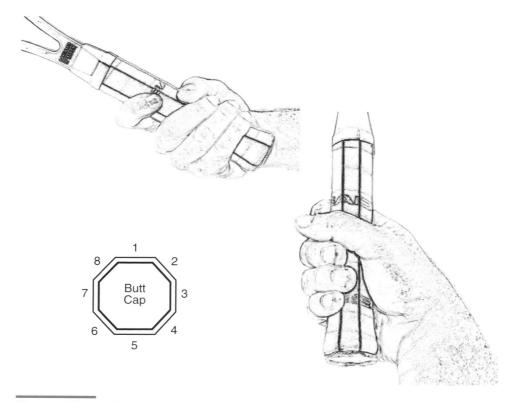

Figure 2.5 The semiwestern forehand grip is located by positioning the base knuckle of the index finger on bevel 4 and the heel pad of the palm on bevel 4.

Semiwestern Backhand

The semiwestern backhand is the same as the semiwestern forehand in reference to the hand and the racquet, but reversed. This grip offers considerable topspin but requires strength and ability to accelerate the racquet on contact. This grip tends to cause the player to lead with the elbow during the forward swing. See figure 2.6.

A more advanced player might consider this grip. Professional players use it frequently when hitting topspin lobs and angle shots. I do not recommend this grip for the majority of players.

Advantages

- Applying topspin
- Specialty shots—angles and topspin lobs from medium-height balls
- Heavy spin from high rally balls

Disadvantages

- Difficult to apply underspin
- Difficult to hit drop shots
- Difficult to hit the flat drive
- Difficult to hit very low balls

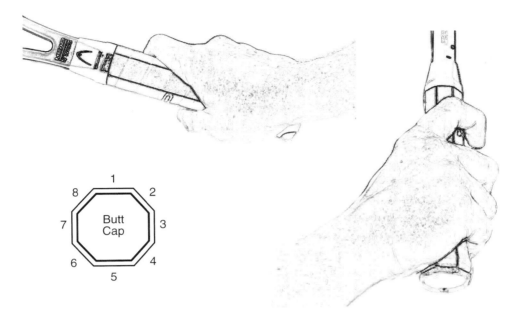

Figure 2.6 The semiwestern backhand grip is located by positioning the base knuckle of the index finger on bevel 8 and the heel pad of the palm on bevel 8.

Western Forehand

This grip originated on the high-bouncing cement courts of the western United States. The drawback of this grip is that it closes the racquet face too soon before contact. This is an excellent grip for high balls and topspin but is awkward for low balls and underspin. See figure 2.7.

Players who use a great deal of topspin, like Thomas Muster, Sergi Bruguera, and Alberto Berasategui, use this grip. Unless the player has an immensely strong wrist and impeccable timing, a western grip will cause problems. I do not recommend it for most players.

Advantages

- Best for very high balls
- Can attack high balls
- Can generate immense racquet-head speed
- Can produce considerable topspin
- Good for topspin lobs and angles from medium-height balls

Disadvantages

- Very difficult to lift low balls
- Cannot slice, chip, or hit drop shots
- Very large grip change required
- Difficult to drive the ball—passing shots

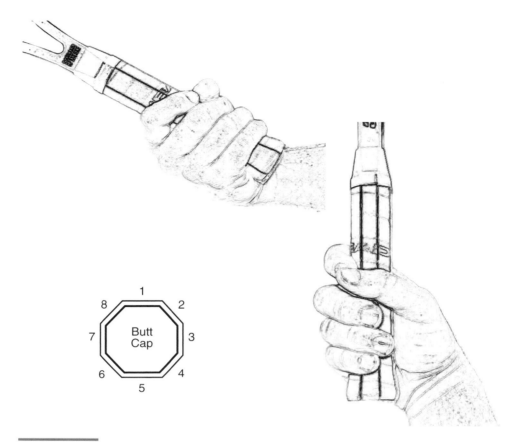

Figure 2.7 The western forehand grip is located by positioning the base knuckle of the index finger on bevel 5 and the heel pad of the palm on bevel 5.

Double-Handed Grips

Double-handed forehand grips. Pancho Segura, Monica Seles, Jan-Michael Gambill, and Fabrice Santoro are just a few of the players who have had success using a double-handed forehand. Gambill and Santoro, outstanding players who use two hands from both sides, vary in style. Jan-Michael is much more aggressive and hits out with less spin, whereas Fabrice is a counterpuncher with all sorts of specialty shots.

If a player hits with two hands off both sides and does not change the position of the hands, the top hand is not able to play a dominant role on both sides. For example, Monica Seles's left side is not as strong as her right because the top hand cannot push the racquet head through as it does from the right side.

One of the key ingredients to using two hands from both sides is foot speed. The limited reach offered by this grip demands great speed and agility.

Tour Tip

The 1999 circuit clearly established that Monica Seles is slower than she was a few years ago. She can no longer dominate against the power and athletic ability of players on the ladies tour. She now hits defensively when forced wide or when moving up for short balls. She is even beginning to hit several single-handed forehands.

The grip variations for the double-handed forehand are essentially the same as those of the double-handed backhand. The only difference is whether the right or left hand is on top. The grip reference table on page 78 outlines the double-handed grip variations for both right- and left-handed players. The table identifies each of the double-handed forehand grips.

Double-handed backhand grips. As with the forehand, several grip combinations are available for the double-handed backhand. Each has advantages and disadvantages.

Grip Variations

Several variations of grips are used today when hitting with two hands. They apply to both the double-handed forehand and double-handed backhand. The illustrations are of a right-handed player, but the grip reference table will help locate grips for the left hand.

Bottom hand	Top hand
Eastern forehand	Eastern forehand
Eastern backhand	Semiwestern forehand
Eastern forehand	Western forehand
Eastern forehand	Semiwestern forehand
Continental	Eastern forehand
Continental	Semiwestern forehand
Continental	Western forehand

Role of Each Hand

When discussing double-handed grips it is important to distinguish between the role each hand plays when hitting a backhand.

Bottom Hand

During the swing the bottom hand always plays a supporting role, helping with timing, racquet-head stability, and control. I prefer that my students use a continental grip with the bottom hand because they can hit with one hand on wide balls, slice approaches, and volleys. Mats Wilander used this style successfully.

Top Hand

Players must accept that the top hand plays a dominant role and leads the show! The top hand generates both power and racquet-head acceleration. The power comes from the top hand (left side for a right-handed player), much like a left-handed forehand that allows the shoulder to rotate through the ball. This circumstance is in contrast to a one-handed backhand, in which the front shoulder is the main factor and the left side plays a supporting role by shifting leverage to the right side.

Double-Handed Backhand—Eastern Forehand/Eastern Forehand

With this grip the bottom hand (wrist) must be laid back on the backswing, making it more difficult to control the racquet head as well as increasing the tendency for the racquet face to open slightly on contact. The eastern grip of the bottom hand can be used for slices and volleys when the top hand is released. See figure 2.8.

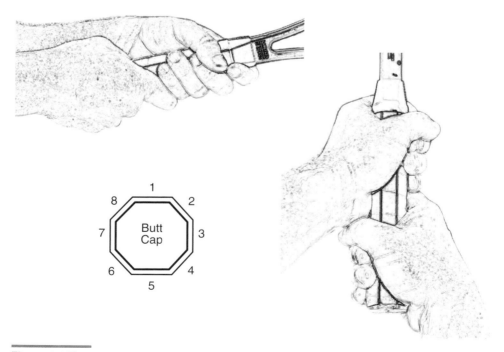

Figure 2.8 The eastern/eastern grip position is located by placing the bottom-hand base knuckle of the index finger on bevel 3 and the heel pad of the palm on bevels 2-3. The top-hand base knuckle of the index finger is placed on bevel 7, and the heel pad of the palm is placed on bevels 7-8.

Double-Handed Backhand—Eastern Forehand/Semiwestern Forehand

This situation is similar to the continental/semiwestern and comes down to individual choice. The bottom hand can execute the slice and volley satisfactorily, but a grip change is required if the player is to find the ideal slice-and-volley grip to the continental. See figure 2.9.

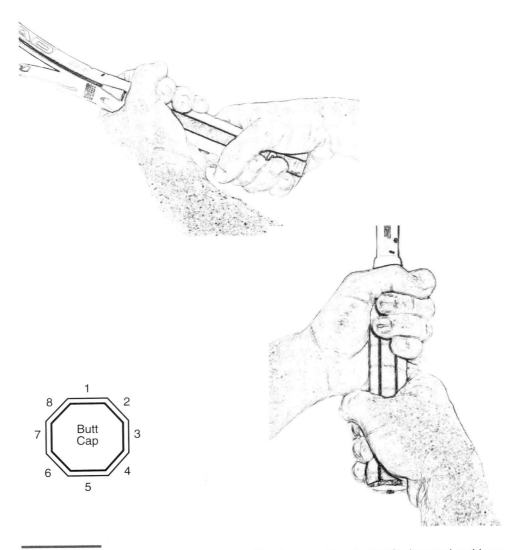

Figure 2.9 The eastern/semiwestern grip position is located by placing the bottom-hand base knuckle of the index finger on bevel 3 and the heel pad of the palm on bevels 2-3. The top-hand base knuckle of the index finger is placed on bevel 6, with the heel pad of the palm on bevel 6.

Double-Handed Backhand—Eastern Forehand/Western Forehand

This grip combination requires the top hand not only to control the contact point but to dominate the stroke with a complete follow-through around the opposite shoulder. See figure 2.10.

Jim Courier used this grip in his first few years on the tour, and he was attacked on this side until I suggested a much bigger follow-through. The top hand played a more dominant role because Jim's left hand was so strong that it was difficult for him to have a long follow-through. With this grip the player must treat the backhand like a left-handed forehand, hitting it with a complete follow-through around the opposite shoulder. Courier was able to dip the ball against a serve and volleyer and hit more depth with spin because of the change.

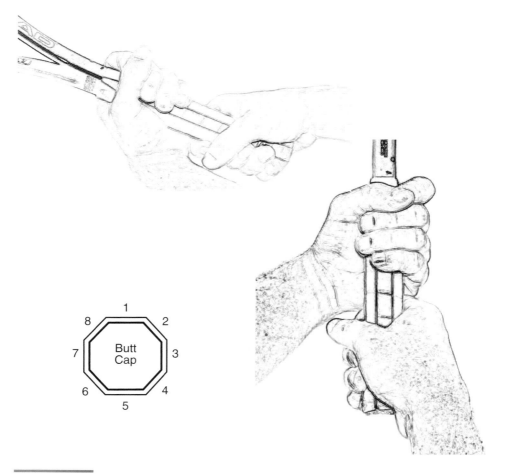

Figure 2.10 The eastern/western grip is located by positioning the bottom-hand base knuckle of the index finger on bevel 3 and the heel pad of the palm on bevels 2-3. The top-hand base knuckle of the index finger is placed on bevel 5, and the heel pad of the palm is placed on bevel 5.

Double-Handed Backhand—Eastern Backhand/Semiwestern Forehand

This unusual grip combination comes down to individual choice. One feature is that the player does not have the variety of options when the top hand is released. The eastern backhand grip of the bottom hand is not ideal for the slice, approach, or volley. The semiwestern grip of the top hand, however, provides an ideal amount of support, allowing it to play a dominant role during execution. See figure 2.11.

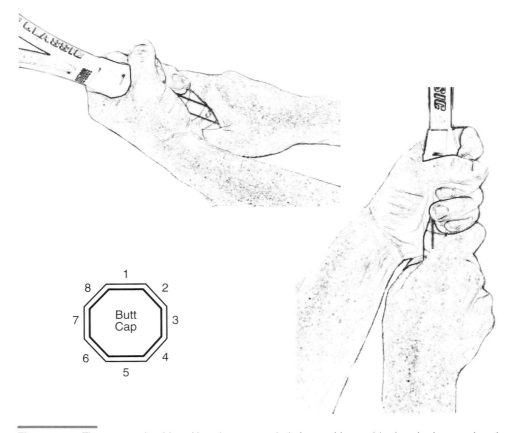

Figure 2.11 The eastern backhand/semiwestern grip is located by positioning the bottom-hand base knuckle of the index finger on bevel 1 and the heel pad of the palm on bevel 8. The top-hand base knuckle of the index finger is placed on bevel 6, with the heel pad of the palm on bevel 6.

Double-Handed Backhand—Continental/Eastern Forehand

This grip allows the player to let go with the top hand on contact and hit a single-handed slice, drop shot, or volley with a continental grip. Although the top hand does not provide as much support as it does with a semiwestern grip, this grip combination will serve the player well. See figure 2.12.

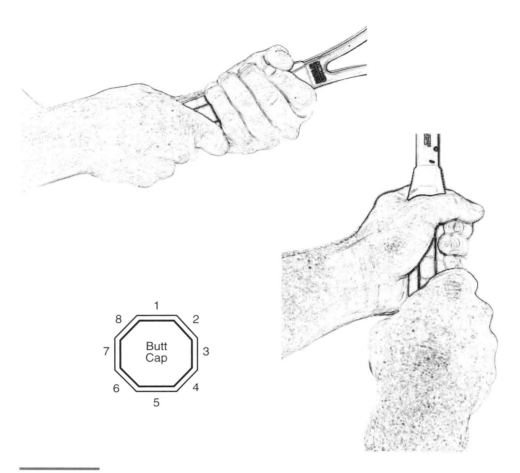

Figure 2.12 The continental/eastern grip is located by positioning the bottom-hand base knuckle of the index finger on bevel 2 and the heel pad of the palm on bevels 1-2. The top-hand base knuckle of the index finger is placed on bevel 7, and the heel pad of the palm is placed on bevels 7-8.

Double-Handed Backhand—Continental/Semiwestern Forehand

This is my grip recommendation for the double-handed backhand. The semiwestern grip of the top hand is in an ideal position to play the dominant role, with the palm of the hand being under the grip, providing maximum support. The continental grip of the bottom hand gives the player the option to slice, drop shot, volley, and reach wide balls when the top hand is released. See figure 2.13.

To reinforce the dominant role the top-hand plays, I have my students practice hitting with one hand, the top hand, in a semiwestern grip, teaching them to use the top hand to drive the racquet head forward. Martina Hingis and both Williams sisters do this exercise every day as did Andre Agassi.

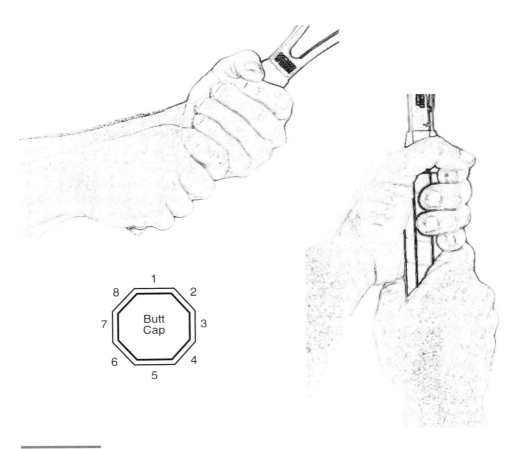

Figure 2.13 The continental/semiwestern grip is located by positioning the bottom-hand base knuckle of the index finger bevel on 2 and the heel pad of the palm on bevels 1-2. The top-hand base knuckle of the index finger is placed on bevel 6, with the heel pad of the palm on bevel 6.

Continental/Western Forehand

This grip is very similar to the continental/semiwestern backhand grip. The top hand is located slightly more under the grip, causing it to play a more dominant role throughout the swing, especially during the follow-through. The continental grip of the bottom hand gives the player the option to slice, drop shot, volley, and reach wide balls when the top hand is released. See figure 2.14.

   With this grip the backhand must be treated like a left-handed forehand, hitting it with a complete follow-through around the opposite shoulder.

What Grips Are Today's Players Using?

The top men and women players predominantly use forehand grips ranging from an eastern to a semiwestern.

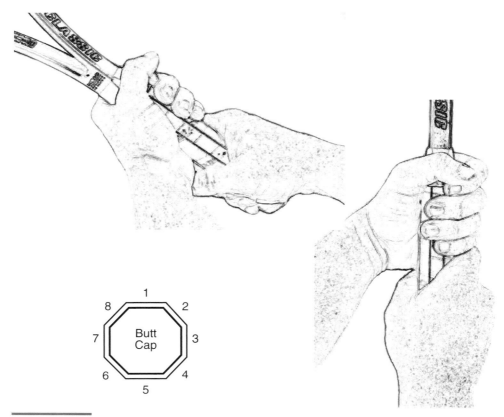

Figure 2.14 The continental/western grip is located by positioning the bottom-hand base knuckle of the index finger on bevel 2 and the heel pad of the palm on bevels 1-2. The top-hand base knuckle of the index finger is placed on bevel 5, and the heel pad of the palm is placed on bevel 5.

Top players' forehand grips

Men

Pete Sampras—eastern
Marcelo Rios—eastern
Patrick Rafter—eastern
Carlos Moya—western
Petr Korda—eastern
Andre Agassi—semiwestern
Alex Corretja—semiwestern
Karol Kucera—semiwestern
Tim Henman—eastern
Yevgeny Kafelnikov—strong eastern/semiwestern

Ladies

Lindsay Davenport—eastern
Martina Hingis—strong eastern
Jana Novotna—eastern
Arantxa Sanchez-Vicario—semiwestern
Venus Williams—semiwestern
Monica Seles—two hands both sides
Conchita Martinez—semiwestern
Nathalie Tauziat—continental
Patty Schnyder—semiwestern
Dominique van Roost—eastern

Grip recommendations

Basic strokes, forehand

Strong eastern to semiwestern

Basic strokes, backhand

Single-handed (beginner): eastern to semiwestern

Single-handed (advanced): eastern to semiwestern

Double-handed—top hand: strong eastern forehand to semiwestern forehand

Double-handed—bottom hand: continental

Slice: continental to eastern

Serve

Developing stage: strong eastern to eastern forehand

As player develops—first serve: continental

As player develops—second serve: continental to weak eastern backhand

The trend within the professional ranks is for the serve grip to move from the continental to a weak eastern grip to an eastern grip. Boris Becker and Pete Sampras followed this pattern.

Overhead

Developing stage: strong eastern to eastern forehand

As player develops: continental to weak eastern backhand

Volley

Developing stage: eastern forehand and eastern backhand

Single-handed: continental

Double-handed—top hand: strong eastern forehand to semiwestern forehand

Double-handed—bottom hand: continental

As a player develops, move the volley grip toward a continental that requires no grip change.

Specialty shots

Topspin lob

Forehand: strong eastern to semiwestern

Backhand single-handed: semiwestern

Backhand double-handed—top hand: strong eastern forehand to semiwestern forehand

Backhand double-handed—bottom hand: continental

Underspin lob

Forehand: continental to weak eastern

Backhand single-handed: continental to weak eastern

Backhand double-handed—top hand: strong eastern forehand to semiwestern forehand

Backhand double-handed—bottom hand: continental

Topspin angles

Forehand: strong eastern to semiwestern

Backhand single-handed: strong eastern to semiwestern

Backhand double-handed—top hand: strong eastern forehand to semiwestern forehand

Backhand double-handed—bottom hand: continental

Drop shot

Forehand: continental to weak eastern

Backhand single-handed: continental to weak eastern

Backhand double-handed—top hand: strong eastern forehand to semiwestern forehand

Backhand double-handed—bottom hand: continental

Half Volley

Some players make a quick transition into the volley grip from their approach shot, but others do not. Using a continental grip for half volleys allows the player to get under the ball, but it is difficult for the player to apply topspin when forced into a half volley. I recommend that my students use the following:

Forehand: strong eastern

Backhand single-handed: continental to weak eastern

Backhand double-handed—top hand: strong eastern forehand to semiwestern forehand

Backhand double-handed—bottom hand: continental

The benefit of using a continental grip for the bottom hand includes being able to release the top hand and open the racquet face to apply underspin. The player must be careful when making grip changes for the half volley. This shot is often hit under pressure. When making a reflex shot, it is difficult to find a new grip. The student may become stuck halfway between the old grip and the new one. In general, I would make changes to the half-volley grip only for the student who has extreme ground-stroke and approach-shot grips.

Tour Tip

Strongly encourage your students to move in quickly after an approach and make up their minds not to hit a half volley. The objective is to eliminate indecision about hitting the half volley and volley. Remember that counterpunchers like Agassi, Courier, and Hingis find half volleys a delight.

Tips on grips

1. The grip is fundamental to every shot. Making adjustments may feel uncomfortable in the beginning, but with practice the grip will become second nature and the student's game will surely improve.
2. The grip should be constant throughout the stroke.
3. The student must be patient with the grip and become comfortable with it.
4. The student should not be afraid to change a grip if doing so can help his or her game.

Although grips, stances, and swings have all changed over the past 20 years, exceptions remain the rule. My suggestion has always been for the player to find what works for him or her, discuss it with the coach, and stick with it!

Grip Reference Table

Table 2.1 has been designed to provide an overview of all grips for both right- and left-handed players. We hope that you find it useful in gaining a greater understanding of each grip. See also figure 2.15.

Building a Strong Foundation

The player's game starts with a strong foundation. We can talk all day about the best way to prepare, make contact, and follow through, but it will make little difference to the outcome if the player sets up and makes contact from a weak foundation. A strong foundation gives the player the best opportunity to react quickly and remain balanced when executing a shot.

Center of Gravity

Controlling the center of gravity is critical to excelling in tennis. Great players like Michael Chang, Thomas Muster, Martina Hingis, Steffi Graf, and

Table 2.1	Grip Reference Table

Single-handed grip	Right-handed player		Left-handed player	
	Base knuckle	Heel pad	Base knuckle	Heel pad
Continental	2	1-2	8	1-8
Eastern forehand	3	2-3	7	7-8
Eastern backhand	1	1-8	1	1-2
Semiwestern forehand	4	4	6	6
Semiwestern backhand	8	8	2	2
Western	5	5	5	5

Double-handed grip	Bottom hand		Top hand		Bottom hand		Top hand	
	Base knuckle	Heel pad	Base knuckle	Heel pad	Base knuckle	Heel pad	Base knuckle	Heel pad
Eastern fh/Eastern fh	3	2-3	7	7-8	7	7-8	3	2-3
Eastern fh/ semiwestern fh	3	2-3	6	6	6	6-7	4	4
Eastern fh/western fh	3	2-3	5	5	7	7-8	5	5
Eastern bh/ semiwestern fh	1-8	8	6	6	1-2	2	4	4
Continental/eastern fh	2	1-2	7	7-8	8	1-8	3	2-3
Continental/ semiwestern fh	2	1-2	6	6	8	1-8	4	4
Continental/western fh	2	1-2	5	5	8	1-8	5	5

Amanda Coetzer possess exceptional movement skills. Have you ever wondered why they are capable of such great feats of athleticism? Several key concepts may give you insight into their success:

• **Center of mass.** The center of mass is the hypothetical balance point of the body. On average it is 55 percent of height for women and 57 percent for men. The center of mass is a constant balance point that always lies within the body. Three factors affect the center of mass— height, body shape, and gender.

• **Center of gravity.** The center of gravity is a balance point that shifts within the body when it moves. If a person stands static and upright, the center of gravity will be the same as the center of mass. When a person moves, the center of gravity shifts within the body and may even move outside the body. The shift of the center of gravity away from the center of mass creates movement.

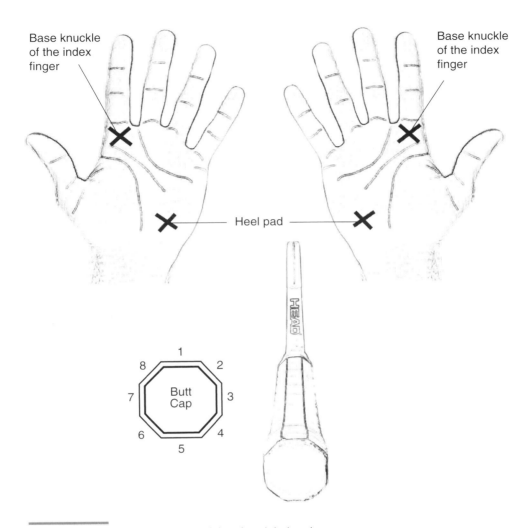

Figure 2.15 Finding grips for the left hand or right hand.

• **Balance.** A person remains balanced when he or she creates neutral equilibrium and stays within the base of support. An example of a base of support in tennis is when a player comes to the net and goes into a split step. The goal of the split step is to change forward momentum into a well-balanced stance, enabling the player to react to forehands or backhands or move diagonally in either direction.

• **Moment of inertia.** To overcome the moment of inertia, it is critical to have a lower center of gravity within the base of support.

• **Positive angles.** The base of support must elicit the proper positive angles to be able to apply force, react, and move in any direction. These angles help to obtain great reaction, first-step quickness, acceleration, deceleration, and redirection in 360 degrees.

Factors Influencing Movement

We often see an advantage in movement by shorter people over taller ones. Several factors cause this circumstance. The first is how athletes develop. Tall children are often selected to play roles not requiring great movement, like the post in basketball, the line in football, or a one-dimensional, serve-dominant player in tennis. This specialization will ultimately limit the quality and number of motor programs and coordination the athlete might have. The athlete who misses out early in development will always be at a slight loss despite later attempts to master movement.

Taller players with long limbs are usually at a slight disadvantage to shorter players who tend to be quicker because they have shorter limbs. If a taller person has the same relative flexibility, mobility, elasticity, and strength as a shorter player, and both have equally efficient biomechanics, the advantage switches to the taller player because of the longer limbs. It is often difficult, however, for the taller player to match the movement speed of the more compact player.

Easy Balls

Tennis offers several examples of how movement skills are applied. During close proximity shots, good athletes can easily maintain their balance. A perfect example is Steffi Graf, who appears to float on court. Like many players, she keeps her hips down, but she does an exceptional job of maintaining her base, of keeping her feet apart, so that her center of gravity floats within her base with positive angles. This stance is critical for successful tennis movement.

Wide Balls

When playing a slightly wider ball, a player might either play with a closed stance and then square up or hit with an open stance. Either way the player finishes squared up to the net. By finishing squared up the player brings the foot around so that at the completion of the shot, he or she is back in a base of support with positive angles that permit redirection back toward the center of the court. One of the great advantages of hitting open is that the player can apply positive angles and stop the momentum from carrying him or her outside the court.

On the Dead Run

On shots that force the player to accelerate and lunge for the ball, the center of gravity shifts outside the base of support toward the head. An extra step or two will be required to stop this momentum and redirect it toward the center of the court.

Coming Forward

When accelerating from the baseline toward the net to volley, the player should lean forward to displace the center of gravity in front of the center of mass. This leaning action will allow forward acceleration. Once the player has momentum forward, he or she must lower the center of gravity, use leg strength to bend and decelerate, and maintain a new position of balance to be able to react efficiently for the volley.

All great athletes possess supreme mobility, balance, movement mechanics, elasticity, power, and strength. When athletes struggle to achieve outstanding movement, one or several of these abilities are missing. Regardless of the center of mass, it is far more advantageous to return to the base of support to keep an optimum center of gravity. By controlling the center of gravity, the player will have taken the first step toward efficient and successful court movement.

Three Ready Postures

The ready posture is a comfortable athletic position that is the core of all movement in tennis. Establishing and maintaining a ready position is the first step in achieving a strong foundation.

The ready position can be viewed in three ways:

1. Normal ready posture
2. Setup posture for the swing
3. Recovery posture

In all three cases the player needs to maintain a strong foundation. Understanding the difference between the three postures will emphasize the importance of maintaining a strong foundation. It is sometimes simple to maintain a sound ready posture and move to the ball easily. Obviously, if the opponent hits a weak shot, the player has a good chance to maintain a strong ready position for all movement, including the swing. But if the opponent hits a strong penetrating shot, the player will find it more difficult to establish a sturdy ready position.

Normal Ready Posture—Strong Athletic Position

A comfortable, strong, athletic posture is fundamental to movement and hitting. Staying comfortable and athletic during play is crucial to success at all levels. See figure 2.16. The keys to establishing a strong athletic posture are

- maintaining a base (feet wider than hips),
- keeping a low center of gravity (hips low with knee bend), and
- holding the arms bent.

Figure 2.16 Monica demonstrates the normal ready posture. Notice how her feet, hips, and shoulders are square to the net. Her base (feet) is wider than her hips, and her knees and arms are slightly bent with the racquet head up. Note also that her eyes are looking forward and focused. In this position Monica can react in all directions—right, left, forward, backward, and diagonally with equal ability.

The base should be wider than the hips. To lower the center of gravity, the feet must be far enough apart to allow the player to bend the knees while keeping the weight on the balls of the feet. Getting low offers the best opportunity for a quick, powerful first step. In addition the arms should be bent. All players are different, but the position of the racquet must allow the player to prepare for the tough shots as well as the easy ones.

Achieving a low center of gravity and maintaining it as long as possible are vital to developing a strong athletic posture.

Setup Posture for the Swing

When preparing for the ball, the player must maintain a strong athletic posture, demonstrated in figures 2.17 and 2.18. He or she should pick up the flight of the ball as soon as possible after it leaves the opponent's racquet. The

a   b

Figure 2.17 Open-stance posture. Monica illustrates both a strong (a) and weak (b) athletic posture from an open-stance forehand. In the first example she has maintained a solid base and is in good position to hit a well-timed forehand. The second example shows Monica off balance and out of position from the same stance.

a   b

Figure 2.18 Neutral-stance posture. Monica illustrates both a strong (a) and weak (b) athletic posture from a neutral stance. In the first frame she maintains a solid base and is in good position to hit a well-timed forehand. The second frame shows Monica off balance and out of position from the same stance.

first step should be quick, balanced, and powerful if the opponent has hit an attacking shot that forces a sprint. The player will normally step out to the ball even if using a drop step.

Recovery Posture

The recovery posture is just as important as the normal ready posture and the setup posture. Maintaining a strong foundation while recovering is the key to improved speed and agility. The player must learn to use the outside leg to push off while remaining balanced with shoulders level and hips and shoulders square to the net. See figures 2.19 and 2.20.

Note that in both examples Monica has finished with her racquet around the opposite shoulder, hips square to the net, and in good position to move to the next ball.

a

b

Figure 2.19 Open-stance recovery posture. Monica demonstrates the recovery posture from an open-stance forehand. (a) Monica has set up with her weight on her right foot, forming a strong athletic base. (b) Monica pushes off her right foot and transfers her weight toward the inside foot after the follow-through.

Figure 2.20 Neutral-stance recovery posture. Monica demonstrates the recovery posture from a neutral-stance forehand. (a) Monica has set up with her weight on her right foot, forming a strong athletic base. (b) Monica's left foot has come around square to the net after the follow-through.

Hitting Stances*

The four stances are neutral, open, semiopen, and closed.

Neutral Stance

The neutral stance serves as the cornerstone for all others. I still teach this stance first even though the open and semiopen stances are becoming increasingly universal. The neutral stance allows the student in the early stages of development to experience shifting weight and body rotation toward the target area.

From the normal ready posture the player begins the backswing by turning the hips and shoulders, stepping out, and shifting the weight to the outside foot. The player steps forward with the inside foot and shifts the weight onto it before starting the forward swing. The weight stays on the front foot until after contact. The player remains balanced during the follow-through and recovery. Bringing the back foot up and around naturally to maintain a strong foundation will ensure that the player remains balanced and ready for the next shot. This sequence is illustrated in figure 2.21.

Initially I instruct my students to hold the back foot behind the front after contact. This allows the student to follow through toward the target with shoulders balanced. The next progression is to move the back foot up and around naturally, transferring the weight after contact.

The neutral stance is the preferred stance to hit both single-handed and double-handed backhands because it allows the player to move body weight in the direction of the target. The neutral stance provides the best foundation from which to execute, follow through, and recover efficiently unless the player is facing a very difficult ball on the run.

Until the last few years, the neutral stance (some call it the closed stance) was the accepted way to hit the forehand, single-handed backhand, and double-handed backhand. I still maintain this selection for the beginner and low intermediate, but I keep them on notice to adopt the open stance, especially on the forehand and two-handed backhand.

If for some reason your student hits with a semiopen to open stance, do not panic and say, "No, No, No!" Simply observe the results and make an adjustment if necessary. Let the player do either if the result is positive.

Open Stance

The open stance is becoming more widely taught and used at all levels of play. It introduces the student to the principles of stepping out, shifting weight to the outside foot, hip loading, and the unit turn.

---

*This section by Nick Bollettieri and Peter D. McCraw.

a

b

Figure 2.21 This sequence of shots illustrates John setting up to hit a forehand and backhand from inside the baseline. Front views of (a) forehand, (b) normal ready posture, (c) backhand; side views of (d) forehand, (e) normal ready posture, (f) backhand.

c

d

Figure 2.21 *(continued)*

e

f

Figure 2.21 *(continued)*

From the normal ready posture the player begins the backswing by turning the hips and shoulders, stepping out, and shifting the weight to the outside foot. See figure 2.22. The player keeps the weight on the outside foot until after contact and remains balanced during the follow-through and recovery. I see too many players shift their weight during the swing and pull off the ball from this stance.

The open stance is ideal for situations when the player has little time to prepare, when the opponent forces the player out of position at the baseline, or when the player must react at the net. The "killer forehand" and all high forehands should be hit with this stance because it allows the player to load up on the outside hip and explode into the shot. With more players using semiwestern and western grips, the open stance is here to stay. Players should practice hitting forehands, backhands, volleys, and return of serves from this stance.

I see two common mistakes with the open stance.

- The first mistake is shifting the weight from the outside leg to the inside leg before making contact, often caused by being too close to the ball.
- The second mistake is loading the hip and stepping onto the inside foot before or during contact.

A simple drill to offset this problem is to have your student lift the inside foot slightly off the ground, thus forcing the outside leg to be the foundation of the stroke.

Coaching Tip

When working with a beginner to low intermediate my choice is the neutral stance. But pay attention to what stance your student uses. If the player naturally hits with a semiopen to open stance, it's OK. This indicates that he or she is developing a comfortable personal style.

Semiopen Stance

The semiopen stance is based on the same principles as the open stance. I teach this stance from the normal ready posture and instruct my students to use it freely within their style of play.

a

b

Figure 2.22 This sequence of shots illustrates John setting up to hit an open-stance forehand and backhand from inside the baseline. Note that the open stance gives John an element of disguise because it is difficult to anticipate in which direction he will hit. Front views of (a) open forehand, (b) normal ready posture, (c) open backhand; side views of (d) open forehand, (e) normal ready posture, and (f) open backhand.

c

d

Figure 2.22 *(continued)*

93

e

f

Figure 2.22 *(continued)*

94

From the normal ready posture the player begins the backswing by turning the hips and shoulders, stepping out, and shifting the weight to the outside foot. As with the open stance, the key to the semiopen stance is maintaining a strong foundation. The player must keep the weight on the outside foot until after contact and remain balanced during the follow-through and recovery. See figure 2.23 for this sequence.

The semiopen stance, like the open stance, is ideal for situations when the player has little time to prepare, when the opponent forces the player out of position at the baseline, or when the player must react at the net. The player should hit the "killer forehand" and high forehand with this stance because he or she can load up on the outside hip and explode into the shot. With more players using semiwestern and western grips, the semiopen stance is here to stay. The student should practice hitting forehands, backhands, volleys, and return of serves from this stance.

There are no hard-and-fast rules as to when a player should use one stance rather than another. I encourage my students to use either stance based on their style of play, grips, movement skills, and stage of development.

Both the semiopen stance and open stance are products of today's power game and the more widespread use of the semiwestern and western grips. The speed and power of professional tennis has dictated that players adapt their games to the way the game is now played. In addition, the more widespread use of both the semiwestern and western forehand grips allows players to generate tremendous racquet-head acceleration and power from either a semiopen or open stance.

While the neutral stance is still my preferred stance for most levels of play because it provides the best foundation and balance for the stroke, the shift toward the semiopen and open stances is becoming more evident as the game evolves.

Technique Tip

Players should practice setting up with both a semiopen and open stance on the forehand, backhand, volley, and return of serve. They should learn to recognize which balls they can step in and hit from a neutral stance within their style of play.

Closed Stance

The closed stance should be avoided when hitting forehands and double-handed backhands from a stationary position.

Figure 2.23 This sequence of shots illustrates John setting up to hit a semiopen forehand and backhand from inside the baseline. Note that the semiopen stance gives John the element of disguise because it is difficult to anticipate in which direction he will hit. Front views of (a) semiopen forehand, (b) normal ready posture, (c) semiopen backhand; side views of (d) semiopen forehand, (e) normal ready posture, (f) semiopen backhand.

c

d

Figure 2.23 *(continued)*

e

f

Figure 2.23 *(continued)*

The drawbacks of this stance are that

- the weight does not move in the direction of the target area,
- it is almost impossible for the hips and shoulders to open when making contact with the ball,
- shot options are limited, and
- recovery requires more time.

Players sprinting to get a wide ball will find it difficult to adjust the feet and step toward the net at contact. As a result, players should make contact on the run, take an extra step or so after contact, and then recover as quickly as possible. A closed stance delays recovery, so players must be sure to offset this with a powerful recovery. See figure 2.24.

It is acceptable and even recommended, however, to use a closed stance when hitting on the run. Although the closed stance is a poor cousin to the neutral stance, the player should hit both the forehand and single-handed backhand from a closed stance when forced wide and on the dead run. The player must remember that hitting from a closed stance delays recovery and leaves him or her momentarily out of position.

Neutral Stance Versus Closed Stance

Years ago I labeled the neutral stance as a closed stance. But with most professional players hitting from semiopen and open stances, I now call it the neutral stance. The neutral and closed stances are significantly different when discussing a stationary hitting stance.

The neutral stance allows the player to

- maintain a strong foundation and good posture throughout the swing,
- transfer the weight toward the target area, and
- maintain a balanced recovery with the back leg moving up and forward, bringing the shoulders and hips square to the net.

The closed stance hinders the player by

- closing out the hips, eliminating any hip rotation during the forward and contact segments of the swing, and resulting in hitting with only the arm,
- preventing transfer of weight toward the target area, and
- forcing the player to take additional recovery steps before squaring to the net with the hips and shoulders.

Note that at times a closed stance is preferred when on the run.

a

b

Figure 2.24 This sequence of shots illustrates John setting up to hit a closed-stance forehand and backhand from the baseline. Note how this stance has closed the natural opening of the hips and shoulders at contact. Front views of (a) closed forehand, (b) normal ready posture, (c) closed backhand; side views of (d) closed forehand, (e) normal ready posture, (f) closed backhand.

c

d

Figure 2.24 *(continued)*

e

f

Figure 2.24 *(continued)*

Stances in Review

Throughout a match the player will be forced to use a variety of stances. Overall, the stances the player uses are both individual and a natural extension of his or her style of play. The "natural" stance for any shot is ultimately influenced by position on the court, the difficulty of the oncoming ball, the player's grips, and his or her physical conditioning.

In the next session on the practice court, the player should take a moment to evaluate his or her stances. Making a slight adjustment may improve the player's shots. Above all, my advice to players is to maintain a strong athletic posture at all times and use a stance that complements their style of play.

Contact Zones

In the figures on pages 104 through 111, Greg demonstrates the contact points for the neutral- and open-stance forehand. The front and side views illustrate the different ideal contact zones for a continental, eastern, semiwestern, and western grip.

As a rule, the more the hand is on top of the grip (continental), the more comfortable a low ball will be. The more the hand is under the grip (western), the more comfortable a high ball will be.

Refer back to the section on grips to review the advantages and disadvantages of each. Remember that no grip does it all. The player must ultimately find a grip that feels comfortable and suits his or her style of play.

Open stance

Continental grip, front view

Continental grip, side view

Eastern grip, front view

Eastern grip, side view

Semiwestern grip,
front view

Semiwestern grip, side view

Western grip, front
view

Western grip, side view

Neutral stance

Continental grip, front view

Continental grip, side view

Eastern grip, front view

Eastern grip, side view

Semiwestern grip, front
view

Semiwestern grip, side view

110

Western grip, front view

Western grip, side view

Killer Forehand

A killer forehand is a lethal weapon in a player's strategic arsenal.

Over the last four decades, I have developed and trained more junior players than any other coach in tennis history. Among these players have been numerous world champions, collegiate champions, everyday warriors, and some of the future's brightest young stars. As president and founder of the Bollettieri Tennis Academy, I have established a trademark that my players possess huge forehand weapons.

Perhaps my greatest assets are my ability to inspire and motivate my students to improve and my ability to instill in them the confidence they need to succeed. My formula for developing new technique and building it into habit involves progressive steps:

- Step 1: "Just hit it." As Andre Agassi's father said to him when he was young, "This is the way you refine your swing and improve your power. For now, don't worry so much about accuracy and consistency. Just relax, groove the swing, and hit big."
- Step 2: Target training. Once you have established your stroke and improved your skill, you should build and test that skill under pressure conditions in practice. Use target zones and drills that test your accuracy and

consistency. (Remember, it may take months of practicing step 1 before you progress to step 2.)

- Step 3: Become match tough. The final stage is to test your skill under match-pressure conditions to see if the habits maintain effectiveness. To be successful, you must believe in your skill. Never fear making a mistake and always execute with a full follow-through under pressure.

What Is a Killer Forehand?*

A "killer forehand" is a lethal weapon in a player's strategic arsenal. All other forehands in a specific rally must be aggressive, controlling the center of the court until the killer forehand either ends the point or forces a weak return for you to attack and volley. Not all forehands are hit with the killer mentality. You must create the situation while keeping your opponent always under the threat of the killer shot.

The ingredients of the killer forehand call for refined and efficient movement skills. The idea is to get into position to hit the killer forehand. Use drop shots and angles to set up your power game and keep your opponent guessing.

A baseball pitcher may have a good fastball, but it will be the variety and disguise of his other pitches (i.e., curve, change-up, etc.) that maintain the effectiveness of his fastball. This is the balance of touch and power that world-class players possess on their killer forehands.

Grips

How you choose to hold the racquet as a habit has great effect on the stroke itself. If I were to start you as a beginner today, I would most likely encourage you to use an extreme eastern or semiwestern grip.

- Continental grip (palm faces down)—It is difficult to achieve killer-forehand power with this grip, although there are a few exceptions. Personally, I prefer to work with grips that offer a higher percentage of success.

- Eastern grip (palm faces forward)—This grip provides good leverage and power, works well with both higher and lower balls in the strike zone, and enables the production of spins and power.

- Semiwestern grip (palm faces forward and upward)—Common in today's pro game, the semiwestern grip offers great power and spin options, especially higher in the strike zone.

---

*This section by Nick Bollettieri and Pat Dougherty.

- Extreme western grip (palm faces upward)—This grip is capable of good power and spin on balls higher in the zone, but low balls are difficult to work with.

To be effective with your forehand, you have to be able to hit balls in all parts of the strike zone. The eastern and semiwestern are the most common, versatile, and powerful options overall.

Using the proper grip pressure is important, regardless of your grip. Holding the grip too tightly, a common problem, will restrict your flexibility. Keep your hand relaxed, especially between shots, and let the racquet do the work. (Try squeezing hard on a tennis ball. See how quickly you begin to lose feeling and how quickly your arm becomes tired.)

Remember to develop one primary grip and practice it with your forehand. A lot of practice is required to ingrain the habit and make it reliable.

Strong Foundation

Athletes can be defined by the body position of a strong foundation. Examples include Boris Becker, Michael Chang, and Martina Hingis.

A strong foundation includes several elements:

- Good back posture
- Low center of gravity (hip area)
- Solid base of support (stance)

The two things that help everyday players the most are early preparation and a strong foundation.

First-Step Reaction

The mentality must be "I will get to every ball."

Gifted players move with speed, agility, balance, and strength. They never think about movement. They are natural athletes who move to the ball and recover to a court position that suits their style.

Other players have to work constantly to start swing preparation with the first step and make the first-step recovery part of the swing itself. They must work daily on preparation and recovery because it does not flow naturally.

Footwork Patterns

Like the dance steps of a ballerina, various footwork patterns allow players to appear smooth and agile as they move. These patterns are used for specific purposes and situations.

1. Crossover—The crossover pattern is often used for lateral movement. This is especially important for run-around forehands and overheads that require backward movement.

2. Cross-behind—The cross-behind is used in situations similar to those that call for the crossover, but the player is usually moving laterally and back in the court. You will also see the cross-behind used with slice approaches.

3. Shuffle—The shuffle step is also used for lateral movement, but for shorter distances. This pattern is not efficient for extreme distances but is effective for balls within a few steps of the player.

4. Adjustments—The adjustment steps, or cut steps, are important for fine-tuning your balance and positioning in your hitting stances. In conjunction with good racquet preparation, these stutter steps help you avoid becoming wrong footed or caught in a closed stance.

5. Drop steps—One foot will drop back slightly to make the second step strong and efficient. Most players use the drop step when moving forward and laterally.

Early and Correct Racquet Preparation

Good preparation habits create more options for you to work with the ball, allowing you to hit more offensive shots, adjust for a bad bounce, disguise your shots, and so on. There is nothing I emphasize more than the importance of early preparation. Lack of preparation is often why a stroke breaks down.

Early preparation also has an effect on your footwork. Remember, your feet are either working to set up a balanced stance or adjusting to hit on the run. Your preparation tells your feet how to set up. Without early preparation, your feet do not have time to adjust to the situation.

Correct preparation is the concept of sending the right message to your feet. The analogy of the flashlight in the butt of the racquet can help you understand this concept. When you use an excessively large backswing and the racquet gets behind you, the beam of light begins to point off the court, parallel to the baseline. The message this sends to the feet is that you are directing your power in a sideways direction, placing you in a closed stance. By keeping the racquet ahead of your body, the beam of light points toward the net, sending the correct message to your feet about where you intend to direct your power.

The entire preparation process should have you arriving to the ball in an open stance, with the option of stepping into the neutral stance if you have time.

Hitting Stances

There are three main stances—open, neutral, and closed. For further details on stances please refer back to chapter 2.

• The open stance is like one used by a batter stepping into the batter's box with only the back foot and hitting. This stance offers all the shot options, and if you have time to step into the shot, you can. Under pressure of a hard-hit ball, you will usually be forced to hit in an open stance. Avoid transferring your weight off the back foot, pulling your body off the shot, in this stance.

• You reach the neutral stance by starting from an open stance, driving your weight forward, and pointing the front toe toward the net. You will often use this stance, along with the open stance, for the killer forehand. The neutral stance has both feet in the batter's box.

• Using the closed stance is a common problem that should be corrected through early and correct racquet preparation. The closed stance reduces power, diminishes control and balance, and offers limited shot options.

Pulling the Trigger

This concept will allow you to maximize racquet speed and power. In the same way that you would pull a towel, you pull the racquet out of a backswing, driving the butt of the racquet toward the ball. This action allows you to use your racquet as a tool and apply leverage. As you pull forward, keeping your arm flexible and swinging out across your body, the racquet head will meet the ball with maximum force.

You should not accelerate the racquet by snapping the wrist and slapping at the ball or by throwing your body into it. Developing the swing line and "pulling the towel" more quickly will achieve acceleration.

Contact Zone and Follow-Through

A full extension of the hitting arm on your follow-through will help you maintain a good swing line.

Preferred contact zones for grips are the following:

• Continental—lower

• Eastern—middle

• Semiwestern—middle to higher. Very low balls will force you to adjust your swing.

• Western—higher. The lower the contact point, the more difficult the shot because the position of the wrist is awkward.

For several reasons, partly because players are starting younger, the semiwestern and western grips are more common than in years past. While you are small, these grips may seem the most comfortable. As your game develops, you should use grips that complement the style of play you like best. A grip adjustment requires patience and hard work.

Opposite Arm

Beginners typically don't use the opposite arm for any benefit. Often it stays limp and at the side.

Your opposite arm can add balance and power to your stroke. When you are wide in the court, the opposite arm adds balance and has an anchoring effect, acting as the balance pole does for a high-wire aerialist to keep the shoulders level.

To generate killer-forehand power in an offensive situation, the opposite arm works like the glove arm of a pitcher that stretches the chest muscles into the stroke. This sweeping action makes for a longer lever that is capable of generating more power while maintaining swing balance.

Hip Loading

This technique involves centering your body weight into the back of the stance and down. As this happens, the body coils like a spring, allowing you to uncoil into the shot. Practicing your stroke while maintaining your balance on the back foot throughout will help you develop the feel for this power source.

Average players take the racquet back without shifting their body weight back and coiling to prepare the racquet. The perfect hip load has you preparing and turning as one unit, as Jimmy Connors does. Even on the run, players like Sampras use hip load for power and disguise.

Recovery

This position may vary, especially if you prefer hitting more offensive weapons, including the killer forehand. Jim Courier and Steffi Graf would often recover to a position that would give them the best chance of hitting a big forehand. Your playing style, and your opponent's returns, may affect your recovery position.

The mentality must be "I will get back into position after every shot." In few sports do you concede open court or field position to your opponent.

Training Methods and Drills

When developing habits take one new thing at a time and be patient. Remember, when you either add or take away something from your stroke, your success and confidence may drop for a while. Don't worry! You should expect this decline, but it should be temporary if you are willing to work hard. Once you overcome it, you will be playing at a higher level. This is the only way you can become better.

Grips

Build through repetition and follow my formula for development:

Step 1: "Just hit it."

Step 2: Target training.

Step 3: Become match tough.

Choose your grip and stick with it through all repetition drills. Remember that gripping too tightly will sacrifice flexibility and racquet speed.

Backboard and ball-machine sessions are great for quality repetition.

Strong Foundation

Focus on maintaining good posture while lowering your playing height 6 to 12 inches below your standing height. As you practice your movement, try to be smooth in your footwork, keeping your head as still as possible. Work on a level, gliding effect.

First–Step Reaction

To practice the drop step, spread your feet one and a half to two shoulder-widths apart as part of your strong foundation ready position. Mark the positions of your feet. Practice the drop step move until you feel an explosive first step. Videotape yourself and compare it to the "kilastrator" graphic in the tape.

A positive first-step reaction will increase your chances of good timing. The ball-hit reaction drill is great for establishing good timing and rhythm. Audibly saying "Ball" at the moment your opponent makes contact forces you to react simultaneously. You will consistently get a better jump on the ball.

Saying "Hit" when you make contact helps you establish a rhythm for the rally. With this exercise, you will also realize how quickly you need to recover your court position before the ball is returned. You must read, react, and recover to stay up with the pace and timing of the points. You can add "Recover" to the drill as well, so it's "Ball, hit, recover."

Footwork Strides

To achieve quick acceleration, you must use first-gear footwork, pumping the feet quickly and powerfully. To practice this, use resistance training to mimic a dog pulling a sled. You can do this in several ways. It's as simple as tying a rope around your waist and having someone hold on and resist your movement. With resistance, you will naturally shorten your stride lengths. You should do several repetitions with each footwork pattern every day. Eventually you will develop the quick, fluid footwork necessary to cover the court effectively.

Footwork Patterns

As mentioned above, practice the crossover, cross-behind, and shuffle steps in specific drills, focusing on quickness and fluidity while keeping your head level. Resistance training will help you develop better quickness and power in a shorter time. You can create your own types of drills with the focus strictly on footwork patterns.

Early Preparation

"The true measure of a great player can often be the discipline to prepare early."

I use this standard to rate players on their preparation skills:

Average—as the ball bounces on your side

Good—as the ball comes over the net

Better—as the opponent hits the ball

Best—before the opponent makes contact

From your shots you can often anticipate the area where the opponent's ball will go. You might also pick up clues from your opponent if he or she has certain tendencies with ball placement.

You can practice the preparation process in several ways. For early preparation get in the habit of establishing your backswing before the ball reaches your side of the court. This means preparing as you move to the ball. For correct preparation the butt end of the racquet must be slightly behind and below and pointing at the incoming ball. The low-to-high movement with the racquet to the ball will create the spin needed to make the ball fall into the court. Correct preparation also keeps the racquet on the right side and ahead of the body if you are right-handed or on the left side and ahead of the body if you are left-handed. If the racquet extends to the opposite side of the body, you are getting in the danger zone. A good way to get a feel for how your feet work together with your hands in preparation is to practice the baseball glove drill.

As you position to catch the ball, you will see how your feet set up automatically into the open stance. This drill also establishes the proper alignment to the ball flight with your preparation.

Hitting Stances

If racquet preparation and your movement work correctly, you will have the open stance or neutral stance available as options. As you learn to hit from an open stance, you should avoid the common problem of transferring your weight, thereby pulling off the ball. Keep your chest over the contact zone all the way to follow-through.

You can try mini tennis games in which both players must compete within the service area and always hit with an open stance.

From the open stance, you should practice driving your weight toward the target in the neutral stance. This weight transfer forces you to rotate your hips to begin the stroke.

Pulling the Trigger

This concept allows you to establish the right swing line and develop maximum racquet acceleration. Use the towel test to create a feel for the arm speed and swing line. When drilling try using a practice swing before you hit each ball by swinging without actually hitting a ball. Doing this can help you increase your swing speed.

To check your swing path, have someone hold the racquet lightly as you start the pulling action. Remember to drive the butt of the racquet straight forward out of the slot as seen in the video.

Opposite Arm

To use the opposite arm in your stroke more effectively, try putting a small weight in that hand. The added weight will allow you to feel the counterbalance effect.

The hand-on-the-hip drill will enhance your feel of how the anchoring effect works and what you should feel when you use the sweeping action.

Hip Loading

From an open stance, you should practice hitting while maintaining your balance on the back foot throughout the stroke. Slowly work on lowering your position and shifting deep into the back of the stance. You should feel your hips and body coil in preparation and uncoil into the ball as your weight stays centered over the back foot. Avoid launching upward through the stroke.

Recovery

The main point of focusing on recovery is demanding a positive first movement and being prepared to make any changes of direction required.

Practice Mentality

Venus Williams, Serena Williams, and Martina Hingis have the mentality of Bjorn Borg, Martina Navratilova, and many other great champions. They approach practice with great intensity, set goals, and have an all-business mind-set.

Be patient with yourself, establish your goals, and work daily on achieving them. You should strive for perfection but understand that you will make mistakes along the way. The player who can best manage mistakes and failures is the one who will most often achieve greatness. Avoid doubting your abilities and being negative about yourself.

There is no substitute for hard work. Practice intelligently by working on specific developmental goals. Accept constructive criticism from your coach and those who understand the game better than you do.

Match-Play Mentality

Don't fear making mistakes or hitting the ball out, or you will become tentative. Use your forehand as often as reasonably possible as the basis of your ground-stroke attack. Your backhand can also be a weapon, but there is something about ending a point with a huge forehand that intimidates even the best players. Andre Agassi provides the perfect example. His backhand is a weapon, but when he wants to dominate play, he hits as many forehands as possible. Show versatility in your ground strokes by mixing up the pace with spins and other kinds of shots to keep your opponent off guard. Set up combinations of shots that highlight your forehand strength. Build points around your strengths and stay positive, even when you are down. Being confident is essential to accomplishing your goals.

CHAPTER 4

Boll-istic Backhand

A number of top players possess truly "Boll-istic" backhands.

The game of tennis is constantly evolving with the influx of bigger, stronger, better-conditioned athletes who compete on faster surfaces with the latest equipment. Athletes today are more talented and have few, if any, flaws to attack. The bottom line is that years ago you could overcome your weaknesses by focusing on your strengths. You could run around most of your backhands and pound your forehand weapon on a regular basis. But today's players possess more balanced weaponry throughout their games. They have developed their ground strokes to near, if not equal, strength, and a number of top players possess truly "Boll-istic" backhands.

What Is a Boll-istic Backhand?

We borrowed the title "Boll-istic" from a military term referring to a guided missile, a missile that seeks and destroys its target. Naturally, we had to change the spelling to make it an appropriate signature of Nick's teaching methods.

This chapter by Pat Dougherty and Peter D. McCraw.

For our purpose Boll-istic refers to

- maximizing power, accuracy, and consistency with your backhand,
- being able to vary the spin and trajectory on all shots,
- understanding how to integrate these skills into a game plan that remains effective for your style of play.

Got Foundation?

The challenge is not about generating speed on your shots. That's the easy part. The true test is in the foundation. If your body position and footwork provide control for your swing, you have a weapon!

Athletic Foundation

We begin the process of understanding the Boll-istic backhand by starting at ground level and working our way up. You must realize that the stroke itself is nothing more than an extension of your foundation. Without a strong foundation you will never achieve Boll-istic status. Athletic foundation is a body position that you develop into habit through training. It involves lowering the overall height of your body by as much as a foot. How you position your body determines whether it can function like a machine.

Think of the design of a Ferrari automobile. It is built low to the ground with the wheels spread wide, giving it a stable base. As a result, the Ferrari handles extremely well through sharp curves at high speeds. A tractor traveling at the same rate of speed through the same course would surely roll over many times.

When it comes to court movement the same forces affect your body foundation. For you to move more like a Ferrari than a tractor, you must stay low to the ground for better stability and power. To accommodate the heavier load on your thighs created by the down position, you must proportionately broaden your base by spreading your feet to between one and a half and two shoulder-widths apart. Positioning your feet farther apart will provide more power, control, and accuracy when you are reacting and preparing your hitting stance.

Your back posture is critical to the integrity of upper-body mechanics. The pivoting action of your shoulders must rely on the strength of your back muscles and the position of your posture to keep the action efficient. As you'll learn, your arms and legs are levers that function from the strength of the core body foundation. You apply intensity to your muscles throughout specific parts of your body to control and support your foundation. Using correct posture allows your body to function like a machine.

The muscles that support your lower-body foundation to your upper-body posture are activated into a firm yet flexible mode. They must be flexed but not rigid, similar to the tight suspension of the Ferrari, capable of operating tight through the turns. With your body core flexed and firm, you can shift gears into a quick, explosive mode, working sharply in reaction, tight through the turns, and under complete control.

The hitting arm or arms are able to function with an even higher degree of flex than the foundation. Regardless of the role the arms and hands play (based on grips), they use flexibility to create whiplike action and speed in the swing. In fact, they have very little tension in their grip. They don't choke the life out of the racquet. If they did, flexibility would be reduced. The hands hold on just tight enough to keep the racquet stable.

The athletic foundation is the key to controlling the result of any action created by your arms and legs. You must train and develop the athletic foundation to form a habit. An inconsistent foundation creates inconsistent results. Remember, physically speaking, tennis is a sport of movement and strokes.

These drills can help you improve your athletic foundation.

1. Tug-of-War—Grab a friend and a length of rope. Face each other and stand a few feet apart. Work at pulling your friend off balance. You will notice that by widening your base and lowering your center of gravity, you can stay balanced and powerful.

2. Take a Stance—Continue the tug-of-war and alternate between the open, neutral, and closed stances. Have your friend take the same stance, then alternate between different stances.

Art of Movement

The art of movement encompasses the understanding of how to choreograph your plan of attack, how to best defend your territory, and how to decide when to attack. Far more is involved in victory than the strength of any one weapon. For consistent success you must develop a competitive mentality.

Movement and positioning are both instrumental to developing a Boll-istic backhand. You should know the direction and speed of your shots, which strongly affect your ability to move into recovery position on time.

If a point averages three or four shots, then close to 80 percent of the time you are hitting to continue the point. Only one time out of four does your hit involve the end of the point. If you are unable to maintain effective court position, your opponent ends up with open-court opportunities. Recovery of your court position is critical 80 percent of the time, but you must make it a habit 100 percent of the time. As we look more closely at the art of movement, keep in mind the importance of maintaining good position through an understanding of timing and correct positioning for each shot selection.

Timing and Rhythm

A good analogy for understanding timing and rhythm is to look at how we dance to music. When we hear a good dance tune many of us will automatically start the body into movement. The timing of the music beat, the rhythm of the instruments, and the style of the song seem to engulf good dancers as they synchronize their movement with the music. The beat of a tennis match is established by the speed at which two players rally. The quicker the exchange of the ball, the quicker each player must respond and move to keep pace with the beat. Like great dancers, tennis athletes move to the beat with fluid grace as they run everything down and then recover.

We can break the process into five stages of action as the ball travels from one player to the other and back. To stay up with the timing, you need speed (or more important, quickness), and you must choose shots that allow you the opportunity to recover at least 80 percent of the time. At the highest level of play, you must be extremely efficient to maintain the pace. Let's look at each stage of the movement process.

Stage 1—Ready to React

As the ball is starting up off the bounce to your opponent during a baseline rally, you prepare for your initial reaction to his or her shot. Even if you haven't fully recovered court position from your previous shot, you should hold your ground so that as your opponent makes contact you can read the direction and depth of the shot and move toward it. This is when you set into your ready position, your athletic foundation, with your Ferrari ready to race.

Stage 2—Read and React

As your opponent begins to stroke, you should be looking for any indication of where the ball will be going so that you can begin to anticipate your next move. At the moment of contact, you read your opponent's shot and start into motion. Because the ball travels the length of the court in only one to two seconds, you have to react quickly.

Stage 3—Footwork and Preparation

You have reacted sharply to your opponent's shot and are tracking down the ball. Your footwork should be quick and fluid as you maintain your low athletic height. Early preparation and correct positioning of the racquet is critical to your footwork for the stroke. By the time the ball bounces on your side, you have prepared your racquet and adjusted your feet to execute.

Stage 4—Set Up and Execute

When you have time you'll load into a hitting stance and be ready to fire, able to make any last-second adjustments for the bounce. In situations when you must hit on the run, your feet will adjust according to your racquet preparation as you prepare to execute.

Stage 5—Recover

Great athletes learn to recover as part of the natural follow-through of the stroke. As they stroke, they have already begun to recover, especially when they are on the run and have to change direction on recovery. You only have the time it takes for your shot to reach your opponent to recover your court position. This means that the harder you strike the ball, the less time you have to reposition. The position on the court for recovery varies according to the direction you hit the ball.

You should make every effort to recover fully in time after every shot. Otherwise, you leave the court open for your opponent. By the time the ball has bounced on the opponent's side, you are back into position and ready to start the process again.

Court Positioning

As we explained in detail in the video *Winning With Your Game—Part I*, the objective on recovery is for you to position yourself halfway between your opponent's best possible shots. You must eliminate open-court opportunities for your opponent by keeping yourself in reach of any shot he or she might hit. As you learn more about your opponent and become more skilled at anticipating his or her shots, you can start to hedge your position.

Correct Movement Technique

Like the Ferrari, we want to be quick off the start, sharp and stable as we change direction, and in control of our momentum. By design, we must stay low with a solid base and foundation. Remember that for each situation you must develop the habit of creating a base between one and a half and two shoulder-widths apart. This width allows your lower body to distribute the forces created by being low. Establishing a strong back posture and developing the muscles that support your upper body are integral to the overall performance of your foundation.

Back posture is like a bridge that connects the lower body to the upper body. The power created through the lower-body weight transfer starts a pivoting action in the hips, passes up through the posture of the back, and pivots the shoulders into action. Good posture allows you to maintain strength and consistency in your stroke and sharpness in your movement.

First-Step Reaction

Your technique on first-step reaction will be rigorously tested on damp, slippery surfaces like hard courts after a light rain or clay couts that have dried out and become dusty. But if you learn to use your body weight and drive off the correct foot each time, you'll have great success moving as court conditions worsen.

From the wide footwork base of your strong foundation position, we recommend the drop-step-and-drive technique to take you from rest into motion. The most critical factor to quick reaction time is the first-step move, which should immediately establish momentum.

Consider a car driving in snow. To increase traction in snow, front-wheel-drive cars use the heavy weight of the engine to provide the grip of the tires to the ground. Rear-wheel-drive cars often spin their tires in the snow because most of the weight of the car is over the front tires. The rear tires have no weight to provide traction. This analogy parallels the concept behind the drop-step-and-drive technique.

The drop-step maneuver uses body weight for traction as the foot positions underneath the midline of your body. For a right-hander reacting to the ball coming to the backhand side, the left foot will drop underneath the torso, positioning the upper body for momentum. The left foot has the traction to explode and drive into motion as the right foot crosses over.

If you drive too hard off the right foot, you may lose your footing just as a rear-wheel-drive car might lose traction on snow.

Footwork Patterns

Thinking of footwork patterns as the gears of a 10-speed bicycle will help you understand stride length. For quickness off the start, you shift into first-gear footwork, which consists of short, chippy, yet powerful steps that accelerate quickly up to speed. Long strides or big steps are like the 10th gear on a bicycle, slow at getting you up to speed. To be quick, you must work with first-gear strides.

The footwork patterns are designed to accomplish specific tasks. To move to your left or right over a distance of more than a few steps, use crossover footwork. This movement pattern allows you to travel quickly yet be able to flow into the setup and execution stage. When the ball is only a few steps away, shuffle footwork allows you to position and adjust to the stroke. In many situations you'll need adjustment steps to arrange your feet for the stroke. These tiny stutter steps, which often make a squeaky sound on the hard court, help you set up your footwork for shot execution.

Racquet preparation is important not only to the stroke itself but to the footwork that must support it. If you prepare your racquet ahead of your body enroute to the ball, your feet will receive the correct message about how to set up and support your stroke. If you prepare your racquet so deep into the backswing that it gets behind your body enroute to the ball, you will send a conflicting message to the feet, which often results in a closed hitting stance. By preparing early in the movement of the ball, your feet will have the necessary time to set up.

A useful reference is to imagine that the butt of the racquet is a flashlight. You want the beam of light to be ahead of your body, pointed toward the net. The flashlight beam represents the direction in which you intend to drive your power. Your feet respond to this preparation by setting you into an open stance, with the option of driving your weight forward into a neutral stance.

Hitting Stances

There are three basic hitting stances:

- Open
- Neutral
- Closed

Using the face of the clock to better understand each one, a right-handed hitter has the left foot at the center of the clock for the backhand. In an open stance the right foot is positioned toward three o'clock. This stance is common in extreme situations when setup time is limited, such as on the return of serve. Two-handed backhand players use the open stance more commonly than one-handers do. By practicing the open stance from a variety of court positions, you can develop it into a powerful stance.

When time permits and when the ball is rather short, the neutral stance becomes a strong option. With the left foot again at the center of the clock, your right foot drives toward twelve o'clock. The neutral stance is the predominant stance for both one and two-handed backhand players, providing the best balance and power to the stroke.

From the open stance, driving forward on the right foot toward twelve o'clock causes the weight transfer to occur with all your power going in the same direction as the stroke and target area.

The closed stance occurs when the left foot is at clock center but the right foot steps across toward nine o'clock. This stance is especially problematic for two-handed players because it prohibits the body from being able to rotate in a pivoting action. In addition, hitting from a closed stance creates balance problems, limiting power and shot options. But one-handed players can be quite effective in a closed stance because they don't use the pivoting rotation that two-handers do.

To avoid taking the closed stance, you must learn to prepare for the stroke correctly with the racquet ahead of your body as you set up.

Recovery

The recovery technique when hitting on the run can begin as you execute the stroke. Just as a downhill skier shifts the lower body outward to carve through a slalom turn, the great athlete can shift momentum in one quick move. You should use primarily crossover and shuffle patterns to recover court position. It is important to have your shoulders facing the net as you recover, at least until the opponent makes contact. This will allow you to change direction sharply if the ball is hit behind you.

We dedicated a large portion of our discussion of the Boll-istic backhand to movement-related concepts because we want you to understand everything involved in developing a weapon and effectively applying it in your game plan. Movement is as important to the result as the stroke itself.

Boll–istic Strokes

Now that you have a better understanding of the movement skills that add fluid and smooth mobility to your weapon, we continue the process by looking at stroke mechanics. You now have a better knowledge of the importance of the body position referred to as the athletic foundation and how it contributes to both movement and stroke.

The lower half of your body is responsible for providing stability to the stroke through either a balanced hitting stance or the correct footwork to hit on the run. Through weight transfer the lower body also generates power to the pivoting action of the body.

The torso region of the body, through strong back posture, works to maintain level shoulders through the stroke and add stability to upper-body mechanics. With the foundation being sturdy yet flexible, we are ready to build stroke mechanics. The shoulders, arms, hands, and racquet will work in harmony with the foundation to generate power in the swing. To maximize your power and minimize your effort, you must learn to create leverage in your stroke.

Leverage of the Machine

The concept of leverage refers to the function of your arms, hands, and racquet working efficiently. A general definition of leverage is "the action of using a lever, such as a metal bar, pivoting against a fixed fulcrum to gain mechanical advantage."

A visual image that represents the definition would be the action of a seesaw. Sitting on one end of the seesaw lifts the other end as the seesaw pivots against the support fulcrum. The function of the seesaw has long been applied to lifting heavy objects with greater ease. Leverage refers to using a tool to make work easier and more efficient.

Another example involves the action of the hammer. To drive a nail into a piece of wood, the hammer, positioned at a 90-degree angle with the forearm, becomes a lever. The downward action begins by driving the butt of the hammer toward the nail. The head of the hammer follows. As the butt drives downward, the energy of the action transfers up to the hammerhead and on to the nail. We call this downward-leverage action.

With this example in mind, think of striking a tennis ball as forward-leverage action. In the backswing the butt of the racquet is positioned to drive forward toward contact. The energy generated by driving the butt of the racquet forward accelerates the racquet head through the contact zone. Similar to the action used with a hammer, the action of the racquet creates leverage.

As we move into the finer details of the strokes, keep the images of leverage fresh in your mind because they will become the key to producing Boll-istic results.

One-Handed Boll-istic Blast

The most critical aspect in the construction of the one-handed blast involves the grip and the position of leverage in the wrist. The eastern backhand grip provides the strongest position of support in the wrist, which prevents the stroke from breaking down at contact.

With the eastern backhand grip intact, the stroke begins with the backswing position. The key element in the backswing is to position the butt of the racquet to drive forward to start the forward swing. Various styles are used to take the racquet back, and often the arm is bent in the backswing. As the stroke begins the forward action, the arm extends fully and becomes a lever. Extended, but not locked at the elbow completely, the arm is firm yet flexible. Boll-istic power is generated when the hitting arm (lever) incorporates the rib cage as a support fulcrum.

The rib cage, mimicking the action of a seesaw, is used to spring energy into the stroke, working with an extended and flexible arm to propel the stroke before the butt starts forward toward contact. The butt is aligned with the path of the incoming ball and beneath the height of the intended contact point. The butt end starts forward toward contact and then follows a path across the body as the arm travels out toward the target.

The racquet head accelerates rapidly into the contact zone as it follows the swing line of the butt end. As the arm continues to full reach in the direction of the target on the follow-through, the racquet head will have passed through a contact zone that provides great margin of error and directional control for the various shot selections. How the racquet head finishes at the end of the stroke will depend on the amount of spin versus driving flat power that was applied in the stroke.

The role of the foundation in the one-handed backhand is to resist the tendency of the body to rotate open. The pivoting action of the body stops completely as the forward action of the racquet begins. By stopping the pivoting action, the energy from the foundation is transferred into the power of the stroke.

The opposite arm counterbalances the shoulders, keeping them level through the stroke and preventing them from rotating as the stroke begins.

The one-handed backhand operates most effectively from a neutral hitting stance that allows the power of the weight transfer to work in the same direction as the stroke. One-handers, however, have the luxury of being effective from the closed stance as well. The open stance is slightly more difficult for one-handers, although they can use it for returns and in other situations when time is limited. You must develop the ability to execute from all of these hitting stances.

> **Boll-istic backhands, whether one-handed or two, operate within a game plan with a constant objective in mind.**

You must establish a threat in the mind of your opponent that at any given moment your backhand could end the point. Still, most of the time you are working at various rally speeds with variations of trajectory and spin to establish more margin for error in your game plan, so that over the course of a match you wear your opponent down with consistent, accurate placements. By using your Boll-istic put-aways sparingly, you will have a more effective result in your game plan.

Remember, when you decide to pull the trigger you can't second-guess yourself and become tentative. Always maintain positive expectations and a confident outlook.

Try the following drill, called the Towel Test—Grab a towel, set up in a neutral stance, and position your wrist in an eastern backhand grip. Have a friend hold the towel behind you close to your hands. Now pull the towel out of your partner's hands and swing forward as though you were hitting a ball. Repeat several times to feel the swing line and shape that your arm and wrist create. The harder you pull, the more racquet-head speed you generate.

One-Handed Knifing Slice

A Boll-istic stroke with underspin, the one-handed knifing slice serves as the strategic counterpart to the blast. Even most two-handed players learn to develop a more biting action by using just one hand. In the most difficult forcing situations, the knifing slice is often the only option you'll have. It is a versatile tool capable of offering disguise in both preparation and execution because you are able to attack both deep and short. Used effectively and set up well, the stroke leaves the opponent on the heels every time you drop shot.

On approach shots, the slice enables you to attack deep and occasionally short. You can move through the stroke with your footwork more readily and have more time to position yourself. Finally, a well-executed slice gives the opponent less to work with because the ball skids low off the bounce.

The preferred grip for the knifing slice is the continental grip. This grip allows a perfect balance of underspin and driving power in the stroke while offering great control and feel on touch shots.

In the backswing we want to prepare the butt of the racquet behind the incoming ball, beneath the intended contact point. The racquet head is tilted back, making an L-shaped position with the arm and racquet. The shoulders rotate to a position perpendicular to the net and level.

To begin the forward move, the hitting shoulder starts to rotate open as the butt of the racquet drives forward toward the contact point. The opposite shoulder, working as a counterbalance, prevents rotation, maintaining the perpendicular relationship of the shoulders to the net. This anchoring function of the opposite arm and shoulder provides the pulling action of the hitting arm with more power and helps maintain the swing line.

The butt end starts forward and then arcs like a waterfall down and across the body, sending the racquet head up into contact. The racquet head then follows the path of the butt end.

The arm should remain flexible as it extends in the backswing. As in the one-handed blast, the arm becomes a lever and uses the rib cage for support as a fulcrum. The hitting arm works with the rib cage to create power and support for the stroke. As the stroke passes through the contact zone, the arm separates from the rib cage to a full reach toward the target on the follow-through.

The foundation of the body works to restrict full rotation of the hips and shoulders. The shoulders, level and perpendicular to the net, lean toward the net ahead of your stance. You might think of how a football player, using the shoulders to block, leans forward for momentum.

To understand the benefits of having a slice in your game plan, think of how a pitcher in baseball uses a variety of pitches—curveballs, change-ups, sliders, and so on—to provide contrast to the fastball. By mixing up the pace, placement, and spin on the ball, the pitcher doesn't permit the batter to become too comfortable anticipating the next pitch.

Your slice adds similar variety to your game plan and has the same effect on your opponent. In addition, the disguise in preparation opens up more opportunity for use of the drop shot and other specialty shots. Steffi Graff, perhaps the greatest woman player in history, had a devastating slice backhand and rarely hits over the ball. For most players, however, learning to mix the slice into the game in contrast to the Boll-istic blast will prove to be most effective.

Two-Handed Boll–istic Blast

The two-handed backhand functions quite differently from the one-handed backhand relative to the use of the foundation and the importance of the hitting stances. Whereas the one-handed stroke works more efficiently without full rotation of the body, the two-handed stroke creates its power through an aggressive hitting stance that must allow the body to rotate fully through the stroke.

The grips for the two-handed stroke determine the look and the function of the stroke and the hands. Depending on the grips the stroke will become left-hand dominant (in right-handers), have a balance of dominance, or become more right-arm dominant. The grip position of the bottom hand determines the dominance factor for the stroke.

We will begin our exploration of the various grip combinations at one extreme and progressively work toward the other extreme, looking at the strokes that match each set of grips.

Grip combination 1

Top hand—eastern forehand

Bottom hand—semiwestern or eastern forehand

Most players are introduced to the sport by learning the forehand ground stroke. As a result, they develop great comfort in the grip they use for their forehand. When they begin to learn the backhands, they are naturally resistant to making any change in the bottom-hand grip. With a forehand grip on the bottom hand, however, all the power for the stroke must come from the top hand. The bottom-hand position is too weak to provide support. The bottom hand will assume the role of anchoring down the butt of the racquet through the contact zone. With the bottom hand creating a pivot point, the top hand provides the driving force behind the stroke.

The preferred contact zone relative to the bottom-hand grip is back off the hip. This contact zone is much farther back, less out in front of the body. When the bottom hand is positioned in a semiwestern or eastern forehand grip, the arm and elbow rest against the stomach through contact. The stroke for these grips is a top-hand forehand with the bottom hand anchoring the butt of the racquet through contact. We do not recommend this grip combination.

Grip combination 2

Top hand—eastern forehand

Bottom hand—continental

The shift of the bottom hand into the continental grip will not change the fact that the stroke will still be top-hand dominant. The preferred contact zone, however, shifts forward from the zone used with the previous set of grips.

The bottom arm will remain slightly bent at the elbow throughout the stroke. Again, the right hand will work to pivot the butt of the racquet as the left hand creates the driving force. The pivoting action of the body begins the stroke as the swing line drives the butt of the racquet toward contact. The hands then travel in a line across the body.

You should develop the ability to hit this stroke from both an open stance and a neutral stance.

Grip combination 3

Top hand—eastern forehand

Bottom hand—eastern backhand

The bottom hand now shifts into a nearly full eastern backhand grip. Several factors change, making this combination more bottom-hand dominant.

Because the wrist in the bottom hand has more leverage, the arm can extend fully through the stroke. This means that the bottom arm can function more like a one-handed backhand, using the extended arm against the rib cage to generate power. The contact zone is now well out in front of the body, allowing you to benefit more by using the body. The strong grip can be released for a one-handed follow-through as well. This is the strongest combination of grips for the backhand, used by Andre Agassi, Yevgeny Kafelnikov, Bjorn Borg, Chris Evert, and many other great champions.

Note that the hands function in a different way than they do in the top-hand dominant grips. The bottom hand pivots the butt of the racquet through contact, drawing it back toward the body, and the top hand provides support in the leverage process.

Try the following drill, called Mirror Image Shadow Swings—Find a mirror or window so that you can see your reflection. Begin to swing, relaxing your hands to feel the weight of the racquet and the pivot action of your hands. Use the towel drill (on page 132) to explore the role of each hand and feel the mechanics of the stroke.

Court drills—backhand

1. Time It—All players will benefit from this drill. No doubt you have seen it before, but it's a classic! "Bounce-hit" or "Ball-bounce-hit." There is no better way to improve your timing than to use all your senses—auditory, visual, and kinesthetic. Yes, the drill is simple, but we at the academy consider it a fundamental drill.

2. Groove It—Gaining feel and racquet awareness on your backhand is the first step to improving your consistency. Find a partner or use a ball machine or backboard. Start slow and work your way up to 20-ball rallies on both crosscourt and down the line.

3. Spin It—Now begin to vary the spin. Be creative, using underspin and topspin on your shots. If you find your consistency dropping, back off the power until you find the right blend of speed and spin on your shots.

4. Place It—Now that you have a feel for your backhand, add targets to take your game to another level. Vary the size and placement of targets for both crosscourt and down-the-line backhand patterns. Challenge yourself to hit 20 or more balls consecutively to each target. It's not easy!

5. Hit It—Finally, add the power component to your backhand. Resist the temptation to go for it right away. Remember, power without consistency or placement is power you don't need! Gain control over your swing and the ball—then turn up the heat!

Conclusion

To improve your mental image of the strokes, we highly recommend repetitive viewing of the Boll-istic backhand video. Merely reading about these techniques may not provide sufficient instruction about how to apply the stroke. Take the information we have presented and work on each part a bit at a time.

Be patient and stay positive. It will take time for you to develop new and improved habits. The fundamentals are essential to the results, so the time you spend and the investment you make now will pay off in the future. All it takes is smart practice and hard work.

CHAPTER 5

Sonic Serves

The serve arsenal today is often equipped with a "sonic boom" first serve capable of eclipsing 140 miles per hour.

Like the game itself, the service motion has evolved to levels of power and control never imagined a decade ago. With bigger, stronger athletes, more powerful racquets, and total precision in body mechanics, the serve arsenal today is often equipped with a "sonic boom" first serve capable of eclipsing 140 miles per hour. Backing up that powerful serve, top players have the support weapons of the wicked slice and kick serves as well as off-speed change-ups. Mixing the rotation in the first-serve position while using variation of placement in the attack, the artful server has the opportunity to play "king of the mountain," allowing no one to rule his or her turf. Holding serve becomes a breeze against most players, allowing the sonic server to focus on achieving the one break of serve needed to take the set.

Some of the professional men who demonstrate the potential of hitting sonic booms at more than 140 miles per hour along with the variations are Max Mirnyi, Greg Rusedski, Mark Philippoussis, Goran Ivanisevic, Richard Krajicek, and Marc Rosset.

But we should recognize that there is more to holding serve than just the serve itself. Pete

This chapter by Pat Dougherty and Peter D. McCraw.

Sampras, whose power potential may not reach the 140s, clearly commands one of the most dominant serve games of all time. It was the combination of the serve and volley strengths that made Pete so effective. The variation of speed, spin, and placement and the quality and consistency of his attack allowed Pete to claim "king of the mountain" status for a long time.

In Pete's most dominant era he would often get himself in a little trouble, down 15-40, but you knew, like everyone else including his opponent, that he would serve his way out of it. He wouldn't necessarily blow the serve by the opponent with the speed of Rusedski, but his creative use of spin and placement would expand the range that the returner had to cover, opening more opportunity for the ace when he most needed it. Sampras knew by where he placed the ball what he would most likely see on the return, and he was able to anticipate and look for the volley opportunities. Everyone can learn much from the competitive mind-set and strategic method of attack of players like Pete Sampras.

Haves and Have Nots

If you were to take the top 100 men and women on the professional tours today and compare serve techniques, you would see quite a variety of styles as well as some similarities.

But if you isolate the 10 players who have clocked the fastest recorded speeds on the serve, you'll likely find among them the servers with the best slice and kick serves as well. What's more, the serve techniques of those 10 players will look nearly identical in the key fundamental aspects. Not by accident, these players have discovered and developed precise mechanical actions that have raised the bar on what was thought humanly possible. When you compare these 10 elite players to the rest of the pack, you will see distinct differences in their motions.

Because the serve is a conceptual motion it is subject to the mental impression and interpretation of the individual. Having the ball in your hand to start the point puts you in control of the situation. You have the option of executing the motion any way you choose. But if you are seeking to reach your ultimate potential, you must develop the precise fundamental technique common among great servers. You can still have your own style, but you must be sure to include the fundamentals.

The serve is nothing more than a pitch, or is it?

The best analogy for many years in teaching the service motion was the comparison to the pitch in baseball. To pitch the baseball, the arm and shoulder mechanics produce a kinetic chain, a sequence of movement driven by shoulder mechanics, passing energy into the throwing arm to propel the ball.

Flexibility throughout the arms and chest muscles allows the energy to build in the sequence of movement, stretching and releasing in a transfer of energy like the crack of a whip.

With the exception of the throwing mechanics, however, there are many significant differences in the overall technique of the serve and the pitch.

The pitch includes the following elements:

1. The front foot takes a big forward stride.
2. The shoulders maintain a level plane in line with the catcher's mitt (target).
3. The throwing elbow follows a forward track in motion.
4. The throwing arm releases the ball with the arm bent.

The sonic serve includes several contrasting elements:

1. No step is taken with the front foot.
2. The shoulders tilt to a position nearly perpendicular to the ground.
3. The hitting elbow follows an upward track on line with the point of contact.
4. The hitting arm straightens into contact.

We see distinct differences in the motions because the throwing actions are directed at dissimilar targets. The pitch uses mechanical characteristics that create power toward a forward target, the catcher's glove. The sonic serve has the characteristics required to direct power toward an upward target, the point of contact. The best way to describe the sonic serve mechanics would be the "upward pitch."

It is extremely important to understand what you are trying to do in the serve motion. Most players have developed their serve technique believing that the target of their throwing motion and power is forward toward the service box. Working from this mental blueprint, they have built a technique that may be adequate but will never reach sonic proportions. It is not until you change the mental blueprint to the upward pitch that you can begin to develop the sonic technique.

No matter how hard I throw a ball forward, it will never travel up unless I aim my throw in that direction. If I want to increase power on my serve, I must direct my power toward the point of contact. By doing so my hitting arm will more efficiently function at contact, releasing more power on the ball. When throwing upward toward the point of contact, the hitting arm straightens at contact, creating a forearm rotation and wrist snap that takes the ball down into the service box. So, to develop the sonic serve, we must focus on the upward-pitch technique.

Like a Pole-Vaulter's Pole

Using a long flexible pole, a pole-vaulter sprints down a runway, plants the end of the pole into a fixed base, and uses the energy of the forward momentum to bend the pole. As the vaulter positions for the upward lift, the pole releases the energy that thrusts the athlete nearly 20 feet in the air and over the bar.

The human body can learn to function like the pole-vaulter's pole to snap energy to the throwing mechanics for the upward throw. By stretching the hips in the positioning of the serve and tilting your shoulders back, you achieve a launch position with the potential energy of the pole-vaulter's pole. The hips work to straighten the body just before contact on a lean over the court. This hip snap often generates enough energy to lift the body off the ground.

At the same time as the hip snap, the toss arm begins the shoulder rotation and initiates the throwing mechanics. The toss arm works to pull the upper body toward contact, tucking and starting the upward rotation of the shoulders. As the shoulders rotate to a position perpendicular to the ground at contact, the hitting elbow follows in sequence on a straight upward track in line with the point of contact. Once the body and arm straighten together before contact, all the energy from the motion passes into the racquet head, sending it over the top into contact and then leading the way back down on the follow-through. With the hitting arm flexible and relaxed throughout this motion, the arm straightens to create the wrist snap. You will only slow down the energy created in the sequence of movement if you consciously force the snap using your forearm muscles. Direct your power toward contact, extend your arm fully into impact, and the rest will take care of itself if you use the continental grip correctly positioned in the hand.

Grab-It Habit

It is extremely important that you position the racquet in your hand correctly. If you have a forehand grip, the wrist action and forearm rotation required for creating the downward action on the ball could be restricted and not function properly.

To ensure that you use your most important wrist action through contact, you must develop the habit of serving with a continental grip. You must place the heel of your hand on the top edge of the grip. This grip will allow you to produce the action required to execute the sonic serve.

To create more spin, you have the option to shift your grip slightly toward the backhand side, which alters the angle of the racquet head. You can become creative with different spin actions by shifting in varying degrees from the continental grip toward the backhand side. Avoid shifting to the forehand side of the grip or you will lose the action you need in the wrist at contact.

Toss

The preferred contact point for the various flat and spin serves is different for each type of serve. Although you toss well into the court for your biggest sonic booms, the preferred position of contact for the kick serve is much closer to the baseline, barely inside the court. This means that you must have command over the placement of your toss to execute all types of serves.

The tossing motion should lift the ball into the air to approximately one foot above the point of contact, allowing the ball to drop into the point of contact as your racquet head makes contact. The desired height of your toss is subject to variation based on the tempo and rhythm of your motion. We call this your "toss-hit" rhythm.

Toss-Hit

Your toss-hit rhythm is the measure of time between the release of your toss and the point of contact. If your toss is rather high and you are slow in creating the set-to-launch position, you will likely prefer a more extended toss-hit rhythm. If you prefer a lower toss and can quickly establish the set-to-launch position as you toss, you can work with a much tighter toss-hit rhythm. When you are serving well, you are usually in a groove, maintaining a consistent toss-hit rhythm.

When you begin to struggle with your toss placement or the motion in general, your timing will be thrown off and it will become difficult to right the ship. Become familiar with the toss-hit rhythm that works best for your motion and do everything possible to maintain that timing for every serve. When your serve seems to leave you in a match, go back to the toss-hit rhythm that works best as the first course of remedy.

To establish your optimal toss-hit rhythm, use the verbal cues of saying "Toss" as you release the ball and "Hit" on contact. Repeat this until you begin to find the timing that works best for you.

The toss itself is a rather simple part of the motion. Nevertheless, players struggle with it, especially under pressure. If you eliminate some of the moving parts, you can gain better control.

If you extend the toss arm to a straight position and firm up the wrist position, your arm will work as one unit in a lever action. Lifting from the shoulders with just enough power to achieve the desired toss-hit, you release the ball at eye level as the toss arm continues upward until it lines up with the point of contact. With the ball positioned within the fingers and thumb, the hand opens up at eye level, releasing the ball, preferably with little spin. If you allow your hand to snap on the release of the toss, your fingers will create spin on the ball, often flipping it back over your head.

Toeing the Line

To avoid the dreaded foot fault, you must be able to toe the line without stepping on or inside the baseline before making contact with the ball. Although players use many stance variations, the primary contributions of the stance are to provide balance throughout the motion and maximum reach at contact. The starting stance we recommend has the front foot pointed in the direction of the net post. The back foot positions perpendicularly to the front foot, lined up with heel of the front foot. With this starting stance, your body can stretch inside the court and maintain the best lower-body support and balance. As the body shifts forward into the set-to-launch position, the back foot will typically slide forward next to the front foot.

It is common to see players line up sideways to the baseline, a la John McEnroe. This stance can prevent full rotation of the body in the motion unless your feet leave the ground and you are skilled at rotating your hips and shoulders in the motion. Maintaining your balance in this stance is difficult because your front knee is unable to extend inside the baseline to support and balance the body. You can make it work, but we don't recommend it.

When your opponent uses this McEnroe-style stance but does not seem to have the entire motion mastered, he or she will likely have difficulty serving to certain targets. For a right-handed server with a closed stance, the best serve will be down the T in the deuce box and out wide on the ad court. Serves to these locations are likely to be your opponent's choice under pressure.

The real test will be when you change court position on the return, taking away the preferred target and forcing your opponent to display the skills of hitting wide in the deuce court and down the T in the ad court. You may find that your opponent has difficulty reaching those targets, allowing you to cheat on your return position for better coverage of serves that your opponent can hit.

Our recommended stance will provide the best control of your balance and allow you to access all the targets in both the deuce and ad courts without being limited by the mechanics of your motion.

Set to Launch

The set-to-launch position, a critical factor in producing the sonic serve, creates the potential energy for the mechanisms of the upward-pitch action. With the body in a flexible yet controlled state, the hips stretch forward under the toss as the shoulders tilt and align with the point of contact, enabling the body to simulate the action of the pole-vaulter's pole. The body stretches, bends, and then snaps the throwing mechanics toward the point of contact.

You will need some time to discover the set-to-launch position, a position of balance centered on the front foot. You will need to relax and release the muscles and tendons along the front side of your body and across the chest and arms. Doing this will allow you to become more flexible.

As you work to learn the stretching of the hips, avoid excessive bending of the front knee in the action. If you use too much knee bend, you will have more difficulty finding the right hip position. Once your hips are familiar with the stretched position, you can begin to add more knee bend but make sure that the additional bending does not compromise the positioning of the hips.

Think of the face of the clock as you tilt your shoulders and arms into alignment with contact. Your toss arm will point in the direction of one o'clock, and the hitting elbow will point toward seven o'clock.

You should feel the potential energy build as you stretch into set-to-launch position, providing explosive energy for the upward launch.

Launch to Contact

You have stretched all the energy into your hip position in the set to launch, and you are aimed and ready to fire toward the point of contact. The key to the hip snap upward is to maintain your hips inside the court. When you force your hips to stay fixed in position, the energy of the upward snap will drive the upper body toward contact, achieving a straight position leaning over the court before contact. On the follow-through you will find yourself inside the baseline with forward momentum pulling you toward the net. You can create enough power in your upward snap to lift your feet off the ground as you reach to higher contact points. When you see the top players leave the ground on the serve, the action is not a jump with the legs and a hit. The snap of the hip is what creates the liftoff.

As your body straightens into the court, all the speed and energy created sends the racquet head up to contact as the hitting elbow travels on a straight track up toward the point of contact, traveling 180 degrees in the process. We call this the "power curve." To achieve racquet-head speed, you must provide enough distance in the swing for the racquet head to generate speed. The sonic serve works with 180 degrees of arc, making contact at the end of the power curve. With all the power of the throwing action directed up toward contact, the hitting arm straightens into contact, forcing the racquet head up over the top, snapping the wrist, and rotating the forearm to follow-through. The result is high net clearance and sharp downward action that sends the ball into the service box.

The problem that most players have is trying to change from creating their power forward to directing it upward. A lack of power and failure to reach aggressive placements frustrate these players. By focusing throwing action and power forward, players shift the power curve forward and down, greatly reducing the distance the racquet head travels heading into contact. This affects the function of the hitting arm at contact, leading to a highly accelerated follow-through made up of wasted power that the player intended to apply to the ball. This causes serves that struggle to clear the net yet have difficulty coming down inside the box.

To overcome the mental blueprint of the forward action and to shift to the upward action, you almost have to trick yourself into discovering it. You truly have to believe that you are creating action on your serve that will result in the ball flying 100 feet in the air. If you do so and extend to the highest point of contact, you will be amazed when you see the ball fire down into the service box. Instead of trying to force your wrist to snap to direct the ball down into the court, the action begins to happen like the crack at the end of the whip snap.

Be prepared to spend considerable time and practice developing the upward-pitch technique in your serve. You will need to work hard at making the mental adjustment. Overcoming an old habit that has likely been set in stone will be more difficult than simply developing a new habit. Under pressure and in the fatigue of match play, don't be surprised if your old motion occasionally reappears. Patience and determination will get you there, if you work at it.

Style

Players develop personal styles built on preferences that feel most comfortable to them. Although players share the vital fundamental components, slight variations of the sonic serve technique will always exist. For instance, the stretching of the hips into the set-to-launch position varies from leading with the front side of the hips into the stretch to extending the rear end to create the stretch. When you stretch the front side forward, you achieve a more powerful and effective snap action that doesn't rely so much on your leg strength.

In any deviations that you make as you create your signature of style, just make sure that you do not sacrifice any of the key elements. Be careful—the more unorthodox your style, the greater the likelihood of injury.

Drills and Exercises

Where Is the Whoosh?

Simply listening to the sound of your swing will help you understand whether you are directing your throwing action and power in the right direction. Without using a ball, go through your normal serve motion, swinging at full speed. Listen to the sound of the racquet and try to determine where the whoosh sound is the loudest. If the swing is loudest in front of your face, past where the contact would occur, you are directing your throwing action and power forward, not up.

If you direct your power up toward the point of contact, the whoosh sound will be above your head through the contact zone. As you practice your serve, do what is necessary to move the whoosh sound before contact.

Mastering the Throw

1. If your throwing motion needs some work, you should practice playing toss and catch with a partner on a daily basis. Start close to each other and then slowly extend the distance until you are able to throw from baseline to baseline with some accuracy.

You will improve your throwing speed and distance if you learn to use shoulder rotation and both arms to accelerate the throwing action. Begin with your arms and shoulders level and your opposite arm lined up with your partner, the target. Use your opposite arm to drive the shoulder rotation, stretching the chest muscles in the sequence of movement. Your chest will rotate and face your target as you release the throw. Try to spread your elbows to increase the stretching of the chest in the action. As you develop your throwing skill, you can progress to the next challenge, the upward pitch.

2. Simulating the full sonic serve motion, work on creating the set-to-launch position by throwing toward a target where the point of contact would be on your serve. Work on improving your hip snap as part of the motion. Try to see how high you can throw the ball. If you do it correctly, the ball will come down in the service box area on the bounce.

3. The last progression of the throwing exercises requires two balls, one for each hand. Toss the first ball into the air to the desired height of your serve. In the timing and toss-hit rhythm of your serve, throw the second ball toward the point of contact and attempt to make the two balls collide. You must not let the tossed ball drop below the height of contact for the serve.

Pivot in the Tube

This exercise tests your ability to control all your body movements. You will also develop a better feel for how the body can efficiently transfer energy to the racquet head as the body straightens before contact in the full motion.

Before you can take total command of your motion and create precision in the positioning, you must eliminate unnecessary parts of your motion that take away from the result. If movements are occurring that you are unaware of, you need to work on taking command of your motion and balance. The pivot-in-the-tube exercise will require firmness in the core of the body to maintain alignment within the tube and relaxation in the throwing mechanics to achieve speed.

Your objective is to establish a position inside an imaginary tube that fits tightly. You will try to maintain your upright alignment within the tube as you toss and hit. From the start of the motion you will need to establish strong upright back posture and use the muscles in your legs and hip area to gain control and resist bowing out. As you swing, you should try not to break through the sides of the tube, allowing only your hips and shoulders to pivot within the tube. Your head should hardly move as you complete this exercise. You may find it easier to face the net more in your stance.

This exercise may look easy, but mastering it requires a lot of patience. When you become proficient at it, the full motion of your sonic serve will be more efficient and powerful.

Balance Until the Bounce

The test of your set to launch is whether you can maintain total control of your balance. As you create the position of potential energy for the upward snap, you need to be in command of your balance so that you can direct your power and energy up toward contact without losing control of your motion. You must have enough flexibility to stretch and snap with your body but not be so loose that your movement becomes sloppy. You must develop a precise habit that you can duplicate. The set-to-launch position is something you can practice off court as well, in front of a mirror. On court you can use videotape or your shadow to check for the qualities you should see. You need to become familiar with your technique. Learning the look and associated feel of this position is integral to the development process.

To create the set-to-launch position, set up in a stance so that your front foot points toward the net post in front of you. Your back foot should be a comfortable distance behind the heel of the front foot. Extend your arms at shoulder level to create a straight line from hand to hand. Now turn your shoulders sideways until the tossing hand is over the toes of your front foot. You are now set to stretch your body over the front toes, under the point of contact. The best way to stretch the hips forward is over the toes of the front foot. Rather than stretching the rear end inside the baseline, you want to stretch the front side from the front knee up to the front shoulder. If you were to put a ball in your pocket in line with your kneecap and at hip-socket level, that would be the ideal stretch point. As you stretch, the ball in your pocket should shift straight forward over the toes of the front foot.

In the drill, keep your arms and shoulders in line with the front foot as you tilt upward in the toss action. Without a ball or racquet, begin in alignment with the toss hand over the front foot. Tilt the shoulder line until it is almost perpendicular to the ground as you shift the ball in your pocket over the front foot. You should find a balanced position with the weight of your stretch positioned behind the ball in your pocket. If your front knee is quivering to support your weight as you stretch, you don't have the position set correctly. Straighten the front knee more and focus on even more stretch in the hips until you feel the weight of the stretch in your hip area, not down by the knee.

When you think you have it, try the balance-until-bounce test. Using a racquet and ball, go through the motion and freeze in the set-to-launch position.

Toss to the desired height of your serve and see if you can freeze on balance until the tossed ball bounces on the ground. Practice this until you can balance totally under control. Check a video of yourself to see if you are stretching your hips enough and to see if your shoulders reach a line with contact. All your body weight should be the front foot as you set.

Upward Launch

You have stretched the energy into the hip area and are balanced and prepared to launch. The hip-snap action works to drive power to the throwing mechanics, snapping the upper body up and out toward contact. For correct function, the hip position must maintain the fixed position inside the court. Once your hips stretch forward, they must stay forward and use the energy to lift the upper body.

It is common to see players reach a perfect set-to-launch position but then allow their hips to pop backward in the upward launch. As the hips pull back, they lose all power as the body collapses, sending the ball down into the net. Force your hips to stay inside the baseline as you create the upward launch.

Remember your throwing action and power aim. Fire up toward contact, not forward. Remind yourself before every serve where you want to direct your energy.

If you have any adjustments to make in the grip, check before every serve. Make sure you don't readjust your grip in midmotion. That action is common, so watch out for it!

Crossing the Finish Line

On the follow-through of the serve, you should find yourself completely inside the baseline. If you create enough upward snap, your feet will leave the ground. If your hips work properly, you will land in a forward-momentum position with your upper body. Like the body of a sprinter crossing the finish line, your body should be leaning forward on the finish, making the serve and volley a natural progression of the follow-through.

CHAPTER 6

Right-Back-Atcha Returns

In a world where sonic serves rule the turf, you do not stand a chance without returns that are right-back-atcha.

When you are facing an opponent who is launching a full-scale aerial assault, you have the choice to either run for cover or hang in there and send them right-back-atcha.

Even if you had the exceptional skills of Andre Agassi, you would need more than just quick reflexes to break the offensive. You need powers of intuition to anticipate the action before it happens. You need to learn the techniques for gaining more control of each situation and the indicators that can help you detect the server's intent. You must have a game plan for breaking serve and the mind-set and discipline to execute it. With less than a half second to read, react, and execute, you should have a plan for the return before the serve is struck because you will not have time to decide later.

Cracking the Safe

Highly skilled returners are capable of hacking through the security codes, of cracking the safe, to gain access to the server's classified strategic documents, allowing them to anticipate every move of the server. Within the first few games of a match,

This chapter by Pat Dougherty and Peter D. McCraw.

they establish their timing and rhythm as they zero in on the server's routine and patterns. Like a computer, they log the data of the previous points played, tracking trends or tendencies that may be predictable. The intuitive returner eventually figures out the server's favorite serves in both courts and the decisions he or she makes under pressure. Such an opponent becomes aware of the placements the server has difficulty with and challenges the server on them. Like a cat baiting the mouse into a trap, the proactive returner will add pressure to the situation, using court position and action to manipulate the server's thought process.

You too can become adept at delivering right-back-atcha returns by leaving no stone unturned and by understanding that the battle is often won before it is ever fought.

From the moment you step on the court, you should feel like you are on the hunt, stalking your prey, looking for signs of weakness and moments of vulnerability that allow you to strike. Your intensity must build up to the moment you react, letting nothing distract you from the task of returning the ball back in play. Convince yourself that returning serve is a challenge you love. You expect, you want, every serve to be in. You need that mind-set to be fully prepared for the return.

You Make the Call

Unless you are a regular on the professional tour, it is a rare occasion when you have the luxury of an umpire to call the lines for you. You must be able to determine whether a serve is in or out without losing focus on executing your return. You will improve this skill with experience.

When you see that a serve is out, be quick and decisive, making sure the server is aware of your call. You can gesture with your arm, raise your index finger, or make the call verbally, but you do not want the server to feel that you are indecisive. If you seem unsure, your opponent will challenge you and often convince himself or herself that you are playing unfairly. Sometimes it can be difficult to make a clear judgment, which can occasionally lead to making a bad call unintentionally. If you are wishing the ball to be out, or hoping it goes out, under pressure you can convince yourself it went out, even when it hit the line!

Intentional Hook

For one reason or another, some players are so obsessed with winning that they cheat on line calls. You do not want to have the notorious reputation of lacking character as a competitor. Nobody has ever cheated on the way to becoming a true champion in any sport. Good players can often tell if their ball went in or out by the feel of the shot at contact. When the server makes contact he or she can feel as well as see whether the ball is in. If you repeatedly make bad line calls, you can be sure that your opponent is aware of it. Once you establish a pattern of making bad line calls, you can expect your opponent to do the same. It is a no-win situation for both players and an ugly match from that point on.

In the end, you are much better off playing it straight. If you feel you are getting hooked, call an umpire. Do not try to beat a cheater at his or her game.

Serve Strategy

To improve your anticipation skills as a returner, you need to understand the server's thought process. Within the first few service games, you should have a good idea of what you are up against. You cannot allow yourself to become frustrated if you do not break serve early in the match. You need to give yourself an opportunity to establish your timing and your feel for the serves as you gather information to help you break serve later in the set. If you can hold serve regularly, all you need is one break of serve to win the set!

Level I: Living on Second Serves

The first level of serve strategy has little thought behind it. Blast the first serve and see if it goes in and then use a "push" second serve. Players who use this strategy do not have a lot of confidence in their serve and have no idea how to use it strategically.

Typically, the majority of these first-serve blasts are faults, and the first-serve percentage falls off the charts. If these players survive the battle, they will be using their second serves to do it.

Servers with methodical serve routines are easy to break because you have so many second serves to work with. If you add a little more pressure to the situation, you can easily force them to double-fault.

Level II: Attack the Weakness

The next progression of serve mentality recognizes the value of attacking weakness. Rather than just getting it in, such servers will place their serves. Servers will often assume that your backhand is the weaker side, so with great predictability they focus most of their serves toward the returner's backhand. Unless you prove to them otherwise, they will continue to play to your backhand most of the time.

Level III: Rotation of Placements

Still working with the hard first serves and spin second serves, level III evolves from predictably attacking a weakness to making a more calculated change of placement. Your return timing should be easy to establish because the serve speed is still not changing much; only the placement varies. These players will begin to challenge your range and reach on the return as they work you side to side.

Level IV: Full Rotation of Speed, Spin, and Placement

"Say hello to my little friend. . . ." You are up against a serve weapon! If the server can maintain a high percentage of first serves in play while varying the speed, spin, and placement, you will have to overcome a complete serve arsenal and a server who knows how to use it.

The server's ability to work the variation of placements keeps the returner uncertain of which side to prepare for. The variation of speed and spin on the first serve toys with the returner's timing. When the server can sense that the returner is expecting the big flat serve, he or she can effectively mix in the off-speed spinner.

The server who has an effective and reliable second serve is likely to be more aggressive with the first serve. But the server should understand that living on the second serve too much is flirting with disaster. On first serves the pressure is on the returner, who is preparing in a defensive mind-set. On second serves the pressure shifts to the server. Like a baseball pitcher with a 3-2 count, the server has no room for error. The returner can begin to assume a more offensive role when facing a second serve.

Showdown

When sonic serve weapons clash with right-back-atcha returns, be ready to rumble. Like two boxers staring each other down at the weigh-in, the game of intimidation begins long before the ball is even in play. With no fear on their faces, the two gunslingers stand off, neither backing down to the other's threat.

The server begins a routine of rituals that he or she methodically performs before every serve, bouncing the ball several times to prepare for battle. The server takes one last look to make sure that the returner is ready and then makes the final decision about what to do with the serve. Meanwhile, the returner studies the server's every move and prepares with similar rituals. In a rocking side-to-side motion and a bounce in his or her step, the returner prepares to react quickly when the server strikes the ball. As the toss goes up in the air, the returner starts moving forward.

To add a little punch to the block returns, the returner wants his or her body to have a little forward momentum on the split step and reaction. Before the serve is in play, the returner has predetermined his or her actions.

When the serve is struck, all the returner has to do is read and react according to plan.

You can answer several questions before playing the point:

1. Considering whether it is a first or second serve, will I block, chip, or drive the ball back into play?
2. Is the server likely to attack the net behind the serve?
3. In what direction will I attempt to execute—down the line, to the middle, or crosscourt?
4. Do I plan to attack or stay back after the return?
5. Will I attempt to pressure and influence serve selection?
6. What can I anticipate happening off my return shot?

Going into points with the answers to these questions in place will better prepare you to make the right decisions in the reaction mode and may allow you to anticipate the action before it happens.

Server's Perspective

As the server takes one last look at the returner before sending the toss into the air, he or she is looking to see if the returner is ready to play. The server is also determining whether the returner's court position will affect the type of serve and placement he or she should use.

During the first few games, the server is collecting information about the returner and logging the data. Once the returner establishes a starting position in both the deuce and ad boxes, the server adjusts his or her visual perspective to those positions.

Where you typically position yourself side to side and up and back in the deuce and ad boxes is your neutral position. You are neutral because you are at the midpoint between the two extreme placements on the serve. Your position gives you a range of coverage that matches nearly all serve possibilities. The server quickly becomes familiar and comfortable with your neutral court position. Each time you take that neutral position, the server feels a little less pressure in selecting the serve, and you'll play an increasingly smaller role in his or her choice. When you use your court position to alter the server's perspective, you can become part of the decision, manipulating the server into thinking that an opportunity is available for exploitation. As you become more proactive by sporadically varying your court position, you can affect the serve, narrowing the possible options and allowing you to anticipate the serve with greater accuracy.

Powers of Influence

As in a game of poker, when the opponent has revealed his or her hand and shown you every weapon available, you might find that he or she has difficulty with particular serve placements. You may be able to predict the serve a split second before it is hit by picking up on certain indicators—how the server stands to serve, how the server adjusts the toss, or how the server positions differently on particular serves.

When your opponent shows limited use of the service boxes, neglects certain targets, or provides you the indicators you need to anticipate the serve, you have more control. You may need to adjust your neutral-court position to create better opportunities for your returns. Suppose the server is clearly struggling on the wide serves, hitting most of them into the net. Most of the time the server is serving down the T and coming to net, a pattern that has been working well for him or her. Your adjusted neutral-court position favoring the T placements will give you a better opportunity to return the strongest serves while challenging your opponent to go for the wider placements that he or she is struggling with.

Bait and Switch

To throw off the server's perspective, you use a different starting position this time. In taking that last look before the toss, the server notices that your position seems to be favoring one side. The server feels that you are looking for the down-the-T placement, offering a challenge to go for the wide ace. But as the server looks away from you to begin the motion, you shift your position back to true neutral with a good idea of where the serve might be going. Even if the server doesn't take the bait and serves down the T, you are reacting from the neutral position so you give the server nothing open down the T either.

When you shift your starting position right or left of neutral, the server tends to choose the part of the court you leave open, that is, until he or she becomes wise to your tricks. When you position farther back from neutral, deep in the court, you challenge the server to go for more angle and spins to beat you, lessening the effect of a powerful first serve. If you position a step or two closer to the service line, inside of neutral, you challenge the server to overpower you. To force the server to double-fault or use a second serve, you can close in tighter to make the service box seem much smaller to the server.

Neutral Then Commit

Against the biggest servers you often have to rely on an educated guess to get you through. They have seen all the tricks and do not fall for them much any more. Your best chance is to figure out the pattern of attack. When you have a good sense of what is coming, especially in a second-serve situation, you can play it neutral until the server looks up with the toss. You then commit yourself to run around what would be a backhand and nail the forehand return. Because you are committing yourself, however, you run a risk of being burned if you do not guess correctly.

Work sparingly with your court-position tactics and make your adjustments subtler. If you adjust too often, you will fail to affect the server. You do not want the server to be aware that you are baiting the serve selection to increase your control of the situation. Save these tactics for the most crucial points and do not expect them to work all the time, especially against servers who know better.

How to Read Serve Technique

The server's stance to start the motion, the toss of the ball, an adjustment to the swing, or even a change of position on the baseline are possible indicators of the server's limitations or intent on the serve.

If the starting stance has the server turned sideways with the front foot parallel to the baseline, you should look to see if the feet leave the ground on the serve. If the server's body rotates completely, the server faces the net on the finish. If the server does not launch up off the ground and completely rotate, he or she will have trouble with certain placements. A right-handed player serving into the deuce box will always struggle to reach the wide and up-the-sideline placements unless he or she leaves the ground and rotates well in the motion. This server's best and favorite serve is likely to be down the T in the deuce box. In the ad box the same server will favor the wide serve to the right-handed returner's backhand and will have more difficulty down the T. Left-handed servers with this stance problem will have the opposite occur—strong wide and weak down the T in the deuce box, strong down the T and weak wide in the ad box.

When the server is facing the net with the front foot pointing more toward the net post, you cannot assume by the stance any patterns of strong versus weak placements.

What can you learn from watching the server's toss? Unless you are up against a highly skilled server who knows how to adjust the toss for the slice, kick, and flat serves under complete disguise, you can often predict the serve by the toss placement.

If you know the look of the toss for the server's biggest hard, flat serve, you can use that as a guide. If the right-handed server tosses the ball over the head, from the returner's perspective that toss would be well *right* of where the server tosses on the flat serve. You can expect to see the kick serve, probably to your backhand side if you are right-handed. If you see the toss to the left of the hard, flat toss, you can expect a slice serve, likely into your body or to the forehand side much of the time.

Do not expect the better servers to telegraph their toss adjustments this way, but if the opportunity arises, take advantage of it.

At times you will see players position wider than normal behind the baseline. Agassi would at times position out by the doubles alley when serving to the ad court to give him a better angle, pulling the returner off the court. Any time you see the server in a wider position, be ready for the wide serve because there is a good chance you will see one.

Right-Back-Atcha Versus Serve and Volley

Big servers will often establish a pattern of regularly attacking the net behind every first serve and often behind the second. Breaking this offensive can be challenging unless you know how to adjust on your returns. Preplanning the point before your return is especially important against the serve and volleyer because your returns have to work as passing shots. To overcome the serve-and-volley attack, you must make several adjustments.

1. **Shot selection.** Rather than using deep crosscourt returns to get a rally started, you should have as your primary targets the feet of the incoming server, down the line, and angle crosscourt.

2. **Stroke selection.** Rather than blasting the topspin drives that are high clearing over the net, work with slicing, chipping, and blocking on the returns to give the server less to work with on the first volley. If you can force your opponent to volley with the ball at the feet, control of the point often shifts to you.

3. **Varying court position.** The serve and volleyer relies on a specific timing of the serve, moves in a few steps, makes the split step at your contact with the ball, and then moves in for the volley. As the returner, if you change the distance between you and the server by adjusting up and back, you will make it difficult for the server to establish consistent timing for the attack.

Rather than maintaining the same neutral-court position for each serve, move in a step or two for some points and move back a step or two at other times. If you don't permit the server to become comfortable with the depth of your court position, he or she will have more trouble getting into a strong groove.

4. **Think two shots to pass, not one**. If you feel immense pressure to hit passing-shot winners off every return, you are likely to end up making many errors. Get yourself into the point on the return and go for the pass on the second or third shot you hit. The longer the point extends, the more the odds favor the returner at the baseline. If you neutralize the first serve and keep the return low or difficult to reach, you can take control of the point and then close on the following shots.

Right-Back-Atcha Versus Baseliner

When you are not under pressure from a serve and volleyer, you want to maintain the primary objective of getting the ball into play a high percentage of the time. You have to be disciplined in your game plan to overcome wanting to do too much with the returns, which will lead to unnecessary errors. Unless one player comes to the net behind either the serve or return, the point will progress into a rally off the return ball. If both players are right-handed, on the deuce side if the server pulls you off the court with a wide serve, a return crosscourt will allow you to recover for the next shot and will likely create the forehand-to-forehand crosscourt rally pattern. A return of the wide serve to the deep midcourt will give the server the option of hitting to either corner. A return down the line will likely lead to a crosscourt shot that could easily catch you out of position, having to hit a low-percentage return. Wide serves in the ad box work much the same way. If you return crosscourt you will likely establish a crosscourt backhand-to-backhand rally. Serves to the T placement in both boxes present the option of hitting to either corner depending on which rally pattern you wish to establish.

Big D

Although the serve can be a player's biggest offensive threat, the return should be a player's biggest defensive threat. The server is providing the power for you and is hitting the ball in your general direction. All you have to do is get the ball back into play. Of course, against the bigger servers this is a task easier said than done. Your goal is to neutralize the opponent's weapon and get the server into the point. You may wonder why the players with the most powerful serves aren't always winning all the tournaments. Well, it takes more than a big serve to win. All too often, the big servers struggle to come up with needed breaks of serve because they are deficient in other parts of the game. So if you can just get past the serve and return the ball back into play, you may find those big servers much easier to beat out of the rally. Thinking offense and always going for return winners on first serves will lead to errors in starting the point. That is not the correct strategic mind-set!

Thinking defense naturally puts you into a reflex-reaction mode, simplifying your ground strokes for quickness and permitting better timing on the return. You begin to see the value of blocking, chipping, and slicing as well as compact driving returns. You should feel like a backboard, setting up a wall of defense like the one that a volleyer creates at the net. You are defending your territory against an aerial assault, using a shield to deflect the incoming serves back into play. In any way you can, you seek to neutralize the server's strength, get the point started, and gain offensive control before the point ends.

If you can lure the server into going for more aggressive placements and more powerful serves to overcome your tenacious defensive stand, you will likely see more faults on the first serve. The second-serve opportunities are your best chance for capitalizing. Now you have the option to be more aggressive and think more offensively, depending on the strength of the second serve. You can become more active in adjusting your court position, pressuring and baiting the server. You can think about driving the ball rather than just blocking it back. On occasion you might attack the net off the return, forcing the server to try to pass you on the second shot. What you do not want to do is squander opportunities by always going for too much. The return must get points started in your mind. When you try to end points with the return, your percentage of errors to winners favors the opponent.

Establishing Your Neutral Ground

When facing a server you have never played before, you will have to learn about the serve strengths and weaknesses in the first few games. You will have to defend against all potential serve placements until you learn otherwise. Find a position that locates you at the midpoint of the server's best possible serves. You should be one step and a full reach from covering the down-the-T placement and the same distance from covering the wide serve. Make sure you factor in the spin effect of the right-handed server versus a left-handed server. The power potential of the server will often determine how close or far back from the service line you should be. Once you establish that center point, your neutral position, you are ready to go.

If the server is neglecting certain areas of the service boxes, he or she may not be able to reach all the targets in both boxes. If the server focuses most of the serve placements to one side or the other, you can shift your court position accordingly. There is no sense in positioning to cover parts of the service box that are never used. Now you can narrow the possibilities and give yourself a better chance of covering the parts of the court your opponent is using. At the same time you challenge the opponent to go for difficult placements.

Early in the match you are better off giving yourself a little more time to react against first serves by taking a position a little deeper in the court. As you begin to zone in on the return and establish your confidence, you can take a more aggressive position a few steps closer to the service line.

The problem with closing in too tight in the return position is that you limit the time available for reaction to the power serve. Positioning very deep in the court opens the opportunity for angle spins, which pull you even wider off the court on the return and allow the serve and volleyer to move in closer. You need quick feet to play deep behind the baseline on the return because you have more ground to cover. So find a middle ground that works for you and be willing to vary your court position as part of your attack.

Same Old Routine

The rituals and routine leading up to executing the return have an important role in your readiness to react and your ability to execute. Although routines will differ from player to player based on style and preference, you must include some key elements if you want returns that are right-back-atcha.

We determined that your neutral position is the location you normally take before the server's toss is in the air. Your split position to react to the serve may or may not be the same as your neutral position. The split position involves the split step timed to the moment of contact on the serve. The split step creates a wide base of support in your stance. From this position, with your feet nearly two shoulder-widths apart, you are down and ready to react quickly to either the forehand or backhand side. The key to having better reach and range of coverage begins with a wider split step, precisely timed to the server's contact.

Some players make a habit of starting in a neutral position well inside the baseline. As the server puts the toss in the air, the returner backs up a few steps before creating the split step. This routine is fine as long as you are able to position quickly and get your body weight forward as you split. If the server catches you leaning backward, you will have problems controlling the return.

Most players are better off in a neutral position a few steps back from where they want to split step. As the toss goes into the air, they move forward to make the split, giving more punch to the defensive return.

You will find other players who start in a neutral position and never move forward or back. Your routine may change from first- to second-serve situations and as you work court-position tactics. Whichever routine you choose, make sure you include a well-timed, wide split step.

Defensive Stroke Production

Most ground strokes are hit offensively with bigger strokes to generate power. On the return you must adjust your forehand and backhand ground strokes for a more defensive application. The serve speed generally provides plenty of power so you will not need big offensive swings.

You need to work with compact, abbreviated versions of your ground strokes, using the existing power on the ball to create your shots. You should use relatively no backswing and a focus on the contact point and follow-through. When using the block return you do not have much backswing or follow-through.

Jack-in-the-Box

A common problem for many players on the return is what we call jack-in-the-box. As the server prepares to serve, the intensity of the moment builds and the returner's excitement and energy rises to a peak. At the moment the server strikes the ball, the returner springs up off the ground like a jack-in-the-box.

At the moment the server makes contact, your feet should be on the ground in the wide split, ready to make a move. The jack-in-the-box returner is a foot off the ground at the moment of contact. By the time Jack's feet land on the ground, it is too late to react. If springing upward is part of your routine, do it early enough that your feet are on the ground and you are down in your split step at the movement of contact on the serve.

How About the Stance

Against powerful serve weapons, you barely have time to get your racquet on the ball, let alone set up the perfect stance. You have to learn to execute from the open stance on both the forehand and backhand sides. When the power serve is placed well within your reach, all you have to do is rotate your hips and shoulders, never moving your feet out of the split step. If the ball is one step away, you will still set up in the open stance to execute.

If you try to adjust your feet quickly into a more comfortable neutral stance, you will often be too late to execute! Avoid becoming wrong-footed. Minimize the footwork involved and develop your skills in working with an open stance.

The ultimate test for a returner is having to move and reach to execute the returns. Most players have far more success with their returns on serves hit to them compared with serves that make them move. If your hitting stance changes from open to closed, your options on the return become much more limited and predictable. Unless you are hitting a one-handed backhand return, the closed hitting stances will cause problems. The open and neutral stances are the ones to use in all circumstances to keep your return options open.

Real Test

To return a ball that is within reach is one thing, but to be able to stretch, reach, and lunge for a return and still do damage is the mark of a skilled returner. Some of the most spectacular returns by players like Jimmy Connors and Andre Agassi occurred when they had to lunge and reach. Most players break down significantly when you test their reach and range of coverage on the return. They experience a lack of control and a total loss of power in that situation. The reason for most of their problems has to do with stroke technique. The best returners do not take a backswing and then stroke out to make contact. The technique used by Connors, Agassi, and all the other great returners is different from the approach the average player uses.

Full-Reach Returns

As if trying to catch the ball with a baseball glove, outstanding returners first react by positioning the butt of the racquet in line with the incoming ball. As they reach out to get the hitting hand behind and beneath the ball, their feet automatically adjust to support the stroke. Driving out of an open stance, they lunge on a diagonal toward the point of contact and generate a powerful pulling action across the body. They reach out and then pull the stroke back across the body, producing a powerful result on contact. This action is very different from that of the average returner, who reaches back into a backswing then strokes out to reach the ball. If you work on the advanced technique for full-reach returns, you will strengthen your range of coverage and frustrate your opponents with your titanium wall of defense.

Mental Adjustments

For most players, making the mental adjustment from thinking offensively on the return to thinking defensively will boost success on the return. Opening your senses and becoming more aware of the patterns and tendencies throughout point play will help you anticipate the action before it happens.

Getting into the habit of preplanning the start of the point will help you make better decisions in the reflex mode. Finally, learning to love the challenge of returning the big serves will put you in the mind-set for creating positive results. Before you know it, you will be sending those returns right-back-atcha!

CHAPTER 7

Tenacious Net Play

The game of the future will see more players dominating with the attacking style of play, getting to the net as often as possible.

This chapter offers insight into the mentality of the attacking player and the art of developing a game plan. We will look at the tools of the trade and how they work together within the flow of building a point toward your desired outcome. You will see that building a game plan around the right objectives takes the pressure off hitting individual shots. You use the power of shot combinations to do the work. The quality of your game plan determines whether you are gambling against the casino or you are the casino! With statistics on your side and an understanding of how to stage the end of points, you will beat the house even against players of greater skill. It all starts with your will to be tenacious at net.

To understand the purpose behind your strokes and shot selection, we begin with a focus on your point-ending objectives. Close your eyes and play the perfect point in your mind. . . .

How does that point end? Were you serving? Was the end of the point something heroic on your part that might appear on ESPN Sports Center highlights? The action you created in your mind likely represents what we refer to as the "want

This chapter by Pat Dougherty and Peter D. McCraw.

circle." Three influences affect every decision you make during a point. Represented by a Venn diagram (figure 7.1), these influences are what you can, want to, and should do in a given situation.

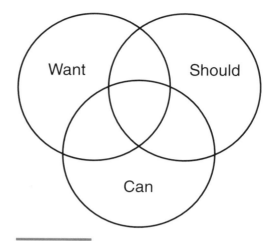

In a rally, suppose the short-ball opportunity arises. What are you going to do with it? What you probably *want* to do is to step up and crush the stuffing out of it for a winner. What you *can* do depends on the pressure of the situation and your ability to execute the desired shot. What you *should* do is make the shot that works

Figure 7.1 The "want circle" illustrates the influences on decision-making.

best within a game plan that favors you statistically. Although you may come out of a losing effort thinking that your strokes let you down, the fact may be that you lost because of all those decisions you made to try for bigger, more difficult shots that you are not capable of executing consistently. Remember, if you were so good that you could hit balls off the lines at will, you would not need a game plan. All you would have to do is hit a put-away winner every time you swing the racquet. Why doesn't Pete Sampras just ace the guy on every first serve to win the point? Why doesn't Andre Agassi just smack those returns away for winners? Well, the greatest players of all time were smart enough to know that they needed a game plan built of shot combinations. If they were to attempt first-ball winners every time, they know that they would beat themselves with errors in the end. If you average two double faults for every ace, you are giving your opponent twice as much as you are getting and it's your strategy that's doing it.

Point structure	Stroke inventory
1. Start	Serves and returns
2. Set up	Ground-stroke rally
3. Attack	Approach shots, angles, drop shots
4. Finish	Volleys, overheads, passing shots, lobs

A game plan establishes an objective for every shot, organizing your skills into shot patterns and combinations so that you can build points toward a desired outcome.

The game plan is your plan of attack. It highlights your strengths and protects your weaknesses. You can adjust it to court surfaces, playing conditions, and opponents. To execute a game plan, you must trust its effectiveness enough to stay on track and not let your raw emotions dictate your decisions under pressure. After all, a game plan should make your job easier while making the opponent's task more difficult.

Think of your skills, strokes, and shots as the tools you have to work with. For your game plan to flow smoothly, each tool must function in harmony with the others. The concept of point structure shows us the purpose behind each tool and how it best functions within your plan.

By building points within point structure, you will see that the serve and return are intended to get points started. When you attempt to end points with your serve or return, do not be surprised when your percentage of getting points started drops dramatically. To work successfully with a game plan, you must understand the decisions you have to make. You must know what you *should* do. What you *want* to do should support that decision. Then you hope that you have the skills to execute.

All too often temptation becomes so great that you choose to go for more than you need. Worse yet, you are torn between what you *want* to do and what you *should* do, and you make an error because of your indecision. When you know you have a solid game plan, you must be disciplined enough to stick with it or, when fighting a losing effort, to adjust it to increase your chances for success. You may find that the big forehand weapon that you normally build your points around isn't quite as big as the forehand you are facing! If your opponent outmatches your strength, you need a fallback position in your game plan. If the forehand crosscourt rally pattern isn't working out, you may be able to build your rallies in the backhand-to-backhand pattern. It's OK to adjust your game plan! After halftime of a football game, you will often see teams come out with a completely new approach for the second half, changing their initial game plan to an adjusted game plan based on the first half. The adjusted game plan allows them to work their way back into a game they were losing at the half. A team's ability to adjust to adversity and come from behind to win is the measure of greatness.

If you are one of the hopeless many that still work with no real game plan and rely on defying the odds with winner after winner, you should not expect to win matches often. You should just learn to enjoy the game for the opportunity to hit your shots and show off your occasional winners. There is nothing wrong with that now, is there? That style of play is what keeps the driving range crowded with people trying to be like Tiger Woods and attempting to hit 300-yard drives. But you will find that the best competitors are not satisfied with individual shots. They want to compete head-to-head and use their shots to beat every opponent.

Point-Ending Outcomes

If you were to chart match statistics, the end of every point would fall into one of three categories:

- Winners
- Forced errors
- Unforced errors

These terms have clear-cut definitions:

- A winner occurs when you successfully execute a shot that goes untouched by the opponent to end the point.
- A forced error occurs when your shot forces the opponent to execute without having time to set up mentally or physically and the opponent makes an error.
- An unforced error occurs when the opponent has time to set up mentally and physically for the shot and the opponent makes an error.

When you compile all the statistics at the end of a match, you will find some interesting results. If you focus on creating winners at every opportunity, you will beat yourself with errors in the end. Nothing feels better than hitting the outright winner, but nothing feels worse than turning a perfect opportunity into an unforced error. Even the easy sitters are easy to miss when the pressure is on. Winners are even more difficult to execute consistently when the opponent is forcing you to go for it.

Against stiffer competition, just keeping the ball in play and waiting for the opponent to make an unforced error will not be enough to win the match. Good players may give you a few unforced errors, but rarely will they give you enough to determine the match. Because you have no control over when and how often the opponent makes unforced errors, you cannot really build a game plan around it.

The player who can more often force the opponent either to produce a winner or to commit a forced error will usually be the winner in the long run. Forcing errors is the focus of a winning game plan.

You put yourself under less pressure on each shot when you hit with the intent to force the opponent rather than hit to produce the outright winner. This does not mean being tentative. The mentality shift requires you to become more disciplined with your opportunities and force the opponent to execute difficult shots. Remember, of every 10 short-ball opportunities, you want to create 7 or 8 difficult situations for the opponent rather than make 6 or 7 unforced errors as you go for winners and miss. You must keep in mind this ratio of winners to errors in building your game plan.

As you work through the stages of point structure in setting up the situation for your desired outcome, you build your points using shot patterns that allow you to recover behind each shot. The ball travels from baseline to baseline in less than two seconds on a ground stroke of average speed. The time that it takes for the ball to reach the opponent is all the time you have to recover before your opponent hits the next ball. How many steps can you take in less than two seconds? Not many. If you do not reach full recovery in time, you leave the court open for your opponent. If you use five shots to set up and end the point, you need to recover behind four of them.

Where do you recover? The recovery position behind every ground stroke should be behind the hash mark at the center of the baseline, right? Wrong!

Percentage-Shot Selection—Rally

You are positioned wide in the court in a rally if you hit the ball crosscourt to shot selection 1. This is the highest percentage shot because it allows you to recover fully. You would recover behind the center hash mark only if you were to choose shot selection 2. Otherwise, the recovery position shifts as you hit to different targets. These recovery positions allow you cover the sharp angles as well as the down the line, putting you halfway in between.

The problem is that you have less than two seconds to reach these positions. When you drive the ball for an attempted winner to shot selection 3, you must hope to end the point on that shot. Unable to recover in time, you will leave the crosscourt open for the opponent. To preserve adequate recovery time, players maintain crosscourt rallies as they build points. If their intent is to hit down the line within a rally to force a change in the rally pattern, they do so with underspin or high loopers to give themselves enough time to recover.

Percentage-Shot Patterns—Attacking the Net

When advancing to the net, you have even less time to reach proper position, and you must avoid leaving any openings for passing shots. The shot direction that provides the shortest distance for improving your net position is down the line. When you are approaching off balls in the midcourt, straight down the middle is the highest percentage shot.

To become more tenacious at the net, you must realize that your positioning at the net is more important than your power! Regardless of the strength of your net game, your ability to achieve position poses a great threat to the opponent. Without the skills to defend the net effectively, however, your threatening position there will lose its influence. The approach shot determines not only your ability to position but also the difficulty you will face in volleying.

**To err is human.
To force is divine.**

Your ability to force your opponent will depend on many factors, including the quality of your opponent. When we think of a forcing shot, naturally we think of a deep shot to the baseline, penetrating and powerful. A drop shot set up with disguise and used correctly is a forcing shot as well. An opponent who positions deep behind the baseline in the rally is much more difficult to force on deep balls than an opponent who positions right on the baseline.

Many players who excel at attacking the net use a variety of shots on the approach. Besides driving with topspin, they will use the slice and chip approaches, which allow them to adjust the depth of their shots from deep shots to drop shots.

Working with a slice or chip allows you a little added time to reach better net position. Mixing up the attack and using a variety of shots on the down-the-line approach will keep the opponent confused about how deep in the court to play.

If I always follow the percentage rules of maintaining crosscourt patterns in rallies and approaching down the line, won't I be too predictable?

Being predictable is not all that bad when you maintain your patterns and provide little opportunity for the opponent to capitalize. Although percentage rules may dictate the direction of your shots, you can vary the depth of your shots without changing the direction. What is important is that you understand what happens when you decide to deviate from the percentage rules.

If you are playing someone with a huge forehand but no backhand threat, you may be able to attack on crosscourt approaches into that weak backhand, even though you leave much wider passing lanes. If that tactic proves to be a risk that is not paying off, however, you may want to rethink your approach.

The last thing you want to do on the approach is provide the opponent with the type of shot he or she loves to work with for hitting passing shots. Most players prefer an approach shot hit with some power, a little topspin, and a bounce within a few feet of the baseline right up into their preferred height of contact. All too often, players approach repeatedly on this type of shot and then wonder why the opponent is having a field day passing them.

The use of variety on the approach is about giving the opponent less to work with on the pass. Learning to vary spin, speed, and depth on the attack will force opponents to work outside their comfort zone, to generate all their own pace, to earn every pass. If you want to improve the conditions of play at the net and increase your effectiveness on the attack, then don't feed the giant!

Don't feed the giant!

Closing Position

When you work your way into closing net position, you should be within one step and a full reach from the sideline, within one step and a full reach of the angle pass, and within two steps of covering the lob. When you approach down the center, your net position is in the center and you force your opponent to create angles to pass you. The closer you get to the net, the better you can cover the angle pass but the more vulnerable you are to the lob. If you hang back to cover the lob, you leave the angle open. So you must develop a sense of when you can close in tight by considering the strengths and weaknesses of the opponent.

Tools of Tenacious Net Play

Your objective on approach shots should be to get the ball in play with the intent of forcing the opponent while you move into the net. You must learn to move through the approach shot with your footwork without missing the shot as a result. The underspin approaches are easier to move through than the flat drives. The footwork patterns commonly used for the approach shots are the cross-behind step, in which the back foot crosses behind the front, and the kick step. For the flatter drives, you will find the open stance most suitable.

You should advance to the net in stages. Move in as much as you can behind your approach for your first volley, but when your opponent is about to make contact, you have to split step to play the next shot.

The split step positions you back into reaction mode so that you can correctly and quickly respond to the opponent's next shot. You do not have to plant your feet in stone when you split. You want your body to have a light feel so that you can react quickly. You just want your feet to touch briefly so that you can make your next move. You have approached down the line, and you split step as the opponent hits. If your first volley is below the level of the net, you will likely need a second volley to close the point. In this case use the first volley as another approach, going back down the line as you close in farther to the net. On the second volley you will have a better opportunity to angle the ball away. Remember to use your position to pressure the opponent and create a wall of defense that the opponent cannot easily penetrate.

Tenacious Grip

For the underspin approaches, all volleys, and your overhead, you should be using the continental grip. By using the continental grip you will not be caught between grip changes in reflex situations. The continental grip can be equally effective on both the forehand and backhand sides, allowing the wrist to establish a strong position of leverage to support the racquet head. When the wrist is positioned correctly, the racquet and arm will form an L.

Reflex Ready

When in net position you need quick and compact preparation to reflex volley, so you need to be sharp in your ready position. Make it a habit to keep the racquet head up in front of you so that you can react quickly to both sides.

If you are to favor one side or the other in your ready position, remember that your backhand volley covers your body whereas the forehand gets jammed. When in doubt react with the backhand volley.

Catch Mentality—Forehand Volley

To develop quick and compact volley technique, you have to overcome the urge to add power. You must think defensively. Your first reaction to the volley should be to prepare as you would to catch the ball. On the forehand side, if you had a baseball glove instead of a racquet in your hand, your natural reaction would be to reach forward to catch. You would not react by moving the elbow back. The same should occur on the volley. Your hitting elbow reacts in the first move by going forward to meet the ball out in front of you as you pivot your hips and shoulders to face the contact point.

When you need to add some pop to an incoming floater, you should not add any backswing. With the elbow moving forward, angle the racquet so that the butt of the racquet points toward the point of contact. Driving the butt of the racquet forward and down, the racquet head will produce a pop with a little underspin for control. This only works well when the ball is near shoulder height at contact.

Overhead

When the contact point is much higher than shoulder level, you should prepare for the overhead. To react to the overhead, point your hitting elbow toward the back fence, keeping it with the shoulders, parallel to the ground. Use your footwork to position the contact point in front of you whenever possible. The overhead is like a half-serve motion, compact and easy to time. The hitting arm should be relaxed and the back posture straight throughout the motion.

Backhand Volley

You should react to the backhand volley with the hitting elbow again moving forward to meet the ball. React with a hip and shoulder turn to face the point of contact as you position the racquet for contact. You should work to maintain the L shape of leverage in the wrist position and use the opponent's power to block the ball.

When you need to add a little power, point the butt of the racquet toward your point of contact. In an action forward and down with the butt of the racquet, the racquet head will accelerate into contact as the elbow straightens.

To execute the backhand overhead, point the butt of the racquet straight up toward the point of contact. Then drive the butt of the racquet up, straightening your arm into contact and sending the racquet head over the top. It is like a service motion, only in reverse!

Drop Volley

When you find your opponent comfortably deep in the backcourt, do not forget the drop volley. The occasional drop volley forces the opponent to cover the short court and play closer to the baseline. Then when you volley deep, you have a better chance to force the opponent.

To drop volley effectively, your arm and racquet must work together as a unit to absorb the impact of the incoming ball. Your preparation looks identical to the deep block volley, so the opponent never expects it. Like a shock absorber, you want to absorb the shock of impact. You do not want to try for perfection on the drop volley or you will miss more than you make. By merely forcing your opponent with a drop volley, you will often win the point on the next shot.

Two-Handed Backhand Volleys

Although some top players are two-handed volleyers, you will never reach your full potential unless you can reach with one hand and volley as well. When just starting out, using two hands can help you develop a feel. But you must begin to work with one hand if you are to maximize your potential at the net.

Swinging Volleys

The swinging volley is nothing more than a regular ground stroke without letting the ball bounce—same grips, same level swing, same footwork. Adding some topspin to this shot will add more control.

You can use the swinging volley on a surprise attack out of the rally, especially when the opponent uses the high looping rally balls. Treat it like an approach shot and follow it in to the net.

Shot Combinations and Tactics

The skills required to dominate the net are not that difficult to acquire. You just have to remember that you are defending your court rather than always attacking. The power of your shot combinations will make you tenacious.

Serve and Volley

For many players the serve-and-volley tactic is a natural progression to the finish on the serve. Those players usually have the serve weaponry to come in behind and capitalize at the net. When you use your serve as an approach shot, you should remember the percentage rule—straight ahead. If you serve to the T, you reduce the passing lanes and force the returns back within your volley reach. When you serve wide you open the passing lanes, making it more difficult for you to cover the net.

Return and Volley

Usually used in second-serve situations, the return and volley is a tactic you can use to put immediate pressure on the server. Players often use a slice or chip so that they can adjust the depth of their returns more effectively. Commonly referred to as "chip and charge," this tactic can pressure the server into going for more on the second serve, thus producing more double faults.

Again, the return down the line provides the best opportunity for you to reach position at the net.

Drop Shot and Lob (or Pass)

Out of the rally you can learn to disguise the drop shot by mixing in deep slices. As the opponent becomes more comfortable with your deep slice, he or she becomes vulnerable to a well-concealed drop shot. When you drop shot out of the rally, you want to close in to protect against the opponent's possible drop shot.

If the opponent is able to get to your drop shot and put it back in play, the lob is a great option to finish off the point. If you create enough open court you might have an open passing-shot opportunity as well.

Approach and Volley

Whether you use a swinging volley or a conventional approach shot, attacking down the line with the short-ball opportunity will allow you the best position to angle the volley away. This short combination is deep down the line followed by an angle crosscourt. Remember that you have the option of varying the depth on your approach when using underspin.

Developing your net skills is certainly a must for you to be truly tenacious at net, but you can take some of the pressure off by becoming more effective with transition shots that get you to net. You will need to work at developing the mind-set that will challenge the opponent to come up with greatness or go down trying. Your objective is to build the points and set the stage for your opponent to fail. Remember that winning matches is about managing which player produces the most forced errors. When playing against a tough opponent you want to see the majority of your winners on closing shots like volleys, overheads, passing shots, and lobs. Focus your mind on the next point and try to develop your skills for mapping out the first few shots of the point *before* playing it. Your ability to anticipate the action enables you to plan. When an opportunity presents itself you can then say, "There it is!" rather than, "There it was!"

CHAPTER 8

Specialty Shots

Drop shots and lobs are valuable tools when you're playing against an aggressive net player.

While not many players focus solely on generating power, it is the ability to create the specialty shots that often determines your ability to finish points effectively. These "touch" shots—like the drop shot and lob—require practice to master, but they can mean all the difference when you're competing against an aggressive net player.

Underrated Weapon: The Drop Shot

I can promise you that after reading this section you will have newfound respect for the potential of the drop shot. Characteristic of classical players in the early years of tennis, the drop shot was a cleverly disguised weapon built around a game of attacking with the use of underspin. The deep slice ground stroke and the chip-and-slice approach are examples of shots that combine well in a one-two punch with the drop shot.

It is not enough to work your opponent side to side to create open-court opportunities. Learning to work with deep and short shot combinations can add another dimension to your game.

This chapter by Nick Bollettieri and Pat Dougherty.

Definitions of a Drop Shot

An effective drop shot crosses the net with a margin for error and bounces twice before the opponent's service line at a height no higher than the net.

Attempting to hit the perfect drop shot as a winner too often results in an error. By setting up the situation through combinations and disguise, even an overhit drop shot can still be effective. In other words, you need not put pressure on yourself to hit the perfect drop shot. Set it up and give yourself a margin for error.

Why Use a Drop Shot?

The drop shot is the key element to many combinations of shots that use disguise to create deep and short opportunities in the court. Power players are effective at moving their opponents left and right, keeping them positioned deep in the back of the court. Touch players use deep slices and chips together with the drop shot to create opportunities and manipulate their opponent's position.

Having a balance of touch and power allows you to keep your opponent guessing about what you are going to do. When your opponent is deep in the court, you beat him or her short. When you pull your opponent off the court to the left, you hit a winner to the right (or sometimes deep). Combinations with a drop shot add a new dimension to a power game by making each shot more effective.

When to Use the Drop Shot

Many players use the drop shot at the wrong time, without setting it up. For example, in a long rally from the baseline, you may become anxious about the length of the point and want to end it with a winning drop shot. You might occasionally be successful in this scenario, but more often than not you'll lose the point because you didn't set up the drop shot with a combination. Your opponent is able to read your drop shot, run it down, and put it away.

Once you have established the use of chips and deep slices, you have conditioned your opponent to associate your drop-shot preparation with your hitting the ball deep. An opponent in that mind-set is vulnerable to your drop shot.

Other variables that affect the use of the drop shot include your ability to disguise it, your opponent's strengths and weaknesses, the weather, and the playing surface.

Disguising the Drop Shot

The whole concept of disguise is to get the opponent to believe that he or she is seeing one thing while you deliver the opposite. For example, when you appear to have hit a deep slice backhand, your opponent begins to lean and step back, waiting for the ball to come back deep. As the ball begins to cross the net, your opponent realizes that you have really hit a drop shot, but by then it is too late to react in time.

We could say, therefore, that your drop shot is only as good as the shots you use to set it up. If you don't have deep, penetrating slices and ground strokes, your drop shot will not be very successful.

Note that you can also hit effective drop shots using your regular swing when hitting drives or shots with spin. You can still have adequate disguise, but you must not change the backswing and body motions you apply on your ground stroke.

Elements of disguise include the following:

- **Set up.** You have to show your opponent the use of underspin deep from the same preparation you use for the drop shot. By using the deep slice regularly, you establish disguise for the drop shot.

- **Preparation.** Players anticipate the shot that you will hit based largely on how you prepare. If your backswing loops back and down, they will expect a drive or topspin. If the racquet stays up in the backswing, they will expect underspin deep or short. The preparation of the drop shot should look the same as the preparation of your regular ground stroke.

- **Swing and execution.** The disguise you establish in preparation extends to the swing. The swing path on the drop shot can look like your deep swing with a slight adjustment in the angle of the racquet face to create more spin and less power and depth. What opponents see is a deep swing. What they get is a drop shot.

- **Footwork.** When using the approach combination, it is especially important that your footwork and movement add to the disguise. Try to maintain identical footwork for all your strokes with only slight adjustments.

- **Direction.** Experts say that the human eye can accurately judge depth only up to a distance of 15 or 20 feet. You can therefore use the direction you hit the ball to further the disguise. Let's look at two scenarios:

  1. Suppose a car is some distance away and traveling toward you in a straight line. How close must it get to you before you can estimate its speed?

  2. In the same situation, if you were to change your position to the side of the road, could you better judge the speed of the car?

Scenario #2 provides the best perspective for your depth perception and for determining the car's speed.

Let's apply this to disguising a drop shot. If you hit the drop shot away from your opponent, the flight of the ball will alert the opponent to respond because of the direction of the ball. But if the situation has your opponent out of position deep in the backcourt, you've created a great opportunity to hit the drop shot away from him or her.

A drop shot hit straight toward your opponent usually best disguises the shot. For example, if you regularly mix a deep slice backhand into your ground-stroke rally, you're in a crosscourt pattern when you drop shot. If your pattern is down the line to approach, you would mix in the drop approach down the line.

• **Height.** Deep slices and chips can themselves be penetrating and offensive weapons. When you use them to set up a drop shot, you need to hit with more height (or trajectory) over the net. Likewise, you want the same trajectory on your drop shot as on your deep shots. So to disguise your drop shots effectively, you should increase the height of your deep balls and avoid popping the drop shot up in the air too much.

Developing the Drop Shot

Three major technical aspects are involved in executing the drop shot:

• **Grips.** Players will vary their grips when hitting the drop shot, including the regular grip they use on ground strokes. Most will adjust to a continental or eastern backhand. But Jim Courier, a master of the drop shot, used his semifull western grip.

• **Preparation and swing.** Again, for disguise, you should use the same backswing for the deep slice and the drop shot. The stroke is the same, although for the drop you may use less follow-through because you are applying less power and more spin. Avoid bunting the ball with your swing.

• **Balance and foundation.** As with all shots, your balance and foundation often determine the success of the shot. To establish consistency with the drop shot, you need a delicate touch, which requires full control of your balance and foundation. Establish a strong foundation and relax your front knee as you step forward.

Drop-Shot Combinations

Serve and volley is an example of a combination in which the serve creates the opportunity for you to advance to the net for a point-ending volley or overhead. If you are serving and volleying, you want to get your first serve in play.

If you try to ace your opponent with the serve, you are not thinking of the combination, and your serve percentage will be low. The same idea applies to the drop shot.

By trying to hit the drop shot as an outright winner, you put pressure on yourself to make the shot better than it needs to be. Your success will be limited. Used in combination, however, the drop shot offers a new dimension to your strategy.

Combination 1: Forehand Loop and Drop Shot

The strategy is to push your opponent progressively to a position deeper into the backcourt, where he or she becomes vulnerable to a drop shot.

Combination 2: Backhand Loop and Drop Shot

Using the same strategy, you can use the looping ball with spin to force the opponent back. From this position you can expect several defensive short returns. You can then move forward and apply

- the drop shot,
- the killer forehand (see chapter 3), or
- an offensive placement that allows you to move in and end the point with a volley or by an unforced error.

Combination 3: Backhand Deep Slice and Drop Shot

Like bread and butter, these two shots were made to go together. Use this combination to bring to the net someone who likes to be there, though not on your terms.

   By using the deep slice in the rally, you set up the constant threat of your drop shot. Your opponent should see your drop shot only often enough to know that you will hit it when the opportunity arises.

Combination 4: Forehand Deep Chip and Drop Shot

Only a handful of players use a chip forehand from the backcourt. As demonstrated by Jimmy Connors and Chris Evert, however, it can be a very effective tool. Like the backhand slice and drop shot, this combination poses a deep, short threat to your opponent in the crosscourt rally. The Williams sisters and Martina Hingis apply the chip forehand.

Combination 5: Backhand Slice Approach and Drop Shot

Attacking the net on underspin gives you the flexibility to adjust depth effectively while still hitting down the line to position yourself at the net. Most of the time, you can knife the ball deep to attack. But bringing the opponent closer to the baseline in fear of your drop shot will make your deep balls more forcing. As your opponent starts playing back more, you mix in the drop approach or other options, including the angle.

Combination 6: Forehand Chip Approach and Drop Shot

Martina Hingis has revived the chip approach from the era of classical and traditional tennis. One of the few who use it regularly today, she can attack you deep and short. The deep chip often has a sidespin-underspin that makes it difficult to pass with. Try it!

Combination 7: Drop Shot and Lob

Here you can use a three-ball combination to end the point. Your opponent can often recover a well-executed drop shot but only with a defensive return. With your opponent's weight coming forward, the lob is the perfect win-win situation.

To position yourself for the opponent's weak return of your drop shot, move inside to guard against a possible drop shot. You may wind up using a lob volley on occasion as well.

Combination 8: Drop Shot and Pass

When your drop shot puts the opponent in a vulnerable position, you can use an average-quality passing shot to the open court. Players who execute the drop shot effetely will often move in a step or two to guard against a short return.

Variables and the Drop Shot

How often you use the drop shot during a match depends on several factors. As a rule you should use it sparingly, just often enough to affect your opponent's positioning and anticipation. On windy days or on days when the ball becomes heavy because of humidity, you might use the drop shot more frequently. If the opponent's weaknesses or an injury makes him or her particularly vulnerable, use the drop shot more often. Clay and grass surfaces are more conducive to successful drop shots than hard courts are.

You must cater to the conditions and your opponent to determine how frequently you use the drop shot. You need to open your senses to what is around you and take everything into consideration—where the sun is, which way the wind is blowing, and what works against your opponent.

Winning With a Drop Shot

Because the appearance of the drop shot so closely resembles the look of deep slices and chips, you should be able to execute the deep counterparts to the drop shot. If, for instance, your slice backhand is unreliable, your drop shot will be less effective and vice versa. Hopefully you've learned to respect the use of deep underspin enough to work on these strokes. If you want to realize the full potential of the drop shot, you need to be skilled at the deep counterparts to it.

Through developing these skills, you will begin to get a sense of how you can hinder your opponent's ability to anticipate both the direction and depth of your shots. Formidable competition, however, will require you to be crafty in how and when you employ your combinations. You'll need keen senses to tell you how often you can incorporate your drop-shot strategy. Against stiff competition, it is especially important for you to structure your game plan around combinations rather than blasting winners.

Smart players make winning easier by doing what it takes, whereas lesser players have to rely on brute strength and perfection to achieve.

Conclusion

With this newfound fascination about the drop shot, I'm sure many of you can't wait to get out there and try it. I must warn you not to be surprised if it doesn't work right away.

You must develop your disguise and learn to sell the situation so that the opponent is thinking deep when you hit short. In the early stages of integrating the drop shot into your game, it is likely that you will use it too often in a match. Keep at it.

You will enjoy the game even more now that you know about the underrated weapon—the drop shot. Good luck!

It's a Lob!

Like the drop shot, the lob is misunderstood and underused in both singles and doubles. The lob can be hit in various ways to accomplish both offensive and defensive objectives. In this section we will explain the many facets of the lob and show you how to integrate it more successfully into your game.

Stigma

The lob tends to get a bad rap. Many power players tend to think of it as a sissy shot. The most dominant players in the world, however, understand that the lob and its variations are important ingredients of a complete game. The lob is a specialty shot like the angle, drop shot, and high looper.

To have a complete game, you must be able to use both power shots and touch shots. By possessing a combination of power and finesse, you can force your opponent to defend in all four directions—left, right, up, and back. When you draw your opponent in tight to the net, the lob or the lob-volley allows you to attack the open backcourt to win the point.

You will need to hit the lob at times, so don't allow hitting it to unnerve you. If you treat it like a regular ground stroke, you'll find more success.

Who Do You Lob?

You will often confront opponents who stay back on the baseline and never advance to the net. One of the best strategies you can use against these players is to set up a situation that forces the opponent to come in. Short, defensive ground strokes, dinks, and especially drop shots can pull the opponent out of his or her comfort zone to the net. The opponent's skill level at the net will determine your success with the lob or passing shots. If the opponent is weak at the net, you can exploit his or her position tirelessly.

Even players who choose to come in and are effective with the volley and overhead should be lobbed on occasion. The lob creates another opportunity to beat your opponent and improve the effectiveness of your passing shots.

Allowing opponents to advance to the net on their terms may make it difficult for you. So a good strategy against net players who come in at the first opportunity is to bring them in intentionally so that they are at the net on your terms.

Pushed Deep? Send a Lob

When your opponent's approach forces you deeper into the backcourt, it is advisable to lob rather than hit a passing shot. The lob will allow you time to reposition and continue the point. Besides, your passing shots are more susceptible to being picked off because they have to travel an extra 8 to 10 feet because of your position on the court.

Opponent's Position on the Court

What ultimately determines when you should lob and when you should pass has much to do with how well positioned your opponent is. If your opponent closes tight to the net as a habit, you can lob until the opponent gains respect for it and adjusts position.

When you lob occasionally, your opponent will begin to adjust position to prepare for the possibility of the lob. The opponent then becomes vulnerable to your passing shot.

Alternating between the crosscourt pass and the down-the-line pass forces your opponent to move left or right. Using the lob will force a move back. Using all three shots forces your opponent to adopt a more neutral position at the net, increasing the effectiveness of your pass or lob.

Basic Lob Technique

The simple low-to-high lob is hit relatively flat and is disguised as a regular ground stroke with a slightly open racket face, aiming 10 to 15 feet over the net and using less power.

The underspin lob, which looks more like the slice or chip ground stroke, is the easiest lob to execute when in trouble. The underspin works well in the wind because it hangs in the air, making for a more difficult overhead.

The topspin lob is executed with a low-to-high motion together with excessive racquet-head speed.

Combinations of the Lob

In singles the simplest combination using the lob is the drop shot–lob. In this combination your drop shot will bring your opponent in. With your opponent's body motion coming forward to retrieve the drop shot, your lob is the perfect answer.

When set up effectively, the drop shot–lob combination can be used sporadically throughout a match with great success. Using this combination will make your opponent respect your drop shot, thereby forcing him or her into a position closer to the baseline, making your deep shots more forcing in nature.

The combination of drop shots and angles forces the opponent to move closer to the baseline. Now your deep, aggressive ground strokes become weapons.

Passing Shot–Lob

As mentioned earlier, you must show capability of hitting all three shots and be willing to use them at the right times. You are constantly adjusting the opponent's court position through the shots you've hit previously in points. The opponent who never sees you lob stops positioning to guard against it. You must use the lob to push the opposition back from the net to open up opportunities for you to pass.

As a Defensive Weapon

In a match you will occasionally be caught in a defensive situation and have few options. The lob can be the answer to keep you in the point, allowing you time to establish better court position and force your opponent to put you away with an overhead. If your opponent misses the overhead on a key point, it can be a big momentum breaker. So when you are in deep trouble, send up the lob and give your opponent a chance to humiliate himself or herself!

Under Adverse Conditions

When the weather begins to play a big role in a match, either through wind, sun position, or intermittent drizzle, your specialty shots can become more effective. A lob into the sun or into a crosswind can create a challenging overhead for your opponent. Make yourself aware of how to use the elements to advantage and note how conditions shift with each changeover.

Doubles Anyone?

A good doubles team uses angles, drop shots, and lobs to create opportunities to close out points. The lob is invaluable in doubles for backing a team off the net and creating openings for you to pass.

You will see the lob used much more frequently in doubles than in singles, ranging from lob return of serves to topspin lob winners.

Conclusion

To master the lob, you must be able to hit it in all situations—on your back foot, when off balance, or on the dead run. Developing this versatility takes time and practice, so make a point of practicing the lob under all conditions and circumstances.

The lob, useful at all levels of play, should be part of your game. Even if you have little success with it early in the match, the lob sends a message to your opponent that you are able to use it. You then have a better chance of passing because your opponent must always be concerned that your next shot will be a lob.

You may lose some points as the opponent painfully punishes your lob with overheads or a swinging volley. Do not let that discourage you from using the lob when the time is right. The more you practice and use lobs in match play, the more successful you will be at executing the stroke.

CHAPTER 9

Doubles Techniques

The game of doubles can be exciting and challenging when players know how it should be played.

Throughout my career I focused on developing singles players. Before long, I realized that people continued to play the doubles game long after their singles careers were over. Doubles is a social game that lends itself to recreation as well as business. Paul Annacone and Mark Knowles are just two of my students who went on to develop successful careers as doubles players. This chapter is designed to provide insight into the game of doubles to a wide range of players. I hope to help the millions of players who love the camaraderie and recreational interaction that doubles offers. By providing you with imaginative, tried-and-true techniques, I hope to make you a little bit better and perhaps add to your love of the game. Cyril Suk, one of the finest doubles players of all time, has assisted me in this chapter. The following resume will show you that he knows what he's talking about.

Cyril Suk: Doubles Champion

Career Highlights

1998 U.S. Open doubles champion (with Stolle)

1997 Wimbledon mixed doubles champion (with Sukova)

1996 Wimbledon mixed doubles champion (with Sukova)

1992 Wimbledon mixed doubles champion (with Neiland)

1991 French Open mixed doubles champion (with Sukova)

Career doubles titles—22

Doubles finalist—18

Cyril Suk, longtime ATP Tour veteran, shares some insight into the game of doubles for the benefit of club-level players.

Q: Give us some background on Cyril Suk.

CS: In 1985, Petr Korda and I, both from the Czech Republic, teamed up and won the ATP Tour World Championship in doubles. As a professional in doubles, I have 20 major titles, was a finalist 18 times, and captured four Grand Slam doubles titles, including the U.S. Open in 1998.

Q: What can club-level players learn from watching the professional game?

CS: At club level, there are two types of games—social and competitive. So you must first determine whether you are playing to have fun and make friends or whether you are out there to win. In competitive doubles, there are many things you can do to help your team win (e.g., create distraction for your opponents) and you can't be afraid to hit the opponent on occasion with a shot.

Q: When you see club players, what do you think they could do to improve?

CS: What separates club level from professional, other than skill differences, is communication. Before each point, I discuss and plan with my partner the tactic we should use for the next point (e.g., where I will hit the serve, whether my partner should look to poach, these kinds of things). This helps us both anticipate the action. Club players seem to start points without any plan at all and their teamwork suffers. Communication is the biggest area where club players can improve.

Q: What should a player consider when choosing a partner? What do you look for in a good partner?

CS: On a professional level, you have to evaluate what is going to bring the whole team up. For instance, you don't want to create a team of two big servers who have return weaknesses or you'll never break serve. You have to weigh the options and try creating a team whose players complement one another. A contrast of skills tends to make an effective team.

Q: How important are the personalities of the two players and getting along with your partner?

CS: On any level of play, competitive or social, it is extremely important to get along with your partner. He should be someone you can feel comfortable communicating with when discussing your strategies and so on. As a professional team, we are under a lot of pressure and must play nearly every day with each other so we must be able to maintain a positive relationship.

Q: Do you find yourself as a partner almost playing a coaching role at times to help your partner?

CS: I think it is important for both players to act as a coach for a partner who is not playing well on a particular day. It's going to happen. You'll always have good days and bad. Your partner must be there to help pull you through the bad times.

   You have to do this for the sake of your team or it is never going to work. Often you can help pull your partner out of a slump within a few points, games, or maybe a set. But if you just give up and lay the blame, your teamwork will suffer.

Q: How should partners determine who plays the deuce side and the ad side at a club level?

CS: Professionals spend years playing and developing strengths, and we usually know what side we prefer. You try to find a partner who prefers or has the skills to play the other side. For club players, the best advice is to try playing both ways. One week you take the deuce court. The next week you play the ad side. See what works better and produces the best results.

Q: Would a weakness, let's say a bad backhand, have an impact on what side you play?

CS: Most of the intense action in pro doubles is down the center of the court. I think on a club level the action tends to be on the outsides of the court. If you have a strong forehand and weak backhand at the club level, playing deuce side will be more effective. If you play the ad side, you won't have the same opportunities.

Q: What is the objective for the serve position?

CS: Club players don't always have to serve and volley like the pros. It is the objective of the server to get as many first serves in as possible. You don't have to push it to get it in, but there is a great advantage to having a high

(continued)

Cyril Suk: Doubles Champion *(continued)*

first-serve percentage. Use a pace with good placement and build up from there. Don't give opponents too many second serves because they can step up and take control of the point.

Q: How does a team decide which player should serve first set?

CS: This is the beginning of teamwork. You must weigh the options and consider the circumstances, especially if both players have fairly equal serves. For instance, I don't like to serve when the toss goes into the sun, so when we choose the side of the court to start the match, I take this into consideration as to whether I want to serve first. Sometimes weaker servers want the wind behind them. In general, the strongest server serves first to highlight the team's strengths. Sometimes, you consider the net player as well and who is best at holding serve.

Q: How important is the net partner in the team's ability to hold serve?

CS: A good partner at net can poach, fake poach, volley well, and so forth and can add distraction to the situation for the return team. On the other hand, someone who stands like a statue at net and doesn't volley or make any moves can make it hard for you to hold serve. The other team feels no threat and can get comfortable hitting their best shots.

Q: In the pro game, there are many tiebreakers because breaking serve can be difficult. How important is holding serve at the club level?

CS: At any level, holding serve gives you a mental advantage and adds confidence, allowing you to focus on breaking serve. It also allows you to take more risks on the return games to force a break. If you don't hold serve well, that becomes the focus for you, often making it more difficult to break.

Q: What is the objective for a player returning the serve?

CS: I think it is important for the returner to establish a target of where to hit the ball before the serve. You don't want to have to make last-second decisions based on five or six options or you will often make mistakes. Knowing where to hit is one thing you shouldn't have to worry about once the ball is on top of you. This will make you more consistent.

Q: What would be a good general target area on the club level for returns?

CS: In club doubles the serving team often stays back, and the server's net partner is very little threat to the returner. In that case, a deep crosscourt return target will be effective. A poacher at net will have you hitting more of a crosscourt angle, which also works well against serve-and-volley players, with the down-the-line return used occasionally to keep a poacher honest.

Q: What is the objective for the net player on the returning side?

CS: This player must position himself based on the strength of his partner's returns. If the returner doesn't hit his targets well, you can become the victim of a net poacher. You may be forced to position farther back. However, your focus is on the return getting past the server's net player. They are moving into a position to play out the point better.

   You can base your moves on the quality of the return. If you see that the return is good, maybe down to the feet of the incoming server, you can fake a move or pick off the next shot by crossing over.

Q: For club doubles, often you see one player at net and the partner on the baseline. Must they play either both at net or both at the baseline to be effective?

CS: If you prefer one up and one back and you are very successful that way, then stick with it. However, if you are losing because your opponents are always hitting between you to put the ball away, try the alternative. Both players at net is better for maintaining an offensive position and reducing the gap between partners, as is both players back. If you are losing, try different things to get yourself into the match.

Q: Are there strokes or shots used more often in good doubles?

CS: My strength in both singles and doubles was always my volley, so I always looked to get to the net as often as I could to highlight my strengths. But in general, you will use the skill, or specialty, shots more often in doubles, such as the lob, sharp angle, chip shot, and so forth. You must work on these touch shots to become a good doubles player.

Q: What do you talk about in planning a point?

CS: If we are serving, we discuss the pace and placement of the serve and the action the net partner will take so that the first two or three shots will follow our attack plan and we can anticipate each other's moves. That is what we try to accomplish before each point, even when returning.

Q: Would club players benefit by using the alternative setups like the Australian or I formations?

CS: Anything you can do that is different or that the other team thinks is weird can distract them and work well for you. Often, we used the I formation against one player who was returning very well because it was the only way to distract and force the player into last-second decisions. It works well on

(continued)

Cyril Suk: Doubles Champion *(continued)*

the pro level so you can imagine how effective it could be on the club level if done for the right reasons and at the right time.

Q: How important is shot selection to the concept of teamwork?

CS: It is crucial to teamwork, but remember that we know ahead of time the shots we plan to hit based on weaknesses of the other team and discussions before each point. Shots like down-the-line returns, lobs, and off-pace serves are all tactics based on the opponents' ability.

Q: What major things could benefit club players the most without their having to improve their technical skills?

CS: Learning how to use tactics and shot combinations for shots they already have and discussing tactics they will use before every point with their partners. Overall, these players need to move more at net and become a factor in points. Practicing reflex volleys would be a great benefit to becoming more comfortable around the net.

Q: Any last comments?

CS: Find a partner you enjoy playing with and you'll have a good time. Try to copy some of the tactics the pros use because it can work for you too. It helps, I think, to watch pros play.

Doubles

When I think about the doubles game, my mind entertains all kinds of exciting thoughts:

- The start of a car race when the drivers all jockey for position after the green light flashes
- A battle between two people trying to protect their property
- A social event in which each person tries to avoid putting any pressure on his or her partner

By this you can see that doubles can be anything you can imagine. When it boils down to a simple explanation, however, we can say that when players lack a plan and do not communicate, doubles cannot reach the high level of excitement that is possible.

In watching a game of doubles, note where players get into position, especially the server's partner and the receiving partner. Unless the ball comes directly at them, some players never move from their starting positions. For the most part, the game is played by two players who stay at their baselines. They might as well play singles.

There are four levels of communication in doubles:

1. Constantly blaming a partner
2. Partners never saying a word to each other and playing each point as if they were playing singles
3. Asking the partner for forgiveness after making a mistake
4. Using positive communication about how the partners can protect each other to set up necessary strategies

The game of doubles can be exciting and challenging when players know how the game should be played. Let it be a challenge and an amusement to learn the strategies of the game. One more thing—if you want to test your relationship with your spouse or significant other, play mixed doubles. You will either break up or stay together forever!

This chapter is designed to discuss the science of doubles. It will provide fundamental tactics and options that will allow each of you to experience personal growth. If you identify techniques that you don't currently employ, be daring and work on some of them. Recognize the techniques in which you excel and continue to improve them. You must also recognize the techniques that you are not so good at and work to improve them.

Singles Versus Doubles

The main difference between doubles and singles is that doubles is a game of court positioning. Singles is more about shot making and the building of points through combinations of shots.

Having two players on one side of the court automatically means less open space. Singles will thus have many more variations because open space requires more movement. Variables in the game will always result.

In doubles the reduced court space limits creativity and results in specific shots being hit more often. Doubles teams can use different formations to find the most effective way to play against another team. Variety will play on the opponents' minds.

Coaching doubles is somewhat different because the coach must determine which two players fit together and at the same time evaluate their separate skills.

Quite often doubles teams clearly indicate an advantage by their lineup. But results will often be negative because of lack of communication.

Although the court is basically the same, the addition of the doubles alleys (and the additional players) changes the strategy.

Singles strategy

- Movement
- Power
- Serve and volley not mandatory

- Use of shot combinations
- Strategy based on individual strengths and weaknesses

Doubles strategy

- You must know your game, maximize the strengths of your partner, and minimize the weaknesses of your partner.
- Your shot must take into consideration not only where your partner may be but also your opponents' court position.
- Because there are two players on each side, defensive and tentative shots must be executed more accurately.
- Players must know and accept their roles on every point.

Perhaps the biggest difference between singles and doubles is that the pressure of singles can often prevent a player from reaching his or her potential. Doubles players often find that a strong, intelligent partner can pull them through if they have skills, constant communication, and support. The teamwork factor can change self-esteem from negative to positive and may have an impact on an individual's singles play at a later stage. For example, Max Mirnyi, who holds three doubles titles and the 1998 U.S. Open mixed doubles title (with Serena Williams), made a breakthrough with singles wins over Jim Courier and Vincent Spadea in April 1999.

Why play doubles?

- You can play your entire life.
- Players of any level, even those with only modest skills, can enjoy the game and have a physical workout.
- Doubles can be played in leagues, as well as on the high school or college level.
- College scholarships often go to those who can play both singles and doubles.
- The variety of shots and knowledge of team play is enriching.
- Doubles will force you to return at a higher level to prevent the server's partner from poaching.
- Starting positions give the tentative volleyer a chance to be closer to the net when attempting to volley.
- Servers come in behind the serve knowing that they have to protect only half the court.
- Levels of play can be uneven because players can make up their partner's shortfalls.
- As you grow older, movement, reflexes, timing, and so forth begin to slow. Doubles requires you to protect only half the space, so you'll be able to prolong your participation in the sport.

- Doubles is easy to incorporate as part of school functions or fund-raising events.

On a much higher level, including college and pro ranks, doubles has come into its own, much as snow boarding has emerged from skiing. Many players seeking a professional career have found the dream of becoming a top singles player out of reach for several reasons:

- They can't endure the pressure of one-on-one competition.
- The modern pro game has reached a level that requires players to have certain dominant shots. With creativity, imagination, and thoughtful selection of a complementary partner, players with less dominant weapons can be successful in doubles.
- To some, team competition is the formula for success.

Strategies of the Game

Before we get into who does what, we must understand exactly what the four players do. Start with court position. The positions must be flexible, depending on each player's strengths and weaknesses and the strategy used for each point.

Server and Returner

These two positions start every point and determine not only where partners select ready positions but also what they will do from the instant the ball is in flight. Within seconds, players jockey for position.

Advanced Doubles

This section discusses the roles of the different positions in advanced doubles: the server and receiver and their partners.

Server

The serving team has the first opportunity to strike the ball, giving it the advantage if the serve is aggressive and used correctly. As the server, you must keep the returner off balance by mixing up serves just as a baseball pitcher varies the pitches to a batter.

- Serve the majority of serves down the middle, making it more difficult for the receiver to hit angles. If the receiver's strength is down the middle, however, serve out wide. Serve to the returner's weakness and mix it up.

- Spinning the first serve into play will allow you to get closer to the net for the first volley.
- On the first volley, hit the majority crosscourt.
- Use the I formation to break the rhythm of the receiver.
- If you elect to serve and stay at the baseline, hit your ground strokes deep to keep your opponent at the baseline. Look for the first short ball and approach the net.

Variation will confuse the receiver and cause the occasional "boom-boom" first serve to be more productive.

The placement of your serve should keep your opponent off balance and guessing. If the returner has an obvious weakness, exploit it until the receiver finds a rhythm. But remember, when the receiver focuses on protecting a weakness, you might serve effectively to his or her strength. It boils down to mixing it up!

Service options to the deuce court

- Serve to the opponent's weakness.
- Serve down the middle.
- Serve into the body (jam the opponent).
- Wide serve to mix it up and keep your opponent honest.

Service options to the ad court

- Serve to obvious weakness.
- Serve down the middle.
- Serve into the body.
- Use a wide, high kicking serve to mix it up and keep your opponent honest.

As a rule, especially with players with a one-handed backhand, the high bouncing serve to the backhand is very effective, especially if the server's partner poaches. For a left-hander, this applies to the deuce court.

Don't believe that the deuce side is easier. When hit crosscourt, the inside–out backhand return is one of the most difficult shots to master.

I have explained where the serves should go based on statistics and probable angle of returns. Now let's throw everything out the window and give some advice.

The strengths and weaknesses of both the serving and returning teams must be considered in doubles. Don't let anyone tell you not to serve out wide. Your opponent's ability to execute the shot will govern your use of this tactic. In simple language, serve wherever it's most effective!

Do a little of everything and more of anything to weak positions of both returns and the opponent's entire game. Too many times games are played based solely on form books.

Receiver

The doubles return is less forgiving than the return in singles play because the returner has only half the court to hit to, especially if the server's partner volleys effectively and poaches. The receiver's partner is also vulnerable to a formidable poacher.

Communicate with your partner about which side of the court you prefer to return from (deuce or ad). Don't commit to a side until you've spent enough time to make a decision based on results.

- Communicate to your partner about which formation you prefer.
- You should hit most returns inside out or crosscourt. When playing a team that poaches often, however, hit down the line every once in a while to avoid being predictable. Even if you lose the point, you have delivered a message that you can go down the line, thereby keeping the net person honest.
- Don't try to hit outright winners. Use the return to set up the next shot.
- Pick out a target on the return.
- Don't play your opponent. Focus on the ball.
- Don't forget to hit your return directly at the server occasionally.
- An aggressive play is to return serve and immediately follow it to the net. This puts the pressure on the serve and volleyer to make a good first volley. If the opponent pops it up, the point is yours. Quite often, the serve and volleyer will watch you instead of the ball.
- As a surprise tactic, lob on the return, especially when defending against an aggressive serve and volleyer. This tactic can catch the server's partner off guard, and you can get an error off the overhead or be able to take the net if the net player cannot reach the ball.
- Occasionally hit the return right at the net player as a surprise tactic or if the net player is not comfortable at the net. Beat them up!—I mean keep going at them until they change their formation.

Options for receivers

Returning against a strong serve and volleyer with net person ready to pounce on any defensive return:

- Go for a bigger-than-normal return of serve.
- Try to get the ball to dip as quickly as possible.

- Hit directly at the net person.
- Back up from your regular position and lob.
- Change your partner's position. Move him or her back to the baseline when you return serve.
- Change position for your return and try to break the server's concentration.

Return of serve when in full control of the return:

- Move in closer for earlier contact, making the server hit the first volley behind the service line.
- Chip and charge.
- Hit directly at the net person with a killer-forehand mentality.
- When you are in control of the return, move your net partner closer than the normal position just inside the service line.
- Your returns should include all shot options—down the middle, to the outside, down the line, at the person, the lob.
- You must take advantage of tentative serves every time. Consider the advantages you gain from the few choices the server has when tentative:
  - The server must serve and stay back.
  - The server must cut down the power of the first serve because he or she has little chance to win off the second serve.
  - Your partner will gain confidence by being closer to the net, thus able to poach and volley.

First Volley

The general rule is to volley deep down the center of the court, especially if contact is made near the service line. The deep volley will make it more difficult for your opponent to hit angles.

How close you are to the net will determine the aggressiveness of your first volley. Because of this, the server will vary the first serve with spin and placement to gain more time to close for the first volley. In addition, the height of the return will make a difference as to what the serve and volleyer can do on the first volley.

If you consistently find yourself volleying up on your first volley, your chances of holding serve diminish. The level of play will be determined by the first volley or the poaching ability of the server's partner. Doubles specialists learn their personal preferences through trial and error.

A big issue is whether the server will make an aggressive first volley and, along with his or her partner, continue to close in, causing the receiving team to hit their best but riskier shot.

Server's Partner

The server's partner is key for all positions at the beginning of each point. The partner has the ability to protect the serve, put fear into the returner about what he or she will do after the return, and scare the dickens out of the returner's partner, especially by popping that player a few times from the poach.

Helpful tips

- When poaching, always try to move in closer to the net.
- Do not stop poaching after missing a few balls. Even when you miss, the receiver knows that you'll poach, forcing an attempt to make a better return.
- If you are not using signals with your serving partner, the weight shift of the receiver may tell you where the serve is going.
- Both the server and the receiver will determine your ready position. The ability to return can alter your own position.
- Always be in a ready position that will enable you to defend against any type of ball.
- Once the ball is in play, your position will vary during the rally.

Receiver's Partner

Communicate with your partner about where you should position yourself—at the net, at the baseline, or at one of these variations:

- Well inside the service line (when your partner has displayed good control of the return).
- Between the baseline and the service line (when having difficulty returning the first serve).
- On the baseline (if the serve is sufficiently strong that the server's partner consistently poaches). Note that this positioning will change depending on whether you are returning the first or second serve.

The receiver's partner is on the back burner by not being in the initial action. But in the end, this position can become valuable for several reasons:

- Immediately after the return of serve, the partner's position can put fear into the server's first volley. With a ready position near the service line, the returner's partner can focus on the partner's return and move in closely. This will not only put the returner's partner in better position to receive the server's first volley but will also disrupt the concentration required for the first volley placement. If the volley is anywhere near the returner's partner, he or she will go for the interception. If the returner controls the return, the returner's partner will move well inside the service line for the ready position.

- This aggressive movement toward net creates doubt in the opposition. This is all that the team needs for a chance in the point.
- The partner must have imagination and anticipation and be bold enough to step right into the firing line, no matter what the return of service is.

At the Net

Net position may vary depending on how comfortable you are with your partner's return and your own volley skills. Position yourself closer to the net if your partner has had success returning serve. Back up a few steps if you're unsure. Always be ready to move forward to catch the ball at the highest level. This will enable you to hit down at your opponent's feet. Remember, your first responsibility is to cover your half of the court.

Be Active at the Net

The priority to cover half the court does not mean you can't cut off easy floating balls. In fact, your partner expects you to help by moving on easy, as well as difficult, shots. Remember that a good fake can fool the returner into hitting right to you at the net. When you are active at the net, the receiver will lose focus. Your first priority is to cover your side of the court, but there are no laws prohibiting you from poaching on other territories. Your partner expects this, knowing that your movement might break the focus of the serve and volleyer.

At the Baseline

When your opponents have a big first serve or your partner is not having success returning serve, you have the option to move back to the baseline. This happens even at the pro level, but here the receiver's partner will be at the net for the second serve return.

If the opponents are in a one up–one back formation, direct your ground strokes to the player at the baseline. Make sure you get good depth to keep the baseline player from advancing. Any time you receive a short ball, hit your approach to the baseline player and come to the net.

Working As a Team

It is imperative to find a doubles partner compatible with your personality and style of play. Good communication will make or break a doubles team. A good doubles player will pump up a partner who makes an unforced error. Both must stay positive in the heat of the battle.

No matter the level of play, players with certain strengths and weaknesses can complement one another. Here are a few examples:

- A player with a consistent baseline game who does not enjoy the net should find a partner with a good net game.
- A player with a weak serve should identify a partner with a good serve.
- A player with a weak return should look for a partner with a good return to break serve.
- A player lacking power should find a partner with the strength to put the ball away.
- A player with limited movement should find a partner who is active and moves well.
- Whether gregarious or reserved, a player must find a partner that he or she can get along with and communicate with.

Which Side Do I Play?

Which side you return best from is the most important point in determining your position. If your partner likes to return serve on the same side that you do, the player with the most confidence about switching sides should yield. Remember you can switch sides after each set if you need to make a change.

Let's be friends off court. Right now we are partners in the heat of the battle.

Many coaches feel that the best returner should play from the ad court because most of the key points are played from there. Others say it is more important to win the first point, and that the most difficult serve to return is the ball served down to the middle, forcing a difficult inside-out backhand crosscourt return. Partners and coaches will have to decide which way to play it.

I'm Left-Handed; Where Do I Play?

Opinions differ on where the left-hander should play:

- It is natural for the left-hander to hit crosscourt from the ad court on the return of serve, which is the best return.
- The left-handed returner can protect the kicker serve into the alley on key points better than a right-handed player, who must defend with the backhand.
- The left-hander can use more shot variations, making it more difficult for the opposing team.
- Having both forehands in the middle is a great selling point. Here the left-hander plays the deuce court. Simply put, partners should play where they feel they form the most effective team.

Additional doubles tips

- When crossing sides, always communicate with your partner and determine whether you need to make changes.
- Tell each other what shots you feel most comfortable with. By doing this, your partner can help out. For example, one player may have difficulty going back to hit overheads.
- Try to make all of your moves so that that the team will not split up.
- If you are forced to split court position, you have two options:
  - Go for a big shot.
  - Buy time to regroup.
- Don't discourage your partner from poaching, especially if he or she misses a few easy volleys.
- Don't hide the lob in your racquet bag. It is one of the best shots in doubles.
- Try to control the net. Attackers win more matches.
- Establishing sound positions is good strategy in doubles.
- When in doubt, hitting down the middle is the best shot selection.
- The last person to hit a volley or an approach has the best feeling about where the ball will come back. He or she should be the hitter of this ball.
- The more angles you hit and the less you hit at the players or down the middle, the more you reduce your percentages because you give up more of the court.

The closer you get to the net, the bigger and wider your opponent's court becomes. At the net, you can play aggressively and put pressure on your opponent to hit a good shot or lob. Remember, the team that plays together, supports each other, and knows exactly what the other can do will usually win the match!

Advanced doubles: player roles and positions

Receiver

- Decide on a formation with your partner.
- Use the return to set up the next shot.
- Change your position to break the server's concentration.
- Attack second serves.

Server

- Make a high percentage of first serves.
- Serve a majority of balls down the middle.
- Serve out wide for variety and to attack a weakness.
- Spin serve to get closer to the net for the first volley.

Options

- Follow the return into the net to pressure the server.
- Use lobs to take control of the net.
- Hit straight at the net player as a surprise tactic.
- Hit down the line to keep your opponents off balance.

Receiver's partner

- Your first responsibility is to cover your half of the court.
- Decide on a formation with your partner.
- Be ready to move forward to hit the volley.
- Be active at the net—poach, fake, cut off floating balls.
- Stay focused during the point—don't relax.
- Move forward as you volley.

Options

- Move back to the baseline when in a defensive situation.
- Move back to the baseline when the receiver is having trouble controlling the return.
- Hit overhead or switch sides to cover open court.

- Hit the majority of first volleys crosscourt.

Options

- Serve and volley on both first and second serves.
- Stay back and rally from the baseline.

Server's partner

- Your first responsibility is to cover your half of the court.
- Decide on a formation with your partner.
- Know where your partner is serving both serves.
- Watch the receiver react to the serve.
- Be active at the net—poach, cut off floating balls.
- Stay focused during the point—don't relax.
- Move forward as you volley.

Options

- Move back to the baseline when in a defensive situation.
- Hit overhead or switch sides to cover open court.

Adult Doubles

As we get older and our physical skills begin to decline, we gravitate to doubles. Doubles is a game that offers many rewards that singles can't provide. Doubles is competitive. It has specific tactics and maneuvers that enhance enjoyment of the game. We have all participated in clinics, classes, and leagues and know that it should be every player's goal to rush the net to finish the point. But realistically, how often does this happen? At the professional and college level it certainly occurs often, but at the club level it is less likely. Let's face it, at the club level the only people at the net are the server's partner and the returner's partner. The server and returner are usually locked in a game of singles, playing crosscourt using half the court. The only time you're involved is when you return or serve. Let's look at some tactics that will improve every phase of doubles play at the intermediate club level.

Server

- Don't panic because the returner probably won't come to the net unless you hit it short.
- Try to hit the strokes you're most confident with.
- Try to take something off your first serve to get a higher percentage in.
- If the returner's partner does not move, you can always hit at the player's feet and look for him or her to panic or hit up on the ball.
- If the opponents lob over your partner, make sure you communicate. Switch sides and get ready to start the point again.
- Try to play inside the baseline as much as possible, especially if you want to hit short to bring your opponent to the net.
- If your opponents have superior strokes, bring your partner back to the baseline with you and offer a steady diet of lobs.
- Be careful if you take a shot that is on your partner's side. This confusion can only happen down the middle. Play the ball crosscourt to avoid hitting your partner.

Server's partner

- That's your real estate. Defend it with your life!
- Try to watch your opponents, not your partner, when the ball goes past you.
- If your partner does not come to the net: encourage your partner to come to net, when the ball goes to your partner pay attention to the receiver's partner after the ball is hit, and get ready to switch sides because they will probably lob over you (especially if you have a consistent partner).
- When you have the opportunity to get a shot, don't panic and take a big swing. Try to hit to the returner's partner, who is closer to you and will have less time to react.
- Be careful if your partner has trouble controlling the direction on the serve. Either move closer to the doubles alley or go back to the baseline with your partner.
- Don't become bored if you're not active in the point. Be patient and ready because when you least expect it, one will be coming your way!

- If your partner is forced deep into the backcourt, be ready to move back a few steps to reduce the distance and close off the opening created down the middle of the court.

Receiver

- Put the ball in play, crosscourt if possible.
- Lob to create confusion.
- Don't worry about the server's partner. He or she is not going anywhere. Just hit it back to the server until you feel comfortable with a more offensive shot.
- Go at the net person when you get a weak shot.
- Move way up on a second serve. Make your opponents think that you are going to attack the serve.
- If you are in control, move inside the baseline and encourage your partner to move forward to the net.
- Don't play back too far. Balls are easier to control when you strike them between the knees and the waist.
- With an aggressive return, you'll seize the offensive advantage.

Receiver's partner

- You are not involved in the first phase of the point, so keep your eyes forward and be alert!
- Don't watch your partner hit the ball.
- Be prepared. If you don't move closer to the net or all the way back to the baseline, they'll hit balls at your feet and you'll need a shovel to dig them out.
- If you do get a shot, try to hit to the net person on the other side for a surprise.
- If both opponents come to the net, get the heck out of Dodge and lob, lob, lob.
- If your partner comes to the net, look for your opponents to lob.
- If you are lobbed, don't forget to tell your partner that you are going to switch to the other side.
- If you and your partner are at the baseline together and don't lob, try to hit to the weaker opponent.

Helpful hints

- Always try to hit to the weaker partner, regardless of whether that person is at the net or on the baseline.
- Always encourage your partner, especially after he or she makes an error.

- Don't be afraid to play both back, especially if your opponents play one up and one back. Sometimes you can hit a shot between them.

- When you are lobbed, move quickly. Don't wait to see if the ball makes it over your head before you retreat.

- If your opponents are very aggressive and both play up, load up your lob and start firing!

- Be extremely patient when playing junkers and pushers. Your shot will come.

- Move back on hard serves and move up on easy ones.

- If you choose to go down the line, try a lob. If the net player is not asleep and can get the racquet on the ball, he or she naturally (not instinctively) will hit the ball crosscourt between you and your partner.

- Remember, both up–both back and one up–one back are proper positions if you know what to expect!

Adult doubles: player roles and positions

Receiver

- Decide on a formation with your partner.
- Never miss a return wide— always make your opponent play the ball.
- Use the return to set up your next shot.
- Make contact with ball in your strike zone for control.
- Attack second serves.

Options

- Follow the return into the net to pressure the server.

Server

- Make a high percentage of first serves.
- Serve the majority of balls down the middle.
- Serve wide for variety and to attack a weakness.
- Spin serve in to get closer to the net for first volley.
- Hit the majority of first volleys crosscourt.

Options

- Serve and volley on both serves.

Receiver's partner

- Defend your half of the court with your life!
- Keep your eyes forward— don't watch your partner hit the ball.

Server's partner

- Defend your half of the court with your life!
- Keep your eyes forward— don't watch your partner hit the ball.

- Encourage your partner to come to the net.
- Get ready to switch sides if the opposition lobs you.
- Be prepared to hit a reflex volley. Hit to the server's partner, who has less time to react.
- Although you are not directly involved in the point, stay alert and be ready.

- Be ready to switch sides if the opposition lobs you.
- Be prepared to hit a reflex volley. Hit to the receiver's partner, who has less time to react.
- Although you are not directly involved in the point, stay alert and be ready.
- Move back a few steps to cover the opening in the middle when your partner is forced behind the baseline.
- If both opponents are at the net, move back and lob.

Conclusion

Doubles is a game of strategy and position as a team. A team that has the proper position will win the majority of points. You have already met a master player, Cyril Suk. He has won numerous Grand Slams doubles titles, yet he doesn't possess a major weapon like a big serve or forehand. He knows and understands the game of doubles and is a master at being in the proper position.

Another athlete who understands the importance of position is NBA player Dennis Rodman. His seven rebound titles in the National Basketball Association are no fluke. His knowledge and desire to get to the correct position, whether to prevent a score or snare a rebound, are unparalleled.

As you play doubles, move your feet and anticipate your opponent's next shot. Proper position will win you the majority of points. Doubles is a lot like chess, always requiring you to anticipate your opponent's next move.

CHAPTER 10

Practice With Purpose

I have often heard athletes as well as people from all walks of life say, "Holy mackerel! Everything went my way."

It would be wonderful if you could step on the court, hit a few warm-up balls, and then magically play the perfect match. In the real world, though, it doesn't work this way. Day in and day out, when the perfect anything happens it's not just luck, it's the result of preparation. Fortunately for the sports enthusiast, from the once-a-week hacker to the tournament player, the one ingredient separating levels of play is practice.

Accomplishing the perfect anything depends on getting your performance as close as possible to your ability. Performance is a broad term. Let's list the variables that contribute to performance:

1. Attitude
2. Physical fitness
3. Mentality
4. Court strategy
5. Techniques
6. Nutrition
7. Tactics
8. Playing strengths and protecting weaknesses
9. Outside pressure

This chapter by Pat Dougherty and Peter D. McCraw.

10. Inner pressure
11. Serving to win
12. Doing anything you can to win!
13. Being able to adjust

Working properly with these variables won't happen through inertia. For the most part, it begins with practice. People must practice in a way that works for them. Jimmy Connors made a statement I have always remembered: "It's not the quantity but the quality that counts."

How to Practice Perfectly

People often ask me about my philosophy toward creating champions. The truth is that champions create themselves because within their make-up they have what it takes to be champions. They have God-given athletic talent, the burning desire to win (losing is simply not in their vocabulary), and a mentor who guides their development.

My role is that of a mentor, the shaper of talent at every level. My philosophy, directed throughout the Bollettieri Tennis Academy, is that anyone with enough desire on court can be his or her best. That's all we can do. In the end, as history has shown, this philosophy produces champions.

Not everyone can be a champion. But everyone, even recreational players, can be their best. How? My suggestions have nothing to do with changing grips or altering hitting style. Instead I offer simple suggestions about how you can elevate your game to another level.

Learn to Concentrate Like the Pros

Not a day goes by at the academy that some student or coach does not ask me how to improve that key element to winning—concentration. Bjorn Borg, perhaps the foremost model of court concentration, once gave a motivation speech at the academy. On the subject of concentration Borg was very clear: "The second you step onto the court, the match begins. Every movement, every contact of the ball, every shot hit must be played with the concentration of match point." If you practice this way, you will improve immediately. You will learn the art of focusing, which in time you will translate into match play.

It's important to remember that most players are unable to concentrate for more than a few minutes. Concentration is a learned art, and with effort, you can develop it. Borg and Chris Evert were extreme examples. They could maintain intense concentration for a match, a week, a year if necessary. Theirs was a remarkable skill but one that you can copy by raising the concentrated intensity of your practice habits.

Monica Seles—Hit the Ball Early

Monica Seles was not an athletic person. When it came to foot speed, coordination, body build, strength, and the ability to recover when falling, Monica had to work at it. You'd never see her playing basketball or roller blading. From Monica I learned the importance of good eyes, quick hands, and playing to your strengths.

Monica can pick up the ball early and play it from a part of the court that everyone else thinks is weird, from inside the baseline. When she is six feet behind the baseline and running laterally, Monica is just ordinary. But with her unbelievable practice habits and ability to hit with two hands off both sides, she could cover up her inefficiencies by playing inside the baseline.

You can learn the value of practice from Monica's unparalleled work ethic. She would practice a single shot for a week, two weeks, three weeks—whatever it took to master it. She'd put a basket on the far sideline five feet in front of the baseline and then just hit ball after ball down the line between the basket and the baseline. She and Andre Agassi would play angle games for hours. They got so good that they could hit hard angles to the sidelines just five feet past the net.

Like Monica, you should spend half your practice time inside the baseline learning to hit the ball early so that you can hit solidly from there without thinking. Practice until it comes naturally.

Reduce Your Unforced Errors

Day in and day out, tennis players who play for the lines will lose, just as gamblers who defy the odds and double up when down will lose.

When you practice (even when rallying back and forth), visualize target areas that allow you to move the ball while maintaining a degree of margin for placement. If you need help, mark the area of the court you know to be effective—deep in the corners and shallow angles near the service line. By practicing with targets you will improve your visualization, which you will soon be able to translate to matches.

The same can be accomplished regarding pace and the ball height. At the academy, part of our System 5 accessory package includes target markers, practice-drill cones, and an adjustable height marker. Practicing correct habits will improve your match performance. It's possible to beat the odds only if you understand the lessons involved.

Why Can't I Reach Every Ball?

Before starting this section, let's bring out the single most important cause of unforced errors—technique breakdowns and lack of movement and balance on contact.

Think about what really happens when you see the ball barely drop over the net and you are standing at the back of the court. What do you do? Nothing? Having concluded that you have no chance to get the shot, you don't even try. Right?

In your next practice session, try something different. Many of the balls that you believe you cannot reach, you can. If you make a mental determination to chase down every ball, you will surprise yourself. On balls that you try to reach and don't make, the message for your opponent is clear. Unless he or she hits a perfect shot, you're going to run the ball down.

Will it be different simply because I'm telling you it will be different? Yes. Telling yourself that you can do it will categorically improve your performance, your self-esteem, and your opponent's respect for your effort.

Anticipate and Watch the Ball

To improve your preparation and response time, watch the ball leave your opponent's racquet. The speed of your movement is secondary to getting a feel for your shot. This feeling, coupled with the knowledge of your opponent's capabilities, is the first step to better preparation.

The next step is to focus on the ball as it leaves the opponent's racquet, not when it appears on your side of the court. Pick up small clues while the ball is still in flight to facilitate early preparation. Too many players permit the ball to bounce before they start to react. By then it is too late. Even if you get to the shot, your timing will be poor and your shot will be defensive or badly prepared.

Rather than just hitting the ball back and forth in your next practice, ask your practice partner to hit the ball away from you. Set yourself a goal to run for everything, no matter how impossible. Try watching the ball come off your opponent's strings. Watch closely and you will learn the art of reading the ball's direction. By incorporating this technique into your practices, during matches you'll feel that you have more than enough time to prepare for the next shot.

I know from my years at the academy that these suggestions will help you play better tennis. None are earth shattering. They are simply commonsense ideas. The point is that regardless of ability, you can improve by practicing with the same focus you use in match play. Remember, the more your practice reflects actual match play, the faster you'll improve.

Translating Practice Tennis to Match Tennis

How many times have you signed up for a clinic at your local club or municipal court and arrived at the courts excited only to leave afterward disappointed? What you expect and what you get often don't match up. Here are tips on what you should ask about prospective clinics before taking out your checkbook:

What is the clinic's context?

What is the coach-to-student ratio?

How match specific are the drills?

Will the clinic be mechanics specific?

Does the clinic cover doubles?

In all forms of practice, especially match practice, it angers me to see one of our pros drilling with no regard to where the ball is going or what the student should be doing next. All drilling should be designed to ensure that the exercise has carryover value into match play.

Take a simple example—a drill designed to reinforce the value of an approach shot followed by a volley. The first ball, hit relatively short by the coach, should usually be struck up the line, especially if the ball is below the net when the student gets to it. Having struck the ball, the student should follow the flight of the ball to the net covering the line and then finish with a crosscourt volley.

At this point most coaches would stop the drill. At the academy, however, we insist that our students continue to concentrate and follow the volley, thereby covering any possibility of a foe's great shot and subsequent passing shot.

This is not genius. It is simply a point-specific drill for predictable movement rules, set up to teach mechanics and strategy simultaneously.

Another good example of a practice that can be match specific is the serve. To practice match-specific serves, the returner must be as serious as the server, thus creating a learning environment for both players. Beyond the important discussion of serve mechanics, this manner of practice permits the pro to discuss, in real time, the direct result of a miss or badly placed serve.

The same can be said for hitting passing shots on the run. It's simply not good enough to have students run from one side of the court to the other, attempt a passing shot down the line, and stop. Having attempted the passing shot in match play, the instinct must be to reposition for the next return. This too should be part of the practice drill.

In summary, to transfer skills from practice into matches, all repetition drills should mirror match possibilities.

Errors, mental or mechanical, should be immediately corrected, and an explanation on how these errors relate to match success or failure should follow. Because most of the adult tennis community plays doubles, a clinic not dealing with doubles is useless.

If your practice lacks the benefit of an instructor, my suggestion is to practice what you should be doing during a match. If your preference is baseline tennis, practice hitting the ball back with depth and consistency. If your preference is serve and volley, work on the location of your serve rather than pace.

Don't neglect hitting returns, the placement of which is especially important in doubles. Have your practice partner serve from inside the baseline (more power and consistency) while you work on a short backswing, meeting the ball out front and, most important, moving the return around the court. If your opponent serves wide, a good return is up the line. If your opponent serves up the middle, a crosscourt return is your best choice.

Don't neglect doubles drills. While you and your partner work on hitting crosscourt, practice coming to the net. At the service tee, practice quick volley drills to improve your reflexes and make those impossible shots routine. Again, when practicing this drill, keep your backswing short, make contact out front, and, most important, concentrate on control and placement.

Remember, when practicing match play it's not the quantity of practice that matters, it's the quality. Make a practice plan, center it on your style of play, and work it to a successful conclusion.

Drilling With Purpose

This section is not about 1,001 drills for every possible situation, nor is it about the most exotic drills ever conceived. Let's face it—drills are drills! This section will give insight into what we do at the academy and show you how you can put more purpose into your drilling. Our *Practice With Purpose* video supplements this by illustrating how I manage my drills and the positive effect the drills have on my students.

We don't use mystical drills that no one else does. We never have. What makes us different is the way we run them. If the coach, parents, and students don't look forward to drilling, then the drills are not being run correctly. Drilling should be a fulfilling challenge to the coach and student. It should expose the program, bring it alive, and create an experience that inspires everyone to perform to his or her highest ability.

How you run your drills will separate you from your competitors. Our drilling methods have kept us at the forefront of the game for many years.

As far back as I can remember, drills have been used to train tennis players at all levels. Drilling offers significant benefits over hitting and playing practice sets. First, drills are specific. They can be tailored to the exact needs of a player and allow the coach to train a variety of skills, including technique, consistency, power, spins, hitting to targets, movement, conditioning, recovery, attitude, point development, strategy, and tactics. No one took better advantage of drills than Monica Seles did. Monica squeaked and grunted her way to the top of the world by consistent and determined use of the drilling court. Drilling allows the coach to reinforce the fundamentals of the game, building the foundation for improvement in all aspects of a player's development.

1. **Safety procedures.** Safety is the single most important aspect of conducting a drill. You must structure the drill so that it does not put either the student or the feeder at risk of being hit by balls and racquets.

- You must have the proper equipment. The feeder must have a large basket of balls so that the drill is productive for an extended period. Buckets or smaller baskets should be placed deep in the backcourt of the feeder to provide students a margin of safety when picking up the balls during the drill. When the feeder's basket is depleted it can be refilled from the bucket or smaller baskets, thus ensuring that no time is wasted in picking up balls. You must also have sufficient cones or markers to construct recovery alleys where students can safely recover off court to pick up balls or return to the back of the line (see figures 10.1 and 10.2).
- Never have students go to the opposite side of the court during the drill to pick up balls and put them into the feeder's basket. Never ask students to recover near the line of fire.
- Students should not stand too close to each other when in line because they need room to handle a bad feed from the coach. Getting students to shadow swing when in line requires them to be a safe distance from one another. Emphasize this from the outset.
- Students must be taught to clear all balls they hit into the net at the completion of their rotation. Stray balls on the court are the single biggest cause of ankle injuries when drilling. Coaches can continue the drill by hitting balls to the next hitter at a different location.
- Bags and equipment are not to be left on court. The best place for them is outside the fence. Drink bottles and towels should be placed together out of the way. Apart from the safety aspect, having the drink bottles in one place keeps the group together during breaks. This enhances group dynamics enormously because everyone feels a part of the action.

2. **Setting a specific goal.** Any drill, no matter how simple, must be appropriate for the level of the group and be run in a manner that accomplishes a specific goal. Each student should understand the goal and how it will benefit the player. Drills can focus on a variety of goals:

- Technique—working on specific shots to generate power and to determine if the technique breaks down during a specific sequence of feeds
- Hitting to targets—creating awareness of the court and providing feedback to students about their accuracy, consistency, and placement
- Movement—improving the ABCs, that is, agility, balance, coordination, and speed

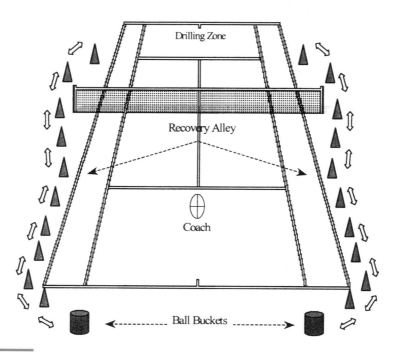

Figure 10.1 Ball buckets should be placed deep in the backcourt of the feeder to provide students a safe environment when picking up balls during the drill. When the feeder's basket is depleted, it can be refilled from the ball buckets, thus ensuring that no time is wasted in picking up the balls.

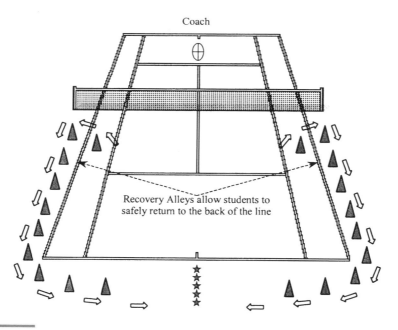

Figure 10.2 You must have sufficient cones or markers to construct recovery alleys where students can safely move around the court to pick up balls or return to the back of the line.

- Conditioning—improving cardiovascular fitness, endurance, and overall stamina in the ABCs

- Point development—breaking down points into start (getting the point started), build (building the point), and close (finishing the point)

- Strategy and tactics—improving ability to control the center of the court and build points against different styles of play

Be aware that you can't work on all these goals at once. A logical progression is to begin with an emphasis on technique, then introduce targets, movement, and conditioning, and finally incorporate the particular stroke into point-development drills and patterns of play for strategy and tactics. This progression ensures that the student learns *how, where,* and *why* to hit. Too often coaches focus solely on technique when drilling. In competition technique begins to break down because the student has not practiced the other components of the shot.

3. **Introducing the drill.** Coaches often fail to provide sufficient explanation of a drill. As a result the drill breaks down. The coach must include several points in the explanation:

- Setting the scene—Bring the students together, get their attention, and explain the importance of the drill.

- Explain the purpose and benefit of the drill—Students need to understand the purpose of the drill and how it relates to their game.

- Explain the role of each student—Informing the students of their roles will increase the effectiveness of the drill immensely. Those waiting in line can move their feet or shadow swing in time with the hitter, pick up balls, or recover to a certain location on court. An effectively run drill keeps the group together while each individual executes the drill.

- Demonstrate the drill—A picture is worth a thousand words, so demonstrate the drill visually and verbally and cater to the learning modes of as many students as possible. This is particularly important when you have students from various nations with language differences.

4. **Students with mixed abilities.** Rarely will students within a group be of equal ability. Drilling allows the coach to cater to each student's needs by altering the difficulty of the feed, speed of the drill, target area, and pattern of shots. This is the best way to work specifically on each student's game in a group setting.

5. **Progressing the drill.** Almost every drill can be progressed to make it more challenging for the group while still emphasizing the needs of the individual. You can progress the drill by

- adding another ball to the sequence,
- increasing the speed of the drill,
- decreasing the speed of the drill to emphasize technique,
- emphasizing hitting to targets, movement, conditioning, point development, strategy and tactics, or
- adding games to determine who can win, no matter what!

The list is endless. The coach must always adjust the drill to match the abilities of the group and student.

6. **Moods and attitudes of students and group when drilling.** Another aspect of effective drilling requires the coach to observe the mood of each student and the groups. Each student reacts in a different way to the tasks and demands you set. Some will withdraw within themselves; others will maintain a constant flow of outbursts and facial expressions during the drill. As a coach, you must be aware of these differences and regulate your feedback accordingly. At times you will have to knock them down, while at other times you will need to build them up. Be attentive and give appropriate feedback to each student as well as to the group. Dealing with the mood of each student correctly will dramatically increase the effectiveness of the drill.

7. **Video drills.** Videotape your drills occasionally and watch them with the group. This is a fantastic way to give students another type of feedback. Review your own level of intensity, enthusiasm, projection, and overall performance. Small changes in the structure of a drill can mean the difference between a good drill and a terrific one. Students often think that they perform a drill in a certain way, but review of the videotape convinces them otherwise. Seeing makes believers!

8. **Dealing with parents who think drilling is a waste of time.** You will always find someone to tell you that drilling is a waste of time and that his or her child should be playing points or matches. Alerting parents to the overall picture often helps them see the importance of drilling. The amount and type of drilling will vary as the student passes through different stages of development. A development program must include some form of drilling to allow the coach and student to isolate and analyze certain aspects of the student's game. For those parents who continue to believe that a drill-based system does not produce good players, I submit the following names:

Andre Agassi	Paul Annacone	Jimmy Arias
Pablo Arraya	Bobby Bancks	Carling Bassett
Kristina Brandi	Boris Becker	Martin Blackman

Lisa Bonder

Sandra Cacic

Jim Casale

Weylie Chang

Denis Dayan

Mary Joe Fernandez

Chris Garry

Donna Gilbert

Tommy Haas

Rodney Harmon

Claudia Hernandez

Kathleen Horvath

David Kaas

Kim Kessaris

Eric Korita

Aaron Krickstein

Jeff Lersh

Jean Rene Lisard

Cecil Mamiit

Lisa Pauaintauri

Terry Phelps

Noelle Porter

Amy Schwartz

David Skoch

Sarah Taylor

Kristina Triska

MarianneWerdel

Steven Wymer

Alex Bose

Marco Cocopardo

Pam Casale

Weylu Chang

Michelle DePalmer

Doug Flach

Gail Gibson

Justin Gimelstob

Elly Hakami

Dan Henry

Gregg Hill

Sonya Jeyaseelan

Yevgeny Kafelnikov

Mark Knowles

Anna Kournikova

Michael Lang

Max Mirnyi

Iva Majoli

Caryn Moss

Bedi Papell

Mark Philippoussis

Raffaella Reggi

Monica Seles

Susan Sloane

Andrea Temesvari

Michelle Torres

David Wheaton

JenniferYoung

John Boytin

Kristina Cante

Michael Chang

Jim Courier

Mike DePalmer

Chris Garner

Brad Gilbert

Anne Grossman

Matt Hanlin

Dierde Herman

Chip Hooper

Raphael Jordan

Brice Kersh

Petr Korda

Eugenia Koulikouskaya

Emily Leonardi

Dexter Nevares

Xavier Malisse

Allison Nash

Al Parker

Mary Pierce

Pete Sampras

Karen Shilhate

Mandy Stoll

Laurence Tieleman

Glenn Weiner

Anne White

Parents, if you think drills are unimportant, just ask any player on the list.
  These players are among the thousands who have passed through our
portals and drilled their way to excellence. Some names are more familiar
than others. Most played on college teams, many played on the satellite
circuit, several played at the world-class level, and a few reached the
pinnacle of tennis as no. 1 in the world. Clearly, drills are valuable tools for
learning. But players must be disciplined and drill with a purpose.

9. **Talking to students who need private lessons.** Group drilling is an ideal way for the coach to assess the overall progress of each student in the program. Some students may need a follow-up for extra work on a certain stroke. Private lessons allow the coach to work on specific parts of a student's game.

10. **Comments about the theory that too many on a court is counterproductive.** The number of students on a court will vary according to the drill. Fast action drills (including two on twos, windshield-wiper drills, around the world, etc.) require large numbers of students because of the cardiovascular demands and the large number of balls being hit.

Types of Drilling

We have included a sample of drills from our *Practice With Purpose* video to illustrate what we do at the academy. The video gives a first-hand look at how I run the drilling courts at the academy.

Fed–Ball Drills

Fed-ball drilling offers many benefits to both coach and student. The coach is able to control the situation when players of varying ability are on court. The coach can observe the students' preparation and movement habits while focusing on repetition of technique. Targets can be introduced to add variety and pressure to the drills. In addition, the coach can test fitness by using endurance drills to push the limits of a student's cardiovascular condition and see when technique breaks down.

Fed–Ball Drills With Target Scoring

Target scoring determines the structure and length of the drill and takes us one step closer to true match conditions as the competitive element plays a bigger role. This drilling style allows the coach to control the situation to some degree and measure students under a new level of pressure.

Live–Ball Drills

Live-ball drills are most beneficial to players who can consistently control the ball. These drills take us closer to match conditions by having the students drill in head-to-head competition. Students must work together to ensure that the drill is successful and doesn't break down.

Live–Ball Workout

The next progression to live-ball drills is the live-ball workout. This drill promotes consistency and discipline and moves the students even closer to match play by simulating controlled rallies and combinations. For live-ball workouts to be successful, students must use teamwork to prevent chaos.

Training on Your Own

Many developing players need to practice but don't have anyone to work out with. Such players can use a backboard or wall to work by themselves on every aspect of the game—ground strokes, half volleys, volleys, overheads, serves, and even playing out points. Adding music can increase the fun.

Fed-Ball Drills

Warm-Up Drill

Objectives

Establish an all-business mind-set for a productive practice session.

Establish early preparation and timing for your contact point.

Warm up your foundation and focus on good technique repetition.

Hit to targets with high net clearance to promote depth.

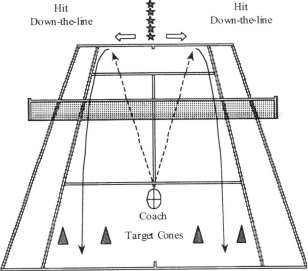

Operation

The feeder hits two balls from the service line to alternating sides of the court.

The student hits both balls down the line to the target area.

The student rotates to the back of the line.

All students move their feet.

Alternatives

Add more balls to each rotation.

Hit four, pick up four—the student hits four balls, then picks up four balls.

Change direction to crosscourt patterns and short angles.

Move students in to hit approach shots and volleys.

Windshield-Wiper Drill

Objectives

Bring the group together to establish discipline, focus, and teamwork.

Work groups of 8 to 12 students, all gaining benefit at once.

Students warm up and focus on good technique repetition.

Students hit to targets with high net clearance to promote depth.

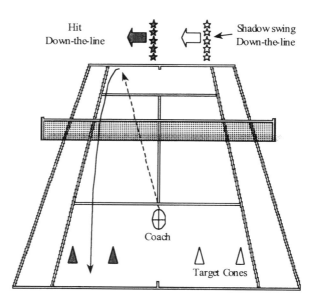

Operation

The feeder hits two balls from the service line to alternating sides of the court.

Students form two lines at the baseline (curl the line around if there is not room behind the court).

Students hit down the line to the target area and shadows to the other side.

Students pick up balls, observe safety procedures, and rotate to the back of the line.

All students shadow in time with the front two hitters.

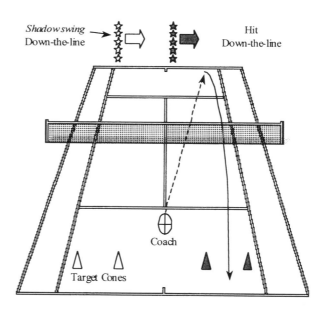

Alternatives

Add more balls to each rotation.

Change direction to crosscourt patterns.

Move students in to hit approach shots and volleys.

When students hit from in the court, lines can go straight back.

Run-Around-Forehand Drill

Objectives

Develop the mind-set of using a weapon.

Aggressively position yourself in the court to take advantage of a big forehand.

Learn to control the point through aggressive positioning.

Hit to the target with power and accuracy.

Operation

The feeder hits one ball from the service line to the student's backhand side.

The student is to run around the backhand and hit an inside-out forehand to the target.

The student rotates to the back of the line.

The feeder must build the confidence and willingness of students to "just hit the ball."

Alternatives

Add a forehand down the line and then position yourself for an inside-out forehand.

Change direction to an inside-in forehand (down the line).

Approach the shot and finish with a volley to the other corner.

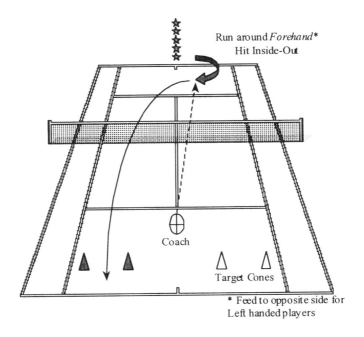

Run-Around-Forehand and Short-Ball Drill

Objectives

Develop a mind-set that you will return every ball.

Develop shot combinations around the inside-out forehand.

Learn to close in and continue to attack the short ball.

Hit to targets with power and accuracy.

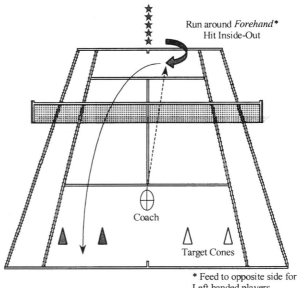

Operation

The feeder hits the first ball from the service line to the student's backhand side.

The student runs around the backhand and hits an inside-out forehand.

The feeder hits the second ball from the service line to the student's forehand side short.

The student closes in and hits the approach down the line to finish the point.

The feeder must build confidence and willingness of students to "just hit the ball."

Alternatives

Add a volley or overhead to the combination.

Change direction to inside-in forehand (down the line).

The student plays out the point after approach.

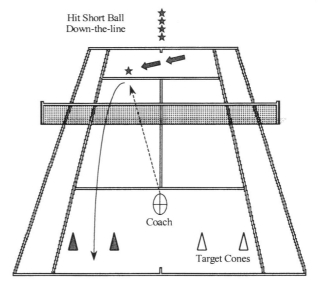

Short-Ball and Short-Angle Drill

Objectives

Develop long- and short-angle ground-stroke combinations.

Develop racquet-head speed and acceleration on the angle shot.

Hit to targets with spin and accuracy.

Operation

The feeder hits the first ball from the service line to the student's forehand.

The student hits a deep forehand down the line with spin (with a margin for error).

The feeder hits the second ball from the service line to the student's backhand.

The student hits a short-angle backhand crosscourt with spin to the target.

The student rotates to the back of the line.

Alternatives

Backhand down the line and forehand short-angle crosscourt.

Forehand crosscourt and backhand short-angle crosscourt.

Backhand crosscourt and forehand short-angle crosscourt.

Students play out the point after the short angle.

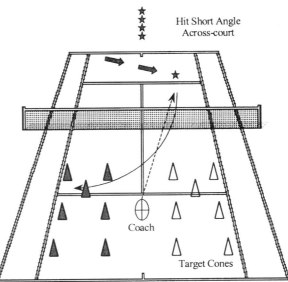

Short-Angle, Short-Angle Drill

Objectives

Develop short-angle, short-angle ground-stroke combinations.

Develop racquet-head speed and acceleration on angle shots.

Hit to targets with spin and accuracy.

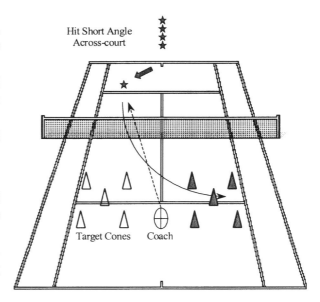

Operation

The feeder hits the first ball from the service line to the student's forehand.

The student hits a short-angle forehand crosscourt with spin to the target.

The feeder hits the second ball from the service line to the student's forehand.

The student hits a short-angle backhand crosscourt with spin to the target.

Alternatives

Add volley and net exchange after the second short-angle shot.

Students play out the point after the short angle.

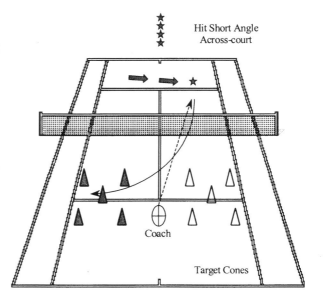

Target Scoring

Objectives

Develop execution skills—hitting to a target under pressure from a fed ball.

Simulate match conditions.

Scoring determines the structure and length of drill.

Operation

The ball is fed to a specific court location.

The student hits crosscourt to the target.

Scoring is +1 for in target and –1 for out of target.

The drill ends when a score of +7 or –7 is achieved.

Students rotate after each ball.

Alternatives

Ground strokes down the line or short angles.

Approach shot, volleys, and overheads.

Multiple-ball combinations—two, three, or four balls.

Score for each target hit.

Increase difficulty—one point if all targets are hit.

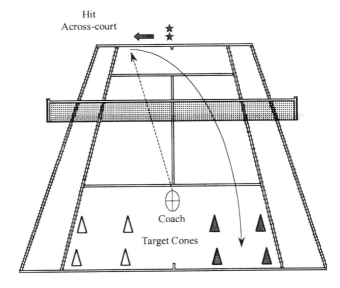

Live-Ball Drills

Box Target Drills

Objectives

Develop execution skills—hitting to a target under pressure from a live ball.

Develop receiving and positioning skills.

Simulate match conditions.

Scoring determines the structure and length of the drill.

Operation

The hitter starts the drill from the baseline.

The student hits crosscourt to the target.

Scoring is +1 for in target and –1 for out of target.

The drill ends when a score of +5 or –5 is achieved.

Students rotate when maximum or minimum score is reached.

Alternatives

Ground strokes down the line or short angles.

Approach shot, volleys, and overheads.

Multiple-ball combinations—two, three, or four balls.

Score for each target hit.

Increase difficulty—one point if all targets are hit.

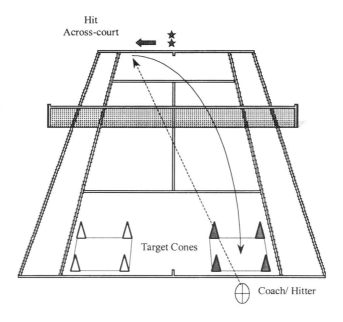

Play to Seven

Objectives

Develop execution skills hitting to a target under pressure from a live ball.

Learn to stay with a task until the goal is achieved.

Simulate match conditions by hitting to the target from all areas of the court.

Scoring determines structure and length of the drill.

Operation

The hitter starts the drill from the baseline.

The student hits to the target from anywhere on court.

Scoring is +1 for in target and –1 for out of target.

The drill ends when a score of +7 or –7 is achieved.

Students rotate when score is achieved.

Alternatives

Play from inside the baseline at all times.

Approach shot, volleys, and overheads.

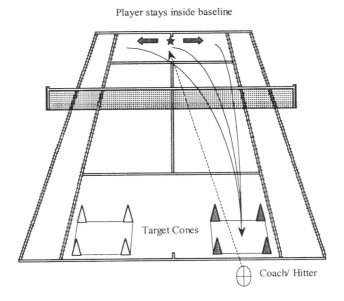

Player stays inside baseline

Target Cones

Coach/ Hitter

Alley Drill

Objectives

Develop concentration skills.

Develop execution skills hitting to a target under pressure from a live ball.

Learn to stay with a task until the goal is achieved.

Simulate match conditions.

Scoring determines the structure and length of the drill.

Operation

The player starts the drill from the doubles alley on the baseline.

The partner hits into the doubles alley only.

Scoring is +1 for in alley and –1 for out of alley.

The drill ends when a score of +7 or –7 is achieved.

Alternatives

Volley, volley.

Ground stroke, volley.

Restrict players to one shot only, for example, forehand or backhand.

Players hit certain spins only, for example, underspin or topspin.

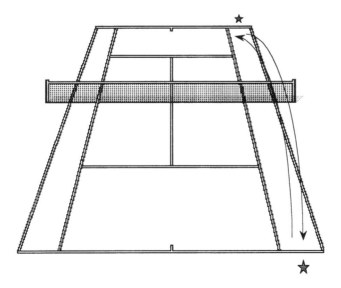

Controlled-Volley Drill

Objectives

Develop ball and racquet control on volley.

Develop receiving and positioning skills.

Follow shot patterns.

Operation

Four players are at the net inside the service line.

Players establish volleying exchange.

Players hit volleys to continue the drill and control the ball.

Alternatives

One player can change the pattern at any time.

#1—up and back with the same partner.

#2—diagonal with same partner.

#3—cross and down.

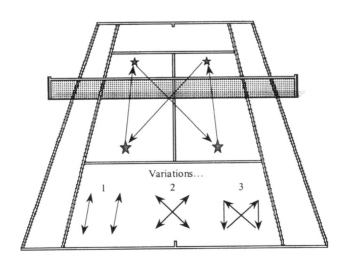

Controlled-Volley 3-on-1 Drill

Objectives

Develop ball and racquet control on volley.

Develop receiving and positioning skills.

Follow shot patterns.

Work as a team.

Operation

Three players rotate after one or two volleys.

Three players must position themselves in and out of the rotation.

One player on the opposite side controls the ball and keeps the drill going.

Alternatives

Use forehand or backhand volleys only.

Increase number of students, for example, 3-on-2 or 3-on-3.

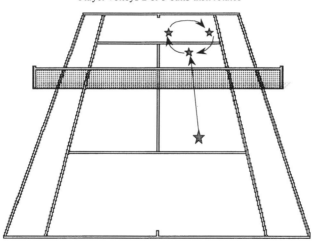

Player volleys 2 or 3 balls then rotates

2-on-1 Drill

Objectives

Develop movement, reaction, and recovery skills.

Develop consistency and discipline.

Define players' rally speed.

Operation

Two players hit down the line.

Solo player hits crosscourt.

Alternatives

Solo player hits forehands only.

All players work within the baseline.

Solo player uses volleys or overhead-volley combinations.

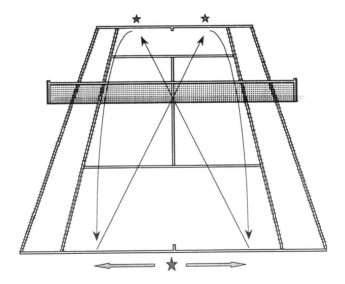

Successful Drilling

Remember, a drill is a drill. How you run it is what makes it effective. Take some time to evaluate your drills. See if you can improve the way you run them. Chances are you can create a new level of enthusiasm among your students if you make a few small adjustments to how you run your next drilling session.

Conclusion

Navy Seals toss into a swimming pool a fighter pilot dressed in full combat gear and strapped in his cockpit seat. The idea is to provide an experience that will help the pilot respond with confidence in a critical situation. If he must ditch his plane in the ocean, he has been conditioned to act from experience and memory. The navy wants its people to experience each crisis in a controlled environment. This process of education is, in many instances, merely a process of repetition.

Similarly, drills should allow a student to repeat a stroke so often that he or she becomes comfortable with it. Under the pressure of a match situation, the player realizes that he or she has hit the same shot a thousand times before. A person can acquire this sort of confidence only from experience. Now the player only needs to learn how to win because the structure and experience of producing shots is in place.

CHAPTER 11

Physical Conditioning

> "It takes 10 years of extensive practice to excel in anything."
> —Herbert Simon, Nobel laureate

Since we began teaching the sport of tennis, we have been studying the physiology of movement and conditioning. For four decades we have been able to focus on injury prevention and rehabilitation. Because of our location, our history of producing outstanding tennis players, and the credibility derived from our success, we have been a fertile training ground for top sports psychologists and fitness trainers. Today, we know far more about fitness and nutrition than we even dreamed about 40 years ago. This chapter, written by the best in the business, provides the latest information for athletes striving to reach their potential. Open your mind and learn how to be the best you can be.

FUNdamentals of Long-Term Preparation*

In tennis, as with all sports, the ultimate goal of athletic preparation is to produce peak performances at the required time or time series. Successful performances at major games and at important

*This section by Istvan Balyi, PhD, and Ann E. Hamilton, MPE Advanced Training and Performance Ltd, Victoria, BC, Canada.

tournaments depend on the coach's ability to produce and implement an effective long-term training plan.

To achieve a peak performance, a player must train in such a way that he or she peaks simultaneously in several areas—technical, tactical, physical, mental, and nutritional. In addition, the medical and environmental elements of training must be optimized. This task is the ultimate coaching challenge. An average of 8 to 12 years of general and specific preparation are required before an athlete can achieve peak performances consistently throughout the competitive season.

In North America, athletic preparation in tennis is often characterized by a low ratio of training time to competition time. The structure of the competitive system promotes this situation of short athletic preparation time and frequent competitions. Too often, coaches and parents overlook the importance of training. They focus on competition and winning rather than the acquisition of fundamental skills and fitness. Coaches, sport scientists, and sport medicine specialists agree that athletes achieve success in sport only through a long-term approach to training.

Ideally, training for the novice player should focus on the acquisition and mastery of the basic technical and tactical skills within a supportive and enjoyable environment. Although games and sets can be played, the competitive aspects of tennis should be deemphasized. Once the player has mastered basic skills and tactics, the coach may gradually shift the emphasis of training as indicated by individual needs.

Early Specialization

During the past few decades, early specialization in sports training has been one of the main topics of discussion for coaches, sport scientists, sport administrators, and parents. The salient success of the former communist countries at international competitions, especially at the Olympic Games, demonstrated the benefits of a fully aligned sport system, including early talent identification, early selection, and specialization. This sport system, which produced an unusually high number of champions, has been described and analyzed by Shneidman in *The Soviet Road to Olympus* (1978), Riordan in *Sport and Soviet Society* (1977), and Gilbert in *The Miracle Machine* (1979).

Many Western societies did not accept or endorse the concept of early specialization in sports because of ethical concerns. Harsanyi (1992) noted that communist countries that exploited athletes through early specialization developed a practice without any scientific theory to support it. Winning at all costs became the basic principle of training in some of these countries, regardless of the consequences for the health and well-being of the athletes.

In Canada and the United States, many sports have adopted a generic model of athlete development based on the "pyramid principle" (figure 11.1). In theory, the larger the talent base, the better the chance for talent identification, selection, and optimal training. Athletic development is composed of five components, including talent identification, recruitment, training, competition, and retainment. Current administrative and coaching practices emphasize only two of these components—training and competition. As a result, the balance between the components is far from optimum. Little attention is paid to systematic talent identification and recruitment at early training ages or to the retainment of athletes toward the end of their athletic careers. Competition or winning at all stages and levels is overemphasized, and this practice hinders optimal development.

In both Canada and the United States, there is an emphasis on winning at all ages and at all levels (Balyi and Way 1995, Bompa 1995, Houston 1997), and as a result, basic skill acquisition suffers. This is in contrast to the former Soviet Union, the Czech Republic, Germany, Sweden, and many other countries where basic athletic preparation for children between the ages of 6 and 10 is characterized by overall preparation. This overall athletic preparation includes the introduction of fundamental gymnastic and track and field skills. These two sports are considered the basic sports for all other sports because they develop general movement skills such as agility, balance, coordination, speed, and stamina as well as running, throwing, and jumping.

The concept of basic general athletic preparation is not widely accepted in Canada, the United States, or in many other Western cultures. Coaches and parents too often focus on competitive performance and winning rather than on the acquisition of basic technical and tactical skills and fitness. Canadian and American athletes undergo highly demanding sport-specific training without ever having mastered basic physical skills and fitness.

Figure 11.1 The pyramid principle of athletic development.

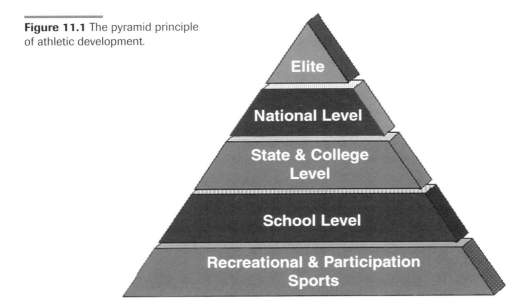

In many sports, including tennis, the elite system of training and competition is used for young and developing athletes.

The North American overemphasis on competition during early athletic development is also partially a consequence of the way that competitions are scheduled. In many sports, calendar planning is sophisticated at the elite levels but largely neglected at the developmental levels. Optimum calendar planning, however, is important at both levels.

Young athletes must often peak year round because the competitive calendar does not allow time for fundamental training. Well-meaning volunteers and administrators who have no expertise in athlete development often compile training or competition calendars for the developmental levels.[1] Scheduling is often done by sport and recreation administrators rather than by technical experts or coaches who realize that the competitive calendar must reflect the developmental level of the players. The competitive calendar is based on and characterized by recreational patterns and trends. Obviously, this kind of schedule is all right when the objective is recreational, but it has a negative effect on optimum long-term athlete development.

Specific Long-Term Athlete Development Studies

Most of the publications on tennis are devoted to skill development, tactical solutions, and drills to enhance technical and tactical improvements. Surprisingly little has been written about long-term player development or physical preparation of the entry level, intermediate, or elite player. In contrast, the importance of long-term athlete development has been written about at length in publications about other sports. Belov (1995) and Durand and Salmela (1994, 1995) on gymnastics, Touretski (1993) on swimming, Holm (1987) on tennis, and Thumm (1987) on athletics are just a few of many authors who have discussed this issue in relation to specific sports. Much of the information contained in these and other models for long-term athlete development is relevant to tennis.

Platonov identified the need for long-term planning in a general (non-sport-specific) context. He included five stages of development and provided normative data about the number of training hours and the percentage distribution of general, complementary, and specific training loads (table 11.1).

Balyi (1978) described and analyzed the socio-politico-economic conditions as well as sport, cultural, and educational policies supporting athlete development in the former communist countries for the University of

---

1 Coaches working with developing athletes have many burdens compared with those training adults. The coach is expected to know the basic facts of biological, physiological, and psychological development and turn this knowledge into practice (Szmodisch 1992). In a rational system the coaches with the best training and education would be employed at the developmental level.

Table 11.1	Stages of Generalized Athletic Preparation			
	Training load (%)			Annual training load hours
Stages	General	Complementary	Specific	
Initial	50	45	5	100–250
Basic	35	50	15	350–500
Specific base	20	40	40	600–800
Maximization	15	25	60	900–1,100
Maintenance	10	25	65	1,200–1,400

Chicago's "Talent Development Project."[2] He concluded that within the communist countries a carefully coordinated and structured policy of athlete development contributed to high performance achievements (albeit often at the expense of other social and cultural sectors).

A large-scale study conducted by Bloom in 1985 focused on the career evolution of individuals who were experts in diverse areas, including tennis players, Olympic swimmers, research neurologists, research mathematicians, sculptors, and concert pianists. Bloom found that although those studied were successful at very different endeavors, their description of their learning environment as they moved from novice to expert was similar. Table 11.2 summarizes his findings.

During the *initiation stage* the coaches or mentors provided a supportive and enjoyable environment, giving positive feedback and rewarding effort rather than achievement. The parents played a significant role by encouraging participation (process) rather than performance outcome.

The coach during the *development stage* was more skilled and demanded greater discipline from the performer as well as a greater commitment to training. During the *perfection stage,* the players sought out the most accomplished coaches, those identified as masters and experts. Players were obsessed with tennis, and their families provided total environmental and financial support, often relocating in search of better coaching for their children.

This study has significant relevance for those interested in long-term athletic development. It underlines the point there are no shortcuts in athlete preparation. Attempting to speed up the training process will always contribute to later shortcomings in the player's abilities.

While summarizing the existing literature in this area, Balyi (1995) pointed out that if children do not acquire fundamental motor skills at an early chronological and training age, they cannot fully develop those skills at a

---

2 Published under the title *Developing Talent in Young People* in 1985.

Table 11.2	Characteristics of Talented Performers and Their Mentors and Parents at Various Stages of Their Careers (Bloom 1985)		
	Career phase		
Individual	**Initiation**	**Development**	**Perfection**
Performer	Joyful, playful, excited, "special"	"Hooked," committed	Obsessed, responsible
Mentor	Kind, cheerful, caring, process centered	Strong, respecting, skilled, demanding	Successful, respected and feared, emotionally bonded
Parents	Shared excitement, supportive, sought mentors, positive	Made sacrifices, restricted activity	

later training age.[3] This is a significant consideration for coaches when preparing a long-term training plan. It touches on the importance of the principles of growth and development in training for children and supports the idea of fundamental skill acquisition during the early years of training.

Holm (1987) identified four developmental stages for tennis players. Table 11.3, modified after Holm, illustrates his developmental concepts and provides valuable normative data for developing tennis players.

Nadori described a long-term athlete development system regardless of chronological age concerns. He also illustrated the "gain" and "deficit" of the traditional and modern methods of athletic preparation, with the traditional method beginning training at age 14 and the modern method beginning training at age 10. Figure 11.2 illustrates traditional and modern athletic preparation models.

Bompa identified a two-phase long-term periodization model, including the *generalized phase* (6 to 14 years old) and the *specialized phase* (15 years old and older). Each phase is broken down into two stages. The two stages within the generalized phase are called the *initiation stage* (6 to 10 years old) and the

3 Further details will be given in the trainability section starting on page 243.

Table 11.3	**Long-Term Athlete Development for Tennis**		
		Age (years)	
Stages	**Biomotor abilities**	**Boys**	**Girls**
Precompetitive 6–10 years	Dexterity and coordination	6–10	6–10
Overall 11–14 years	Flexibility (emphasized)	13	12
Specific 15–18 years	Speed and agility		
	Acceleration run	12–14	10–12
	Slalom run	13	11
	Interval training	15	13
High performance 18 and older	Strength		
	Stage 1: improve neuromuscular coordination	10–14	10–12
	Stage 2: increase muscle mass	15–16	13–15
	Stage 3: develop maximum strength	17–18	16–17
	Aerobic capacity	12–14	11–13
	Commence training	17–18	16–17
	Endurance maximum		

athletic formation stage (11 to 14 years old). The two stages within the specialized phase are referred to as the *specialization phase* (15 to 18 years old) and the *high performance phase* (19 years old and older). Bompa (1985) also underlined the importance of overall athletic development versus early specialization for young athletes.

Balyi (1996) identified early and late recruitment sports and recommended that all sports be classified according to those categories for athlete development projects. He defined early recruitment sports as those that require early specific training for success, such as gymnastics, rhythmic gymnastics, swimming, diving, fencing, and table tennis. Late recruitment sports were defined as open-skill sports, such as soccer, rugby, volleyball, combative sports, and racquet sports, that did not require early specialization for future excellence.

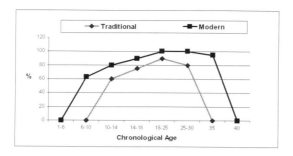

Figure 11.2 Nadori's deficit model.

Balyi identifies four stages of long-term development within early recruitment sports and five stages within late recruitment sports.

Early recruitment sports

Training to train

Training to compete

Training to win

Retirement-retainment

Late recruitment sports

Fundamental

Training to train

Training to complete

Training to win

Retirement-retainment

Note that in the early recruitment sports, in which early sport-specific training is essential, the fundamental and training-to-train stages of training must be combined to optimize the development of young athletes. This means that long-term development becomes a more complex phenomenon.

In summary, those who have developed a theory of long-term athletic development usually use a three- or four-stage model to illustrate their theory and suggest that structured athlete training should begin around the age of eight. In some sports, beginning training at a later age will contribute to salient performances, but in all sports the mastery of the fundamental skills and fitness during the early stages of athletic training is a prerequisite for excellence.[4]

Balyi and Hamilton, while working with the British Columbia Tennis Association, used the five-stage model to develop a sport-specific, long-term player development model for tennis. Table 11.4 summarizes their concept.

At this point in the chapter, a number of terms related to long-term athlete development have been mentioned. Before continuing, here is a brief definition and explanation of some of these terms.

Periodization is the structuring, or cycling, of short- and long-term training programs to provide optimum performance at the required time or time series. The term is a synonym for planning for athletic training and performance. To attain a peak performance, training must be arranged so that the

---

4 It is clearly pointed out, however, that early participation in the form of overall athletic development has a positive contribution on later capacities and skills (Zaichkowsky, Zaichkowsky, and Martinek 1980).

		Table 11.4	Long-Term Player Development in Tennis (Balyi and Hamilton 1998)	
FUNdamental	**Training to train**	**Training to compete**	**Training to win**	**Retirement/ retainment**
Chronological/ skeletal age 5-10 (M&F)	Skeletal age 10-14 (M) 10-13 (F)	Skeletal/ chronological age 14-18 (M) 13-17 (F)	Chronological age 18+ (M) 17+ (F)	Upon retirement
FUN and participation	Emphasis on general physical conditioning	Sport and individual-specific "ancillary capacities"	Maintenance (or possible improve-ment) of physical capacities	FUN and participation
General, overall development	Shoulder, core, and ankle stability	Shoulder, core, and ankle stability	Shoulder, core, and ankle stability	Exhibition matches
ABCs of move-ment: agility, balance, co-ordination, and speed	FUNdamental technical skills progressively more specific skills toward the end of the stage	Sport-specific technical and playing skills under com-petitive conditions	Further develop-ment of technical, tactical, and playing skills	Masters
ABCs of running	FUNdamentals of tactical preparation	Advanced tactical preparation	Modeling all as-pects of training and performance	"Friendlies"
Speed, power, and endurance through FUN and games	Participation in complementary sports (similar energy system and movement pattern require-ments)	Individualization of technical/tactical skills	Frequent prophylactic breaks	Coaching
Proper running, jumping, and throwing tech-nique	Individualization of fitness and technical training	Advanced mental preparation	All aspects of training individualized	Officiating
Medicine ball, Swiss ball, and own body exer-cises for strength	Introduction to mental preparation	Sport and individual-specific physical conditioning	Fine-tune "ancillary capacities;" leadership in	Club pro

(continued)

Table 11.4		*(Continued)*		
FUNdamental	**Training to train**	**Training to compete**	**Training to win**	**Retirement/ retainment**
Chronological/ skeletal age 5-10 (M&F)	**Skeletal age 10-14 (M) 10-13 (F)**	**Skeletal/ chronological age 14-18 (M) 13-17 (F)**	**Chronological age 18+ (M) 17+ (F)**	**Upon retirement**
Introduction to simple rules and ethics of sport	FUNdamentals of "ancillary capacities"			Academy or club ownership
No periodization but well-structured training	Single periodization	Double or multiple periodization	Multiple periodization	Mass media
Racquet sport-specific once a week with participation in other sports 4-5 times per week	Tennis-specific training 4 times per week, with participation in other sports	Tennis-specific technical, tactical, and fitness training 6-9 times per week	Tennis-specific technical, tactical, and fitness training 9-12 times per week	Sport administration
			FUN and participation	Health and well-being

athlete achieves a simultaneous peak in all components of training, including technical (skills), tactical, physical, and mental. In addition, nutritional, medical, environmental and equipment factors must be also optimized. Coaches are responsible for the planning and implementation processes involved in achieving peak performance. Therefore, they must carefully integrate and sequence all the factors of training and performance. The achievement of optimum peak performance requires several years of general and specific preparation to ensure that all components are trained and optimized while avoiding interference between them. Single, double, and multiple periodization refers to the number of seasons in an annual cycle.

Single periodization is characterized by one competitive season. Seven to eight months of training is usually followed by a three- to four-month period of an in-season, or competitive, cycle.

Double periodization is characterized by two major competitive seasons; thus the competitive cycle, or in-season, will take six to seven months, and the training season will be shorter, only four to five months. Only well-trained players able to focus on high-quality training and a long in-season can accomplish double periodization.

Multiple periodization is the framework of preparation for elite players. After 8 to 12 years of training, such athletes should be fully trained. They do not need to take part in general conditioning or fitness preparation. The world's best players can compete year round without detraining or over-training because the high intensity and high frequency of competition and training will maintain their established physical and technical capacities. The high intensity must be complemented by occasional "boosting" sessions when fitness monitoring calls for it and by strategically timed "prophylactic breaks" to prevent physical or mental burnout.

A huge body of literature indirectly supports the activities of the leading coaches, best teams, and elite players. The so-called maintenance literature (about the effect of reduced training on fitness and performance) and the tapering literature (about reducing the volume of training before major tournaments but maintaining high intensity and frequency of training) fully supports the previously described principles.[5]

In many individual sports, such as swimming and athletics, improvements can be measured and empirically tested. Tennis coaches and experts should carefully analyze this. The framework of multiple periodization and the competitive calendar for such sports have been adjusted to accommodate multiple or triple peaks—nationals, selection meets, and major games. Thus, training, preparation, and peaking for the major tournaments (i.e., Grand Slam events and other important tournaments) within the annual cycle are superimposed on the entire training and competitive system.

The terms *growth* and *development* are often used together, sometimes synonymously, but each refers to specific biological activities (Malina and Bouchard 1991).

Growth refers to increase in the size of the body or its parts, including changes in size, body composition, physique, and specific body systems (Malina 1991). *Maturation* refers to the tempo and timing of progress toward the mature state. Skeletal (skeletal age), sexual (secondary sex characteristics), and somatic (age at peak height velocity) maturation are often used (Malina 1991).

Development refers to "the interrelationship between growth and maturation in relation to the passage of time. The concept of development also includes the social, emotional, intellectual, and motor realms of the child" (Tihanyi 1990).

Skeletal age refers to the maturity of the skeleton "determined by the degree of ossification of the bone structure" (Haywood 1993) or a "measure of age that takes into consideration how far given bones have progressed toward maturity, not in size but with respect to shape and position to one another" (Zaichkowsky, Zaichkowsky, and Martinek 1980).

Chronological age refers to "the number of years and days elapsed since birth" (Haywood 1993). According to Malina and Bouchard (1991), "Growth,

5 For further reading, see Hickson (1980), Hickson et al. (1982), Houmard (1991), and Neufer (1990).

development and maturation operate in a time framework—that is, the child's chronological age . . . children of the same chronological age can differ by several years in their level of biological maturation. The integrated nature of growth and maturation is achieved by the interaction of genes, hormones, nutrients, and the physical and psychosocial environments in which the individual lives. This complex interaction regulates the child's growth, neuromuscular maturation, sexual maturation, and general physical meta-morphosis during the first two decades of life."

Childhood ordinarily spans from the end of infancy (the first birthday) to the start of adolescence and is characterized by relatively steady progress in children's growth and maturation and rapid progress in their neuromuscu-lar, or motor, development. It is often divided into early childhood, which includes the preschool children aged one to five years, and late childhood, which includes elementary school-age children aged six through to the onset of adolescence.

Adolescence is a more difficult period to define in terms of the time of its onset and termination. During this period, most bodily systems become adult both structurally and functionally. Structurally, adolescence begins with acceleration in the rate of growth in stature, which marks the onset of the adolescent growth spurt. The rate of statural growth reaches a peak, begins a slower or decelerative phase, and finally terminates with the attainment of adult stature. Functionally, adolescence is usually viewed in terms of sexual maturation, which begins with changes in the neuroendo-crine system prior to overt physical changes and terminates with the attainment of mature reproductive function (Malina and Bouchard 1991).

Puberty refers to the point at which an individual is sexually mature and able to reproduce.

Peak height velocity (or PHV) is the maximum rate of growth in stature during the growth spurt. The age of maximum velocity of growth is called the age at PHV (Malina and Bouchard 1991).

A *critical period of development* refers to a point in the development of a specific behavior when experience or training has an optimal effect on development. The same experience, introduced at an earlier or later time, has no effect on or retards later skill acquisition (Zaichkowsky, Zaichkowsky, and Martinek 1980).

Readiness refers to the child's level of growth, maturity, and development that enables him or her to perform tasks and meet demands through training and competition (Malina and Bouchard 1991).

Adaptation refers to a stimulus or a series of stimuli that induces functional or morphological changes in the organism. Naturally, the level or degree of adaptation depends on the genetic endowment of an individual. The general trends of adaptation, however, are identified by physiological research. The facts and guidelines of the different adaptation processes, such as adaptation to muscular endurance or maximum strength, are clearly delineated.

The term *trainability* refers to the genetic endowment of athletes as they respond individually to specific stimuli and adapt to them accordingly.

Trainability During Childhood

Malina and Bouchard (1991) defined trainability as "the responsiveness of developing individuals at different stages of growth and maturation to the training stimulus." They also referred to "readiness and critical periods" of trainability during growth and development of young athletes. Thus the stimulus must be timed to achieve optimum adaptation with regard to motor skills, muscular power, and aerobic power.

Individual developmental levels also influence trainability during the periods of early and late childhood. Jacquard (1989) suggested that genetic variability is responsible for the appearance of gifted athletes and that these athletes possess more than one exceptional trait. Variables used include weight, height, adiposity, muscular strength, speed, aerobic power, and anaerobic power.

Bouchard et al. (1986, 1992) underlined the importance that heredity can play in determining the pattern of adaptation to training. These studies examined adaptation to training in terms of a high or low response and an early or late response, stating that these four patterns must be considered when evaluating individuals and training programs.

Hamel (1987) stated that heredity has such an effect on adaptation that from a practical point of view, it is almost impossible to predict with any accuracy an individual response to a given training stimulus.

Malina and Bouchard (1991), while summarizing the available data on the trainability of maximal aerobic power, concluded there is little trainability of maximal aerobic power in children under age 10. They stated, however, that "it is not certain whether these results are the consequence of low trainability (a low adaptive potential to aerobic training) or to inadequacies of training programs."

In their article "Endurance Trainability of Children and Youths," Pate and Ward (1996) reviewed the pertinent literature and concluded that children and youth, both male and female, are physiologically adaptive to endurance exercise training if the exercise program meets the criteria for intensity, frequency, and duration. But the literature is so scant as to preclude drawing even a tentative conclusion.

In their article "Trainability of Muscle Strength, Power and Endurance During Childhood," Blimki and Bar-Or (1996) describe morphological and neural adaptations to strength training during childhood and summarized the trainability of muscular strength.

In "Resistance Training During Preadolescence: Issues, Controversies, and Recommendations," Blimki and Marion (1995) concluded that "most, but not all, studies indicate that pre and early pubertal children make similar relative strength gains compared to adolescents and adults, but usually demonstrate smaller absolute strength gains following training." Neural adaptation rather than improved hypertrophy and improved movement coordination seems to be the contributing factor to these strength gains. The authors also provide practical recommendations in point form for coaches about new perspectives in the era of strength training during preadolescence.

Trainability in Coaching Studies

Nadori, summarizing the trainability literature, schematically illustrated the general trends of "critical periods" of trainability, calling them "optimum periods of trainability" (table 11.5). Of course, such generalizations have limitations, but they provide convenient information to help coaches of developmental athletes identify the key factors in the general patterns of trainability of athletes.

Bompa (1995) described the general trends of integrated long-term training plans for various sports including the training phases, skill acquisition, and the training components of skill and physical capacities as well as recommendations for competitive involvements.

Table 11.5	General Patterns of Optimum Periods of Trainability (Nadori 1985)														
Age	5	6	7	8	9	10	11	12	13	14	15	16	17	18
Coordination capacities														
Motor learning			G	G	G	E	E				G	E	E	E
Motor control			G	G	G	G	E				G	G	G	G
Reaction to audio-visual clues			G	E	E	G								
Rhythm/cadence capacity			G	G	E	E	G	G						
Spatial awareness			G	G	G	G	G	E	E	E				
Kinesthetic awareness					G	E	E	G	G					
Physical capacities														
Endurance	G	G	G	G	G	G	G	E	E	E	E	E	E	E
Strength					G	G	G	G	E	E	E	E	E	E
Speed		G	E	E	E	E	E	E	E	G	G	G		

G = Good; E = Excellent

Scammon (1930) proposed that the growth of different tissues and systems could be summarized in four patterns. The growth of each structure is expressed as a percentage of the total gain between birth and 20 years. Size at age 20 equals 100 percent on the vertical scale. Figure 11.3 is based on Scammon (1930), adapted from Malina and Bouchard (1991), and modified by Balyi (1997).

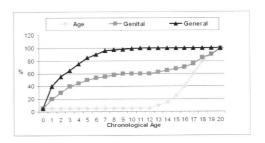

Figure 11.3 Patterns of growth (modified after Scammon, 1930).

The general, or body, curve describes the growth of the whole body. Malina and Bouchard (1991) summarized the model:

"The pattern is S-shaped and has four phases: rapid growth in infancy and early childhood, constant growth during middle childhood, rapid growth during the adolescent spurt and slow increase and eventual cessation of growth after adolescence. The neural curve characterizes the growth of the brain, nervous system, and associated structures. Ninety-five percent of the total increment of the nervous system is attained by about age seven. The genital curve characterizes the growth pattern of the primary and secondary sex characteristics. The genital tissue shows slight growth in infancy, followed by a latent period during most of childhood and extremely rapid growth and maturation during the adolescent spurt.[6]

"Scammon's curves indicate the differential nature of postnatal growth. Growth occurs in different areas and tissues of the body at different times and at different rates. Although somewhat simplified and diagrammatic, the curves give a sense of order to the structural and functional changes that occur with growth and maturation."

Balyi and Hamilton (1997) summarized the available literature on trainability, growth and development, and maturation. Using a modified version of Scammon's model, they identified the "critical" or "sensitive" periods of trainability during childhood and adolescence (see figure 11.4). Of course, as was the case with Nadori's model, this generalization has its limitations, but it can help coaches to understand the complex processes of "optimum periods of trainability."

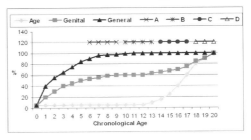

Figure 11.4 Optimum periods of trainability (adapted from Scammon, 1930).

---

6 This description is based on Malina and Bouchard's overview of postnatal growth (1991, p. 8.) The fourth curve, the lymphoid curve, is not included in the figure.

FUNdamental Stage (6 to 10 Years Old)

This stage emphasizes well-structured fun and the development of overall physical capacities, such as the ABCs of movement education (agility, balance, coordination, and speed), the ABCs of running, strength, flexibility, and endurance. Participation in as many sports as possible is encouraged. Parallel with all other participation is an introduction to most of the basic racquet-sport skills, including the skills of tennis.

Training–to–Train Stage, Single Periodization (10 to 14 Years Old)

This stage emphasizes overall sport-specific skills, fun, and games. Structured short- and long-term programs are featured. Growth and development must be carefully monitored. Strength and endurance training and monitoring (medical, physiological, psychological, nutritional, and technical-tactical) are introduced during this phase. The focus is on basic skill development early in the stage. Later, gradual progression is used from simple to more complex skills. Perceptual motor skills are introduced and enhanced. As the stage progresses, players continue to refine skills, learn skill variations, and begin to understand tactical components of play. Individual specific training is introduced.

Training–to–Compete Stage, Double Periodization (14 to 18 Years Old)

During this phase, the focus is on sport-specific skills, conditioning programs, and full individualization. Training is highly specialized. Fully integrated sport science, sport medicine, and sport-specific technical-tactical programs should now be introduced along with regular monitoring of the adaptation and performance patterns.

Training–to–Win Stage, Multiple Periodization (18 Years Old and Older)

The focus is now on high-performance sport, optimum peaking for major competitions or tournaments, and maintenance of established physical, technical, and tactical capacities. Optimum regeneration programs with frequent "prophylactic breaks" and daily or weekly monitoring of adaptation to training and fatigue levels should be established.[7]

Although this model helps the coach integrate the growth and maturation processes with the general trends of trainability of the developmental athlete, the model is limited because it is based on chronological age. Short- and long-term training and competition programs designed according to chronological age rather than maturation or "readiness" levels have nega-

---

7 Tschine introduced the concept of "prophylactic breaks" during the 1970s to refer to preventative breaks or rest periods to avoid physical or mental burnout.

tive consequences. Athletes should be grouped together according to readiness rather than chronological age (Durand and Salmela 1995).

Summarizing the trends of the literature, it seems that trainability after maturation is limited only by genetic endowment. Although adaptation during late childhood is somewhat limited by the developmental or maturation stages, trainability is not as limited as researchers in the 1970s and 1980s thought it to be (Docherty 1985, Blimki and Bar-Or 1996).

Large-scale practical experiences from early involvement sports also proved there is no limit on trainability in speed and power sports (artistic gymnastics, rhythmic gymnastics, figure skating, diving). During late childhood, athletes at the highest training and competition levels can perform extremely complex and physically demanding skills.

Motor and physical maturation or psychomotor development is closely connected with cognitive, affective, and psychosocial maturation. The development of motor skills must occur in harmony with the stages of growth and maturation. Coaches must recognize critical periods and introduce the appropriate training stimuli during each period. Broadly speaking, general, fundamental skills should be taught during early childhood (ages 2 to 5). Fundamental skills include running, jumping, hopping, bounding, balancing, throwing, and catching. Although most children perform these skills, they will display large individual differences in ability to perform them. Specific skills should be taught during late childhood (ages 5 to 10). During late childhood, the generalized, fundamental skills will become more refined, fluid, and automatic, and the child can apply these skills to sports performances. Depending on the volume, intensity, and frequency of practice, children can develop specialized skills from late childhood to adolescence.

Specialized skills may be introduced during adolescence (ages 10 to 18) (Zaichkowsky, Zaichkowsky, and Martinek 1980). Tables 11.6, 11.7, and 11.8 summarize the physical, cognitive, and emotional developmental characteristics and identify the consequences and implications for the coach when making a training plan.[8]

These tables will help the coach make decisions that go beyond the usual technical-tactical focus and include the cognitive and emotional factors. The various stages of physical, cognitive, and emotional development are predictable, but the rate or tempo of that development is specific to the individual and genetically determined (Tenner 1973, Tihanyi 1982, Durand and Salmela 1995). Players will go through the same development but at different time frames or chronologies.

To summarize, tennis coaches at all levels of development must recognize that long-term planning is essential to athletic success. They must also realize that young athletes are not miniature adults and that the emphasis

---

8 Tables are modified after Alpine Canada's Long-Term Athlete Development Model, 1987.

Table 11.6 Physical Development Characteristics and Implications

Basic characteristics	General consequences: Performance capabilities and limitations	Implications for the coach
Larger muscle groups are more developed than smaller ones.	Children are more skillful in gross movements involving large muscle groups than in precisely coordinated movements involving the interaction of many smaller muscles.	Basic skills should be developed during this phase.
The size of the heart is increasing in relation to the rest of the body. The cardiovascular system is still developing.	The child's aerobic system is trainable, but the emphasis of training should be on the anaerobic alactic system.	Short duration, anaerobic alactic activities should be planned. Endurance must be developed through play and games (lack of attention span for continuous work).
Ligamentous structures are becoming stronger, but the ends of the bones are still cartilaginous and continue to ossify.	The body is very susceptible to injuries through excessive stress or heavy pressure.	Use slow progressions in hopping and bounding. Strength training limited to own body weight or use medicine ball exercises (neural recruitment).
Basic motor patterns become more refined toward the end of this phase, and the balance mechanism in the inner ear is gradually maturing.	There is great improvement in speed, agility, balance, coordination, and flexibility toward the end of this phase.	Specific activities and games should emphasize coordination and kinesthetic sense. Activities such as gymnastics, diving, and athletics are appropriate.
During this phase, girls develop coordination skills faster than boys, but the developmental differences between boys and girls are negligible.	Sex differences are not of great consequence at this stage in development.	Training and playing together should be emphasized at this age and phase.

Table 11.7 Cognitive Development Characteristics and Implications

Basic characteristics	General consequences: Performance capabilities and limitations	Implications for the coach
Attention span is short and children are action-oriented. Memory is developing in a progressive way.	Young players cannot sit and listen for longer periods of time.	Use short, clear, and simple instructions. Children want to move and participate in action.
Children at this level have limited reasoning ability. Later in the phase there is a growing capacity for more abstract thought.	Children are generally leader-oriented: they love to be led!	Coaches should adopt a "follow me" or "follow the leader" approach and ensure that all activities are fun and well-planned.
The repetition of activities is greatly enjoyed. Young players improve their abilities through experience.	Children do not learn the skills correctly just by trial and error.	Coaches must be able to provide a correct demonstration of the basic skills required at this level.
Imagination is blossoming.	Experimentation and creativity should be encouraged.	While playing and practicing encourage input (opinion) from the children. They love to try new things.

and content of training differs according to the developmental age of the child.

This is not to say that American players are not achieving great success at the international level, but to point out that significant improvements could be achieved easily by rethinking our long-term athlete development.

Achieving this type of athlete development may involve critically examining our current coaching and training methods. We may want to take a hard look at methods that have led to success in other countries and in other sports. We may also consider reorganizing competition schedules to allow children and developing players to have more time to learn and master basic movement skills and basic technical-tactical skills.

Table 11.8	Emotional Development Characteristics and Consequences	
Basic characteristics	**General consequences: Performance capabilities and limitations**	**Implications for the coach**
The child's self-concept is developing through experience and comments from others.	Youngsters perceive these experiences as a form of self-evaluation: "I am a good person if I do well/ I'm a bad person if I do poorly."	Children need positive reinforcement from a coach on a regular basis. This will provide strong motivation to continue with the activity.
Children like to be the center of focus and attention.	When a situation becomes threatening, they quickly lose confidence.	Structure technical and tactical activities so that success is virtually guaranteed. This means gradually progressing from simple to complex.
The influence of peers becomes a very strong driving force behind all activities.	Acceptance into the peer group often depends upon one's abilities in physical skills and activities.	At this phase the coach must be capable of properly assessing the basic skills and providing a varied repertoire of practical opportunities for technical and tactical development and improvement.
The child begins to understand the need for rules and structure.	Children can understand and play simple games with simple rules and will tend to question rules and expect thoughtful answers.	Participation and fun to be emphasized versus winning. Focus is on the process, not on the outcome (and have lots of FUN!).

The results of these changes may contribute significantly to a higher caliber of skills, fitness levels, and knowledge base (ancillary capacities) among North American players, as well as greater longevity of their athletic careers.

FUNdamental skills will always be useful for young players if they later decide to pursue other sports interests.

Figure 11.5 schematically illustrates the distribution of general (non-sport-specific) and sport-specific training loads from the FUNdamental stage to the training-to-win stage.

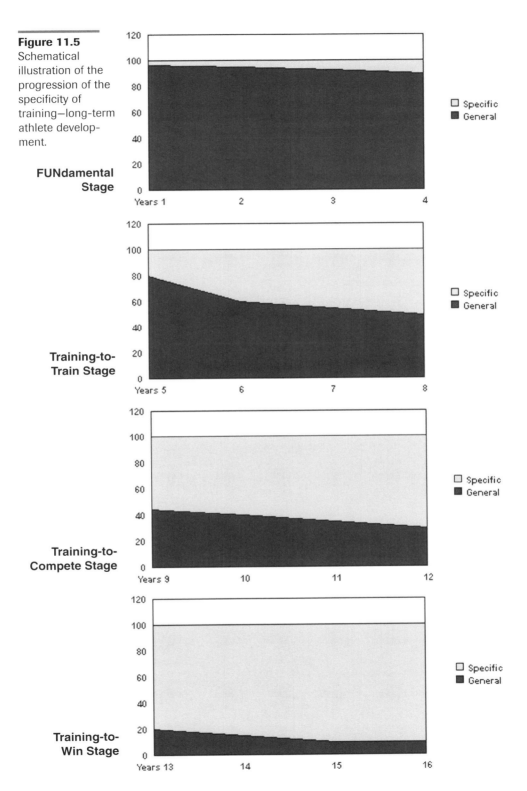

Figure 11.5
Schematical illustration of the progression of the specificity of training—long-term athlete development.

FUNdamental Stage

Training-to-Train Stage

Training-to-Compete Stage

Training-to-Win Stage

Postscript

In my former publications and lectures I devoted more time to sport-specific training during the FUNdamental stage of athletic preparation. I recommended two weekly sport-specific training sessions complemented by four overall developmental sessions. After a few intense discussions with Nick I was converted! From the point of view of optimal development in tennis, only racquet sports, including tennis, are to be implemented during this stage.

The earlier one specializes, the earlier one burns out. This is especially true in tennis!

Empirical experience and scientific observation seem to support the importance of overall athletic preparation and early specialization in the ages from 9 to 12 as far as skill learning is concerned (Rushall 1998). This period is called the "critical" period (McGraw 1935, Magill 1978, and Singer 1975) or the "sensitive" period (Tenner 1978) in the scientific literature. A critical period is assumed to be the point in the development of a specific behavior during which experience or training has an optimal effect. Experience at an earlier or later time has no effect on or retards later skill acquisition (Zaichkowsky et al. 1980).[9] Thus, unless constructive athletic preparation is carried out, athletes will never reach their optimal potential, regardless of the quantity and quality of future training. At the end of the FUNdamental stage and at the beginning of the training-to-train stage, highly sophisticated ABCs (agility, balance, coordination, and speed) training should be implemented together with carefully planned and periodized sport-specific tennis training and competition programs. This method provides the FUNdamentals, prevents early burnouts, and establishes future optimal training and performance factors. Of course, skeletal age must be observed.

References

Balyi, I. "Talent Development in Sport. The Case of the State Socialist Countries." Unpublished paper, solicited and supported by the University of Chicago "Talent Development Project" Workshop (See Bloom 1985).

Balyi, I., and A. Hamilton. "The FUNdamental Phase of Training." *Performance Conditioning for Soccer* 4 (7): 6–12.

Balyi, I., and R. Way. 1995. "Long-Term Planning of Athlete Development. The Training to Train Phase." *B.C. Coach,* pp. 2–10.

Balyi, I. 1996. "Planning for Training and Performance. The Training to Compete Phase." *B.C. Coach,* pp. 9–14.

---

9 Rushall summarizes the literature of trainability well in his article "The Growth of Physical Characteristics in Male and Female Children" in *Sports Coach,* vol. 20, no. 4 (summer), 1998, pp. 25–27, Canberra, Australia.

Balyi, I., and A. Hamilton. 1996. "Planning for Training and Performance. The Training to Win Phase." *B.C. Coach,* 9–26.

Balyi, I. 1998. "Long-Term Development of Tennis Players." Paper delivered at the International Tennis Coaching Conference, Toronto.

Bloom, B. 1985. *Developing Talent in Young People.* New York: Ballantine.

Bompa, T. 1985. *The Theory and Methodology of Training.* Dubuque, Iowa: Kendall/Hunt.

Bompa, T. 1995. *From Childhood to Champion Athlete.* Toronto: Veritas.

Bouchard, C. 1990. "Discussion: Heredity, Fitness and Health." In *Exercise, Fitness and Health,* edited by Bouchard et al., 147–153. Champaign, Illinois: Human Kinetics.

Bouchard, C., J.A. Simoneau, G. Lortie, M.R. Boulay, M. Marcotte, and M.C. Thibault. 1986. "Genetic Effects in Human Skeletal Muscle Fiber Type Distribution and Enzyme Activities." *Canadian Journal of Physiology and Pharmacology* 64: 1245–1251.

Costill et al. 1985. "Effect of Reduced Training on Muscular Power in Swimmers." *Physician and Sports Medicine* 13 (2): 94–1001.

Durand, N., and J. Salmela. 1994. "CGF Women's Artistic Gymnastics Athlete Development Training Model." Unpublished paper, University of Ottawa.

Durand, N., and J. Salmela. 1995. "CGF Men's Artistic Gymnastics Athlete Development Training Model." Unpublished paper, University of Ottawa.

Gilbert, A. 1979. *The Miracle Machine.* Toronto: Longman Canada Limited.

Hamel, P., J.A. Simoneau, G. Lorte, M.R. Boulay, and C. Bouchard. 1986. "Heredity and Muscle Adaptation to Endurance Training." *Medicine and Science in Sports and Exercise* 18: 690–696.

Harre, D. 1982. *Principles of Sports Training.* Berlin: Sportverlag.

Harsanyi, L. 1992. *Az edzes egy even beluli szakaszai.* Budapest: OTSH.

Harsanyi, L. 1983. *A 10-18 eves atletak felkeszitesenek modellje.* Budapest: Utanpotlas-neveles, no. 10.

Hickson et al. 1982. "Reduced Training Duration Effects on Aerobic Power, Endurance and Cardiac Growth." *Journal of Applied Physiology,* no. 53: 225–229.

Holm, J. 1987. *Tennis: Plan to Win the Czech Way.* Toronto: Sport Books.

Houmard, J. 1991. "Impact of Reduced Training on Performance in Endurance Athletes." *Sports Medicine* 12 (6): 929–935.

Houston, W. 1997. "Young Hockey Talent Failed by the System." *Globe and Mail* (May 10, May 12, May 13, and May 14).

International Tennis Federation. 1998. *Advanced Coaches Manual.* London.

Malina, R.M.1988. "Growth and Maturation of Young Athletes. Biological and Social Considerations." In *Children in Sport,* edited by Small et al., 83–101. Champaign, Illinois: Human Kinetics.

Malina, R.M., and C. Bouchard. 1991. *Growth, Maturation, and Physical Activity.* Champaign, Illinois: Human Kinetics.

Matveyev, L.P. 1983. *Aspects fondamentaux de l'entrainement.* Paris: Vigot.

McGraw, M.B. 1935. *Growth: A Study of Johnny and Jimmy.* New York: Appleton-Century-Crofts.

Neufer, P.D. 1990. "The Effect of Detraining and Reduced Training on the Physiological Adaptations to Aerobic Exercise Training." *Sports Medicine* 8: 302–321.

Platonov, V.N. 1988. *L'entrainement sportif: theorie et methode.* Paris: Ed. EPS.

Riordan, J. 1977. *Sport and Soviet Society.* Cambridge: Cambridge University Press.

Rushall, B. 1998. "The Growth of Physical Characteristics in Male and Female Children." *Sports Coach* (Canberra, Australia) 20 (summer): 25–27.

Sanderson, L. 1989. "Growth and Development Considerations for the Design of Training Plans for Young Athletes." Ottawa: CAC, SPORTS, vol. 10. no. 2.

Shneidman. 1978. *The Soviet Road to Olympus.* Toronto: Ontario Institute for Studies in Education.

Tenner, J.M. 1973. "Growing Up." *Scientific American,* 9.

Tenner, J.M. 1978. *Fetus Into Man.* Cambridge: Harvard University Press.

Starischka, S., and P. Tschiene. 1977. "Anmerkungen zur Trainingssteuerung." *Leistungssport* 4: 275–281.

Zaichkowsky, L.D., L.B. Zaichkowsky, and T.J. Martinek. 1980. *Growth and Development.* St. Louis: C.V. Mosby.

International Performance Institute: Training for Tennis*

Top-ranked tennis player Mary Pierce, baseball player Nomar Garciaparra, and Detroit Lions quarterback Charlie Batch, phenomenal athletes who have excelled in their sports, are products of the International Performance Institute (IPI). In a society that demands success, athletes feel constant pressure to keep in shape and perfect their skills. Competition is becoming ever more rigorous in the athletic realm, and each athlete strives to perform at the best level possible. Advances in exercise science are occurring every day, many directed toward enabling athletes to enhance their performance. The advance in performance is evident in the shattering of world records. Great feats of athleticism are seen throughout the world. Athletes are becoming bigger, stronger, quicker, faster, and able to jump higher. Therefore, athletes and coaches in all sports are looking for the competitive edge. Current theory suggests that the most effective sport training uses a progression tailored to the specific athletic demands of the sport (Marcello 1998).

The IPI philosophy conceived in 1995 by Mark Verstegen was developed around three goals:

1. Decreasing the potential for injury
2. Improving performance
3. Motivating through education, teaching the athlete what it takes to be a consummate professional and a better player (Verstegen 1998).

Training is the systematic approach to improving performance (Verstegen 1998). This approach relies on a thorough evaluation of the sport and the athlete's playing style, history, physical parameters, injury potential, and performance characteristics. Training generally comprises four levels:

---

*This section by Mark Verstegen, MS, CSCS, and Brandon Marcello, MS, CSCS.

FUNdamentals, training to train, training to compete, and training to win (Balyi 1996). The key to any successful program is planning, mastery, and progression. This section will discuss a wide spectrum of training techniques employed by IPI that are generally applicable to athletes who compete in tennis.

Many of the training techniques are tailored to meet the specific demands of that sport. Thus the sport needs to be analyzed to determine which variables act as the main ingredients. To determine the needs of tennis, the following areas need to be evaluated: predominant injuries, biomechanical demands, metabolic demands, surface demands, and style of play. Injuries themselves can hinder performance on the court. Sixty-three percent of all injuries in tennis occur from overload or overuse. Repetitive use of a particular part of the body without sufficient rest can lead to breakdown of the area, causing pain and inflammation. This is generally seen in the rotator cuff (shoulder), elbow, stress fractures and shin splints in the legs, and even chronic recurring pain. Traumatic injuries account for the remaining 37 percent and include the more severe injuries. These injuries tend to require long periods off from tennis. Traumatic injuries include ankle sprains, knee injuries, and fractures (Kibler and Chandler 1994). Other often injured areas in tennis occur in the wrist, low back, and leg (abductors, gastrocnemius, and hamstring). If the areas more susceptible to injury can be strengthened in the training regimen, the likelihood of an injury will decrease.

Examination of metabolic demands for tennis indicates that the sport is 70 to 80 percent anaerobic and 10 to 20 percent aerobic (Kibler and Chandler 1994). The anaerobic system powers action lasting up to 25 to 40 seconds, and the aerobic system powers activity lasting longer than two minutes. At the elite level 80 percent of the points last less than 20 seconds (Kibler and Chandler 1994). This shows us that the athlete must train the anaerobic system to compete effectively at a higher level. This is not to say that the aerobic system should be neglected. The aerobic system allows the anaerobic system to recover between points. This type of training will be addressed later.

Playing surface is another variable that should be addressed when examining the training regimen for tennis. Because tennis players play on different surfaces, they must train for changing physical demands required to perform optimally on each surface. Because the type of surface can increase injury potential or manipulate metabolic demands, it is crucial to prepare and train for all surfaces. For example, impact forces greatly increase on a hard court surface, putting greater stress on the legs and back, thus leading to a higher incidence of impact-related injuries such as shin splints and stress fractures. A clay surface decreases impact forces on the legs and knees but increases the likelihood of muscle pulls from sliding.

The final variable is the type of player. There are several different types. A baseliner like Thomas Muster or Amanda Coetzer plays the game deep behind the baseline. An aggressive baseliner like Monica Seles or Andre

Jim Courier—Pay the Price

I saw Jim Courier as a youngster put in endless hours of work. He knew that if he had to hit 50 percent of his shots with the backhand, he'd never make it to the top. His backhand was just a solid neutral shot. Although his opponents couldn't beat him up by hitting to it, his backhand was certainly not a weapon.

Courier knew that he had to protect the backhand. So he learned to run around it and hit a big forehand, even from the backhand sideline. He had the guts to give up 25 percent of the court and at the same time cover 25 percent more of it to make up for running around his backhand. That meant making a tremendous mental and physical commitment.

Courier had to build his legs and do more cardiovascular conditioning than his opponents. He has worked so hard that it has taken a toll on his mind and body. But Courier taught me that if you want to be a champion, you must accept what has to be done and pay the price to do it.

Agassi plays near or inside the baseline. One who always attacks the net, like Patrick Rafter or Jana Novotna, can be considered a serve-and-volley player. Finally, an all-court player like Pete Sampras likes to take chances and uses the entire court for a versatile style.

IPI's Top Training Tips for the Serious Tennis Athlete

IPI has compiled a regimen that addresses every component of training for tennis. Each component contains IPI's top exercises, listed for each of the following: movement prep, plyometrics, speed, energy system development (ESD), strength, and prehab.

Movement Prep

Traditional warm-up for tennis consists of some light jogging around the court and doing various static stretches, both standing and on the ground. Many players fall into the rut of daydreaming through the prepractice stretch, paying little attention to their routine. After athletes attempt to lengthen the muscles by prying them apart, we expect them to hop up and compete. Warm-up is often the least productive period of the practice, even though it sets the tone for the entire day. To improve the productivity of this period, we must determine the purpose of the warm-up and the best use of the time committed to it.

We need to design a warm-up and flexibility program that achieves the following goals in 8 to 10 minutes:

1. Elevate the athlete's core temperature and heart rate
2. Elongate the muscles
3. Decrease inhibition of opposing muscle groups to improve speed and decrease injury potential
4. Maximize teaching time for proper movement biomechanics

Movement preparation is preparing for the way that one plays. There are three main categories: general kinesthetic warm-up, mobility exercises, and dynamic flexibility. Movement preparation uses walking, skipping, jogging, and running movements specifically designed to achieve the warm-up goals in a short time. This routine will increase the core temperature, decrease the potential for injury, and improve athleticism, core stability, proprioception, coordination, and movement speed. Movement preparation will enhance the player's performance by teaching perfect movement patterns. This system will improve the productivity of the 10-minute daily period (60 minutes per week for 16 weeks equals 16 hours per season) to give the athletes an edge over the competition (Verstegen 1996).

IPI's top movement prep exercises

1. **Hip crossover:** Supine and holding your torso flat, twist your bent legs to the right until they reach the floor. Then twist to the left. Repeat the sequence. Advanced: try it with your legs straight out.

2.   **Scorpion:** Prone and with arms and shoulders spread out, stretch your right heel toward your left hand while keeping your left hip glued to the ground. Alternate legs and continue. Advanced: switch legs in quicker succession.

3.   **Lateral lunge with twist:** From a lunge, maintain an upright torso and twist at the hips across the leading leg. Advanced: work to straighten the trailing leg and pivot on the ball of your foot.

4. **Forward lunge to instep:** Stride into a lunge, reaching forward to touch the ground with the forearm from the same side as your forward leg. Advanced: try to get the forearm perfectly flat.

5. **Straight leg march to skip:** Balancing on your right foot, kick your left foot toward your extended right hand and vice versa on the next step, while keeping excellent posture. Advanced: work to straighten the legs.

6. **Hand walks:** Put both hands and feet on the ground. Tighten your tummy and walk your hands out as far over your head as possible while keeping your body straight. Leave your hands there. Then, with straight legs, start walking your feet to your hands. Walk hands back out and repeat.

Plyometrics

The popularity of the training method commonly known as plyometric training is now evident in all sports and at all levels of competition (King 1993). Plyometrics enhances the way a muscle contracts, increasing the power and work that the muscle can produce. IPI has had great success with the integration of plyometrics in strength workouts and believes it to be a crucial part of the training process. IPI carefully chooses plyometric exercises based on the athlete's level, ability, and mastery before advancing the athlete to more advanced exercises. Several basic plyometric exercises can be effectively used to train for tennis.

Rapid response

The goal is to make the feet go as quickly as possible, like a sewing machine.

1. **Base rapid response:** With feet shoulder-width apart, move both feet as fast as you can back and forth across a line. Other variations include moving feet left to right and twisting the hips so that one foot moves in front of the line and the other foot moves behind the line. See top photo on page 261.

Short response

The goal is to develop elasticity by being quick off the ground. Think of a superball!

2. **Reactive step-up:** With one foot on the floor and the other on a box (about midshin in height), leap straight up and land as you started. Advanced: switch legs in midair.

Long response

The goal is to develop power and speed strength.

3. **Split jump:** Leap up from a low lunge until your legs are straight beneath you and land as you started. Advanced: alternate legs in the air.

4. **Squat jump:** From a deep squat position, leap up straight into the air and land as you started.

Speed

The following movement drills have several roles in improving performance. These drills will help develop speed and quickness while improving tennis-specific movement, or footwork. The athlete can improve speed in two ways—by increasing stride length, which means that the player is able to put explosive power into the court to propel the body in the direction of the ball, and by increasing stride frequency, which will improve adjustment steps as well.

   The player should do these drills for quality, not quantity. Our goal is to get the players very quick so that they are able to cover the entire court as Michael Chang does. This work will help develop the nervous system, "wiring" the players to be like superfit players Thomas Muster and Steffi Graf, who appear to float on top of the court.

   1. **Baseline to volley**—Start at the doubles line and shuffle laterally, making sure to keep your feet apart as you do in your split step. On reaching the center mark, explode forward with a positive first step and follow it with three to five attacking strides, pushing back and down into the ground. Keep the hips low, hugging the ground like a fine sports car, and go into your split step. Absorb all the momentum by bending your legs, using them like shock absorbers. Make sure to stop with great balance. This drill may be progressed by having a coach point or drop a ball to signal your burst forward or your volley. Remember: drive, drive, drive, hug the ground, split step, volley, recover.

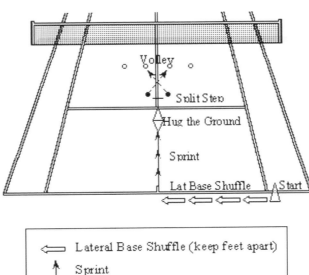

2. **Wide-ball drills**—This drill will improve the efficiency of your recovery from a wide ball. Remember, square up, cross over, and base (or keep the feet apart as you do in your split step).

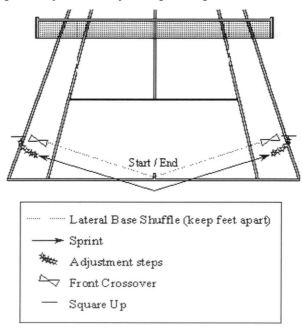

3. **Close proximity drill**—The goal is to develop the ability to move with balance and fluidity in your comfort zone. Start the drill by standing on the center mark and in the middle of four cones approximately four yards apart. Move as if you were going to step up and hit a forehand. Do the same for the backhand, the defensive forehand (pushing back gaining depth), and the backhand. After you have achieved mastery, the coach may progress the drill by randomly pointing to one of the cones. Always return to the center mark.

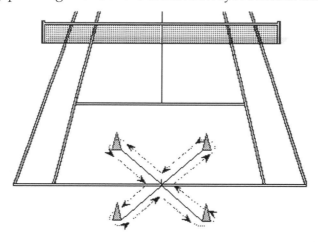

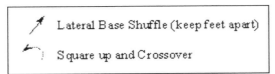

4. **Lateral shuffle**—Keep your feet wide apart, keep your hips low to the ground, and maintain a strong balanced posture as you move. The following photos illustrate both a good and a poor lateral shuffle.

5. **Front Crossover**

Energy System Development

Traditionally, energy system development (ESD) training for tennis has been accomplished through running long, slow distances for cardiovascular fitness. Although this practice improves the cardiovascular system, it tends to become stale and can slow the nervous system. IPI employs a different approach to ESD training for tennis. As mentioned earlier, tennis is predominantly anaerobic rather than aerobic. Therefore, to be specific to tennis, IPI trains anaerobic intervals specific to the work-to-rest ratio of a tennis match. This training has a secondary benefit of improving aerobic power without having to spend additional time. IPI's top three ESD training activities follow. Work-to-rest intervals may vary to give the desired results.

1. **Three cone:** Align three cones as follows: cone 2 above cone 1, cone 3 to the right of cone 2. Start at the first cone, sprint to the second cone, and touch the line. Return to the starting point and touch the line. Then sprint around the second and third cones in a figure-8 pattern, running outside the second cone and finishing where you began.

2. **5-10-5:** Align three cones in a row—cone 1 on right, cone 2 in middle, cone 3 on left. Start at the middle cone. Using a crossover step, sprint to cone number 1 and touch the line. Then cross over and sprint to cone 3. After touching the line at cone 3, cross over and finish by sprinting through the starting point.

3. **Circuit:** Using a bike, treadmill, versa-climber, and jump rope, complete the exercises in a circuit fashion using intervals of 12 seconds of work and 24 seconds of rest. Variations of equipment and work-to-rest intervals can be manipulated to achieve the desired result.

Strength

Strength is a critical part of tennis. Although we can identify as many as 15 different types of strength, we will generalize ours to two main headings—stabilizing and propulsive strength. Stabilizing strength uses a number of little muscles that act to hold everything in an optimal position so that the body can function efficiently, much as guide wires act on a suspension bridge. The development of these muscles is critical to keeping the body healthy through proper alignment, thereby allowing the body to function optimally. Players should try to maintain proper alignment in everything they do, from tennis practice and physical training to everyday activities.

Propulsive strength refers to a tennis player's ability to accelerate and decelerate. Fine sports cars are evaluated by the same characteristics. How quickly can the car accelerate from 0 to 60 miles per hour? How quickly can the car brake to a stop? Tennis players use these abilities with every serve. Acceleration develops great racquet speed. Just as important, deceleration slows the racquet and arm so that the arm doesn't rip out of its socket. Thomas Muster displays these qualities in every point he plays. He accelerates to run down a wide ball, hits his shot, stops on a dime, and springs back to the center mark. To be powerful and strong, one does not need the physique of a bodybuilder. Most bodybuilders are not especially strong given their body weight. If one wants to be a top tennis player, every pound of body weight must be quick and powerful, having the characteristic known as high relative strength.

Stabilizing

1. **Supine hip extension:** Bridge your torso parallel to the ground for three seconds.

2. **Supine lateral roll:** Roll left until only your right shoulder blade rests on the ball. Roll right and continue.

3. **Plate crunch:** Grasp a 10-pound weight, drape your back over the ball, perform a crunch, and hold it for three seconds. Advanced: use a 25-pound weight.

4. **Prone knee tuck:** Roll the ball up under your hips so that you're balancing on the tops of your toes. Hold for a few seconds. Advanced: use one leg.

5. **Supine floor bridge leg flexion:** With your calves on the ball and your shoulders on the ground, curl your legs and roll the ball toward you until the soles of your shoes are on it. Hold for a few seconds. Advanced: use one leg.

Propulsive

1. **Alternate dumbbell bench press:** Lift one weight as you lower the other.

2. **Split squat:** With a straight back, drop the trailing knee almost to the ground. Do all repetitions on one leg before switching.

3. **Dumbbell pull-over extension:** Hold weights straight up in the air, lower them to your ears, and then lower them toward the floor. Lift to the starting position to finish one rep.

4. **Romanian dead lift:** Folding at the hips and with the back straight, lift the barbell to your waist. Then lower the barbell, keeping it close.

Prehab

Prehab is a proactive approach to heading off the most predominant injuries in sport. Tennis is a one-sided rotational sport, and players often begin training at a young age. The appearance of most tennis players reveals that playing the sport forces the body to make physical adaptations. It becomes stronger on one side within all movement planes, from right to left and from front to back. This imbalance occurs in areas of the legs, hips, low back, abdomen, shoulders, and all the way out to the forearms. If this circumstance is not addressed, the athlete may have to compensate biomechanically, predisposing him or her to several kinds of injuries.

1. **Shoulder combo:** Perform these four exercises using no more than five pounds. Point your thumbs down and raise your arms in a V shape. Starting with your arms at the side, raise your arms to shoulder height and shrug. Bend over with your back flat, point your thumbs out, and raise your arms to the side. Starting in the same position, lift bent arms out to the side and rotate arms outward.

(continued)

2. **Lying opposites:** Face down, lift one leg and the opposite hand. Return to the ground and lift the opposite side.

3. **Protraction:** In a push-up position, pinch your shoulder blades together and apart.

4. **Retraction:** Same as protraction, but hanging face up.

5. **Depression:** From a dip position, let your shoulders touch your ears and then push away.

Recovery

Recovery, or regeneration, is one of the most neglected factors in trying to achieve peak performance. A critical factor in the performance of our athletes is their ability to recover quickly. The sooner and more completely they recover, the sooner the next quality training session can begin. Training is the stimulus, but the recovery period is when the athlete adapts and improves. What the athlete does during periods of recovery and regeneration can directly affect the quality of the individual's training. At IPI we employ numerous techniques to facilitate the recovery process. Regeneration permits more rapid recovery between workout sessions, which allows the athlete to feel better day to day, prevents overtraining, and maximizes the benefits gained through the training sessions. Listed below are four simple yet important tips for recovery and regeneration.

Nutrition

One of the most important and complex aspects of training is nutrition. To put it simply, nutrition can make a good athlete great and a great athlete good. Here are the top five tips for nutrition, offered as a way to make a long story short:

1. Eat consistently: One needs to eat five to six medium-size meals or snacks each day (once every three hours).
2. Build the meal with glycemicly correct carbohydrates. Eat low-glycemic carbs throughout the day while incorporating a lean protein source. This diet will keep energy levels up throughout the day.
3. Eat high-glycemic carbs plus a protein *immediately* (within 10 minutes) after intense exercise. The carbohydrate-to-protein ratio should be 2:1.
4. Stay hydrated!
5. Remember that vitamins do not give you energy. The body uses them to help convert food into energy. In the morning take a multivitamin, an antioxidant complex, vitamin C (500 milligrams), and vitamin E (500 milligrams). At night take all of the above except the multivitamin.

Flexibility

Immediately after training, when the muscle is warm, is the best time for various forms of isolated stretching. There are several types of stretching: active isolative, contract-relax, contract-assist, static hold, and others. Regardless of the technique you use, you should stretch the following muscles, which are commonly tight in tennis players:

Calf—bent leg, straight leg

Hip flexors

Hamstrings

Hip rotators

Torso rotators

Shoulder

Internal rotators

Posterior cuff

Triceps and inferior rotator cuff

Forearm

Massage Stick

IPI has found that the massage stick can be a great tool for the regeneration process. The purpose of the massage stick is to increase flexibility, enhance blood flow to the treated area, and break up trigger points (knots in the muscle). Another purpose is to soothe muscle tension so that tight muscles or muscles that are in spasm can relax. The massage stick routine is quick and easy and takes 6 to 10 minutes. IPI recommends the massage stick produced by RPI of Atlanta (1-800-554-1501).

Hydrotherapy

Used frequently by IPI athletes, hydrotherapy is a great way to facilitate the recovery process. After finishing a workout and getting the proper nutrition, head directly for the pool. In the pool, perform some leg swings and swim around at a light pace. This routine helps the body rid itself of the waste it produced during the training regimen. A hydrotherapy session will make you feel better for the next training session. Another type of hydrotherapy is called contrast hydrotherapy. Alternating between hot and cold will have the same effect. You can accomplish this with a hot tub and a pool or just with a shower. Spend three to four minutes in the hot tub first and then one minute in the cold. Repeat this five times, ending in the cold one (Rosenfeld 1996).

Summary

This chapter expressed ideas and thoughts on various types of training. These methods were derived from the experience of IPI in training world-class tennis players. The key elements to a successful program are planning, mastery, and progression. Each program is outfitted to meet the specific demands of tennis; thus these demands must be examined. Injuries, metabolic demands, biomechanical demands, type of surface, and style of play are the areas that are studied to determine how the training should be constructed. To achieve full potential, one must do a great job in technical, tactical, and physical development, both on the court and off. Training for tennis will allow the player to attack the limiting factors. This program is a generalized start in the right direction to achieving tennis goals.

References

Balyi, I. 1996. "Planning for Training and Performance, the Training to Compete Phase." *Australian Strength and Conditioning Coach* 4 (1): 3–9.

Kibler, W., and T. Chandler. 1994. "Racquet Sports." In *Sports Injuries: Mechanisms, Prevention, and Treatment*, edited by F. Fu and D. Stone. Baltimore: Williams & Wilkins.

Marcello, B. 1998. "Effects of Ballistic Resistance Training on the Bat Velocity of the Division I Female Softball Player." Unpublished master's thesis, Marshall University.

Rosenfeld, I. 1996. *Dr. Rosenfeld's Guide to Alternative Medicine.* New York: Random House.

Verstegen, M. 1998. *Adidas Training for Sport.* Video.

Verstegen, M. 1998. "Integration of Speed Development in Soccer." *Performance Conditioning for Soccer* 5 (5): 5–9.

Verstegen, M. 1996. "Warm-Up and Flexibility for Football." *American Football Quarterly* (September).

CHAPTER 12

Mental Training

> "When I step onto the tennis court, whether positive or negative thoughts are on my mind, I try to keep focused on the game."
> —Bjorn Borg

The circular relationship between parent, student, and coach can be difficult. Although I have been a coach for more than four decades, I will attempt to be neutral in addressing my thoughts on the responsibilities of each.

At the outset, it should be clear to all involved that the relationship between parent, student, and coach is sensitive. Each must enter this arrangement with the knowledge that communication, patience, love, understanding, and tolerance must be the operative qualities if the desired result is to be achieved.

To the Parent

Parents bring an interesting perspective to the relationship. Parents often refer back to their childhood, when things were less complicated. Children could walk to school, go to the movies, and go outside at night without fear. This is a different time. Your family values may be the same, and your expectations of your children may be similar to what your parents expected of you, but the world around you is more dangerous and unpredictable. You must listen to your kids more, spend more time with them, and attempt to have open, no-holds-barred conversations.

Put yourself in their place and try to remain open to their feelings about the sport. They are brighter and more aware of their surroundings than kids were 30 years ago. They have to be! When you select a coach, make sure that you do serious research on that individual. Be sure that the coach's background includes notable accomplishments with children and that the coach places no undue pressure on students to achieve. Once you have chosen your child's coach wisely, step back and enjoy the experience. Demand only that the child perform up to his or her ability every day. Remember that you are creating the way in which your son or daughter will deal with your grandchildren. Your children need you more than they realize. In a few years they will be off managing their own lives with the fundamentals you have provided.

To the Student

The student reading this chapter should refer to it periodically. You will spend a significant portion of your youth learning who you are. During this learning process you will be socializing with others who are also preoccupied with learning about themselves.

Recreational activities are exciting and provide an opportunity to let off steam. If you plan to excel at a sport, you will have to meet certain requirements if you want to reach your potential. The same can be said of life. In sports, as in life, success usually requires an educator, a willingness to learn, and ability to focus on a task.

At times your parents will question you, provide their input, and become involved in a big way. My advice to you is simple—be honest and open to both parents and coaches. Communicate!

To the Coach

Accept it or not, the days of your old-fashioned one-hour lesson for each student are over, and for a good reason. You are no longer just a coach. You are a surrogate parent, mediator, peacekeeper, publicist, and motivator. Add one more term to the equation—children need your input more than ever.

If you are half as good at building relationships as you are at teaching tennis, your student will be a winner.

They are young and inexperienced, trying to survive in a new millennium—an age of fast computers, fast cars, fast feet, and absentee parents. Such formidable obstacles would turn back many adults. Don't put aside your principles. Spend more time listening. Children deliver subtle messages. In many instances, those messages are questions you can answer. Be grateful you were chosen to help provide guidance to the child. Accept the challenge and have a positive effect on this young life. But remember, you can't do it alone. You need the cooperation and support of the parents.

Complex Circular Relationship

This complex, tension-filled relationship between student, parent, and coach sometimes defies understanding. But what realistic alternative exists? The youth of today need help just to pass into adulthood. It is inconceivable that conflict could exist over the details of saving a life. But first, let's define the problem.

Of the nearly 1 million students enrolled in the New York City school system, over one third—nearly 340,000—dropped out before receiving a high school diploma. Teacher-to-student ratios were 1 to 623. Sixteen hundred assaults occurred inside school buildings. As frightening as these statistics are, the dropout rate in some other American cities is even higher than the 34 percent rate in New York. American prisons are full, and the number of drug addicts and homeless men and women wandering the streets is growing at an alarming rate. Inadequate education, little or no appreciation for the value of education, low levels of self-esteem, and lowered expectations are the fundamental causes of this decline in the values of American youth. We must address these problems before our children reach high school. Social scientists agree that dropout rates continue to climb because of the decreasing influence of parents on the daily lives of their children.

The situation is complicated by a growing number of latchkey children, a group created by the need for both parents to contribute to household income. America's children are receiving televised megadoses of sex, crime, and violence while their parents are at work. In essence, the standard has been lowered. Television glorifies sex, crime, and violence, and an increasing number of children are committing crimes, including mass murder.

Anthony Robbins, world-renowned author and motivational speaker, has devoted his life to motivating adults who are seeking increased personal productivity. He and I both feel that it is important to create self-esteem in our children before they become so dysfunctional that psychological intervention is required.

This introduction has highlighted the enormity of the problem facing youth in America and around the world. If we can establish a realistic perspective, then disagreements among parents, students, and coaches become insignificant. Considering that most junior athletes never sign a professional contract, we should make it our main priority to establish a proper foundation for growth into adulthood.

The Coach

A coach or tennis teacher is much more than a teacher of tennis. At one time or another, a coach needs to be a mother, father, friend, foe, guide, leader, and psychoanalyst. The student must know that the coach feels every win and loss, but at the same time the coach must be more detached than a parent, especially in the face of a loss. When a student loses, the coach should maintain, or even increase, the student's motivation by pointing to specific things the player did well in a losing effort. Besides being an expert in tennis, a coach is fundamentally a surrogate parent with more objectivity than a real parent. A good coach needs to learn the idiosyncrasies of the student and know when to be positive and when to be negative. Certain students need to be hit over the head with a hammer; others can be spoken to quietly. Because the pupil and coach usually establish a close relationship, parents shouldn't expect their child to come home happy from every lesson.

Overall, the relationship between pupil and coach should be smooth, happy, and enjoyable for the child. A child will grow to be fond of his or her coach and will trust the coach in all matters concerning tennis. A child will see the coach as the ultimate tennis authority. This perspective can sometimes lead to problems between parents and the coach, especially if the parents have definite ideas about their child's tennis career.

Relationship Between Parents and Coach

Parents and coach must forge a working relationship to benefit the child. If they can't come together, the pupil will suffer. This union is often complex and burdened with unusual conflicts. Parents often stubbornly think that their child can do a lot more. Many are unwilling to admit that their child is limited in a particular sport. To accomplish what is best for the child over the long term, the relationship between coach and parents must honest and forthright. The coach must be willing to provide an honest evaluation of the pupil's likelihood of success. A parent will appreciate hearing that a coach believes the student will likely make the high school team. A coach also must be able to say that with a lot of hard work, the student might be able to play college tennis, but that the possibility of a college scholarship or a professional career is remote. Along with honest communication, parental noninterference is an important ingredient to a flourishing relationship. Parents who have selected a professional to guide their child, even if only through a one-hour lesson each week, should show trust and confidence by giving the coach a chance to succeed. Parents must allow the coach time to produce the proper techniques, footwork, or whatever it takes to make the child a player.

Parental Guidance

The greatest error parents can make is to voice expectations for their child beyond having a good time. As soon as a child begins to play for a parent's approval or to maintain harmony in the family, his or her motivation and fun will diminish instantly, no matter how talented the player is. Many young players with potential have been turned off tennis by their parents. Some great talents have been destroyed in the process. Unfortunately, in tournament circles one often hears that "Susie has super talent, but her parents put too much pressure on her. She just gets too uptight to win."

Parental pressure can take many forms. Parents may force a child to practice, take lessons, or compete in a match. An insidious by-product of parental expectations can be excessive criticism of a child's efforts. A child shouldn't be made to feel that every mistake will be thrown back at him or her. It's hard enough to go through the agony of playing badly.

Psychologically, human beings learn just as well, if not better, from positive support as they do from negative reinforcement. It is more helpful to tell a child what he or she did well and suggest what to try in the future than to belabor what went wrong and what not to do. Even after the most disastrous days, parents can say something positive, such as, "I guess you didn't play well today, but I liked the way you kept trying," rather than, "You really played badly today." A child's coach is responsible for the tennis technique, but parents can help create mental well-being. Making unflattering comparisons between a child and his or her peers can damage a child's motivation. Remember, every child is unique and learns at an individual pace; each child's progress is unrelated to anybody else's and should be gauged only against itself.

More important than the establishment of work patterns is how the child feels about himself or herself. Whether a child feels like a winner has little to do with the scores. Rather, the approval the child wins from parents for the effort has everything to do with feelings of self-worth. It is difficult for a child to differentiate between having a bad tennis day and being a bad person. So when a parent criticizes a child for being a bad player, that child may feel that the parent thinks he or she is bad. Tennis in childhood can help form later work habits, and more important, it can help develop the elusive quality of self-esteem. A great deal of that responsibility lies with the parents.

My message to parents and coaches is to consider these issues and make sure that the long-term well-being of the child is your driving motive. Recognize that the coach becomes part of the family. Tennis provides countless benefits. Those disagreements about stroke techniques are insignificant in the larger scheme.

Stimulating the Growth of Tennis in America

If you had a free hand, someone once asked, how would you stimulate the growth of tennis in America and develop players to their highest potential?

That's the wrong question. Ask me how to redirect the lives of America's children. Forget about tennis, baseball, basketball, football, and soccer. Every day our kids have to cope with the issues of drugs, alcohol, violence, and preadolescent sex. Parents can't find affordable day care. In too many cases, our youth are being raised by their grandparents. Our municipal recreation centers are closing or reducing their programs because of a shortage of funding. First, let's address the crippling social problems our children face every day. Then, armed with positive self-images and programs that produce successful experiences, America's children will excel at sports, in business, and, most important, in life.

For me to have a chance at success I'd want a five-year, no-cut, no-buyout contract. That's a bold demand. But complex problems demand complex solutions, and I wouldn't want to be interrupted halfway through the process by petty jealousies and power struggles that have a way of ruining the best plans. Of course, the added benefit of a long-term contract is that the kids experience continuity. America's children have grown accustomed to programs that go away. Programs are established with the promise of helping many youngsters, and then the programs disappear at the end of the summer. This happens every year in communities all across the country. The kids don't expect continuity. As a consequence they don't commit themselves to the program.

Tennis has developed in all sorts of ways, including the technological improvements of racquets, balls, court surfaces, and so on. Attempts to improve players' mental outlook has also been part of this development. Our academy has a separate sport psychology department. Working closely with this department I have produced a CD set. The first set focuses on ACE (attitude, concentration, and effort). The second CD set focuses on MAP (motivation, activation, and pressure).

What Can We Do?

I am associated with a child-development program produced by the New Millennium Company. This program systematically develops the physical and mental skills of youngsters to produce superior athletes. A by-product of this process is that the discipline acquired will spill over into other areas of children's lives.

This program develops the psychological, social, intellectual, physiological, and motor skills of preschool children. Luis Mediero, a USPTA master professional living in Spain, and I have collaborated on the development of this unique program. The program has the endorsement of more than 30 psychologists, 15 physiologists, 8 pediatricians, and a European association of kindergarten teachers. The games and exercises are designed to create skills and to ensure success. In the beginning, the program would consist of easy exercises integrating the process of bringing kids (aged 3 to 9) into the world of sports and, coincidentally, help them discover the joy of balance, general coordination, spatial orientation, catching, throwing, and kicking. The program includes individual participation, team training (any member of the team may score), and a new concept that we call circuitous training, meaning that all the youngsters on a team must participate in a point in order to score. Children learn many physical and social skills using these techniques, but most important they learn to become socially responsible teenagers and adults. The younger the child, the easier it is to succeed at the game. We use sports equipment such as bats, tennis racquets, soccer balls, and hockey sticks so that the children become familiar with the spatial skills required to strike a ball or hockey puck or carry a ball on the face of a tennis racquet. We initially maintain a mass teaching, team concept and make sure that the kids can never feel personally responsible for failure. Statistics show that early success in children increases concentration, lengthens attention span, and decreases behavioral problems. Today's kids have a fear of failure, suffer from poor self-esteem, and possess a depressed sense of self-fulfillment. Children must learn that losing is always a possible outcome, so they must learn to lose with poise and grace. They must learn to seek other tactics leading to a successful result (to change a losing game). All these skills have proved to be transferable from sports to life, and they help youngsters address real-life adversity.

Where Would These Games Be Played?

Implementing this program does not require a major construction project. My program is a turnkey, one-stop developmental program for children, complete with net, balls, blocks, bars, and hoops. The package is sufficiently affordable that every school, day-care center, recreation center, and family in America can own one. A creative mind can find space anywhere—in family garages, family rooms, backyards, school parking lots, lunch rooms, classrooms, day-care centers, or gymnasiums, indoors or out.

Many people ask me, "Am I to understand that you would not begin by teaching tennis to these children?" That's absolutely correct! The tennis court is too big, children can't hit the ball, they can't keep the ball in play, they experience frustration and failure, and then they quit. My program allows children to learn how to perform sports activities by experiencing attainable exercises, social interaction, and loads of fun! Notice that the program focuses on the issues of children, of tilling the soil in which world-class tennis players can grow. Why attempt to develop a tennis player out of a child so crippled by the environment that he or she can't be socialized?

When these kids finally begin to learn tennis, golf, or basketball, they will be prepared mentally and physically for the challenges of competing. The various governing bodies of sports have never attacked the real social issues that prevent our kids from experiencing normal growth. In fact, our society as a whole has failed to address these issues adequately. Consequently, we have produced neither tennis players nor functional, productive adults.

Sure, I could change the condition of tennis, baseball, basketball, and soccer in America, and it wouldn't take me long. In 5 to 10 years I'd have several world-class athletes and an even greater number of world-class American citizens and college graduates with high-energy work ethics.

Cheating

Buried deep within the old saying, "Winning tells something of your character, but losing tells all of it," lurks the psychological cause of cheating. Make no mistake, cheating is not a modern phenomenon. Plato, the ancient Greek philosopher, recognized this human weakness by observing that "You can discover more about a person in an hour of play than in a year of conversation." Over the course of human evolution, why have many of us come to believe that cheating is a reasonable way to avoid defeat? Why have youngsters become convinced that they must win at all costs? Why have they been led to believe that they are OK only if they win? Are they afraid that a loss will disappoint those who love and support them? And how do we begin the process of rebuilding the self-esteem and character of our youth so that they may better serve themselves and humanity in their adulthood?

Clearly, this problem has been around so long that it will not be resolved quickly. Parents, educators, and role models have a huge responsibility. We must address the root causes of cheating because these issues are steeped in poor self-esteem and a lack of self-respect that will not serve our children well in adulthood. We must stress the value of having integrity, the quality that places more importance on effort than result. We must assure our kids that heroes and winners who cheat are frauds. As General Colin Powell put it, "The healthiest competition occurs when average people win by putting in above-average effort."

Those who would teach kids when and how to cheat don't deserve the power that has been given them. They have been entrusted with the responsibility to mold the values that our children will use as adults. They have been given the authority to provide for the emotional direction of children's lives. They have been offered an opportunity to provide nutrition for the minds of young people and then have fed them poison. As surely as small doses of poison will steal the lives of children, learning to win by cheating will steal their futures. Parents, if you or your tennis pro tolerates or encourages cheating, you are both guilty of preventing your child from enjoying the true benefits of this wonderful sport. God gives every bird its food, but He doesn't throw it into the nest. Let your child know that he or she must work hard for victories and compete with integrity. Children must be reassured that, in the final analysis, cheaters lose.

When Frustrated Perk Up Your Play

"I'm not getting any better." "It's boring to lose match after match . . . I can't hit with any power." "I'll never be able to hit a slice serve . . . I'm frustrated." Lame excuses like these are chasing many adult tennis players into early retirement. I reject these retirement papers! With a few simple pointers, all of you can improve and enjoy the game within your own style of play.

Get in Shape!

You may not want to admit it, but the single most important aspect of your life is staying in shape. This holds on court and off. Your strokes do not break down as often as you think. Problems with certain strokes can usually be traced to positioning, footwork, or failing to get to the ball. Bjorn Borg said it best and proved it on the court: "There is no substitute for mobility."

Mobility is something you can work at. Learn to arrange your schedule. Most people waste at least an hour a day. You do not even need that much time to improve your physical condition. Take a close look at your daily schedule and see if you can spend less time on the telephone. Try turning off the television from time to time. Take 30 minutes for lunch instead of an hour. Go to bed earlier. To work in peace and quiet, get up earlier.

You owe it to your health (and your tennis) to set aside a few minutes each day. Once you find the time, it is not that tough to get in shape. If you can attend aerobics classes or Nautilus sessions, or work out at home, fantastic. But if you do not have the time or cannot afford such things, don't panic. You can do plenty of simple activities that require little time or money.

Take a few minutes each day to jog, swim, ride a bicycle (even a stationary bicycle), jump rope, take a walk, or use the stairs instead of the elevator. You can do simple stretching exercises, push-ups, sit-ups, and other exercises at home to shape up.

Develop Your Mental Game

If you want to improve, work on the mental part of your game. Like any athlete, you have to concentrate. Make it a point to block out the office, the kids, and plans for weekend. By concentrating on the moment, you'll play better. The old saying "Work hard, play hard" applies. Keep the two separate, and both will improve.

Have a Goal or Two

If you are going out to practice, have a plan of what you want to work on. Don't go out and just hit. Convince your playing partner that you'll get more out of the session by working on particular drills or rallying exercises. When you go out to play, have a few small goals in mind. Most important, don't judge everything by the result. Look deeper and analyze different aspects of your game to see what has improved and what needs more work.

Don't Let the Game Get to You

Keep tennis in perspective. The game should provide good exercise, fun, and healthy competition. If you start taking it too seriously and put too much pressure on yourself, you're not going to enjoy the game. Rather than releasing tension and working out your anxieties, you'll build frustration; essentially defeating the purpose of playing. The worst thing that can happen when you play a match is that you'll lose, but if you work up a good sweat and enjoy the competition, even a loss is a victory.

Take a Good Look at Your Game

After you have improved your physical condition and mental outlook, talk to a teaching pro. Do not be afraid to sign up for a couple of lessons on an aspect of your game that is giving you trouble. No pro should expect you to make big changes. You have your own style, and a good pro should help you within that style. If you find you are getting frustrated with a particular shot, get some help with it. If you begin feeling better about that shot and develop confidence in it, your whole game will improve.

Another solution might be to attend a tennis camp for a week or a long weekend. You will have a chance to get away from everything and concentrate on tennis.

You can also learn a lot by watching if you know what to look for. Don't try to imitate the strokes of the pros. Instead, concentrate on their footwork, determination, shot selection, strategy, and consistency. Everyone needs to work on these areas.

If you like tennis but are frustrated, give yourself a couple more weeks and try working on a few simple pointers. They will make a difference.

How to Become a Better Hacker

Don't be embarrassed if you fall into the hacker category. Hackers have proved you don't need great natural skills or beautiful strokes to have fun. Furthermore, many hackers walk away from the court with the balls in hand, the signal of a winner. Hackers seem to win more than they lose. But even a hacker can improve on imperfection. Here are some simple tips that will frustrate your opponent:

- Use the elements to your advantage. Hackers need to be smarter and more patient than their opponents. One way to illustrate your superior ability to concentrate is to use the sun, wind, and heat to your advantage.

Don't let the elements frustrate you. There is nothing you can do to change them. Accept the elements and learn to use them to frustrate your opponent. Lob into the sun, attack a weak second serve, hit against the wind, keep your opponent out there for long rallies on a hot day. These are ways that you can mentally and physically control a match.

- Recover. Don't make the mistake that too many "stylists" make during a match by standing and admiring the beautiful stroke you just hit. You've got a job to do. Get back into position and be ready for your opponent's return. Let your opponent watch his or her points. You'll be too busy winning points, games, and sets.

- Follow the hacker's motto. Winning means hitting the ball back one more time than your opponent does. If you concentrate on hitting high and deep with a wide margin for error, you will not only make fewer errors but also frustrate your opponent into making more unforced errors than normal.

- Be proud of your hacker heritage. Two of the sport's best hackers, former pros Harold Solomon and Eddie Dibbs, are also two of the game's richest hackers. If hacker is synonymous with winner, who cares!

- Play the percentages. You should accept the fact that you'll never be John McEnroe. Forget the glamorous ace. Get your first serve in. Place it to your opponent's weakness. If possible, eliminate the double fault from your game. You'll be surprised at how many times you'll hold serve. Resist the temptation to go for the lines or the flashy angles. Too often these attempts become nothing but impressive misses. Remember, the impressive miss that draws "Ahs" from the crowd is still a miss.

- Master the sissy shots. The lob and the drop shot win more matches in hacker tennis than any other shot or combination of shots. Moving forward and backward is tough and tiring. Put your opponent on a lob and drop-shot string and wear him or her down. Female hackers will find the lob and drop shots to be their biggest weapons. In junior tennis, these shots force rivals to concentrate more.

- Work on off-court conditioning. No matter how quick your step is, it's of little value if you're tired by the middle of the second set. You need more stamina than your opponent. Devote a small amount of time each day, or at least every other day, to some type of physical conditioning. Swimming, jogging, jumping rope, and bicycling are simple, fun, and relatively inexpensive exercises that improve your conditioning, your overall game, and, most important, your quality of life.

- Be a better hacker—go for every ball. Never hesitate—take a positive first step for every ball. You'll be surprised at the number of shots you'll reach. Because a hacker normally has few weapons for hitting winners, you have to be a backboard and run down everything.

- Enjoy the challenge. As the famed sports psychologist and former academy employee Jim Loehr says, "Learn to love the battle." The thrill of competition and meeting a challenge, rather than backing away, is what improves your chances of winning. It also helps you achieve your ultimate goal in tennis—to have fun.

How to Change a Losing Game

One of the most difficult tasks any tennis player faces when competing is how to change a losing game. Most good players are stubborn and tenacious. Unfortunately, this stubbornness often makes them stick with a losing game plan.

As an overall strategy for success, any winning plan should include a tactic that changes the rhythm of play, for at least a few games. Michael Chang, whose strength is from the baseline, is as adept at making this change as any of the world's leading players. When his baseline strategy fails, he invariably does his best to mix staying back and approaching the net, giving his opponent something to think about, something to distract his rhythm, something to derail a groove, something, anything, to disrupt momentum.

If this exercise is good enough for Michael Chang and other topflight pros, it's probably worthwhile for your strategy. Develop a game plan. Of course, you'll want to design it around your physical assets and mental capabilities but don't underestimate the importance of changing a losing game.

There is nothing easier than losing a tennis match. As anyone who has coached aspiring pros will confirm, tennis players can find any excuse to lose. I've heard them all—loose strings, cheating, crowds, not feeling well, any number of crazy excuses. Seldom, if ever, did a player lose and confide in me that he or she had simply played dumb or been outthought by the opponent.

While you are playing a game, it is never easy to understand why you're losing. But you can pick up some clues, and they are not necessarily the score.

Look to see how and why you're losing points. If you are netting the ball, then the change is simple—concentrate more on the ball than your opponent does, take the ball early, and hit the ball higher to take the net out of the equation. If you're hitting short and allowing your opponent easy put-away shots, hit the ball higher and deeper. If your opponent is hitting winning shots from everywhere on court, even though you're hitting deep and to the corners, you can't do much other than wait until your opponent cools off.

Much of this is simple, little more than common sense. The real art in changing a losing game comes when you're playing well, perhaps even at your best, and you're still losing. Assume for a moment that you have a character similar to Michael Chang's, that you are a focused player with strong resolve and a disciplined mind. You are a fit baseline player whose strategy consists of retrieving every ball until you wear your opponent down. Assume also that you're playing well. Unfortunately, so is your opponent, who happens to be fitter. If your opponent is fitter and you're both baseliners playing well, the odds are not in your favor. This would be an excellent time to change your tactics, perhaps throw in a few serve-and-volley points or storm the net when your opponent least expects it. If you're losing, you have nothing left to lose. The upside is that by disrupting your opponent's rhythm, you might upset his or her concentration. This circumstance may allow you to crawl back into the game.

If your opponent becomes flustered and the score turns in your favor, you have a difficult choice. You can return to what you're most comfortable with, or you can stay with the change. My recommendation is that you revert to your strengths and win or lose by doing what you do best.

The same is true if your preference is to serve and volley. Don't be so stubborn or stupid that you will not change a losing game. Try something different. Stay back a game or two, push if necessary (particularly if it's a temporary strategy), and all the while think of yourself as a winner.

The art of changing a losing game is to get inside your opponent's head and disrupt his or her concentration. If your opponent is distracted by your tactical change, then you've taken the first step to winning. Having tipped the balance in your favor, it's up to you to hold the momentum through the final point of the match. Do this and you've beaten your opponent physically and mentally. What could be more satisfying?

Be stubborn, practice hard, be disciplined, but don't let a losing game force you into the back draw, at least not without trying some degree of change.

Change a losing game and intensify a winning one. Following this advice will carry you well into the twilight of your game. Try it, and you'll be surprised at how easy it is to turn a potential loss into a satisfying win.

Kids Clutch Too

Take a cue from Jimmy Arias, Aaron Krickstein, Carling Bassett, and Pam Casale, all former tour players. Overcome your fear of failure. Every youngster has a method of dealing with the fear of choking. Jimmy Arias focuses on nothing but the match. Whether he is playing or sitting at a changeover, Arias concentrates entirely on what it will take to beat his opponent. This method relaxes him because he wants no intrusion during play. Pam Casale was the opposite. When she was nervous or uptight, Pam thought of her favorite song; it was her way of relieving the pressure. Carling Bassett took an altogether different approach. She felt she played her best tennis when her mind was blank. Carling preferred not to think about what she was doing. When Bassett thought too much about her strokes, she put more pressure on herself. Aaron Krickstein fought nerves by carrying on a running conversation with himself.

For juniors with less experience, I have some tips for winning the battle of nerves. Always think positively before, during, and after a match. Don't dwell on mistakes and don't fear weaknesses. Accept that mistakes are inevitable. At the same time try to correct some of your flaws. Turn negatives into positives. The same theory holds for the way you view your opponent. Don't fear your rival's strengths; exploit his or her weaknesses. Don't mistake excitement or butterflies for fear. Everyone becomes nervous. Meet your challenge and use your adrenaline in a positive way. Relax and breathe deeply in times of stress. Short, irregular breathing increases tension. Relax, slow down, clear your mind, calm your body, and concentrate on the job at hand.

The worst that can happen is that you'll lose. If you think about it, it's not so bad. Arias often imagines a defeat before he walks on court. As a result, he plays much looser. Keep your feet moving and hit out. When it gets tight, the first thing that happens is that your feet stop moving. You begin shortening your strokes and pushing the ball. Force yourself to keep moving when you become nervous. Exaggerate your follow-through. If you make errors, at least you will be playing your game, going for shots. Put more spin on your serve, more topspin on your forehand, and finish your strokes. Doing that should help you past the pressure points.

Work extra hard in practice. Get your strokes down cold so that when you are in a match, you have less to worry about. With confidence, hard work, and a positive attitude, you can avoid choking. But when choking does get the best of you, remember that misery loves company—you're not the only one out there who is nervous.

Staying Focused

Developing the ability to focus, to center or concentrate, can be difficult because you must filter out your normal awareness of the surrounding environment. People differ in many ways. I have been successful because I try to understand that people have different styles. Although we recognize different styles, let's see what factors are common to the majority. Having worked with thousands of children, adults, and athletes of all levels, including the best in the world, I will apply some of this experience to help your game.

- Monica Seles—For the most part, her focus stays on the tennis court and the tennis ball. It is unusual to see her eyes drift to the outside, even to glimpse her family or coaches.

- Mary Pierce—She finds a way to know where everyone is sitting. I remember Mary always asking where we would sit. Throughout the match, Mary would stop play if people were moving about or phones were ringing. She included gestures of either disgust or excitement with almost every rally.

- Michael Chang—Chang maintains complete court and ball focus, but he always looks to the umpire to change a close line call.

- Anna Kournikova—After every point she looks to her mother. The umpires always look to her box to see if there are any coaching gestures.
- John McEnroe—He argues consistently throughout his matches. Statistics show he was able to focus on the ball right after these outbursts and win 80 percent of the points. Many opponents felt he did this to break their concentration.

It is important for coaches to learn about their students' off-court behavior. By having that information, coaches can determine if their players are being consistent. In this regard I have had experiences with several top players.

- Boris Becker—To stay focused, Boris relieves frustration with controlled gestures of anger. For example, if he missed a shot, he slapped his leg and yelled some German phrase. Or he glared at the umpire, walked up to him, and let everyone in the stadium know that he was putting him on notice.
- Jimmy Connors—He puts on a complete television show with every point, every set, every match.

I could go on forever, but it all boils down to one factor: are you ready for the next ball, the next stroke, the next point, or whatever you are doing? Are your mind and body focused on being ready to get into gear without losing the edge?

I have learned many things from my students:

- What's happened is history. You have no control over the past.
- We are all human and subject to breakdowns.
- The most drastic penalty you can get is one point against you.
- Whatever thoughts you have in mind when you arrive for battle are out of your control until the match is over.

Realistic suggestions

1. Play against the ball only. Make the ball your best friend and never let it out of your sight.
2. Play simple games of catch to practice.

Fear of Competition

Throughout my experience, one factor has repeatedly come into play—many people do not like to compete because they fear losing. Children most fear competition because they fear losing and having to tell their parents the results. Some kids in doubles are even embarrassed to be on the losing side.

Some say that players who are not prepared fear competition. This is not entirely true because many people, no matter how well prepared, just don't like to play competitive games.

Competition lets you know whether you can apply what you work on in practice to matches. In life, success is measured by results.

Expectations can deter players from giving their best. Competition often changes people, especially when they must play in front of a crowd or with their parents looking on. Competition can completely alter a person's style of play and prevent the person from doing what feels comfortable or what he or she has practiced.

Excuses

I could write volumes about excuses. For the most part, excuses result from predicting outcomes. Legitimate excuses are certainly valid, but most are not true. They occur before, during, or after competition. Many excuses come from covering up losses. In this case, a coach needs information to complete a case history of the student. An excuse can be either a cop-out or a valid explanation. The coach must determine what is real and what is imagined.

On the tour, certain players' patterns are pretty much the same. People must be honest to help themselves in this area. Most are not willing to own up to certain patterns of behavior.

Pressure

Today we all face pressure just to survive. Many years ago, life just seemed to go on each day, and many of the social problems that exist today were absent.

Good communication is required to identify the different types of pressures for various students. Until this happens, little progress can occur. Pressure can come from yourself, outsiders (oral or by facial expressions), innuendoes, or by just being part of a specific activity (i.e., competition).

Everyone can improve in this area. First, you must accept reality. You must understand that to survive daily activities you have to stay involved. This is a starting point for finding ways to play the game and cope with pressure.

Although they use different words, all coaches try to express similar thoughts and values to their students. We could find a simple dictionary definition for each of these principles:

- Focus
- Competition (no fear)
- Excuses
- Confidence (building and maintaining, not losing)
- Attention
- Analysis

Once we have assembled these ideas, we can add more information based on our personal experience. The coach can consider different scenarios and see where certain students fit in. Doing this can identify helpful solutions.

Possible scenarios include the following:

- The student is or is not prepared in reference to practice sessions and technique.
- The student is or is not prepared mentally.
- The student is or is not prepared physically.
- The student likes or fears competition.

At this point, the coach has a good foundation of knowledge about a particular student. But the coach may need to consider other factors about a specific competition:

- College coaches may determine scholarships by an event.
- Agents may determine pro status or opportunities at an event.
- Parents may call the student and say, "This is the big one."

The way in which on-court practice sessions are conducted will also vary from student to student. Here is how I conduced practice with some of my students.

- Andre Agassi—Andre had to be treated like an F-18 Hornet with limited fuel in his gas tank. We had to vary the practice sessions to keep his interest. We always had to be careful about telling him that something was not right, especially if an audience was watching. We had to make adjustments without telling him what we were trying to accomplish. Whenever he was in trouble, we let him just hit the ball, using all his shots.
- Monica Seles—For our first practice sessions, we allowed people to watch. Within a short time, however, we took our sessions behind closed doors. I still remember the heavy canvas we had to use to cover the fence. Several times, high winds took the entire fence down.

Practice with Monica meant bringing lots of snacks and not scheduling other lessons after hers. She would stay for hours to work on just one shot. Drills would always have targets. We had to use two to four pros or hitters because she wore them out.

Ingredients for Success

The ingredients for success differ among students. Although their needs are different, we can identify some similarities. There are also some requirements for newly arriving enthusiasts.

To be successful, students should possess a strong sense of urgency to succeed. They should be prepared for our type of coaching, which is perhaps different from what they have previously experienced. Most important, they should be receptive to constructive criticism, discipline, and the constraints of time. Living away from home for the first time can affect life on and off court.

Besides having a strong desire to succeed, our students need to know how to get along with students from other countries. They must leave any ideas of racism or prejudice at home. The Bollettieri Tennis Academy is home to students from around the world, and each of them is part of our family. A family divided by petty prejudices cannot succeed. We don't ask our students to love one another, but we do expect them to respect each other's differences.

Being away from home for the first time can be challenging and emotionally difficult. Students arriving at the academy must commit themselves to the academy's rules and disciplines. Over the past 40 years, these rules have been crucial to our students' continued success. Students who feel that they know more about their needs than we do would be foolish to apply.

Off court, applying discipline is even more difficult. Although we have arranged a structure that makes it difficult for a child to go astray, those determined to abuse their new freedom can and do. The conclusions are never cheerful. We expel students who have discipline problems.

The combination of physical, mental, technical, and competitive instincts are the disciplines around which we develop an individual's game.

During each practice regimen we include all the training necessary to be successful. That training includes match play, performance training, and on-court drilling. Match play is supervised. We offer both technical and strategic criticism during the contest. We provide performance training for fitness, movement, and strength. We test each student on arrival and design a program to suit individual needs. Mental conditioning, or sports psychology training, is offered on court and in the classroom.

If the student is confident, aggressive, organized, and offensive, we design a game plan to fit those attributes. Conversely, if a student is disciplined, patient, orderly, and thoughtful, we design a program to fit that personality. This is our way of saying that each student is an individual even though we are oriented toward group dynamics.

How far can players go? In determining each player's potential, it's important first to establish the player's needs. Establishing long-term and short-term goals and determining how hard the individual is willing to work to get there is a major feature at the academy. Absent a crystal ball, it is impossible to predict the potential of any player. There are too many variables.

Our promise is to allow our students to be the best they can be. To reinforce this philosophy, we ask that they do everything possible to fulfill their commitment. Obviously, not every student succeeds, but those with the correct character mix usually fulfill their potential.

Some students who do not have the ideal character mix surprise us. They simply take longer to reach their goals. This is how it is in life, so we should not be surprised if this is how it is on court.

When Is My Child Old Enough to Play Tennis?

The best time to begin a child in tennis is when he or she is ready. Some children are ready at 4; others are not ready until they're 11. It is hard to attach a standard to such a serious issue. Parents too often push their children at a tender age. What often happens is that the child soon "retires" and never fulfills his or her potential. At the same time, many children who begin late by today's standards, at age 11 or 12, go on to have extended careers. I repeat: the time to consider a career in tennis for a child is when the child is ready.

Children often realize early success in team sports because coaches and positive peer pressure provide motivation. Tennis, on the other hand, takes time and patience. Early and easy success is an exception.

If a child does begin early, he or she should start by playing hand-eye coordination games. These games should be fun and allow the child to enjoy early success and learn the motor skills necessary for tennis success (i.e., footwork). Tennis is a difficult sport to master at an early age. If the games are enjoyable and the child gradually progresses, then I believe that 11 to 13 years of age is a good time to begin thinking seriously about a tennis career. By then the child will be old enough to determine if he or she wants to pursue the game for the right reasons.

Once a child has been introduced to the game, I feel that group lessons should take precedence. Our experience at the academy indicates that group dynamics and peer pressure can help a child decide if he or she wants to continue. Individual instruction is then helpful in expanding and fine-tuning a tennis game.

During this process, parents should provide the child with emotional, financial, and moral support. This is an important but often neglected part of a player's development. In the parent-child relationship, the role of each person must be clearly defined and strictly adhered to. Otherwise, the tennis parent can handicap the child's development.

Does this mean that parents should be excluded from participation? Quite the contrary. Often, parents sacrifice their homes and lives in support of their child's ambitions. When parents do this for the right reasons and within the proper framework, the sacrifice often breeds success.

Like Father, Like Son: Good Behavior Begins at Home

Tennis players handle on-court pressure in different ways. Some keep their feelings inside; others vent every emotion. This is normal; not everyone can be like Bjorn Borg, the picture of quiet concentration.

Self-control and concentration, however, go hand in hand. Most people who break their concentration through outbursts take several minutes to regain their normal thought process. When they play the next few points, what happened a few moments earlier continues to bother them. Sometimes, in a close match, these players never regain their composure, giving their opponents a psychological lift.

Ultimately, parents play the most important role in shaping a child's attitudes. Parents can observe a situation, explain what is acceptable behavior, and set a good example for a child at an early age. How you, as a parent, react, is crucial. It is often difficult to impress upon young players how bad behavior can seriously affect their game. Be patient. Make children understand how certain actions hurt and emphasize how they can achieve positive results.

Parents must develop a realistic dialogue with their children, stressing positive reinforcement. Instead of reprimanding the player, you should say, "I watched you today," and speak about some of the child's positive attitudes. Ask your child about problems he or she might have experienced. Without even realizing it, your child will admit that something went wrong. Then, you might say, "Why don't you and I come up with a penalty for this in case it happens again. Tell me what you would like to do. That way you won't lose three or four points because you've lost your temper." Let the penalty come from the child.

With Jimmy Arias, I tried to understand his point of view. I talked to him before a match, and he would say, "You know, Nick, a short outburst in practice gets me relaxed, and that's me. But, when I get into the tournament, I lose control." So I knew to give him some leeway in practice, which is helpful for anyone.

Still, you must stress the importance of self-control and enforce proper punishment from an early age. It may be necessary to take tennis away from a child for a day, a week, or a month, depending on the severity of the problem. This may sound harsh, but children will probably think twice before they let themselves get carried away. This sort of punishment could prevent more serious disciplinary problems later.

Here are a few guidelines to help you teach your child good behavior:

- Examine your own behavior in stressful situations. Are you setting an example for your child to follow?

- How do you react to your child's performance? My experience shows that a few positive statements pave the way for constructive criticism.

- How much time do you spend with your child? What your child learns from age two to five can shape lifelong attitudes.

- Do you look at your child objectively? Many parents are quick to defend their child's actions before they have realistically evaluated the situation. If your child was at fault, admit it and work with your child to make sure it's not repeated.

- If a pro works with your child, do you let the pro do his or her job? Parents should be concerned with what their child is learning, but if you have hired a professional, work with the pro to reinforce the lessons. If you have questions, talk them over so that you can work as a team.

- Last, be realistic with the standards of behavior you demand. Your child has enough pressure with school, tennis, and just growing up without trying to live up to unrealistic expectations. Asking your child to do too much can cause outbursts and tantrums.

Real Life

With school in session, less has to be more. Your kids have probably been on their own all summer, with plenty of time to train, practice, play tournaments, and relax. Now school bells are ringing, and they have to juggle training, practice, tournament play, and free time with the important demands of studying.

How can you do it? Try following these six pieces of advice.

1. Have your child take 7 to 10 days off from tennis when school starts. He or she should concentrate on getting into the routine of studying and attending class. Your child will get off to a good start in school and will be more eager to hit the courts, practice, and train when tennis begins again.

2. Take these 7 to 10 days to plan the fall, winter, and spring schedules. Accept the fact that less court time will be available and make the necessary adjustments. Set up a schedule to play early mornings, late afternoons, weekends, or evenings. Line up a practice partner for your child because court times will be limited in these months. To avoid wasting time, plan each practice. Step up off-court conditioning.

3. If your budget permits, you might consider a tennis camp or academy for an intense week of work before an important tournament. Participating in a camp is an excellent way to get ready for the big test. If the cost of securing court time or traveling to a tournament is a problem, perhaps your child could work at the club in return for court time, stringing, and so on. Planning tournament trips with others in your area can save on travel and hotel costs.

Schedule plenty of time to study. A good education is indispensable in today's world. Moreover, good study habits can have a positive effect on tennis. Concentration and dedication in school will parallel the approach your child should take to tennis and conditioning.

4. A child should learn to accept sudden schedule changes without becoming frustrated or disappointed. He or she will face adversity throughout life, in and out of tennis. Adjusting to simple changes in a routine can prepare the child to handle greater pressures ahead.

Remember that nothing is more important than maximizing time. Here is where the importance of practicing efficiently comes in. Most kids with plenty of time don't get down to business quickly because they know they have time to spare. During the school year, indoor court time will be limited. As a result, young players must practice efficiently to cover all parts of their game that need work.

5. Don't devote all of the available court time to drilling. Emphasize playing points. Play 10-point games in doubles with two service points by each player down the line. Playing indoors spoils players because there is no wind, no sun, and no blowing dust. Without sun and rain, the court always plays the same. Players should avoid becoming complacent about their play in these ideal conditions.

6. There is no reason why a group can't go to the courts at 6:00 every morning or work out from 6:30 to 8:00 on weekend mornings. Make a deal with management. Offer to clean the place and work on the restrooms from 8:00 to 10:00 in exchange for court time.

Finally, let me offer one more tip. If you had a great summer playing tennis regularly, don't let the cold weather frustrate you. You can still arrange for the fall season and work yourself into games at the club and the parks. Here's a suggestion. Plan to help with special luncheons and functions at the club once a month. Volunteer to bring the food and ask to trade your services for free court time.

Mental Efficiency Program*

By looking at the big picture you can recognize that tennis influences all aspects of your life, just as events in your life influence your tennis development. Consider yourself not only as a tennis player but also as a unique individual who exists beyond the game. Tennis can be a worthwhile part of growing up, a routine aspect of your life, and a favorite pastime. By taking a personal perspective, tennis will provide you with a range of personal development benefits.

---

*Adapted from "The Mental Efficiency Program: Positive Self-Development for Tennis, Sport, and Life," by Nick Bollettieri and Dr. Charles Maher (1984).

- Positive self-development involves making yourself more valuable.
- Personal awareness means knowing your current strengths, limitations, and needs for improvement as a tennis player and person.
- Self-motivation has to do with your desire to make progress and attain your personal goals. To enhance self-motivation, you can set specific and challenging personal goals.
- Self-confidence encompasses the idea of trusting yourself—playing tennis in a relaxed and controlled way, without overanalyzing what you are doing.
- Self-discipline is being able to start your training with a defined goal and to follow through, making necessary adjustments along the way.
- Your ability to experience quality interpersonal relationships occurs when you relate to individuals and groups in mutually beneficial ways.
- When you possess positive self-esteem, you view yourself as a unique individual, happy about who you are and what you do.
- Continuous improvement involves never being satisfied—always wanting to reach another level and be your best.

When you are mentally efficient, you remain balanced and in control. You are personally aware, self-motivated, self-confident, and self-disciplined. You enjoy quality interpersonal relationships, possess high self-esteem, and continually seek to improve yourself.

In this section, we discuss how you can acquire and develop personal qualities and acquire the abilities associated with mental efficiency in tennis. By developing the specific quality and ability in each area, you will contribute to your overall mental efficiency.

The more you involve the entire team—player, coach, and parent—the more quickly and effectively you will be able to become mentally efficient as both a tennis player and a person.

Becoming Aware of Yourself

Personal awareness refers to your ability to know yourself as a tennis player and as a person. You can develop your strong points even further. Developing a sound and thorough personal awareness will help you identify your strong points, limitations, and areas for improvement.

Be honest with yourself. You will be a better planner if you have a vision. Challenge yourself to be a better player. Focus on what is important and what you need to work on. You can obtain information about yourself by asking focused questions. The tennis skills inventory that follows is divided into mental and physical tennis skills. We recommend that you complete this inventory by yourself and then discuss it with your coach and others.

Tennis Skills Inventory

In the space to the left of each item below, rate your current level of skill development. Use this scale for each item:

1 = excellent   2 = good   3 = average   4 = fair   5 = poor

Ground-Stroke Play

____1. Forehand crosscourt

____2. Forehand down the line

____3. Backhand crosscourt

____4. Backhand down the line

____5. Backhand lob

____6. Forehand lob

____7. Forehand inside out

Transition Play

____1. Forehand approach shot crosscourt

____2. Forehand approach shot down the line

____3. Backhand approach shot crosscourt

____4. Backhand approach shot down the line

Net Play

____1. Forehand volley crosscourt

____2. Forehand volley down the line

____3. Backhand volley crosscourt

____4. Backhand volley down the line

____5. Overhead

Return of Serve

____1. Forehand in the deuce court

____2. Backhand in the deuce court

Specialty Shots

____1. Forehand angle crosscourt

____2. Backhand angle crosscourt

____3. Forehand drop shot

____4. Backhand drop shot

____5. Forehand touch volley

____6. Backhand touch volley

Serve

____1. First-serve flat

____2. First-serve slice

____3. First-serve topspin

____4. Second-serve slice

____5. Second-serve topspin

Style of Play

____1. Serve and volley

____2. Aggressive baseliner

____3. Baseliner

____4. All-court game

Mental Approach and Skills

____1. Setting personal goals

____2. Monitoring progress toward goals

____3. Wanting to play competitively

____4. Enjoying the game

____5. Believing I can create shots and strategy

___3. Forehand in the ad court

___4. Backhand in the ad court

Movement

___1. To the wide forehand

___2. To the wide backhand

___3. To the short forehand

___4. To the short backhand

___5. On volleys

___6. For overheads

___6. Concentration and attention

___7. Maintaining poise

___8. Preparing for matches

___9. Having quality practices

___10. Getting along with coaches

___11. Getting along with team-mates

___12. Not getting down on myself

___13. Committed to improvement

___14. Remaining motivated

With the physical fitness and condition rating scale, rate your physical fitness attributes—stamina, speed, strength, mobility, weight, and diet.

Physical Fitness and Condition Rating Scale

In terms of your physical strength and condition, consider the following categories—stamina, speed, strength, mobility, weight, and diet. For each item, rate yourself in the space to the left. Rate what you believe is your current level of development. Using this scale:

1 = excellent   2 = good   3 = average   4 = fair   5 = poor

Stamina

___1. Running

___2. Breathing

___3. Pulse rate

Speed

___1. First-step quickness

___2. Speed endurance

___3. Coping with tiring situations

___4. Quick recovery

Strength

___1. Muscle tone

___2. Endurance

___3. Power

Mobility

___1. Stretching

___2. Lunging

___3. Range of arm motion

___4. Joint flexibility

Weight and Diet

___1. Current weight

___2. Body-fat composition

___3. Prematch diet

___4. Nutrition during the match

___5. Postmatch diet

Rate your daily living activities and personal routines with the personal profile form that follows. Learn what has prevented you from doing as well as you would like in tennis or in other areas of your life. Identify your strong points. Determine areas that you need to develop. List your needs for development on the personal profile form.

Personal Profile Form

Name and date:

My current strong points are the following (specify physical and mental tennis skills, physical fitness and condition, daily living skills):

1.

2.

3.

4.

5.

My current needs for development are the following (specific physical and mental tennis skills, physical fitness and condition, daily living skills):

1.

2.

3.

4.

5.

Limitations that I need to address and rectify are the following (particular knowledge, skills, attitudes):

1.

2.

3.

4.

5.

I plan to discuss my profile with_____

Identify and determine your current personal limitations. Get an outside check on the accuracy of your opinions. A personal mission statement outlines what you want to do as both a tennis player and a person over the next two years.

Your mission statement should be broad-based and clear. It should not refer to external, self-centered achievements. A mission statement is for your personal use and benefit, not for discussion by others. Visualize yourself realizing your mission. Update your personal awareness profile two to three times a year.

Achieving Self-Motivation

When you are self-motivated, you have the interest and desire to attain important goals. The more aware you are of yourself, the more self-motivated you will be. Self-motivation means that you have taken personal initiative to set goals for yourself and do what is necessary to attain them. You do not want other people to be your primary source of motivation. Others can help you set conditions for improvement, but they can't make you take advantage of them. Your motive for action comes primarily from within, not from an external source.

Develop an increased focus on what is important both on and off the tennis court. When you are self-motivated, you have positive energy that helps you control all aspects of your training. Being self-motivated allows you to block out negative distractions. Being self-motivated will give you more physical and mental energy. Identify personal goals that have meaning to you. You will be able to remain self-motivated when your goals are ones that you can control. The driving force to attain a goal comes not from outside but from within. Create a master list of goals and select the ones especially important for you. Select enough goals so that you can stay focused and motivated.

Use the personal goals form to record your goals.

Personal Goals Identification List

Name_____ Date_____

Tennis skills goals:

Physical fitness and condition goals:

Daily living skills goals:

Personal Goals Form

Name_____ Style of play_____

Date goal set_____

Evaluation date_____

1 = excellent   2 = good   3 = average   4 = fair   5 = poor

Personal goals: Progress rating:

1.

2.

3.

4.

5.

Comments:

Select no less than three or four goals and no more than six or seven at any one time. Use this table as a sample for your goal statements.

Example of Personal Goal Statements in Various Categories of Tennis and Personal Development

Mechanical

To improve the accuracy of my first serve

To increase the percentage of my service return

To get more depth on my ground-stroke rallies

To win more first points in a game

To improve my fitness so that I can perform fully in long matches

To add variety to my second serve

Mental

To relax better on important points

To become more disciplined in preparing for my matches

To remain focused between sets

SMART goals have five characteristics found in the letters of the word *smart*.

Specific—You and your coach known exactly what the goal is.

Measurable—You and others can measure your progress toward the goal.

Attainable—You are able to make progress and attain the goal.

Relevant—By attaining the goal, you will have become a better tennis player; the goal is relevant to your development as a tennis player.

Time frame—You have a clear understanding of when you expect to attain the goal.

When setting goals, be specific. Specific goals convey information to both you and your coach. The more specific you can make a personal goal, the greater the chance you will be motivated by it.

Learn how to measure goals so that you can better follow through. Review your practice and match-play performance. Compare your ratings with those of your coach and determine similarities and differences.

Break down personal goals into simpler components if they become too complicated to accomplish. To attain goals, you must know what actions to take. Know and determine why your goals are relevant. Determine goals in terms of short-term and long-term attainability.

Discuss your goals with other people. Use others to give you feedback and monitor your short-term and long-term goals. Discussing your goals with other people is an effective way to get them involved positively in your game. Seek help, guidance, and ongoing support and monitoring by others. Learn to monitor your progress continually.

Establish a benchmark to know where you began to measure your progress. Determine your progress toward each of your goals. Knowing where you are and where you came from will allow you to measure your progress effectively. Know where you are heading. Be flexible and able to adjust your goals based on your progress. Learn to define and monitor the quantity and the quality of your practice and progress. Quantity refers to the number of times you practice. Quality refers to the effort you expend to achieve your goals. Making changes in goals is characteristic of the mentally efficient tennis player.

Visualization is a personal process involving the forming of mental images, or pictures, about your tennis performance. The more often you use visualization, the better your chances of being motivated to hit and execute a specific shot. Through visualization, you can put yourself in positive states of thought and emotion. Make the mental images relate to your goals. Make a list of your personal goals and the associated mental images. Describe the images on the positive image form.

Positive Image Form

Name_____ Date_____

Style of play_____

Images:

Situations when I will use these images:

Visualization should be scheduled, not random. Collect visual images of yourself that you can refer to for reference and reinforcement. Look at your still pictures and videos regularly. Add to your positive images throughout the tennis season. Positive affirmations will aid in maintaining motivation, help you concentrate on what you are trying to accomplish on court, and allow you to reestablish your focus if you lose it. Identify specific positive states that you want to attain as a tennis player. Write a positive affirmation for each specific positive state.

Positive Affirmations Form

Name_____ Date_____

Style of play_____

Positive states: Positive affirmations:

Situations when I will use these affirmations:

Building and Maintaining Self-Confidence

When you are self-confident, you believe in your ability to follow through and accomplish the goals set for yourself. With self-confidence, you are able to maintain poise and perseverance—two important indicators of a self-confident state. *Poise* is the ability to avoid becoming upset with yourself or with what is going on around you. *Perseverance* means being able to follow through with your plans no matter what the obstacles. When you believe that you can compete on the court with players of your ability level or better, your self-confidence promotes and sustains performance.

Trust yourself. Have faith in your training and ability. Balancing the mental and physical aspects of tennis allows you to reach your potential. Believing in yourself helps eliminate negative self-perceptions and feelings of failure, fear, and intimidation. Practice building and maintaining your self-confidence regularly. Make a personal commitment to yourself. Do not doubt yourself or your ability. Strive to improve and play your best.

You must be realistic, of course—you cannot be perfect. But you should challenge yourself to reach your best. Separate your performance in sport from your self-worth in life. Determine your own level of self-confidence.

Believe that you have the skills necessary to perform well or, if you don't, be able to develop them within your training program. Sport is dynamic. You will have to continually change, learn, and refine during development. Determine when you are and when you are not confident.

Tennis Self-Confidence Survey

Name_____ Date_____

1. When am I in a confident state (e.g., during practice, prematch warm-up, match play, other)?

2. In what aspects of my game am I usually confident (e.g., baseline play, midcourt play, net play, mental approach, serve, other)?

3. What is it that makes me confident?

4. When am I not confident?

5. In what aspects of my game am I not confident?

Determine which factors help you to be more confident and which factors hinder your confidence. Know your current skills. You must maintain skills by using consistent, high-quality practice habits. Conduct a routine inventory of your skills. Get opinions from others who are interested in your development.

Examine your skill levels. Appraise your situations and results realistically. You alone determine how you react and view a particular situation. You alone interpret the situations and events in your life positively or negatively. No one is perfect. Those who believe they are perfect approach life unrealistically and set themselves up to fail.

The first step to building self-confidence is acknowledging your mistakes. Try to reduce the frequency of making mistakes. Don't be adversely affected by things beyond your control. Focus on what you can control. Making every situation in tennis and life a learning experience is a healthy, positive way to approach sport and life. Put a particular situation into a fuller context to gain perspective. You alone control your ability to be (or not be) self-confident.

Learn to recognize and monitor three important senses—visual, auditory, and kinesthetic. Learn what factors inhibit or enhance your self-confidence. Learn to identify the situations in which you have the least amount of self-confidence. Once you have identified your low-confidence situations, recognize the feelings associated with them. Learn what negative statements you may be associating with a particular situation. Muscle sensations can also be identified and associated with particular low-confidence states.

Learn to monitor your senses during and before competitive play. Learn to use breathing to your advantage in practice and match play. Learning to regulate your breathing will increase your self-confidence. Use breathing to relax and eliminate negative, unproductive performance states. You need to control what you think and be able to detect differences in your muscle tension. Practicing progressive relaxation will help you learn how to control and relax muscles. Become aware of how your muscles feel when you are tense and how they feel when you are relaxed. Practice the progressive-relaxation procedure often.

Learn to control thoughts to improve your self-confidence. Negative thoughts can adversely affect your game mentally and physically. Learn to say no to negative thoughts. Focus your mind on a positive thought. Use the technique of letting go of negative thoughts. Remind yourself that you can control thoughts and make them positive.

Possessing Self-Discipline

Serious athletes are disciplined in their sport and in other areas of their lives. When you plan what you need to do to attain your goals and then follow through, making adjustments as required along the way, you are actively developing self-discipline.

Self-discipline involves following through on activities not directly related to your primary goal yet important to accomplishing it.

Personal planning offers several meaningful benefits. Being self-disciplined promotes positive, constructive thoughts and behaviors. Being self-disciplined provides positive reinforcement, allows you to use your time effectively, gives you a sense of self-control, and involves you in taking action and moving forward.

Make a commitment to developing a personal plan. A personal plan is a statement of the actions you will take to accomplish something. The implementation of a long-range plan for your tennis development will require you to be patient and to persevere as you make progress toward your goals. A game plan includes one or more specific goals to develop and implement during match play. Game plans involve the use of strategy and tactics.

A continuing education plan targets your development beyond and outside tennis. You can plan all the goals and actions for your tennis and your life. Decide which kind of goals will be part of your personal plan.

On the personal planning form (PPF), list the goals on which your plan will focus. Specify personal actions you will take. Establish a timeline for starting and completing the action.

Personal Planning Form (PPF)

Name_____ Date_____ Type of plan_____

People to discuss this plan with_____

Goals	Personal actions	Timelines	Comments

Make sure that you have a way of knowing that you have completed the listed personal actions. Describe any personal obstacles under the comments section of the PPF. List the people with whom you expect to discuss the plan. It is valuable to have others review and support your plan. Show another person your plan and discuss it in detail. Seek this individual's constructive criticism and comments about your plan.

Take a systematic approach to monitoring yourself. If you are not satisfied with how you have followed through, you can troubleshoot possible reasons. Use the information from your troubleshooting activity to make changes in your plan. Don't be afraid to make changes. Flexibility is an indicator of a self-disciplined approach. Find the most effective and efficient means to achieve your actions and goals. You may have to readjust the timeline for attaining a goal.

Self-reinforcement means that you do something positive for yourself. Compliment and reward yourself for a job well done and enjoy reinforcement from others. Reward yourself occasionally with something tangible or material.

A routine is a standard way of doing something that contributes to your overall effectiveness. Routines help you maintain self-discipline, a sense of balance, and order. A productive routine helps you follow through on your personal actions to attain your goals.

You can develop routines around life areas that are important to your daily effectiveness in tennis and school. You have the option of perceiving a situation as a challenge or as a source of stress. Assess your current routines in relation to the areas you have identified. Make changes in your routines as necessary. Evaluate the productiveness of your routines on a scheduled basis.

Routine Evaluation Form

Name_____ Date_____

For each item below, give yourself a rating in the space provided to the left of each item.

   1 = excellent   2 = good   3 = average   4 = fair   5 = poor

_____ Overall, I am able to manage my entire life.

_____ I devote adequate time to study, which allows me to be successful in school.

_____ I do not put off what I am supposed to do in school.

_____ I make sure that I am ready to train in a quality manner.

_____ I can prepare for matches efficiently.

_____ I am able to add appointments to my schedule without difficulty.

_____ I am able to say no to people when time does not permit.

_____ I do not take on more things than I can handle.

_____ I am able to plan a weekly schedule for my life.

_____ I spend quality time with family and friends.

You can use the process of visualization to help you remain a self-disciplined tennis player and person. Identify images of yourself functioning as a self-disciplined tennis player. Describe and write down these images. Visualize these images of effective self-discipline regularly. The more precise you can be about when you will use positive images of yourself, the more mentally efficient you will be. Use positive affirmations to support your self-discipline.

Maintaining Quality Interpersonal Relationships

In a quality interpersonal relationship, you gain benefit from another human being while providing that person with something valuable in return. You build a quality interpersonal relationship by respecting, trusting, and having a sincere interest in helping another person. If you want to accomplish something worthwhile in tennis and reach your personal best, you need the help of others. You should seek to develop quality relationships with all kinds of people yet know when not to associate with particular people. Having caring relationships with others fulfills a critical but often neglected personal need. When you are mentally efficient, you can address this need.

It is important to gain the cooperation of others. Helping others and being helped by others is a mutually profitable experience. When you respect others and yourself at the same time, you are more likely to enjoy playing tennis and practicing. By eliminating or reducing a self-centered approach to your existence, you can maintain quality relationships with many people.

Your personal network consists of all the people who are important to you and with whom you want to maintain contact. Identify the people with whom you want to maintain quality interpersonal relationships. Place the people in your network in categories and record that information so that it is readily accessible.

By taking the initiative, you can develop and maintain quality interpersonal relationships. Specify your needs and interests to people with whom you want to have quality relationships. Determine which needs your network of people can fulfill. Specify the needs and interests of the people with whom you want to maintain quality interpersonal relationships. By focusing your attention on the other person, you will avoid having a self-centered relationship. One way you can specify the needs of others is simply to ask each person what he or she expects from the relationship. Anyone will appreciate getting respect, a listening ear, help when needed, and compliments.

Assess the status of your relationships. Identify specific actions you need to take to improve each relationship. Feedback will come to you in many different forms, from different sources, and in a variety of circumstances. You will receive oral feedback and written feedback. You will expect some of the feedback you receive; other comments may come as a surprise. The way you accept personal feedback from others will influence future performance and the quality of your relationships. We suggest that you accept all criticism about yourself in a positive way. You can take or leave opinion for what it's worth, depending on the reliability of the source.

- Feedback can be positive and expected.
- Feedback can be positive and unexpected.
- Feedback can be negative and expected.
- Feedback can be negative and unexpected.

Make sure that you understand the feedback, no matter what type it is. Be a good listener. To maintain quality interpersonal relationships, you must give feedback to others. Do unto others as you would have them do unto you. Be specific and clear when providing feedback. Look for nonverbal signs. Provide additional information to the person.

When conflict occurs in an interpersonal relationship, try to manage it effectively. Conflicts between individuals often develop because the individuals involved are not aware of whether they are disagreeing over means or ends. A conflict can be a positive experience and a growth situation for the people involved. Interpersonal disagreement can happen in any setting. Discuss first the areas you agree on and then talk about those you disagree on. Discuss how you can reach an agreement. Restate the compromise as a personal action and follow through on it.

Developing Positive Self-Esteem

Self-esteem is what you think about yourself. You can think about yourself either positively or negatively. Judging yourself by things over which you have no control is setting yourself up for a negative situation. You need to know and believe that you are unique. You must be able to separate the quality of your performance from your overall worth as a person. You should be able to counter and eliminate negative ways of viewing activities in your life.

You can avoid developing a poor opinion of yourself, devaluing yourself as an individual, by practicing and following through on activities that develop and maintain your self-esteem. Your true value does not come from playing tennis. Make a determination to look at yourself in an accurate, positive way. It is important to have an accurate view of what you can and cannot do. Be realistic in what you attempt to do.

Usually, the way we make judgments about who we are comes from what people tell us about ourselves. It is important for you to engage in a variety of activities beyond tennis. You should use yourself, not others, as a basis for comparison. Be satisfied with small but steady gains in all that you do. You risk lowering your self-esteem if you maintain or create irrational beliefs about yourself. You have to be able to let go of self-defeating beliefs. You can be confident about being able to perform well while recognizing that you will never be perfect.

It is important to recognize your anxiety, accept it, and take steps to reduce it. Identify irrational beliefs and dislodge them. Personal awareness of your beliefs can help you dispel them. Substitute an appropriate belief for each irrational belief. Negative self-talk usually leads to lowered self-esteem. Positive self-talk means that you make statements that put you in a favorable light. If you routinely employ positive self-talk, you are likely to be positive about yourself and will enhance your self-esteem. Identify and list the various situations in which you examine how you talk to yourself.

Self-Talk Assessment Form

Name_____ Date_____

Situation	Self-statement	Rating (+/-)	Personal action

For each situation you list on the form, describe the statement you made to yourself. When you are practicing or playing in matches, you can foster positive self-talk by substituting the positive for the negative. Self-esteem has to do with unconditional acceptance of yourself despite mistakes you feel you have made. Change the perspective that you have about the mistake. View a mistake as a signal to yourself. Mistakes occur for everyone all the time—that's part of life. Learn from each mistake and move forward.

Committing to Continuous Improvement

Continuous improvement means being personally committed to using information about your progress and performance in tennis and other areas of your life. If your personal growth is in motion, it will remain in motion until some external force stops it. If it is at rest, it will remain at rest until acted upon. When someone does not seek improvement in a planned way, he or she is likely to become stagnant mentally, emotionally, and physically.

To improve yourself continuously as a tennis player and a person, you must approach the task in a planned, systematic way. By constantly improving your mental, emotional, and physical skills, you will be sharp, productive, and able to maintain a competitive edge. Committing to continuous improvement will steer you away from a complacent attitude and psychological helplessness.

Progress feedback is information that indicates your growth or improvement from one point in time to another. Performance feedback is the data that indicates the results of your play. Ask your coach to provide an opinion about how you are progressing in the area of self-confidence in match play.

Watching videotape can help you compare your current performance to a previous performance. Discuss with yourself the things that you are doing well. Make notes about areas in which you want the opinion of your coach or others. Consider the things you need to improve. List specific items from your discussion with yourself that you want to discuss with your coach. To conclude your meeting, summarize your thoughts and impressions.

Schedule another personal meeting with yourself. You can use the information you have derived from your personal meeting to take initiative for continuous improvement. You can answer the questions by using the feedback about yourself. In addition, you may want to discuss your answers with your coach. Acquire new physical or mental skills that will help your game. Become more respectful and patient with other people. Believe in yourself more consistently.

Taking the Mental Efficiency Advantage

Your commitment to take the mental efficiency advantage can start right now. The mental efficiency program is most beneficial when you make it part of your daily routine both on and off court. Set up a schedule of review and study for yourself. Ask the opinions of your coach, parents, and others who are interested in your improvement.

Mental efficiency can also be considered from a group perspective. Regardless of the size of a group, the participants in the group should coordinate their physical efforts, their common emotions, their goals, and their mental skills. A mentally efficient tennis group is able to identify its collective strong points, limitations, and developmental needs. To perform well, a group also needs to commit itself to pursuing its common purpose. Each of the group members, including you, needs to discuss the setting of group goals. The individuals who make up the group (doubles, tennis team) have a common belief that they can perform well as a unit and accomplish their group goals.

Discipline in a group context refers to the extent to which the group can formulate a coordinated game plan—a team plan—that is over and above any individual plan and then follow through during competition. A mentally efficient group is able to maintain quality interpersonal relationships among all members of the group, as a group, and with people outside the group.

The members of the group use feedback from their performance to develop action plans for their development. As you remain involved with the mental efficiency program, you will witness positive results.

CHAPTER 13

Game Plans and Match Strategy

You should never enter a match without a plan.

Just as you would never enter a sales meeting without a plan, you should never enter a match without a plan. The plan may be as simple as hitting every ball to the backhand or as intricate as coming in on your serve and attacking a certain area of the court.

We intend to draw parallels between sports planning and how it relates to your business, home, or family relationships. The academy produces a very comprehensive master plan for the training year. This plan is then further broken down into weeks and outlines the specific areas in much more detail.

To live comfortably in today's world, often both parents must work to produce income. With a working mother and father already going in different directions and a child off in another, family coordination requires planning and cooperation. Tennis requires similar planning. Planning defines the strategy that gets you from one point to another. In tennis that point is winning. We tell our students and coaches, "Make a plan, then work the plan." That's what every parent attempts. With luck, success follows.

Many lessons learned on the court transcend the game. One of the most obvious is the effect of mood swings. On court as in life, mood swings parallel momentum. Positive and negative attitudes affect more than just hitting a ball across the net; they also affect associates and projects. On court we teach players to keep emotions positive, even under difficult circumstances. By controlling your emotions, you enhance your chances of controlling the court. It works the same way in life. No competitor is more difficult to beat than one who is positive and exudes confidence.

Your attitude to everything you do on the court is far more important than the result.

Strategy and game planning are among the topics that players ask about during coaching seminars. Usually they are searching for secret weapons. There are none. There is good planning, both on court and off. Plans and strategies can be simple or complex. On court keep it simple.

The great Australian coach Harry Hopman, who won more Davis Cup matches than any other coach in history, had the simplest strategy of all. Work harder than your opponents, stay positive, and hit the ball to the open court. His strategy was simple, sweet, and ahead of its time. Harry claimed his success was a result of his players' talent. Smart people knew better. Harry planned and executed. That's what made him a winner.

In the following text we have accumulated articles, lessons, and seminars of our experience, put them on paper, and positioned them for all levels of play. Young or not so young, novice or advanced, you'll find something, guaranteed.

Game Plans

Over the 40 years of the Bollettieri Tennis Academy, we have observed that the most successful players define their game plans around their strengths. With this foremost in mind, they step on court with the absolute belief that to win they must do what they do best. Naturally, they accept a tip here and there about playing a particular opponent. But most are wise enough to know that making too many complex adjustments in their game plan is risky. I can close my eyes during a match and hear people around me describing how a player is doing this or that. What they are actually viewing is the implementation of strategy.

- Techniques—Style is the product of techniques and grips.
- Mental approach—A positive approach is essential because this area alone can break down any game plan, no matter how good.
- Physical conditioning—Levels of conditioning vary, but clearly, athletes are limited by their physical condition.

Other important factors include mental efficiency, nutrition, statistical analysis, and equipment.

Boris Becker—Be Prepared

The most important thing I learned from coaching Boris Becker was this: have a plan and be prepared. When you get on the court forget everything else in the world and be ready to play.

Nobody has ever prepared for a match the way Boris Becker does. He always asks to discuss strategy before a match, sometimes right after he finishes practicing on match day. When he goes into the locker room before a match, he goes through a strict set of preparations and rituals. He comes in with his head down, carrying his own bag (he never lets anyone carry his bag). It's like he doesn't know anybody and doesn't hear anything. He's already into the match. He intimidates everyone around him. At Wimbledon his attitude is one of "Hey, everybody, move out—this is my locker room."

Just before the match, he'll sneak a look at the court he's going to play on, go outside by himself, and do a little running. He pumps himself up before a match starting when he takes his street clothes off. He blocks out everything else. Learn from him: when it's time to play, be ready to play. Be mentally prepared. Have your equipment prepared. Block out arguments with your girlfriend or boyfriend, the business deal that fell through, the test you flunked at school. Everything! When you step onto that court, nothing exists in the world except those 7,200 square feet.

The other thing I learned from Boris is that he's a lot more than just "Big Boom-Boom." All people think about is his big serve and his diving for volleys. But his game is immaculate in almost every way. He can annihilate an opponent—hit the big topspin backhand crosscourt, the inside-out forehand down the line, the little dink angle. His underspin backhand is a good example. He can hit it deep crosscourt, down the line, or even short to the service line. His opponent ends up saying to himself, "What the heck am I doing here trying to hit this low forehand?"

Here's what you can learn from Boris Becker: even if you have one or two big shots, develop the rest of your game as well.

What Does Having a Game Plan Mean?

Having a game plan means devising a winning strategy before entering the tennis court. Your plan should include using your strengths as often as you can. To use your game plan effectively, you must concentrate on building points so that you can use your arsenal in the most effective way.

Here are some examples:

- Jim Courier—Jim has a simple game plan: "I will hit as many forehands as possible from any position on the court." To help himself succeed, he will cheat over to the backhand side of the court on each point.

- Andre Agassi—When on top of his game, Andre will move to (or even inside) the baseline so that he can hit the ball on the rise. This positioning gives his opponents less time to recover.
- Monica Seles—She uses the same aggressive pattern as Agassi.
- Patrick Rafter—Pat will serve and volley almost all the time, chip and charge on return of serve, and stay at the baseline as little as possible.

What Is Your Plan?

Options are always available. What follows are a variety of game plans matched to the kinds of players who use them best. Find your style. The next time you step on court, try building points around a plan that best suits your style.

Baseline Player

Baseline players are situated three to five feet behind the baseline. They move well and for the most part retrieve ball after ball. Their strategy is to keep the ball coming back with high net clearance and to take few chances. The strategy for playing against this type of player includes the following:

- Use drop shots and angles that force the baseliner to move closer to the baseline to a less comfortable position.
- Hit short angles that force the baseliner to run a long distance to the ball and into unfamiliar territory—toward the net.
- Attack short balls.
- Periodically serve and volley.

Net Rusher

John McEnroe was a genius who could drive even the sanest player in the world to distraction, if not disaster. Both he and Pete Sampras can stay back but be at the net in a second to surprise their opponent.

Two-Hander

Two-handed players with excellent movement and recovery are dangerous. Hitting balls to their power zone will prove to be dangerous, often putting you in a defensive position. Players like Michael Chang, Marcelo Rios, Andre Agassi, Martina Hingis, Anna Kournikova, and Serena Williams are always in position to hit their two-handed backhand weapon.

When playing players like this, you must hit balls out of their comfort zone, which includes hitting directly at them. You must stretch them out wide and attack the net.

Semiwestern and Full Western Forehand Player

Players with semiwestern and full western grips often prefer to stay back at the baseline. Michael Chang, Jim Courier, and Venus and Serena Williams all attack the net and make a grip change to their volley grip. Players who hit with full western grips will find it difficult to make this grip change. Therefore, forcing a western forehand player to come to the net will be an effective tactic.

Western and semiwestern players do not like

- playing low balls or wide slice serves,
- being attacked off a slice, or
- coming to the net.

Continental Forehand Player

The continental forehand grip has limitations, especially if you lack strength. The hand on top of the racquet requires excessive racquet-head speed, especially when applying spin or hitting angles and topspin lobs. Mark Philippoussis uses this grip effectively.

Players who use this grip often have difficulty with

- wide forehands hit on the run,
- high-bouncing deep ground strokes, and
- high kick serves.

Power Player

A match between two power players, say Venus Williams and Mary Pierce, is really interesting. These players will just bang and bang until they hit a winner or make an unforced error. This style will not often get you into the winner's circle.

Generally, power players prefer one side to the other, and they gear their efforts to set up their strength. Use a variation of shots, including junk and off-pace balls. Figure out what makes the power player uncomfortable and deliver accordingly on big points.

Baseline Counterpuncher

This player will take a position a short distance behind the baseline and will quite often move forward and hit the ball on the rise. Current top players who use this style include Michael Chang, Andre Agassi, Martina Hingis, Venus Williams, Serena Williams, Mary Pierce, and Iva Majoli.

Against a counterpuncher, use off-pace balls that land deep in the backcourt. Take the counterpuncher out of his or her game and force the player into net. Don't let this type of player get to you—especially when you attack. Some attack patterns can be right at an opponent's body. Counterpunchers will use your power, so hit behind them periodically to upset their balance.

Junk Baller

A match against a junk baller will be a game of cerebral strength. The junk baller with the weird grip will irritate you to death and force you to go for outright winners. Fabrice Santoro is a classic junk baller.

- Move junk ballers all over the court, wreaking havoc on their game by causing them to hit from unstable positions.
- Be ready to move for balls that just don't seem to be there and have all varieties of action on the ball.
- Play aggressively without going for winners recklessly. Attack.
- Bring the junk baller to the net.

Working Against a Game Plan

Here is where brainpower comes into play. You are not the only one capable of devising a game plan. Any worthy opponent will have done the same. Irrespective of whom you are playing, if the game is competitive, you will have to do something to protect your weaknesses. Every ball you hit should have a purpose and be part of a plan. Get into your strengths by creating a combination of shots to the weaker part of your opponent's game, thereby enabling you to attack tentative returns.

Strategy

Say you have a tennis match on Saturday at the club and you know that you will be playing a baseliner. In your mind develop a plan to win the match, a strategy that will enable you to be prepared and capable, both mentally and physically.

Suppose, however, that your opponent changes tactics. Can you prepare yourself in a game or two to change your strategy? Approach each tennis match as you would a battle. Create a strategy to beat the enemy but be prepared to make adjustments.

Consider a general at war. This general develops an intelligent strategy to overtake the enemy's headquarters. He summons his troops, vividly describes the march toward victory, and tells them that under no circumstances can they deviate from his clever plan to surprise the enemy from the west. The troops attack from the west, moving eastward through the heart of the enemy's headquarters. Suppose, however, that as the troops approach enemy headquarters, shells bombard them from the rear. The enemy had stationed soldiers in the woods and crept up behind the troops. The troops who had orders to continue marching east until they reached the enemy's camp are now in an impossible situation. The plan they are required to follow means certain destruction.

The message is clear. Have a strategy but don't etch it in stone. Leave room for change in the heat of battle. Take, for example, the authoritarian football coach who was having a particularly bad year because his team couldn't move the ball on offense and couldn't stop anyone on defense.

So at 0-5 he devised what he thought was an ingenious game plan. He took the quarterback into his office before the game and gave him a strategy, set in stone. "If we win the toss, elect to receive, and we'll do the best we can. On the first play from scrimmage run the simplest play possible, a quarterback sneak. Call the same play a second time and then a third time. On fourth down, punt."

The quarterback said, "OK," and went to the field. His team won the toss and elected to receive. They received and the returner got to the 30-yard line. A big surprise so far. On the first play the quarterback sneak produced a 20-yard gain, on the second play another 20-yard gain, and on the third play the results were even better, putting the team on their opponent's 20-yard line. With that, on the fourth play from scrimmage, the team lined up in punt formation. The coach yelled frantically to no avail. The punter kicked the ball out of the stadium.

As the quarterback came to the sideline, the distraught coach yelled at him, "Son, what in the world were you thinking, punting from so close to the opponent's goal line?" To which the young quarterback replied, "I was thinking what a dumb coach we had."

In battle an enemy particularly skilled on the ground or in the air will possess certain weapons. Similarly, a tennis match may feature an opponent particularly strong in a certain area who relies on certain strokes. Great generals and great tennis players have a sound sense of timing about when to make a change.

Compartmentalization and Strategies

As anyone who has ever tried it will affirm, losing a tennis match is easy to do. Something minor goes wrong. Perhaps a new piece of clothing is uncomfortable. Maybe a close call goes against you. Suddenly, quicker than you can imagine, things fall apart. Every time you miss a shot, you associate it with a cause and, whammo, before you know it you're in the showers, consoling yourself with the reality that you finished second, or impolitely, last.

Imagine now that you're playing in a major event against an opponent who is on his or her home ground. The crowd is foul and against you. They scream, yell, clap, boo, ring cowbells, and beat native drums. Add your customary internal demons to this cacophony, and you begin to understand the value of compartmentalization.

Compartmentalization is the art of separating, setting aside, and antici-pating all eventualities. Players who can do this, like Pete Sampras, can deal with any situation, regardless of the turbulence. A well-learned lesson here will benefit us all. If you're a player concerned about the score, the art of compartmentalization is both necessary and rewarding.

Compartmentalization, while it might sound difficult, is a relatively easy exercise. Given the practical consequences, it's surprising that most training facilities neglect it. It is not overlooked at the Bollettieri Tennis Academy. We have an entire sports psychology department devoted to, among other things, mental efficiency and compartmentalization.

One way to describe compartmentalization is "getting your ducks in a row" before walking on the court. It's a way to check those ducks and anticipate those few that you cannot check. For each of us, these ducks line up differently. Some are petty; others are unconquerable.

The value of compartmentalizing is that it does not ask us to rid ourselves totally of our demons, particularly those that psychiatrists would have difficulty setting aside. Rather, it suggests, in a world of uncertainty, that for the length of our match, we simply set aside (compartmentalize) that which we cannot control.

How can we achieve this? Given that in most matches, everything that can go wrong will go wrong, we suggest setting up a checklist of perfection. Begin simply—the right socks, the right sneakers, enough racquets, sufficient sweatbands, a few towels. Decide when to eat, when to warm up, and so on. The list can be endless—the longer, the better. Your checklist sets in motion a process. By following it, you'll know before you walk onto the court that everything you can control is under control.

Easy, right? Well, not when it comes to what you can't control, which can vary in magnitude with conditions, personality, and even the day of the week.

At a deeper level, compartmentalization is an exercise in understanding the emotional weaknesses that plague your game. Compartmentalization is the ability to anticipate every eventuality, to predict, and then to eliminate. You know, for instance, when you are apt to blow an easy game point or to do whatever you do to self-destruct. Compartmentalization is the art of educating yourself before walking on the court about how you will act when the cowbells and the drums arouse an audience to dance at your failure. This is what happened to the U.S. Davis Cuppers playing in South America. Jimmy Arias and Jim Courier were hit with cans, bottles, and coins. At one point they were threatened with bodily harm. They were expecting this hostility.

At the academy, we teach our students to use a twofold approach before they set foot on the court. First, they compartmentalize. Second, they define a strategy that will vary with the court surface and opponent. In defining strategies, let's look at the games of players who have success on certain playing surfaces.

Grass-Court Strategy

Here are some examples of strategy on a grass court:

- Boris Becker—The serve and volleyer stays back, sneaks in, and has a solid hitting base.
- Jana Novotna—She comes in almost all the time with a slice from the backhand and even a chip from the forehand.

Keep a few factors in mind:

- The early rounds, because the grass is slick, if not greasy, will have shorter points, including more serve and volley. Most successful players will come in.
- Court positions will be much closer to the baseline.
- Flat balls and slices will be in full gear versus the big topspin rallies.

Clay-Court Strategy

The most successful clay-court players hit with heavy topspin off both sides. Because the clay slows the ball, players have ample time to run down ball after ball and hit from a low- to high-breaking topspin stroke. This, in turn, puts the ball much higher over the net than is recommended on grass. Dirt ballers for the most part like to grind and are in top physical shape. Court positions will vary.

Several feet behind the baseline	Fairly close to the baseline	Varying positions
Berasategui	Hingis	Pierce
Mantilla	Agassi	Moya (he has recently changed strategy and moved to the baseline area)
Corretja	Seles	
Sanchez-Vicario	Williams sisters	
	Rios	

Clay-court strokes will see heavy topspin, low slices, and flat drives, all used at various times. In general, points will be much longer, especially if the court is damp and players are hitting the balls a little heavier.

Thomas Muster, along with Michael Chang and Arantxa Sanchez-Vicario, proved that one of the keys to winning is physical conditioning and mental state of mind.

Hard-Court Strategy

Hard courts can produce varying degrees of ball speed and height depending on the final court specs. In addition, some hard-court tournaments use synthetic surfaces placed on top of asphalt, wood, or other material. Once again, each court will be different.

All-court players have more success on hard courts, especially if they are blessed by having

- a sound serve and volley,
- ground strokes flexible enough to win the point outright or control play, and
- a formidable service return to take advantage of tentative serves.

As the consummate all-court player, Sampras reinforces the adage that if you want to win, your best strategy is to force your opponent into a type of game with which he or she is uncomfortable.

To be more effective in your game plans, use drills and practice sets to re-create match-play situations. This is standard procedure at the Bollettieri Tennis Academy. We force our students to do what they do best so that when they receive a ball of choice, they respond automatically.

Remember that you always seek to take your opponent out of his or her game plan, the place where your opponent is comfortable. Make your opponent uncomfortable and you are halfway to winning.

Specific Player-Type Strategies

What type of player will you face?—Baseline player? Aggressive baseliner? All-court player? Serve-and-volley player? To combat these types of players, we suggest the following strategies.

- **Baseline player.** Against the baseline player, use patience and don't overhit the ball. Because your opponent is probably a retriever and won't hurt you, wait for a short ball to end the point. Take your time, use drop shots and angles to open up the court, and then go on the offensive. Control the center of the court with good footwork and consistent shots high over the net with good depth. If possible, look for a looping return and hit forceful, swinging volleys to create your offense.

- **Aggressive baseliner.** Be assertive, take the initiative, and go up the line early in the point. Look to create offense quickly. Seldom hit the ball to the same area twice, except to wrong-foot the opponent occasionally. If your opponent attacks first, try to outrun him or her. If your opponent is overpowering you, move back and lob a few balls to make your opponent generate his or her own power. Use angles and dictate points by running around the backhand and hitting inside-out forehands.

- **All-court player.** Be prepared to anticipate when your opponent will stay back and when he or she will come to net. Determine where your opponent plays best and keep him or her out of that area. If your opponent prefers the net, lob the ball and vice versa. Make plenty of first serves even if you must sacrifice pace. Conversely, make offensive returns of serve and control the point from the start. Respond especially aggressively against second serves. When you have to hit a second serve, go for depth to neutralize the return. Take chances to win the point early.

- **Serve-and-volley player.** You must return the ball consistently low and at your opponent's feet. Make your opponent volley up and be prepared to move in to hit a forcing shot immediately. Pick a spot on your return and focus on it. Your ground strokes should be heavily topspin to drop at the volleying player's feet. Topspin will assist you in hitting angles to make passing shots. Play close to the baseline and pick your spots to make passing shots. Be precise and accurate rather than strong and inconsistent. Use the lob early to make your opponent wary of it for the rest of the match. Attack the second serve, getting to the net first. If you prefer the baseline, go to the net early as a bluff. As the match progresses, settle into your comfort zone.

Remember, these are merely suggestions. The key is to make a plan and work it. If it's successful don't deviate, but if it's a bomb, change. Don't lose sight of another Al Davis quote: "Show me a happy loser and I'll show you a loser."

Statistical Analysis*

"Can we make it better?" is a question that has been posed through the years in sports. Training elite athletes to reach new levels of accomplishment has become a technological race. By nature, humans search for knowledge. The weekend warrior seeks ways of improving. Players want to see improvement in all areas. Tennis teachers must enlighten the top-level athletes, the novices, and those between. How can we do this?

Two ends of our sport—stroke production and strategy—are linked like Siamese twins. The foundation of tennis is having strong, biomechanically correct strokes that give you power and consistency. With power and consistency you can hit to areas of the court from which your opponent must return a shot that you expect. We can deal with anything expected; anything unexpected causes us to improvise. When playing balls that come back at us without purpose, the game favors the strongest. Stroke production and strategy have distinct purposes, but without proficiency at each, a player will find it difficult to move forward.

---

*This section by Lance Luciani, Baseline Tennis Analysis

Technology has given us the ability to move forward on both ends. A teacher must be able to demonstrate to the student why a change is needed. Most people learn best visually. Through video, players can see stroke production and make appropriate changes. Videotaping to teach strategy is a little tougher because the best view is from above and behind the court. The focus should be on court positioning, shot selection, and tactics. Another form of evidence—statistical analysis—can offer key insight into the learning process.

The practice of tracking shots in a game has been around for a long time. It can be as elementary as counting the number of double faults hit in a two-set match (which should be no more than three). On the other end, advanced tracking would measure the level of consistency and the percentage of points won when the ball was served to the backhand side of the ad court. We would do this to establish guidelines and goals. By noting what we do in a match and comparing it to what better players do, we can set realistic goals.

Of course, at first basic information is better. What kinds of errors is a player making? Are most of the balls long, or are they in the net? The mistakes of a novice player usually stem from improper movement to the ball. Statistically, we would see a large number of errors long because the beginner has a tendency to reach for the ball, causing the racquet to veer off its practiced path. If we chart low-intermediate players, we would expect them to get 5 of 10 balls back in play. The majority of their errors would still be long or in the net with few winners. At the high end of the intermediate level, winners would become more common, but unforced errors wide would start to appear as players at this level start to strive for accuracy. The number of balls in should rise to almost 8 out of 10 at this level. At the highest levels the focus is more on comparing the number of errors to the number of winners, a ratio that is directly related to number of crosscourt shots versus down-the-line shots. The critical point is being able to distinguish the ball on which the player can be aggressive from the ball that the player should play defensively to the length of the court for a margin of error. Professionals must get 9 out of 10 balls in to be successful.

Another good statistic to analyze is the serve. The serve is crucial to strategy. At the beginner level, the strategy is simple: get it in the service block and play the point. Giving the fewest free points increases the chance of winning. At the intermediate level, speed becomes a weapon, coupled with spin. At the highest level, placement and speed together can be the difference in a match. A professional must play at high intensity for a long time. Easily obtained points are critical to conserving energy for longer rallies. The serve holds the key to several goals at each level. From starting the point to starting a combination (which might give us an easy point), the serve is critical.

Juniors often neglect the placement of the serve. A player may have fantastic form and great power but be unable to hold serve. Such a player probably serves consistently to the same area of the court, giving the opponent the ability to groove the pace and not worry about where the ball is going. Or maybe the player simply serves flat, a serve that can hurt the opponent only with its speed. On the other hand, adult club players usually don't have good form, but through years of experience they have learned not to serve the ball to locations that result in their having to be defensive from the beginning of the point. At the highest level, players mix up speed, spin, and placement. At times they can leave their opponent standing still, guessing which way the ball will go. The bottom line is that if you can win more than 55 percent of the points that you play in your service, success will probably follow you. The association of a successful serve to having the upper hand is common, but what about the good defense? The final topic to focus on statistically is the return of serve.

The return of serve is the most overlooked area of concentration. In beginner tennis the object is simply to hit the ball back into the court. This sounds simple, but the serve comes faster than any other stroke so reaction time is limited. Intermediate players start hitting with depth and spin to keep the opponent from hitting balls inside the court. At the intermediate level the return becomes more important. The returning player who can be aggressive gains the momentum of the point early. At the highest level an extraordinary effort is needed to be aggressive on the return. Breaks of service are rare, and the returner must act quickly on any weakness by the server. Thus we see low levels of consistency at the higher levels because the returning player must try to do more with the ball.

Additionally, we want to look at the percentage of points won by the returning player when the ball is served to a certain area of the court. A player may have a weakness in a certain area of the court, such as the return when the ball is started to the forehand in the deuce court. That person may be 100 percent consistent in getting the ball back into play but win only 25 percent of the points. That suggests that the returning player is probably hitting safely in the center of the court, allowing the opponent to control the momentum of the point. Consequently, the server wins most of the points. The secret to success is finding the correct mix of consistency and aggressiveness to keep pressure on the server.

The last area of statistical analysis deals with the mental part of the game. How does a player react when he or she has a game point? Or how often does a player win the 30 points? Knowing the answers to these questions can give a player a better understanding of when he or she really concentrates. Good players win 40 percent of game points. Champions usually win about 60 percent of game points because they understand how to play and know how to withstand the pressure associated with the score. These kinds of statistics also give a sports psychologist some understanding of the workings of an individual's game. The player can then make adjustments in rituals, positive reinforcement, or timing.

It is only through knowledge that we move forward. How do we practice? How do we perform in match play? By answering these questions, players can move forward in leveled jumps rather than wait for that one revelation about what the game is all about.

Table 13.1 is a sampling of statistics over the last two years. Each sample of information is based on players who won matches at the various ages and levels of play. The information reveals in a general way what to expect at the higher levels of competition.

To understand what this table reveals we must understand what numbers go into these statistics.

- Return of serve consistency—The return consistency is the number of times the player put the ball back into the court when the ball was playable. Aces and service winners are considered unreturnable and are therefore not included in this statistic. Younger players and lower-level players produce few aces and winners, so consistency means more at those levels.
- Service effectiveness—Service effectiveness is the number of points the serving player wins when serving to a certain area of the court. This statistic can reveal which areas the player serves to when he or she gains control of the momentum of the point right from the service.

Table 13.1 Sampling of Statistics

Age/level	Service return consistency	Service effectiveness	Ground-stroke consistency	One point from game	Points by aggressive play	Points by consistency
Boys 12s	85%	55%	92%	56%	21%	30%
Boys 14s	90%	55%	85%	54%	25%	25%
Boys 16s	79%	62%	86%	52%	31%	20%
Boys 18s	91%	71%	91%	63%	29%	31%
Girls 12s	80%	53%	89%	40%	25%	25%
Girls 14s	94%	49%	87%	60%	14%	41%
Girls 16s	93%	51%	89%	52%	31%	25%
Girls 18s	83%	59%	82%	44%	19%	33%
Women's	85%	51%	87%	59%	23%	29%
Women's satellite	90%	62%	91%	71%	20%	34%
Women's professional	85%	63%	88%	71%	15%	38%
Men's professional	90%	63%	88%	67%	26%	27%

- Ground-stroke consistency—When players are rallying, the number of chances they have to hit the ball back into play can show a stronger or weaker side. Variances of 5 percent between the forehand and backhand can show a weakness.

- One point from game—This statistic reveals how a player performs when playing a game point. A sports psychologist might use the information to look at how the player handles stress. If the player has trouble finishing the game, adjustments in how that point is played must be made. If the player approaches game point as a process instead of a pressure-filled occasion, success will come easier.

- Points won by aggressive play—In a match a player must find the proper mix of consistency and aggressiveness. Being too aggressive raises the number of errors because the risk level of the shots is greater. Being aggressive usually involves changing direction of the ball from crosscourt to down the line. The risk level is higher because the ball must travel over the highest part of the net, the target distance is shorter, and angling the ball correctly is more difficult.

- Points won by consistency—Again, the player is looking for the proper mix to compete in the match. Being too conservative can mean being too predictable. When a player never uses the element of surprise, the opponent can move before the ball is struck and thus have easier shots.

Statistics can be a guide for structuring practices, making small adjustment, and tuning the mental process of winning matches. You wouldn't want to base your whole style of play on statistics because tennis is still an instinctual exercise. But gaining every possible advantage through technology is the future of our sport.

Shot Selection and Court Positioning*

The basic foundation of strategy begins with learning how your shot selection affects court position, recovery position at the baseline and net, reasons for using shot combinations, and patterns of play. Without changing your style, we will show how you can become more consistent at winning by learning to control the center of the court and improve your shot selection in match play.

Your Style of Play

Many factors are involved in establishing your style of play. Your technical strengths and weaknesses, physical condition, movement skills, personality,

---

*This section by Pat Dougherty and Peter D. McCraw.

and temperament all contribute to defining your game and identifying your style.

It's not our objective to persuade you to abandon your style of play. Instead, we encourage you to use what you have and become more effective by changing your shot selection, altering your recovery position, and adding more strategy to your game.

What Can You Control?

We begin by looking at the elements you can control during competition. The sun, wind, court surface, and your opponent's decisions and actions are elements that you cannot control. You can adjust your game for conditions and influence the decisions that your opponent makes, but in general, these elements are beyond your control during a match.

> **Focusing on factors you control and making better decisions are keys to winning with your game.**

Things you can control include your response to your opponent's actions and your decision making. For example, you control the direction, spin, pace, and trajectory of your shots as well as the tactics or strategy you use.

Controlling the Center of the Court

Controlling the center of the court is the foundation on which all strategies are built. This process involves understanding the concept of recovery. Your recovery position is based on the shot you hit and the location you hit it from. The objective of correct positioning is to eliminate open-court opportunities for your opponent as you build the point.

You must learn to defend your court against an opponent's attack, just as you would in other sports. In basketball, a good defense makes it difficult for the opposing team to get the ball up court, take an open shot, or break to the basket. If you leave parts of the court open, your opponent has an opportunity to take control and score.

Basic Court Positioning

This section discusses the factors influencing the server and returner's positions, and your position at the baseline.

Server's Position

In singles the server will usually take a position near the hash mark on the baseline to begin points. By staying back to play the point, the server can quickly recover to a position that is halfway between the opponent's best possible returns (figure 13.1). Note that the server may at times take various positions along the baseline. For example, Andre Agassi stands out wide when hitting a high kicking topspin serve.

Returner's Position

The returner's position is influenced by whether the server is right- or left-handed, the server's ability to produce spin, and the power and range of the server's placement. In general, the returner will position in the middle of the range of possible serves. By adjusting his or her position, however, the returner can influence where the server will serve. Taking a different position can pressure the server and protect the returner's weakness by forcing a serve to the returner's strength. Whether you stand in front of, on top of, or behind the baseline will depend on the strengths and weaknesses of you and your opponent (figure 13.2).

You should take a position on the return that allows you to reach various serves yet gives you a chance to establish some control of the point.

At the Baseline

When you hit balls down the center of the court, you should recover to a position behind the hash mark on the baseline. Again, this position will put you halfway between your opponent's two best shots. The depth of your position will vary based on the strength of your shot, your style of play, and the surface. For example, players tend to position themselves farther behind the baseline on clay courts than on hard courts (figure 13.3).

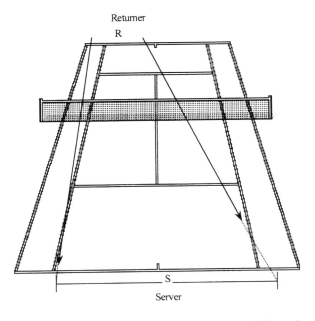

Figure 13.1 The server should stand halfway between the returner's best shots.

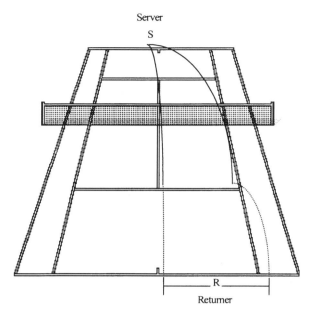

Figure 13.2 The returner should position to cover the server's best serves.

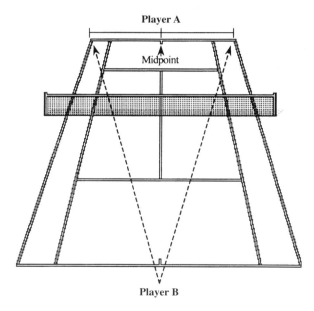

Figure 13.3 Player A should position himself halfway between player B's two best shots.

Although the recovery position behind the hash mark is appropriate for a ball hit toward the center of the court, when you hit to a corner the recovery position changes based on the direction of your shot (figures 13.4–13.7).

A common misunderstanding is that you should always recover back to the middle behind the hash mark in a rally, no matter where the ball is hit. Players who do this often find themselves out of position with no control of points. Even quick-footed players can look slow on the court when they don't know where to position themselves.

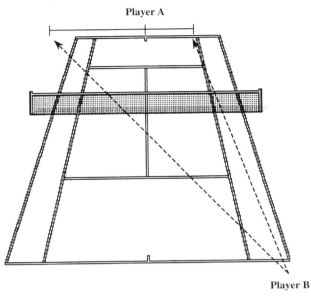

Figure 13.4 After forcing player B into his forehand corner, player A incorrectly recovers behind the hash mark in the center of the court. Player A has left an open court for player B to hit to.

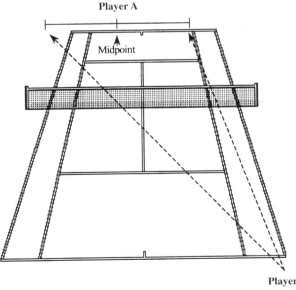

Figure 13.5 Player A correctly recovers to the midpoint of player B's best shots from the forehand corner.

The objective of recovery is to position halfway between the opponent's best possible shots. When your opponent is in a corner and hits down the line, he or she cannot force you any wider than the singles sideline. Anything

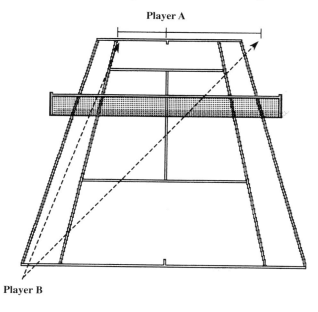

Figure 13.6 Having forced player B into his backhand corner, player A recovers behind the hash mark in the center of the court. Player A has put himself out of position and left open court for player B.

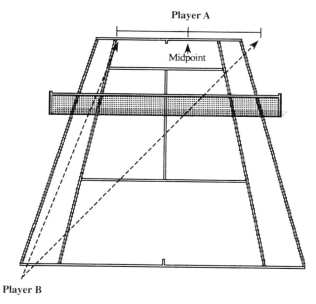

Figure 13.7 Player A correctly recovers to the midpoint of player B's best shots from the backhand corner.

wider is out of play. The opponent who hits a crosscourt angle from that position, however, could force you much wider than the opposite sideline. So if your opponent is in the deuce-court corner, you need to cover against the crosscourt angle by positioning several steps to your right of the hash mark. This position puts you at an equal distance from your opponent's down-the-line and crosscourt shots.

Shot Selection and Recovery in Review

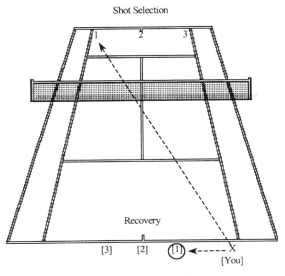

Figure 13.8 When you hit to shot selection #l, you should position at recovery #l.

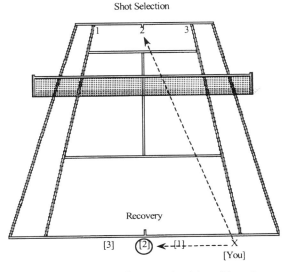

Figure 13.9 When you hit to shot selection #2, you should position at recovery #2.

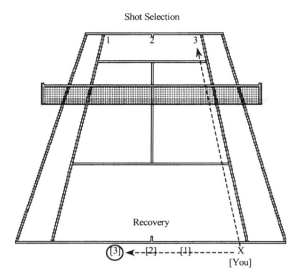

Figure 13.10 When you hit to shot selection #3, you should position at recovery #3.

Learning the Look

Once you get into the habit of finding the correct recovery position, you will find it easier to control the center of the court.

The look of the court will be your guide to finding the correct recovery position. At no time should you look down at your feet to find your recovery position. Instead, you must watch the ball and your opponent as you move to position on recovery and find your way by the look (or perspective) of the court. Initially, you will feel out of position when you are in the perfect recovery spot. You must train yourself to respond to the look and feel of the correct recovery position.

Time of Recovery

After your shot leaves your racquet you have only until the ball reaches your opponent to recover your court position. On average, it takes your shot less than 1.5 seconds to reach your opponent. How far can you expect to move on recovery given that small amount of time? Most players can travel only two or three steps in 1.5 seconds. For this reason, it is important to understand and execute shots that are good for your position when building points.

Shots Good for Your Position

A shot that is good for your position would be one that you hit in a direction or in a way that allows you to recover before your opponent's next shot. For example, when in a corner of the court, hitting in a crosscourt direction would yield the shortest distance to the correct recovery position (figure 13.11).

When in the middle of the court, you can hit a shot in any direction and still have time to recover. No matter which direction you choose to hit, you will be only a few steps from the correct recovery position. Based on where you are positioned, you can hit to any of the three shot selections and recover in time (figure 13.12).

Another option, when in the corner of the court, is to hit a high loop down the line. This shot takes more time to travel to your opponent because of the spin, slower pace, and trajectory, thus allowing you more time to reach the correct recovery position. The objective of hitting the ball in this situation is to force a change of direction in a rally, not end the point. In this example, you use the way that you hit the ball, not the direction that you hit it, to buy time to recover (figure 13.13).

In summary, we now know that when you are near the center of the court on the baseline, you are close enough to all recovery positions that you can hit in any direction and have time to recover (figure 13.12).

If you are forced into a corner, hitting crosscourt provides the shortest distance to your correct recovery position. You use the longest part of the court by hitting from corner to corner, which gives you a time advantage, and you have the benefit of hitting over the lowest part of the net (figure 13.11).

If you hit down the line from a corner, your shot should be a high deep ball that allows you time to recover and continue the point (figure 13.13).

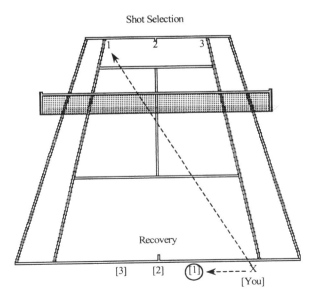

Figure 13.11 Hitting a shot in a direction that is good for your court position.

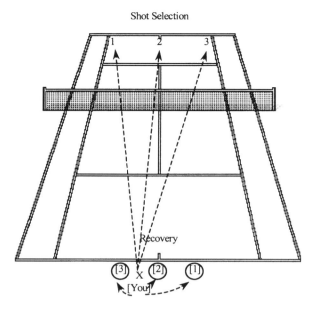

Figure 13.12 Hitting a shot to any of the three shot selections and being a few steps from the correct recovery position.

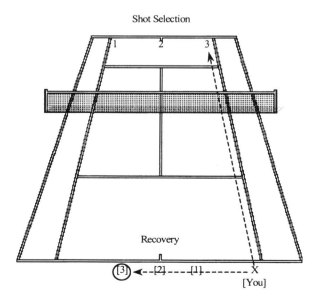

Figure 13.13 Hitting the ball down the line produces the greatest distance to the correct recovery position.

Shot Patterns

Based on what you've learned so far, you can understand why professional players often maintain crosscourt patterns in a rally. They are extremely cautious about driving balls down the line.

Crosscourt patterns result when players protect their positions as they build a point. Neither player wants to leave an opening or waste energy running the extra distance to maintain good court position.

Early in every match, a player must make a basic decision about whether a forehand-to-forehand pattern or a backhand-to-backhand pattern will be more advantageous in highlighting the player's strengths or attacking the opponent's weaknesses.

Positioning at the Net

Your objective at the net is to position yourself at the midpoint of your opponent's possible shots. The three shots you must be able to reach are the down-the-line pass, the crosscourt pass, and the lob. When you approach the net you are challenging your opponent to beat you with one of these shots. The shot direction that works best for your court position is down the line because it provides the shortest distance to good position at the net (figure 13.14).

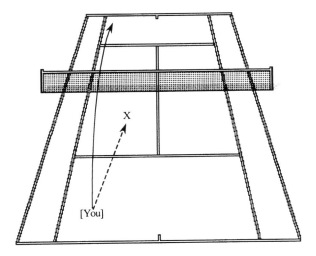

Figure 13.14 Optimum position when approaching down the line. This position allows you to cover a down-the-line pass, crosscourt pass, and lob with the least travel time.

When you work with a short ball near the middle of the court, hitting the approach straight down the center allows you to move into position and limit the angles on your opponent's passing shots.

When you have an opportunity to attack the net, it is important to understand the shot pattern that allows you to establish good position behind your approach shots. When you attack from inside the baseline, your ball will take even less time to reach the opponent, thus giving you less time to move into the correct recovery position.

Approaching crosscourt requires you to run farther to establish net position while leaving an open court for your opponent to pass. But the crosscourt approach that delivers the ball to an opponent's weaker forehand or backhand can prove successful. This is a strategic choice you must make on a case-by-case basis (figure 13.15).

The situation created in the rally can also influence your decision on where to approach. When you have your opponent in trouble, you have more options because you are close to ending the point with your approach. In this instance, position becomes less important in determining the direction for approach. The crosscourt approach thus becomes a more attractive option. But you must still cover the return by proper positioning, always anticipating the ball to come back (figure 13.16).

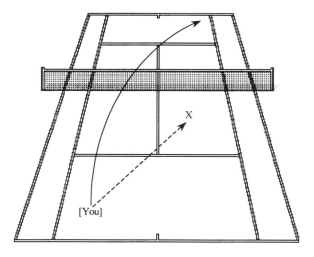

Figure 13.15 Position when approaching crosscourt. Note that the player must travel farther to the correct position to cover the opponent's passing shot or lob.

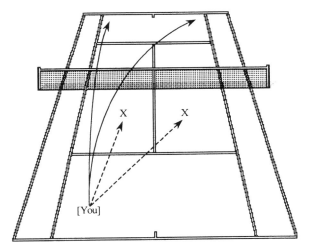

Figure 13.16 The player must travel farther to establish correct position at net when approaching crosscourt rather than down the line.

First Volley

You will often be faced with a first volley and not be in position to end the point. Your objective should be to use the first volley to position yourself better to end the point on the next ball. In this case, think of a first volley as nothing more than another approach shot. Use the shot patterns that you applied to your approach shots. Down-the-line or straight-ahead volleys will allow you to improve your court position for a second volley or overhead to end the point. For a point-ending volley or overhead, hit primarily to the open court. Remember that if you don't hit this volley with enough force to end the point, you'll have to move farther to establish good positioning at the net. Hitting behind an opponent occasionally will prevent an opponent from anticipating your patterns.

Don't underestimate the value of being in a good position at net. By being in good position, you will put pressure on your opponent to hit better shots, often resulting in errors. Penetrating approaches and firm first volleys also produce forced errors.

Good position at the net should place you one step and a reach from a down-the-line pass, close enough to the net to reach an angle pass, and still able to guard against the lob. As you learn more about your opponent's strengths, weaknesses, and tendency to hit certain shots, you can adjust your position accordingly. In general, when you are in good position you will be approximately six to eight feet from the net.

Positioning in review

In the rally

- Crosscourt patterns work best for protecting your position while building points.
- Adjust the speed and loft of shots down the line to give yourself time to recover unless you are hitting behind your opponent or have a point-ending shot.

Approaching the net

- Down-the-line shots provide the shortest distance to a good position at the net while limiting an opponent's open-court opportunities.
- Down-the-center shots work well off short balls in the middle because you can establish good position and limit your opponent's passing-shot opportunities.

First volley

- When you are not in a position to end the point on the first volley, treat it like an approach shot by hitting down the line or straight ahead to establish position for ending the point on the next volley or overhead.

Point Outcomes

In statistical terms, there are three ways to end a match—winners, forced errors, or unforced errors.

A winner is a winning shot that your opponent is unable to touch. A forced error occurs when your opponent is so far in the defensive mode that he or she makes an error. An unforced error occurs when a player has time to set up, has options, is in a position to hit offensively, but flubs the shot.

The objective of many strategic game plans is to use opportunities created in a rally to put opponents in difficult positions, causing them to produce more forced errors than winners. For example, given a short ball, one player may choose to go for winner at the risk of making an unforced error. On a bad day, this player ends up beating himself or herself. Another player in the short-ball situation may choose to approach the net and build the point so that the opponent must hit a passing shot from a difficult position and make an error. This strategy puts more pressure on the opponent and makes the attacking player's job a little safer.

Practice Drills

Down the Line Versus Crosscourt

Start off each rally by hitting the first ball down the center of the court. Your opponent will then start into a pattern. One player is designated to hit everything down the line. Play 10 points and then reverse the shot patterns so that both players experience the two patterns.

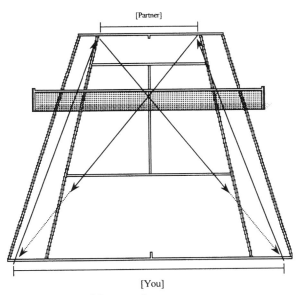

The down-the-line player must work harder to stay in the point because he or she must continually hit shots that result in unfavorable court position. This exercise allows both players to experience how shot selection affects court position and recovery.

Forehand Crosscourt and Recovery

Both players begin in a crosscourt forehand rally (for right-handed players). Alternating the start between players, one player begins the drill by hitting the first ball toward the opponent's forehand corner. The focus is on achieving full recovery after every shot and being consistent rather than powerful.

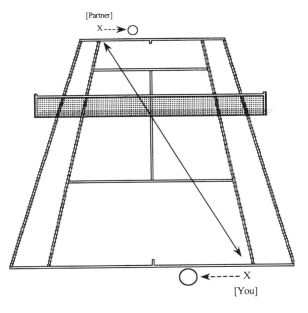

To create a game out of this drill, simply add scoring. Each player begins with 15 points. For every unforced error you commit, you lose a point. The first player to reach 0 loses the drill. This method of scoring helps you develop consistency.

Backhand Crosscourt and Recovery

This drill is similar to the forehand crosscourt and recovery drill except that players use a backhand pattern. Score the same way and compare the results of the two drills to determine your most consistent side.

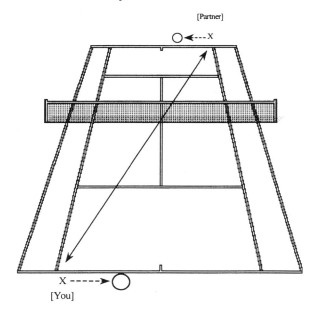

Forehand Crosscourt and Attack

To the second and third drills, we now add the element of attack. Again, we work in a forehand pattern, rewarding the player who attacks and wins the point at net.

The scoring this time starts at 0 and plays to 20. Each player gets 1 point for winning a point and 2 points for winning the point on a volley, overhead, or opponent's forced error. Alternate the start of each point between players.

Backhand Crosscourt and Attack

This drill is run in the same manner as the previous drill except that players use the backhand pattern. Compare the results of the two drills to determine which pattern works better for setting up your strengths for attacking the net.

Change-of-Direction Drill

For this drill we use a rope to extend the height of the net over the sidelines by 10 to 12 feet. Start the rally down the center of the court and use this exercise to practice changing the direction of the rally. When you are positioned toward a corner, work with a high looper down the line over the rope, emphasizing full recovery behind each ball. You can also use a slice down the line that passes under the rope to accomplish a change of direction.

It is best to change direction when you are positioned toward the middle of the court. The ball travels over the low part of the rope, and you are only a few steps from the correct recovery position.

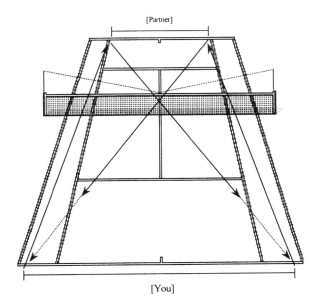

Building Points and Tactics*

Now that you have an understanding of basic strategy and patterns, we will build on this foundation by introducing the concept of building points and tactics.

We will help shape your frame of mind and develop a mentality conducive to building points. You will learn how to apply the various parts of your game in harmony and build a game plan around your style of play.

Match Mentality

Match mentality is the frame of mind you establish in competition. It determines your attitude, thought process, and decision making. Your mentality dictates how you will respond under the pressure of competition.

Some players allow certain circumstances to affect their mentality. For example, players may have difficulty competing against opponents who they know are much better or against opponents whom everyone knows they should beat. Both situations create added pressure that can affect match mentality.

*This section by Pat Dougherty and Peter D. McCraw.

Mentality Traps

When a boy and a girl with similar skills and ability compete against each other, both may find it difficult to maintain the right frame of mind for competition. This type of matchup often leads to one or both players falling into what we call a mentality trap. Any player can fall into a mentality trap when facing a pressure situation.

One example is the go-for-broke mentality trap. This occurs when a player tries to end the point on every swing of the racquet. Players may adopt the go-for-broke mentality if they feel compelled to blow their opponent off the court. They may use this approach against an opponent they know they should beat.

Another circumstance when one might use the go-for-broke mentality is when playing a superior opponent. Here, the player is afraid of playing out the points, feeling that if they keep the ball in play, the opponent will take control and end the point first. Go-for-broke players can have trouble with consistency, often producing more errors than winners. Frustration sets in and they ultimately beat themselves.

At the opposite extreme, players may fall into the tentative-pusher mentality trap. Under pressure, this type of player fears making errors and plays only to get the ball back. Although these players may be consistent, they have trouble controlling points and are always in a defensive mode. The tentative pusher struggles with the concept of forcing the action and finishing the point. Unless an opponent gets impatient with a tentative pusher and self-destructs, the tentative pusher will have a difficult time winning points, especially at higher skill levels.

What Is Building Points?

The concept of building points begins with an understanding of how the parts of your game contribute to a game plan. The idea is to start a point, set it up, create an opportunity, and finish the point.

Why must you build points? Every time you go for an outright winner and make an error, your opponent's score improves. In basketball, if a player takes a shot and misses, the offensive team has a chance to rebound the miss and take another shot. At worst, the other team gets the rebound and advances toward their basket. Missing shots in basketball doesn't put points on the board for the opponent.

In tennis, however, it is much easier to beat yourself because each time you make an error, your opponent scores. This scoring system means that you must be selective about when and how you try to end a point.

Think of how a basketball team builds a play. An inbound pass begins the action. A player dribbles down the court, and the team sets up in formation. As the players pass the ball around, they are constantly trying to create a good opportunity to score. When they find an opening in the defense, they seek to capitalize.

Four Phases of Building Points

Understanding the four phases of building points will help you organize your strokes and shots into a game plan.

Phase I—Start

The point starts with the serve and return. It is important to understand the objective and mentality for phase I—using the serve and return effectively to get the point started. You want to establish control of the point from the first ball. Players are inconsistent in phase I because they use the serve and return to try to end the point. Aces and return winners may result from well-placed shots, but they should not be the focus for most points.

Establishing a mind-set of getting the point started properly in phase I will improve consistency. Being more creative with your options will make you more effective in the start of points.

Phase II—Setup

If the point does not end on the serve or return and neither player advances to net, then the point progresses into phase II—the baseline rally.

Just as a basketball team passes the ball around to search for opportunities, in the rally both players use pace, spin, and trajectory options, while working with shot patterns and directions, to try to create opportunities.

Again, players who make many errors in the rally are often trying to end the point from low-percentage situations. The objective is to work on the setup until you create a high-percentage opportunity.

Your objective in the rally is to establish offensive control of the point and be mentally prepared to hit as many shots as necessary to set up an opportunity. You must stay alert and be able to identify opportunities so that you can quickly capitalize on them when they happen. It is important to use shots and patterns that permit you to maintain correct position while rallying. You want to avoid giving the opponent open-court opportunities during the setup phase.

Phase III—Opportunity Ball

An opportunity ball can present itself immediately off a serve or return, but it may appear on another point only after a 12-shot rally. You should recognize several opportunity-ball situations—the short ball, the open court, and the angle or drop shot.

Short Ball

The short ball, the most recognizable opportunity, often results from a penetrating ground stroke or from a defensive shot by your opponent. The short ball offers you the option to go for an outright winner or to advance to the net on an approach shot.

Open Court

An open-court opportunity usually occurs when you use a combination of shots that pulls your opponent out of position in the court. Open-court opportunities will also occur if the opponent chooses to hit shots that are not good for his or her court position.

Angle and Drop Shots

Angle and drop shots force the action out of the rally, setting up the opportunity to end the point. Much of the time, your sharp angles or drop shots will pull your opponent off court or catch him or her at net.

Phase IV—Finish

The choices you make with the opportunity ball set the stage for what occurs in phase IV—finishing the point. An aggressive shot maker is more likely to try to end the point with an outright winner, whereas players who use other styles of play will prefer to advance to the net.

By advancing to the net, you are relying on the quality of your approach shot to create a difficult situation for the opponent to either lob or pass, make a forced error, or set up a ball that you can volley or overhead away.

The way of thinking for phase IV is to capitalize and finish strong. You are no longer building the point; you are closing.

Be realistic. You can't outslug Monica Seles. You can't outserve Pete Sampras or Richard Krajicek. Pride can make even the top pros stubborn about this. Boris Becker, for example, tried to beat Andre Agassi from the baseline, where Agassi is superior. Becker lost eight times in a row.

Now that you understand the phases of building a point and the objectives of your strokes and shots, you are prepared to create a game plan for your style of play.

Realize that not every point will reach all four phases. Winners and errors anywhere in the building process will end the point. Some tactics, like serve and volley, are designed to eliminate phases of building a point by applying immediate pressure.

Will to Build

You must develop the will to build and believe in the concept. If you are not confident that building points will produce better results, you will never have the right mind-set.

The idea is not just to keep the ball in play, but to do it with a purpose. Understanding the process and the flow of building the point will not lessen the offensive aspects of your game. A strong offense has a balanced attack, using variety with consistency. If you make as many errors as you do winners, they cancel each other.

Be offensive as you build points but be consistent. This means working within your ability and skill level, using all your strokes and shots for their intended purpose.

Don't Fear Your Opponent's Winners

Experienced players delight in the opportunity to play opponents with the go-for-broke mentality. Such players love to trigger the outright winner, and they really compete against themselves and against match statistics. More often than not, their errors stack up more quickly than their winners. A simple strategy that works well against the go-for-broke player is to be steady, taking every opportunity to force your opponent into awkward situations from which he or she will have to hit even more difficult winners to beat you.

Don't let a few winners discourage or frighten you out of your strategy to build points. Stay with your game plan and remember that the percentages are on your side. If it happens that your opponent rises to your challenge by hitting more winners than errors from those difficult situations you've created, you know that your opponent was the better player that day and deserved to win. You've done your best.

Building Points

While building points, you have strategic options available within each phase. Using these options to create variety in your game plan will help you control points and keep your opponent guessing.

Serve Options

Many players think of a first serve as hard and flat and a second serve as spin. This way of thinking produces predictable serves, allowing the returner to anticipate what's coming.

In baseball, if a pitcher were to throw nothing but fastballs, the batters would soon know what to expect and would start hitting the ball out of the park. By using a variety of pitches and changing speed, spin, and placement, the pitcher keeps the batter guessing.

In tennis, the server has the same options. On the first serve, using flat, spin, and kick serves, changing speeds, and varying placements will reduce the effectiveness of the returner. Mixing spins and pace will make it difficult for the returner to establish timing. In addition, changing placements on the first serve will open up opportunities to attack weaknesses and allow you to anticipate the direction of the return.

By maintaining a high first-serve percentage, you can keep pressure off yourself and avoid having to hit too many second serves. Missing too many first serves gives the returner an advantage.

To reduce double faults, use spin serves and aim for the center of the box. Spin allows you to swing aggressively while maintaining consistency. Options include using slice and kick serves as well as mixing placement for variety, but using too much variation can upset the regular rhythm of your swing, causing faults if not double faults. These possibilities are all the more reason to get the first serve in on big points, that is, game point or break point.

Return-of-Serve Options

Getting the point started on return of serve is challenging against a consistently strong server because you have only fractions of a second to react and execute. Your court position is the key. Where you are positioned varies based on the server's strengths, your ability to return, your style of play, and your strategy. In general, you should position yourself halfway between the extreme possible placements of the serve.

Your return position in relation to the baseline will vary according to your tactics, your strategy, and the server's ability. Most players simplify when returning a first serve by using the pace already on the ball and hitting to a predetermined target.

Returning a second serve allows you to stroke more aggressively. On the big points, good returners often use their position to add pressure to the server's second serve, influencing both where and how the opponent hits that serve.

Your shot selection as a returner for both first and second serves will depend on your strategy. Hitting crosscourt on the return works well for getting into the rally, whereas going down the line on a second serve allows you to get into the net and immediately close out the point.

Baseline Rally Options

Based on the shots and patterns that are good for your court position, here are some options to consider in the rally.

Early in a match you must decide whether to use the forehand crosscourt pattern or the backhand crosscourt pattern to build points. To make the decision, analyze your strengths and weaknesses as well as what opportunity you seek to set up.

To anticipate what will happen, know that if you hit a ball crosscourt your opponent is likely to hit back crosscourt or toward the center of the court. If your opponent hits the ball toward the center of the court, you can hit to either corner to set up a pattern. If your opponent hits deep down the line in the rally, you should automatically think about hitting crosscourt to take advantage of the open court or at least take control of the point.

If the opponent hits regularly down the center of the court, you have an opportunity to hit corner to corner and put your rival on the run as you control the center of the court.

As we learned earlier, if you choose to hit down the line to force a change of direction in the rally, you need to hit the ball in such a way that you will have enough time to recover and continue the point.

As you work in crosscourt patterns to create an opportunity ball, you have options to adjust the spin, pace, and trajectory of your shots. Working with this variety will make it difficult for an opponent to establish rhythm. Use angle shots to force your opponent wide to set up further open-court opportunities.

Opportunity-Ball Options

An opportunity ball can be any offensive situation that presents itself and allows you to progress to ending the point. How you choose to work with that opportunity may vary from point to point. Your match mentality and style often determines your choice. Here are options to consider for the various types of opportunity balls.

The short ball offers several options, one of which is to attack the net with an approach shot. As we learned earlier, the shot direction you choose on the approach affects your position at the net. Hitting the approach down the line or down the middle when you are positioned near the center of the court will provide the shortest distance to good position at the net. Using the short ball to approach puts pressure on the opponent as you finish the point at net.

Some players prefer to use the short ball to try for an outright winner toward any court opening, but they run a greater risk of making an unforced error.

The open-court opportunity ball usually occurs because you used a combination of shots to open the court. You can then finish the point with an offensive shot.

Another open-court opportunity could occur because your opponent chooses to hit a shot that is not good for his or her position, thus being out of position to recover.

When you have an open-court opportunity, you should not aim for the lines with your point-ending shot. You risk making an unforced error. Be offensive with your shot but leave some margin for error.

The use of angle and drop shots can force your opponent out of the rally by bringing him or her into the net or off court, putting the player in a defensive situation. Your angles and drop shots need not be outright winners; you can use them to set up for finishing the point.

A textbook finish to a point has the player in control, taking the first opportunity ball and advancing to net. This sequence puts the opponent into a forced situation. If the opponent on the baseline is unable to produce a winning passing shot or lob, he or she will either commit a forced error or hit a shot that you can put away with a volley or overhead.

The player attacking the net uses the opportunity ball to force the opponent to execute winners, relying on the fact that if the approach shots are forced, the baseliner will make more errors than winners or will produce shots that can be put away.

Some players, however, are extremely effective at hitting passing shots and lobs. They look forward to the challenge. These players will often bring you to the net so that they can pass you. The net position is then a difficult place to be. You are caught in a defensive situation and not in control of the point.

When at net, it's important to establish a position that keeps you in reach of the down-the-line or angle pass yet able to guard against the lob.

When facing a net player you must interchange the down-the-line pass with angles and lobs to create opportunities. Keep an eye on the position of the net player. If your opponent plays close to the net, lob until he or she moves back. Your passing shots will then become more effective.

Tactical Combinations

You create tactics, usually built around your strengths, by combining two or more shots to achieve a desired goal—an opportunity ball or an open-court situation. Let's explore the various tactical combinations.

• **Serve and volley.** You use this tactic to apply immediate pressure on your opponent's ability to pass you. This tactic eliminates the rally phase of the point, allowing you to highlight your strengths at net.

• **Chip and charge.** This tactic is used primarily against the second serve when the returner approaches the net off the return. Down the line is preferable for the chip and charge. This tactic adds pressure on a second serve.

• **Sharp angle and crosscourt.** Within the rally, a sharp angle shot can pull the opponent off court and set up an opportunity to hit an offensive crosscourt shot into the open court.

• **Corner to corner.** When the opponent tends to hit the ball deep center repeatedly, you have the option to use the corner-to-corner tactic to put your rival on the run. This tactic will usually cause the opponent to make an error or leave an open court.

• **Corner and hit behind.** Particularly effective when you've successfully used the corner-to-corner tactic, the corner-and-hit-behind tactic takes advantage of the opponent's anticipation of your hitting to the opposite corner. Hit behind the opponent to catch him or her off guard.

• **The long point.** By playing a long offensive point, you may be able to psych out your opponent. The purpose is to outlast the opponent and test the opponent's patience. This is an effective tactic for establishing momentum or breaking an opponent's rhythm in a match. Your opponent's realization that you can dominate long rallies can have a psychological effect on his or her game, leading to more errors.

*   **Swing volley.** Aggressive baseline players use the swing volley to launch a surprise attack off a deep ground-stroke shot. Especially effective on high looping balls, the swing volley allows a player to move to the net without having to wait for a short ball.

*   **Drop shot and lob.** You can set up the drop shot and lob through the rally by using a slice backhand to build disguise for the eventual drop shot. The drop shot forces the opponent into net and allows you to control the point. The lob works well to complete this combination, taking advantage of the opponent's open backcourt. The court will sometimes be open for the passing shot.

*   **Deep down the line and short crosscourt.** This combination works well as a one-two punch, first opening the court, then finishing the point. This tactic can be used in the rally but is most effective on the approach and volley. Approach down the line, take position at the net, and finish the point with an angle volley.

In summary, you have learned how shot selection affects your ability to cover the court, the correct recovery positions for each shot, and how much time you have to recover. You also learned how to establish a match mentality to build points, how to organize and understand objectives for each part of your game, and how to work tactically based on your strengths and style of play.

You are now better prepared to win with your game. Go into match situations expecting long, tough rallies. Be prepared to go the distance. Use what you do best as often as possible and never give up. When you have your opponent down, keep the pressure on, stay on your game plan, and finish strong. If you are losing and your game plan is failing, adjust your plan or even gamble. Do what it takes to break your opponent's momentum.

Learn to become aware of your opponent's abilities and weaknesses. Test your opponent early to see if he or she knows what you know about shot patterns and building points. If your opponent doesn't play smart, your strategy will certainly give you an advantage.

Preparing for Tournament Play

One of the greatest sources of confidence is feeling that you are prepared. You can develop this belief by training with a purpose, by setting short-term goals leading up to the event, and by conditioning your body and mind for the test ahead. By developing reliable and consistent routines in preparation for a match, you can alleviate some of the prematch doubt that affects many players.

The physical part of the routine should include adequate sleep the night before the match, a proper diet, specific plans for transportation to the match site, stretching exercises, and a specific prematch warm-up. Most tennis players learn, over time, to bring the requisite physical items that will help them be ready—racquet, shoes, water, towel, snack, extra strings, extra shoelaces, extra socks, hat, sunscreen, bandages, glasses, extra shirts, extra shorts, a warm-up suit, grips, and so forth.

With the body ready and the physical necessities on hand, we turn to preparing the mind. Despite almost universal acknowledgment that a large part of tennis is mental, few players have developed a consistent, reliable mental preparation plan for their matches. At Bollettieri's we suggest that athletes begin their mental preparation the night before the match.

First, we encourage players to devise a written game plan consistent with their strengths. What are their strong points and how are they going to take advantage of them? How are they going to hide their weaknesses? Then we suggest that players use imagery techniques to see themselves executing their game plan.

The image should be precise. The player must see himself or herself executing forcefully and dominating the opponent, feeling what it feels like to be confident, what it feels like to be a winner.

On match day players should set aside a few minutes in their prematch preparation to get their minds focused on the upcoming task. Exactly how are they to accomplish what they've set out to do? Players must be specific about how they are going to use their strokes and physical presence to dominate the opponent. We suggest that players regulate their prematch arousal level to be neither too anxious nor too relaxed. Relaxation and breathing techniques can help deal with overstimulation. Psych-up strategies are useful for days when a player feels flat.

To build confidence, players should begin to gather more information during the warm-up. Players should become familiar with the court surroundings and look for anything unique about the court's surface with regard to speed, reaction to spin, slippery areas, and so on. They should also assess environmental conditions, such as the sun, shade, wind, and placement of spectators. When warming up, players should evaluate the opponent's strengths and weaknesses and process the information dispassionately. We remind players that this is a time to gather information, not a time to judge whether an opponent is better or worse than they are. By making judgments, players may either lose confidence or become overconfident.

Despite good intentions and well thought-out plans, circumstances will inevitably cause players to make changes on match day. We strongly encourage players to develop contingency plans to deal with unforeseen problems or distractions. Thinking about potential problems and writing down solutions can be helpful.

Here are some examples. What will you do if your opponent is rude to you before the match? How will you respond if your opponent is overfriendly and talkative? How will you deal with a conflict with your coach, playing partner, or parent that takes place just before the match begins? How will you react to drawing a player you've never beaten before? How will you cope with distractions, such as an opponent who cheats or a crowd that cheers more loudly for your opponent than it does for you? Adversity can strike in myriad ways before or during a match. Being prepared to handle all circumstances can help you perform optimally. Dealing effectively with uncontrollable situations can help you stay focused on the things that you can control— attitude, concentration, and effort.

Fighting Back When Losing

Carl Sandberg said, "It's never over until it's over." Or maybe it was Yogi Berra. Either way, the message is clear—keep fighting, keep trying, and maybe you can turn around a hopeless match, game, or set. When it's easier to quit than come back, the real winner keeps fighting until the final whistle. Vince Lombardi, the legendary Green Bay Packers coach said, "We never lose, we just run out of time." All competitors should have this winning attitude.

How do these cliches relate to tennis? Well, coming back from a likely defeat is an attitude. We see evidence of this attitude posted on locker-room walls: "When the going gets tough, the tough get going."

Mental toughness separates great players from good players. Whether winning or losing, great players will fight and claw for each point. They will not give up, regardless of the score. When great players lose, they leave heart and soul on court. These players can look at themselves in the mirror after the match and say, "I gave it my all—I have nothing left." If you have this attitude, any loss means you got beat.

This type of mental toughness is evident in successful players like John McEnroe, Jimmy Connors, and Chris Evert—players who never thought they were beaten. This belief, even though each developed it in a different way, prevailed when defeat was near. Evert says she played not to lose. Connors played only to win, often forgetting to serve and battling until he left everything on court.

Tennis players can develop a successful mental game by forming good habits and continually focusing on mental preparation and concentration. Sports psychologists tell us to visualize winning shots and winning points, one at a time. Maintain your rituals whether winning or losing, staying focused by taking deep breaths and adjusting your racquet strings.

To summarize, winning is a state of mind, a belief that somehow, something is going to happen that will enable you to prevail. The score is secondary. You should manage each point, each game, with the entire contest in mind. If you can accomplish this, you'll end up a winner regardless of the score.

Staying Focused When Winning

One of the toughest areas of sport to master is to stay focused when winning, even though it seems pretty simple—just finish the match. But victory is often elusive, and it can escape the faint of heart.

Giving away a match after leading 5-2 in the third is possible through a combination of events. First, your opponent is at the threshold of defeat and is going to bear down harder than ever. Your rival's renewed focus may eat at you, causing you to play more cautiously. You may completely abandon the game plan that got you to match point. Some call it a shift in momentum, and when momentum starts rolling against you, anything can happen, and it usually does.

A cliche applies here: "Never change a winning game, except perhaps to intensify it." Don't change from a baseline style to serving and volleying. Stay with the game that enabled you to succeed.

Obviously, winning one point at a time and not thinking about the score are the habits of winners. Choking, or giving away a match or game, is something every athlete must cope with. No one is immune. Some mask the feeling better than others do. Losing when victory seems imminent occurs in all sports. There isn't a formula, but there is one thing that you can do to avoid giving away a match. Train yourself through quality practice sessions and learn to put a match away when ahead. Remember, quality practices generate quality matches.

How to Combat the Power Player

Throughout tennis history, players have been more intimidated by power players than by players of any other style. Nothing is more frustrating than watching your opponent smash balls past you. Although you may feel helpless, you have ways to defend yourself. This circumstance is one of the greatest problems that athletes must face and conquer. Tennis players tend to focus on the outcome rather than the process of how to get where they want to go. To attain a victory, you must take one shot at a time and play each point individually.

To understand how to play the power player, you must first understand the strengths and tendencies of the power player. We are not as concerned with technical aspects as much as we are with tactics. Years ago, power players like Roscoe Tanner and Victor Amaya had huge serves but little else. They lived and died with the serve. In the 1980s the power game shifted to big forehands like those of Jimmy Arias and Aaron Krickstein. They too relied on a single weapon. In the 1990s we have players like Andre Agassi and Jim Courier, who have not only big forehands but also the ability to take the ball early on the rise with power. All these players have one thing in common—their survival depends on their ability to hit winners and keep their opponents on the defensive with their weapons.

Power players love to discourage their opponents by hitting a high number of winners and playing quick points. Doing this achieves two things. First, opponents become discouraged because they cannot put the ball in play. Second, opponents make more unforced errors because the power player is hitting a constant barrage of winners. Power players seek to play quick points because their opponents then have little time to gain confidence or develop a good rhythm. The power player's foe thus becomes more uncomfortable as the match progresses. How do you counter and adjust to the big hitter? How do you get back into the match? When you understand what the power player looks for and thrives on, you can more easily develop a game plan to retaliate.

From a technical standpoint, early preparation is a must! Because the ball is coming hard and fast, you must pick the ball up when it leaves your opponent's racquet. You do not have time to wait until the ball crosses the net or bounces on your side of the court. Prepare and move to the ball immediately. You must have good hip and shoulder turn, and the racquet must go back in the same motion to ensure good balance and positioning. You must also remember to shorten your backswing, which will help you keep the ball in front and allow you to use your opponent's power. Play smarter, not harder! Don't try to outhit your opponent in a slugging match because you will lose. You must try to win off your opponent's mistakes, not off your winners. Strive to put as many balls in play as possible.

Be extremely patient. Remember, the power player loves pace and likes to play quick points. Therefore, whenever possible use change of pace to neutralize the power of the incoming balls. The power player will find it much more difficult to create pace off shots landing at the baseline with no speed. Also, don't forget the high looping ball. This shot drives power players crazy! Last, try to move behind the baseline more to give yourself more time to prepare for your next shot. If your opponent begins to hit angles, however, you must move closer to the baseline to reduce the amount of court your opponent has to work with.

Now that we have established a plan to use against the power player, you should be less concerned with the outcome. Remember, it is easier to develop and implement a game plan if you understand what your opponent is trying to do. If you implement these tips each day in practice, victories will come sooner and more often than you thought possible.

How to Handle Cheating and Gamesmanship

During the more than 40 years that I have been teaching tennis, I have never seen a match won or lost solely on the basis of cheating or gamesmanship.

But I have on many occasions witnessed points and even games won by using these manipulative, unethical tactics.

Unlike golf, in which kicking your ball closer to the hole or not counting your strokes is undeniably cheating, tennis does not clearly define cheating. Nonetheless, actions such as questioning every line call, taking too long between points, and quick serving are all tactics that display disrespect for tennis and a lack of personal etiquette.

Certain tactics used to disrupt an opponent's momentum or game, however, are acceptable. For example, a player may attempt to change the tempo of play and upset an opponent's rhythm.

Although at times it may be difficult to distinguish between gamesmanship and acceptable tactics, some actions are obviously unscrupulous, if not obnoxious. I still encourage my players not to jump to conclusions, and to give any opponent the benefit of the doubt. But when a situation arises in which dishonesty is clear, the defense should be to ask your opponent if he or she is sure of the call. At no time should you scream at your opponent or an official or accuse your opponent of foul play.

If the cheating continues, stand motionless by the net and ask your opponent again if he or she is sure. If, in your opinion, your foe needs an eye exam, put your racquet down and ask for a monitor to watch the match.

To neutralize an opponent who employs gamesmanship, I encourage my players to pay attention to their own game and not become caught up in their opponent's behavior. If your concentration begins to fade, focus on the following to regain it:

- Make big serves.
- Get to net.
- Make good shots.
- Play longer points.
- Focus on the ball and think only of the point being played.

As when facing an opponent who is cheating or employing gamesmanship, athletes must learn to cope with umpires or referees and their calls. Regardless of the referee or umpire, players must know how to put a call or no-call behind them and concentrate on their game plan.

For instance, in basketball a player who is fouled hard and stripped of the ball while driving to the basket may anticipate the referee's whistle. But the player may not get the call. The sight of the opposing player streaking down the sideline toward the basket can further antagonize the player. Despite having four fouls, the player may yield to the natural tendency to race back and reach in from behind to get the ball back. By committing a stupid foul, however, this player fouls out of the game and hurts the team. In basketball, players are taught to disregard a referee's horrendous call or no-call and shift focus back to the task at hand—carrying out the game plan and winning the game. No athlete can afford to let a call disrupt his or her focus.

The great Billie Jean King frequently mentions that during a match she was so focused and so into the next point that she would forget whom she was playing. Her attention centered on the ball and the point she was currently playing. This focus and determination is at the core of the mental efficiency program at the Bollettieri Tennis Academy. Mental efficiency is a proactive approach to sport psychology, in contrast to today's reactive methods. As a total-program approach to playing tennis, it combines every aspect of the player's life. Mental efficiency provides the tools to obtain and maintain a higher level of play, even if an opponent displays gamesmanship or cheats. It sets a focus on the main reason the player is out there. As Al Davis of the Oakland Raiders says, "Just win baby, just win!"

Using and Developing Your Strengths

Once you've had your limit of clinics, attended a plethora of workshops, listened to Vic Braden, Dennis Van der Meer, and the others, it is time to develop your game. At the academy, we preach, coach, and teach playing within your style and capabilities. Don't try to be another Mac, Jimmy, Chrissie, or Martina. Be yourself. If you are comfortable at the baseline, play the baseline. If you like to attack, chip and charge, serve and volley, then play what you like best. If you are a counterpuncher, invite your opponent to net by employing dinks, drop shots, and angles. If you like to run and have the discipline to stay on the court all day, then, of course, become a moon baller.

All styles can work. Players from around the world have used them to win championships. Look inside yourself and decide honestly what best suits your capabilities. Having defined yourself, structure a plan of attack. Don't deviate and don't compromise. You will always be at your best working your strengths. To steal from a well-known swoosh, just do it!

Think of the consequences for Jim Courier if a coach had insisted that he change his controversial grips or stop running around his backhand. What would have become of his devastating inside-out forehand? Could he possibly have achieved a no. 1 ranking? What if Becker's coach had insisted that he not dive for volleys? Play in a style that makes you comfortable. Whatever the result, you will walk off court feeling good about yourself.

It's obvious that some players only reach a certain level at net (you might be one of them). They simply don't have the speed or instinct, or they may lack confidence in knowing what to do and where to stand. This does not mean they can't become good players. The list of world-class baseline players is endless, and you might just be one of those players who stay back and hit groundball after groundball.

Obviously, the reverse is also true. If your forehand or backhand is weak, you can minimize the weakness by coming to the net quickly and often.

At the Bollettieri Tennis Academy, our philosophy is to work on our students' strengths 70 percent of the time and on their deficiencies the rest of the time. Never neglect any weakness in your game, but don't magnify it by insisting on a 50:50 work ratio. This sort of schedule will weaken your strengths rather than strengthen your weaknesses. I have seen many players become disenchanted with our sport because they could not overcome a weakness. In my judgment they would have done better to master their strengths.

CHAPTER 14

Racquets, Strings, and Grips

By understanding your individual equipment needs, you will stay healthier and win more matches.

This chapter deals with the equipment needs of players at all levels. Keep in mind that these general statements focus on helping all players get the most from today's complex, high-tech racquet products and services. Experimentation with this knowledge will help you fine-tune your specific equipment needs.

Remember, there isn't a bad racquet, string, or other tennis product manufactured today, but players can make bad choices when they don't understand product specifications and design objectives. By understanding your individual equipment needs, you will stay healthier and win more matches.

Strings

Let's start with the facts. The energy created in a tennis ball that meets a racquet breaks down into the following components:

- 60 percent of the energy comes from the string bed (the strings in the racquet).

This chapter by Tom Parry.

- 30 percent of the energy comes from the ball (a rubber object in motion with its own energy).
- 10 percent of the created energy comes from you and your racquet frame (frame only, not the strings).

A bold statement to remember! This proves the importance of proper stringing, correct tension, string type, quality of strings, and age ("freshness," or resilience) of strings.

With this in mind, let's start with the most important item in hitting a tennis ball, the strings! Whatever type or brand of string you use, the following 10 commandments of strings apply. Study each carefully. They will help explain the many differences in today's string selections and how they can affect your game.

Ten commandments of strings

1. Lower string tension generates more power (providing that excessive string movement doesn't occur).
2. Higher string tension generates more ball control (with less power, placement of the ball improves).
3. A longer string, or string-plane area, produces more power.
4. Lower string density (fewer strings in the string pattern) generates more power.
5. Thinner strings generate more power.
6. Strings with more elasticity generate more power and absorb more shock at impact.
7. Softer strings, or strings with a softer coating, tend to vibrate less.
8. Thinner strings produce more spin on the ball.
9. Lower string density (fewer strings) generates more spin on the ball.
10. The more elastic the string, the more tension is lost in the racquet after a string job (prestretching will reduce this effect).

String Types and Construction

Not too long ago, players had just two choices in strings—natural-gut strings or nylon strings. Natural-gut strings were the strings used when tennis was created. Today, most top professional players still use natural gut because of its amazing characteristics, which are found only in a natural fiber. Because of the complexity of the subject, an entire section of this chapter is devoted to natural gut.

Today, many nylon strings are referred to as "synthetic-gut" strings. This name can be misleading. The most important point to remember is that all such strings are made from a nylon-based product. True, many synthetic-gut strings have special features that make them last longer than regular nylon strings, but in basic chemical analysis they are virtually the same product.

If the added features of a specific synthetic-gut string favor your game, feel confident in continuing to use that product. But remember, a freshly strung racquet with the basic nylon string will greatly outperform an expensive synthetic-gut string that is old and has lost its resiliency.

The basic construction types in today's nylon or synthetic-gut strings can be classified into the following groups. Each construction technique is for a specific purpose.

1. Solid core (polyester strings)
2. Solid core/single wrap
3. Solid core/multiwrap
4. Multifilament
5. Multicore/single wrap
6. Multicore/multiwrap
7. Composites
8. Aramid fiber/hybrids (Kevlar and other materials)

Of these eight construction types, solid core/single wrap is by far the most widely manufactured string, making up over 70 percent of all strings manufactured today. The main reason for the wide acceptance of this string is its overall performance at a price much lower than the price of natural gut.

To define each category better, let's look at the specific groups and their playing characteristics.

Solid-Core Synthetic Strings

Polyester strings fall in the solid-core category. Although they have been around for many years, polyester strings have recently found great popularity among players at all levels. Like all synthetic strings, they are available in different gauges (string thickness) and from a variety of manufacturers. The advantages and disadvantages are as follows:

Advantages	Disadvantages
• Durability	• Tension loss
• Greater control*	• Less ball speed*
• Claims of exceptional feel	• Increased shock and vibration
• Resists notching	• Difficult to install (for stringer)

*Polyester string is less resilient than other synthetics, so a claim of more control also means that the player cannot hit the ball as hard.

Typical examples of this type of string include the following:

- Babolat Strong Play (Poly Mono)
- Kirchbam Super Smash
- Gosen Polylon

Solid Core/Single Wrap Synthetic Strings

Solid core/single wrap synthetic strings make up 70 percent of today's string market. These popular strings derive their durability from having a large solid core. An outer wrap of smaller filaments (or fibers) improves tension retention. The outer wrap assists in two ways—by helping to hold the tension on the string and by protecting the core from notching and other abrasions caused by impact with the ball.

Because of the string's popularity, a wide choice of gauges is available. Manufacturers price their strings competitively. If this is the best-playing string type for you, shop around. You can probably find the same string from several companies, differing only in packaging and pricing.

Advantages

- Wide variety of gauges
- Excellent value for most players
- Very durable (thicker gauges)
- Balance between power and control

Disadvantages

- Too many choices
- Better strings overlooked
- Will go "dead" before breaking
- Shock and vibration to arm

Typical examples of this type of string include the following:

- Babolat Fine Play
- Prince Synthetic Gut Original
- Gosen OG Sheep
- Wilson Extreme Synthetic Gut

Solid Core/Multiwrap Synthetic Strings

Multiwrapped solid-core synthetic strings have recently gained in popularity because of the increased use of wide-body racquets. These strings tend to play softer because the core is smaller. The added outer wraps lend more playability as well as more durability.

Advantages

- Softer feel on the arm
- Resists notching better
- Variety of gauges

Disadvantages

- Feels less crisp
- Greater tension loss
- Less durability

Typical examples of this type of string include the following:

- Babolat Fiberfeel
- Gamma TNT Rx
- Leoina 66

Multifilament Synthetic Strings

Multifilament synthetic strings are coreless and have multiple synthetic fibers twisted together in a manner similar to natural gut. Fibers vary in thickness and number and are not wrapped around a center core. The biggest advantage of this type of construction is playability. These strings are technically difficult to produce and carry the highest price tag among synthetic strings. They are the best playing synthetic-gut strings and most closely resemble natural gut in all characteristics.

Advantages

- Exceptional feel
- Increased power
- Less shock and vibration to arm
- Excellent for wide-body frames

Disadvantages

- Tension loss
- Premature breakage
- Susceptible to notching from topspin

Typical examples of this type of string include the following:

- Babolat Fiberace
- Tecnifibre 515
- Wilson Sensation

Multicore/Single Wrap Synthetic Strings

A relatively new category is the multicore/single wrap synthetic string. Multiple cores improve playability over a single-core string, and a single wrap around these cores improves durability. These strings will generally have playing characteristics somewhere between a solid-core string and a multifilament string.

Advantages

- Soft, forgiving feel
- Less shock and vibration than solid core
- Good blend of power and control
- Fits a variety of players

Disadvantages

- Tension loss
- Not as durable
- Susceptible to notching

Typical examples of this type of string include the following:

- Alpha Gut 2000
- Prince Helix Soft Pro
- Forten Fiber Ace

Multicore/Multiwrap Synthetic Strings

An additional outer wrap distinguishes multicore/multiwrap strings from multicore/single wrap strings. The additional wrap enhances durability and may increase playability because the multicores can be made smaller. This type of string makes up a small portion of the string market.

Typical examples of this type of string include the following:

- Ashaway Vantage Pro
- Forten Fiber Flex

Composite Synthetic Strings

Composite synthetic strings combine different materials to try to bring out the best attributes from each. For example, regular nylon fibers may be combined with Kevlar or Zyex fibers to produce a string that is more durable and playable. Typically, these strings carry a high price and are difficult to find at retail outlets.

Advantages

- Longer life
- Tend to feel softer on the arm
- Excellent for wide-body frames

Disadvantages

- Loss of playability before breaking
- Less powerful
- Higher priced

Typical examples of this type of string include the following:

- Prince Response
- Gosen Arammix Pro
- Forten New Age 18

Aramid Fiber/Hybrids Synthetic Strings

Produced for chronic string breakers, aramid fiber/hybrid synthetic strings are made with aramid fibers like Kevlar or Technora. The main goal is to prevent strings from breaking prematurely. Typically, these strings use a hybrid combination—the main strings are made entirely from Kevlar or a similar material and the cross strings are a regular nylon. As with any string, the main strings of the racquet produce the power. The cross strings serve mostly to keep the mains from wandering around on contact with the ball.

These strings should be the last resort for someone who needs added durability because the excessive shock and vibration to the arm can cause tennis elbow. Junior players who are just starting out or adults who have experienced arm or shoulder problems should try a thick, durable string or a racquet with a tight string pattern before going to a Kevlar-type hybrid.

Advantages	**Disadvantages**
• Excellent durability	• Excessive shock and vibration to arm
• Improved control*	• Low power*
• Holds tension well	• Very low resiliency

*The extremely low elongation and resiliency of Kevlar diminishes ball speed, so the player experiences a feeling of greater control.

Typical examples of this type of string include the following:

- Prince Pro Blend
- Gamma Infinity
- Wilson Hammer-last

String Gauge

The gauge of a string is the thickness (or diameter) measured before traction (tension) is applied. Gauge is measured in millimeters and grouped into reference categories, which are what most people refer to when discussing gauge. By studying table 14.1, you'll see that opinion differs about where certain string gauges fall. It is important to understand these differences as we find out more about how the gauge of a string affects your game. Table 14.1 begins with thick strings and progresses to thin ones.

Of the gauges available, 16 gauge (1.26–1.34 millimeters) is the most popular. For most players this gauge delivers the best blend of power, control, and durability. Thinner strings play better (refer to the 10 commandments of strings) but are not as durable. The following chart shows how string gauge affects playability. Remember what you have learned about how the construction of a string affects its reaction.

	Thicker string	**Thinner string**
Power	Less	More
Control	More	Less
Spin	Less	More
Durability	More	Less
Tension loss	Same	Same

Table 14.1	Gauge Conversion (USA and European String Gauge Specs)		
USA	**Europe**	**Inches**	**Millimeters**
13	12	.065–.071	1.65–1.80
14	11	.059–.065	1.50–1.65
15	9.5	.056–.059	1.41–1.49
15L	9	.052.–056	1.33–1.41
16	8.5	.050–.053	1.26–1.34
16L	8	.048–.051	1.22–1.30
17	7.5	.046–.049	1.16–1.24
18	7	.042–.046	1.06–1.16
19	4	.035–.042	0.90–1.06
20	3.5	.031–.035	0.80–.090
21	3	.028–.031	0.70–.080
22	2.5	.024–.028	0.60–0.70

Remember that thinner strings are more elastic than thicker strings. This means that thinner strings can store more energy at the same *reference tension*. The *actual tension* felt in the racquet will be much different. If you string your racquet at 60 pounds with a 15-gauge string (thick) and like the way it plays but want to test a 17-gauge string (thin), you will need to adjust the tension accordingly. Players should experiment with gauges to find the best possible blend of power, control, and durability. A string of any given type of construction will play differently when used in a different gauge.

Natural Gut

Despite the countless number of synthetics on the market today, most players still judge natural gut the best. String manufacturers try vigorously to duplicate its exceptional feel and playability, but so far they have fallen short. Thus we often hear or read the statement "Plays most similar to natural gut."

Natural gut is made from high-grade beef intestine. Only the upper part of the intestine is used. The process is a delicate, hands-on procedure that requires up to three months from start to finish.

Natural gut is a by-product of the beef industry. No cows are slaughtered just to make gut. The labor-intensive work needed to produce natural gut accounts for its high price compared with synthetic strings.

Natural gut is the best playing string available; its power is unmatched. Natural gut will hold tension much better than any synthetic string, and it absorbs shock and vibration much better as well. The actual "dwell time"

(time the ball is on the string bed) is longer with natural gut than it is with synthetics, so the player experiences a much greater feel. An old saying in the tennis world is this: "Once you have tried gut, you will never go back to a synthetic. You're hooked!"

Over the years, people have questioned the durability of natural gut. These doubts have arisen because some stringers don't know how to handle natural gut. Natural gut is extremely durable when handled correctly and remains playable longer than a normal synthetic string. Synthetic string will lose an average of 15 to 18 percent of initial tension in the first 24 hours after stringing. Natural gut will lose an average of only 5 to 8 percent. The synthetic string will become "dead" (lose its resiliency) after 15 to 20 hours of normal play, whereas natural gut will stay resilient for its entire life.

If you have had arm or shoulder problems, natural gut is the best remedy for you. Natural gut is made from hundreds of individual "ribbons" of the intestine, twisted together to form the string. Each ribbon acts independently as well as with others when a ball is struck. Each ribbon absorbs shock and vibration to deliver optimal power. Natural gut is considered a multifilament string and is available in many different gauges. All that we have learned about construction and gauge applies to natural gut. The following list further addresses the benefits and drawbacks of natural gut.

Advantages	Disadvantage
• Power	• Price
• Control	
• Tension maintenance	
• Best for arm and shoulder	
• Longevity of playability	

Matching Player Styles to String Types

This section addresses generic questions that players ask about string types. Use this guide as a reference to help you find the best string type for your individual game. Refer to previous sections on construction and gauge to fine-tune these recommendations.

Need	Recommended string
More power	Natural gut, multifilament synthetic, thinner gauge
More control	Solid core, solid core/multiwrap, hybrid
More feel	Natural gut, multifilament, thinner gauge
Less shock and vibration	Natural gut, multifilament
Durability	Hybrid, thicker gauge
Firm feel	Solid core/single wrap, aramid blend

Tension

The most important thing to remember is that tension is only a number. What a particular stringing machine is set to when you are having a racquet strung will be affected by the following:

- Type of machine (drop weight, spring type, constant pull, etc.)
- Calibration of the machine
- Person using the machine
- String type being used (gauge, elongation, resiliency, etc.)
- Pattern of the racquet
- Pattern used to string the racquet
- Condition of the racquet

With all these factors, the number requested (tension) will be only a "reference tension." The actual tension of the racquet after stringing can vary from the reference tension by as much as 25 percent, almost always on the low side.

Several other factors affect actual tension:

- Elongation of the string over time
- Exposure to the elements (especially heat)
- Amount of stress placed on the string bed during use (frequency and intensity of use)

Let's look more closely at these variables so that we can better understand their effect on the tension requested.

Machine Types

The first racquet stringers were true artisans who used wooden dowels and makeshift awls to install strings. They achieved tension by wrapping string around the dowels and twisting until they heard the proper pitch from plucking the string. The stringer would then carefully install an awl into the frame hole, pinching the tensioned string to the frame. The entire frame was done this way! Because they achieved proper tension only by hearing a certain pitch, these early stringers varied from one to another. Stringers gave unique attention to each racquet, so players rarely changed from one stringer to another.

The first mechanical stringing machines were in the form of a drop-weight system. By applying a specific weight to a lever that held the string, tension could be applied more uniformly. By using the same drop-weight system, stringers could begin to duplicate each other's work more precisely.

These machines soon gave way to crank, spring-activated machines. The most popular of these was the Ektelon stringing machine (now manufactured by Prince and called the Neos). Many are still in use today and have been applauded for their years of reliable service and adequate consistency.

Electronic (or constant-pull) machines are today's state-of-the-art equipment. By pulling tension at a specific, precise amount, the machines have eliminated almost all human factors. These machines are the only ones that can account for the differences in elongation, friction, and resiliency of different string types. Electronic machines, by far the most accurate machines available today, are used at every major professional tournament.

Typical examples of stringing machines include the following:

1. Drop weight
   - Serrano
   - Alpha Pioneer
   - Klipper Klippermate
2. Crank, spring activated
   - Prince Neos
   - Alpha Dc
   - Ektelon H
3. Electronic
   - Babolat Star-3/4
   - Prince P-200
   - Alpha Tour Edge

Calibration

As mentioned before, tension is only a number. Reference tension and actual tension can differ by 5 to 25 percent. Accurate calibration will help reduce the difference between the two. Because of differences in construction, actual tension produced by the three types of machines will differ even when each is calibrated to be the same. Knowing the specific differences between these machines will help you request a reference tension when going from one machine to another.

For example, suppose you want your racquet strung at a reference tension of 60 pounds. You usually have your racquet strung on an Ektelon (crank, spring-activated) machine. You should request the following for the other machine types (assuming that all machines are calibrated correctly).

- Drop weight: 5 to 10 percent greater reference tension (63 to 66 pounds)
- Electronic: 5 to 10 percent less reference tension (54 to 57 pounds)

This does not mean that an electronic machine strings tighter than a crank, spring-activated machine. It only means that an electronic machine strings more accurately to the reference tension requested! Elongation, friction, and so on have less effect on this type of machine.

Again, remember that tension is only a number! The closer you can get your racquet to the tension you prefer, the better off you and your game will be. Knowing that machines string differently at the same requested tension will help you achieve this goal. Don't become caught up in a number. Be intelligent and play with a string tension that is best for your game.

The stringer should calibrate the stringing machine every day before starting work. By knowing that the machine will perform the same from one day to the next, the stringer will be more consistent. It is your responsibility to ask the stringer when the machine was last calibrated and if it's OK. Each company issues specific guidelines about proper calibration techniques. Shy away from a shop or stringer who doesn't know when or how to calibrate the machine. Chances are that stringers like these are not as serious about their work as you are about your game!

Stringers and Racquet Technicians

The person using the machine must be skilled to achieve an actual tension that is close to the reference tension you request. Players sometimes refer to a stringer as someone who strings tight or loose. This usually refers more to the person's stringing habits, good and bad, than to the machine. Many stringers, for whatever reason, feel they need to be fast to gain a favorable reputation from players. The opposite is usually true. Quality in doing anything takes time, and stringing a racquet is no exception. If a stringer doesn't attend to details and, let's say, clamps off before the machine has finished pulling tension, the string job will feel loose to the player.

The person using the machine and the calibration of the machine are the two factors that most affect tension, but there are others.

String Type Used

You learned in the section on string construction that different types of strings feel different. Even at the same reference tension (tension the machine is set to), different types of strings will vary in actual tension (tension of the frame's strings after stringing). Several variables can cause this difference:

- String gauge
- String construction or composition
- String elongation
- String resiliency (or elasticity)

The conclusion you can draw from this is that if you use a different string in your racquet, your regular reference tension may give you a very different feel. You should do your homework or consult a professional about the differences first.

String Pattern of a Racquet

Different racquets have different string patterns for a reason (see figure 14.1). Denser patterns (more main and cross strings) deliver greater string durability and more control because the strings move less on impact with the ball. Open string patterns tend to enhance power and spin on the ball when struck. Because it has more string, a dense-pattern racquet will feel as if it is strung tighter than a comparable racquet with a more open string pattern.

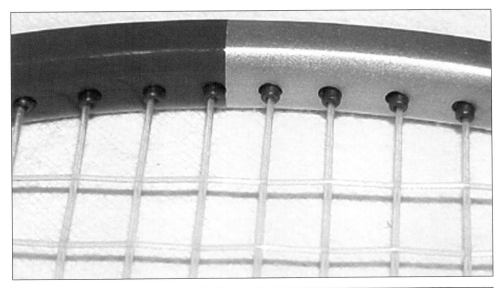

Figure 14.1 Different racquets have different string patterns.

Let's take two identical racquets that only differ in string patterns. One racquet has a dense pattern with 18 main strings and 20 cross strings. The other has an open pattern with 16 main strings and 18 cross strings. The requested reference tension is 60 pounds. A player comparing the two would note the following characteristics (when comparing strings in the racquet, not the frame).

	Dense pattern	Open pattern
Power	Less	More
Control	More	Less
Topspin	Less	More
Durability	More	Less
Vibration	Same	Same
Shock*	More	Less

*Because a dense-pattern racquet is less resilient and creates a tighter string bed, the player would feel more shock with it than with an open-pattern racquet strung at the same tension.

Stringing Pattern

The two ways to install strings in today's racquets are typically referred to as one-piece stringing and two-piece stringing. When implemented properly, both are recommended by racquet manufacturers. Some racquets call for one or the other. The stringer should know which is correct for a particular racquet, but some overlook the distinction and don't understand why there is a difference. Some stringers will be lazy and simply install the strings into the racquet as fast as they can.

As a serious tennis player, you should know the correct way to have your racquet strung. Improper stringing is a major cause of premature racquet fatigue and can create a different feel on the string bed.

The United States Racquet Stringers Association (USRSA) is the only worldwide organization that actively tests stringers around the world. Look for the worldwide symbol of a USRSA certified racquet technician (CRT), the designation of the highest level of competence.

Racquet (Frame) Condition

The last issue related to tension is the condition of the frame. An old and worn frame will most likely be fatigued and unable to hold the tension placed on it during the stringing process. The reference tension applied by the machine will be OK, but the actual tension will typically be much less than it was when the racquet was new. The fibers of the frame can't withstand the forces placed on the frame and tend to give, causing the string bed to be softer than it should be.

On the other hand, a new frame that has never been strung will tend to string up looser on the initial stringing, mainly because the grommets haven't yet been "seated" or "conditioned" by having tension applied to them. Many professional players request that a new racquet be strung two to four pounds tighter than normal.

Never attempt to string or play with a cracked or broken frame. Serious damage to yourself or others may occur! Be respectful of others and discard the racquet properly so that no one will attempt to use it.

Prestretching String

Some manufacturers recommend prestretching for highly elastic strings. This process slows the initial string stretch (loss in tension) prevalent among these type of strings. The process is accomplished by uncoiling the string set and wrapping the entire length of string around a smooth pole. The stringer then pulls both ends of the string in a slow, gradual motion, holding the string at full resistance for 20 or 30 seconds. The amount of force needed to accomplish a proper prestretch is 45 to 50 pounds of pulling force. A proper prestretch should result in the coil being taken out of the string so that it lays flat.

Many stringers prestretch natural gut so that it is easier to handle. Doing this will help reduce the initial tension loss in natural gut, but the prestretch will not have as great an effect on natural gut as it does on multifilament synthetic string.

If you are accustomed to having your strings prestretched, be sure to tell your stringer each time you need service. Don't assume that your stringer will do it just because the string package recommends it!

Prestretching will make the string bed of your racquet feel somewhat tighter at the same tension than it would feel without prestretching. This characteristic can be helpful to someone who wants a bit more control but can't afford to string tighter because of arm or shoulder problems.

Effect of Weather on Tension

The elements play a big role in the tension of the strings in your racquet. Heat is the most damaging. Exposure to excessive heat will reduce the ability of the strings to deliver the energy they had when fresh, before exposure.

We have all heard that you shouldn't leave your racquet in the car on a hot day, especially in the trunk. What does this really mean? How long is too long? How hot is hot? The best way to explain this is by looking at test results about the effect of heat on a freshly strung racquet.

Two racquets, identical in every aspect, were strung with the same string at 60 pounds of tension. Immediately after stringing, all possible measurements were taken on the string bed. These tests included tension from a Beers tensometer and bed deflection from a Babolat RDC. The string beds of the two racquets were the same in all test parameters. One racquet was then placed inside a car with the windows rolled up. The other was placed in an air-conditioned house. The weather was normal for a spring day in Florida, 75 degrees Fahrenheit and mostly sunny. The temperature inside the house was a climate-controlled 70 degrees Fahrenheit.

A thermometer placed inside the car measured just how hot the interior of the car would get during the test. The temperature inside (with the windows up and in the sun) reached 140 degrees! The racquets were checked on the test equipment after 30 minutes, 60 minutes, and 120 minutes. Table 14.2 displays the results.

This was not an extreme test—people leave their racquets in the car all the time! We performed the test to show that heat becomes excessive in a closed-up car. What is it that causes the string to lose so much tension and resiliency in such a short time?

Well, the molecules of the nylon under traction (tension in the racquet) become farther apart and lose their ability to resist the force of the tension. Once this ability is lost, it will not return. Although the racquet placed in the car had yet to strike a ball, for all practical purposes it was "dead" and should

Table 14.2	Effect of Heat on String Tension and Bed Deflection	
Start	**Fresh frame**	**Frame in car**
Strung tension (machine set to)	60 pounds	60 pounds
Tensometer reading	60 pounds	60 pounds
RDC bed deflection	76 units	76 units
After 30 minutes	**Fresh frame**	**Frame in car**
Tensometer reading	59 pounds	55 pounds
RDC bed deflection	74 units	70 units
After 60 minutes	**Fresh frame**	**Frame in car**
Tensometer reading	58 pounds	50 pounds
RDC bed deflection	73 units	65 units
After 120 minutes	**Fresh frame**	**Frame in car**
Tensometer reading	57 pounds	47 pounds
RDC bed deflection	73 units	63 units

have been restrung. Two hours in the heat had stressed the strings as much as 20 to 30 hours of normal playing would.

You may be telling yourself, "If heat is this bad, then cold must be good!" All tests have shown that although extreme cold doesn't affect tension as heat does, it will make the strings (as well as the racquet frame) brittle. If you live in a climate where you must leave your racquet in the car during extremely cold (below-zero) weather, you need to allow ample time for the racquet and strings to warm up before playing. Remember, a racquet is a nonliving thing that will lose heat faster than it will absorb it. Wait until the racquet has a normal temperature to the touch. Thirty minutes should be enough. I hope you are playing inside! You will have plenty of time to stretch and prepare for your match.

When to String

Unfortunately, most people restring their racquets only when the strings break. The opposite occurs on the professional tour. Pro players restring before every match, and many do so during a match! What is best for you depends on the following:

1. Are you above the novice level of play?
2. Are you serious about your game? (Is top performance important to you?)
3. Do you often break strings? (Will you be caught without a racquet in a match?)
4. Do you have arm or shoulder problems? (If so, fresh strings are a must.)
5. Do you expose your racquet to extreme conditions (excessive heat, airline flights)?
6. Do you play primarily on clay courts? (Clay tends to wear out strings faster.)

If you answer yes to any of these questions, you probably need to be more aware of when to restring.

A good benchmark for normal recreational use is to restring your racquet after every 30 hours of play. The more serious you are, the more often you should restring. Remember that 60 percent of the energy delivered to the ball comes from the strings. Even if you are just an occasional player who plays seasonally, you should restring before each season.

Stringing at Tournaments

Nearly all tennis players who travel will occasionally need to have a racquet restrung by someone other than their regular stringer. Tournament players at all levels often have this need. For the professional player, it is the norm rather than the exception.

How you handle the situation will determine whether you gain the satisfaction you're looking for. What you really want is for your racquet to feel like what you are accustomed to. Here is what you need to know:

- What type of machine (electronic or spring activated) is your racquet regularly strung on?

- What pattern is used on your racquet? (One-piece? Two-piece? Count the knots.)

- What string do you use exactly? (Brand, gauge, and color are important!)

- Does your regular stringer prestretch your string? (If you don't know, ask.)

- If your regular stringer has made any comments, pass them along.

All too often people take proper stringing for granted and fail to pay attention to these simple issues. Have your stringer write you a "racquet prescription" on a note card and keep it in your racquet bag. You will thank yourself when you need service from someone else.

Don't blame a stringer for spoiling your vacation or causing you to lose an important match because you couldn't play with your racquet. Chances are that if you had known the answers to the preceding questions, you wouldn't have experienced a problem.

You should carry extra strings and grips of the exact type you use, especially if you use a string that is somewhat special or hard to find. Not every shop will carry the specific products you use.

All players who travel must be able to arrange for a restringing. Tournament players must do the following additional things.

- Immediately after arriving at a tournament, check-in a racquet for stringing. This is crucial! Don't wait until you have to get a racquet strung. Chances are that the stringer will be busy, and you may not get your racquet done as quickly as expected. More important, by having a racquet done before you need one, you'll be able to judge the tension.

- Even if you need to get more than one racquet strung when you arrive, have only one strung at first. When that frame is completed, test the tension. If you need to change your request, you will have wasted only one stringing.

If you prepare yourself successfully and professionally, be prepared to be professionally successful!

Stringing Process

Whether you are a stringer or someone who is having a racquet strung, this section is important. It deals with the process of installing the strings into a racquet and the basic things you should know.

The first item is a frame inspection. Before any racquet, regardless of age, is restrung, a visual inspection of the following items should be conducted:

- Check for any visible cracks or stress marks in the frame. You should never restring or play with a cracked racquet. If you are a customer just wanting to get your racquet strung, knowing about any cracks will help answer questions that might come as a surprise later. If you are a stringer, checking the racquet before doing any work can save you from trying to explain to a customer returning to pick up the racquet that he or she has a broken frame. It is best to do this visual inspection while the customer is present.

- Check the condition of the grommets (plastic protective strips that protect the string and frame). You can often have these replaced for a nominal charge, and doing so will lengthen the life of both the racquet frame and the strings.

- Check the condition of the grip. This is an excellent time to receive a complete tune-up of your racquet. Also, be sure to check the butt cap for loose staples.

Cutting Out the Strings

The next step is to cut out the old strings correctly. To minimize the stress to the frame when relieving the tension, begin cutting in the middle of the string pattern (see figure 14.2). Cut mains and crosses together in a uniform system as you work to the outer edge of the racquet. Cut at a diagonal direction going up, then down, then up.

Carefully remove the old string and again look closely at the grommet strips. Check the holes for any cracks and check the bumper guard (on top of the racquet) for excessive wear. Replace them as needed.

Tubing and Padding

If you can't find a replacement grommet kit for your racquet, or have only a few holes that need attention, you can use tubing to protect the string from the frame. Any qualified stringer has plenty of experience using tubing and should have an adequate supply on hand.

Sometimes a stringer will install leather pads (referred to as power pads) in certain areas of a frame. These pads protect the string from breaking prematurely by creating a rounder turn for the string to follow, which helps

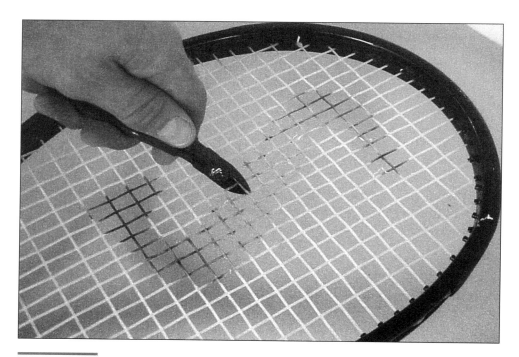

Figure 14.2 To minimize the stress to the frame when relieving the tension, begin cutting in the middle of the string pattern.

alleviate sheer or grommet breakage. Pads are usually used with natural-gut strings in higher tension.

If you continue to break a string in the same area close to the frame and have tried replacing the grommets, try having power pads installed in that area. As with all special stringing variations or additions, consult a professional racquet technician first.

Frame Mounting

Proper mounting of the racquet in a stringing machine is essential to maintaining the integrity of the frame (see figure 14.3). Shy away from purchasing an inexpensive home machine because you want to save money on stringing. The stress load placed on a tennis racquet during the stringing process is the most strain and stress it will ever experience. If stringing a racquet causes its shape to change, chances are the machine is inferior or the racquet was mounted incorrectly.

Knowing how to use a particular stringing machine is just as important as knowing how to install the strings. The manufacturer provides a complete set of instructions with the stringing machine. The stringer should understand and follow these instructions. If you have purchased a used machine that doesn't have instructions, call the manufacturer and request a copy before you use the equipment.

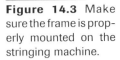

Figure 14.3 Make sure the frame is properly mounted on the stringing machine.

Racquet Patterns

We are getting closer to stringing a racquet! Now that we have checked and properly mounted the racquet, we need to know what pattern to use. Every manufacturer has a diagram of the pattern for stringing every racquet they sell. You may need to request one if you don't know the correct way.

There is only one way to string each racquet! We need to know what holes the main and cross strings skip. The integrity of the racquet frame will be seriously compromised if the racquet is not strung as it was designed. In addition, a racquet may be illegal for tournament play if the pattern isn't consistent. The USRSA provides a yearly digest to its members. Each edition is updated with all the newer models on the market. With this book, the stringer can quickly find the pattern for every racquet.

If as a last resort you are attempting to string a racquet for which you have no directions, look carefully at the existing string pattern. Do not cut it out until you are sure of the correct pattern. If the frame has no strings but has been strung before, look carefully at which way the grommets go. With luck you will be able to distinguish the mains from the crosses.

Custom Stringing Techniques

Undoubtedly, most stringers consider themselves the best. Many attempt to differentiate their work from the work of others by stringing in a special way. Usually the knots will be in a different place. Stringers may use creative knots or add pads on every frame. In any case, as long as these specialized techniques don't jeopardize the integrity of the frame or strings, you shouldn't worry.

In many cases these special techniques stem from knowledge about how certain strings react to particular frames, and the techniques can make an important difference. Be sure that this is the case and that the stringer did not use a "special" technique only because he or she didn't know the proper way to string the racquet!

Machine Maintenance and Calibration

Anyone who uses a stringing machine needs to clean and calibrate the machine at regular intervals. If you travel with a machine, you must have the calibration checked and adjusted before using it. Machines that stay put in a shop should be cleaned and calibrated daily.

Racquet Grips

Here we discuss grip sizes, how to size a grip for your hand, grip types, and customization techniques.

Grip Sizes

The size of the pallet (the handle of the racquet) when it has a grip installed is measured around the circumference of the grip. The smaller the measurement, the smaller the grip size. The most commonly produced sizes available today are the following:

- 4 $\frac{1}{8}$ inches (L-1)
- 4 $\frac{1}{4}$ inches (L-2)
- 4 $\frac{3}{8}$ inches (L-3)
- 4 $\frac{1}{2}$ inches (L-4)
- 4 $\frac{5}{8}$ inches (L-5)

Two numbers are listed for each grip size. The size in parentheses is how grips are usually described in European countries.

Proper Sizing of the Grip

The best way to determine your correct size is to hold the racquet comfortably in your playing hand. Turn the racquet over to expose your palm and fingertips. You should be able to place the pinkie finger from your free hand comfortably between the heel of your palm and the ring finger of the hand holding the racquet. You should have enough room to just touch each (figure 14.4).

If you overlap, the grip is too small. Having too small a grip is one of the primary causes of tennis elbow. If you are uncertain about which size to use, play with the larger one. By doing so, you will experience less twisting and torque and thus less shock to the arm.

Figure 14.4 If your pinky finger fits comfortably between your palm and fingers, your grip is sized correctly.

Grip Feels

Two grips of a given size produced by different companies may feel quite different from one another. The circumference may be the same, but the sizing of the bevels (the eight sides of the pallet) will vary, which may cause an entirely different feel in your hand. You may experience playing discomfort with a grip of the size you normally use.

When choosing a grip, find one of the proper size that feels correct. When changing from one racquet to another (usually one from a different manufacturer), many people don't give the fit much thought. They will say, "I am a 4½-inch grip size. There's no need to check—that's what my old racquet was." You always need to check the way a new or different racquet fits your hand. Don't become caught up in a number.

Grip Types

The first racquets had no grip material at all on the handle. The grip was simply the wood as it continued down from the head of the racquet. As the game and the technology of racquet manufacturing progressed, players found it increasingly difficult to hold on to the racquet because they were hitting the ball harder. Manufacturers started to produce racquets with a covering of natural leather over the pallet. Leather grips are still used today, but in recent years they have given way in popularity to synthetic grips. Each type has benefits and drawbacks.

Leather Grips

Because leather grips are made from a high-grade calfskin, they offer the best absorption of perspiration. Like any skin, the leather grip has many pores that breathe so it absorbs moisture well. The durability of a leather grip surpasses that of any synthetic grip. The biggest complaint about leather grips is that they have a much harder feel on the hand. The average recreational player may develop blisters and perceive more shock to the arm. On the professional tour, most players use a leather grip. Most racquets manufactured today come with a synthetic grip because the cost of a leather grip is much greater.

Synthetic Grips

Bright colors, various textures, tacky feel, and extra cushioning are some of the stated benefits of today's synthetic grips. Low durability, poor absorption, and a feel that quickly becomes slippery are more the reality. The synthetic grips feel good when new, but many recreational players fail to replace them regularly. Synthetic replacement grips are economical, and you can maintain the feel you loved when the grip was new by frequently installing a new one. If you tend to perspire a lot or play in a hot, humid climate, be aware that synthetic grips do not absorb moisture. They shed water at first and then become saturated and slippery. The benefit of the extra cushioning is a positive. If you want to reduce the vibration from your racquet, a cushioned synthetic grip will help. Be aware that these synthetic grips do not have a life expectancy similar to that of the racquet frame. A good guideline is to change the synthetic replacement grip every other time you have the racquet restrung, if not more often.

Overgrips

With the overall appeal of modern synthetic grips, overgrips, or overwraps, have become popular. These thin grips are installed directly over the main grip of the racquet. Inexpensive and usually sold in multiple-unit packages, they are intended for short-term use. Literally hundreds of overgrips are available, but they fall into two different basic categories—sticky (or tacky) and dry (or nontacky). Because each of us has a different pH balance, we produce different kinds of perspiration. So for each of us, some grip styles will become more slippery than others. No type is better than another. The following product examples can help you find one that fits your needs.

Players who sweat a lot or play in a hot, humid climate should try a dry overgrip:

- Tournagrip Original
- Babolat Team Grip
- Prince Dura Zorb

Players who want a sticky feel should consider one of these tacky overgrips:

- Gamma Grip 2
- Prince Duratred
- Babolat ATP Tour Over-Grip XL

These are just a few samples of the hundreds available. By experimentation or by asking someone qualified, you will have no problem finding a perfect type for your specific needs.

Grip Installation

Any grip or overgrip must be installed correctly. If you are attempting this for the first time, you need to be aware of a few simple things.

- You must first remove the old grip.
- If you are replacing the main grip of your racquet, you will probably have to remove a staple at the end.
- You will need scissors, a stapler, and grip tape (usually supplied with new grip).

- Be attentive to how the original grip was installed. You should try to duplicate the wrap.
- All racquets come gripped right-handed from the factory. If you are left-handed, see the section that follows shortly.
- You always start from the bottom of the racquet!

Almost all of today's replacement grips come with instructions. If you are installing a leather grip, you will also need some double-sided tape to secure the grip to the racquet pallet.

If you are putting on an overgrip, simply install it directly over the main grip of your racquet. Try to follow the pattern of the main grip, starting at the bottom of the racquet.

As mentioned earlier, all racquets from the manufacturers come wrapped right-handed. If you are left-handed, you should be aware that the grip on your racquet is "backward." If the handle doesn't feel comfortable on either side or if you tend to tear up grips quickly, chances are that you can solve the problem by having the grip installed for a left-handed player.

If your grip is old or has been used, you will need to buy a new grip before making the change. When removing the current factory grip, notice the direction of the wrap. You will simply need to reverse the procedure and go the other way. Figure 14.5 illustrates the difference.

Grip Customization Techniques

If you can't get comfortable with the dimensional shape of your grip or you need to enlarge or reduce the size of the pallet, you can customize the grip. Few professional players use the grip size and shape that their racquets come with. On this level, professional racquet technicians remold the shape to one that is different and personal for each player. This technical service carries a premium price tag.

Although the recreational player wouldn't think of having this done, individual attention to grip shape is sometimes necessary. To increase grip size, several reliable options are available:

- Add-ons—Available at many tennis shops, the add-on is placed between the pallet and the main grip to add one full size.
- Heat sleeves—Installed on the racquet pallet with a high-temperature heat gun, heat sleeves also add one full size.
- Thicker replacement grips—Some manufacturers sell a synthetic replacement grip somewhat thicker than normal, which increases the size.

Reducing the size of most modern racquets is more difficult. Many of the frames produced today don't have a foam pallet that can be shaved down. These solid, one-piece-construction racquets can't be reduced in size. You

Figure 14.5 Right-handed and left-handed grips are different.

can try a thinner replacement grip or simply rewrap the existing grip more tightly to produce a slightly smaller dimension.

If you have a racquet that can be shaved, you should seek a qualified person to do the work. Once the process has started, it can't be undone! If you make a mistake you will have to replace the racquet.

Other customizations for the grip of your racquet include the following:

- Use a larger or smaller butt cap to create a larger or smaller feel at the end of the racquet. Try a larger one if you have a hard time holding on to the racquet when serving.

- If you have a two-handed backhand, you may want to wrap a new replacement grip far up the shaft. Most frames today apply grip material only high enough for one hand to have full touch.

- By wrapping the main grip tighter or looser, or by overlapping the material more or less, you can create a unique, personal feel.

Racquet Selection

Just as we offered the 10 commandments of strings, we offer the 12 commandments of racquet frames, basic guidelines that apply to all racquets:

1. A heavier racquet frame generates more power.
2. A heavier racquet frame vibrates less.
3. A heavier racquet frame has a larger sweet spot.
4. A stiffer racquet frame generates more power.
5. A stiffer racquet frame has a larger sweet spot.
6. A stiffer racquet frame transmits more shock to the arm than a more flexible racquet frame.
7. A stiffer racquet frame provides a more uniform ball response across the entire string bed.
8. A larger racquet frame (larger head size) generates more power.
9. A larger racquet frame (larger head size) is more resistant to twisting.
10. A larger racquet frame (larger head size) has a larger sweet spot.
11. A longer racquet frame (total length) generates more velocity and therefore more power.
12. The string bed in a longer racquet frame generates more spin because the long frame produces greater velocity.

Refer back to these guidelines as we further discuss the aspects of the frame.

Frame Construction

The first tennis racquets were wood. Different types of wood created different feels or different kinds of playability. These first racquets varied little in head size, string pattern, or length. The biggest drawback to wood was its weight and stiffness, which limited technical innovation. Equipment had little effect on the game for many years.

A big step for racquet production came with the use aluminum alloys, which allowed companies to make larger, stiffer, and lighter racquets. These new frames allowed the user to hit the ball harder and more accurately. Power quickly overtook finesse among tennis players at all levels.

Soon after their introduction, aluminum frames had to share the spotlight with something even more powerful—composite frames made of graphite and fiberglass. The age of power tennis had arrived.

As we discuss racquet frames, keep in mind that they vary in two ways—construction type and frame type.

Construction types

- Alloy (aluminum)
- Fiberglass
- Graphite
- Fused (alloy and composite)

Frame types

- Constant beam
- Taper beam
- Wide-body
- Thin beam (player's frames)

Racquet companies match the various frame types to the different frame constructions to attempt to bring out the best combination of attributes. Playing style has a crucial role in how a racquet will perform. Keep in mind that there are no bad racquets, only bad choices in racquets!

By the laws of physics, all tennis racquets are governed by the following items:

- Weight of the racquet—the total mass of the racquet
- Balance of the racquet—how the mass is proportioned
- Stiffness of the racquet—flexibility
- Inertia of the racquet—swing weight of the racquet in motion

Beyond these basic principles are other items that can enhance how a racquet will play, including head size, length, beam width, frame type, and material (construction type). Remember also what we have learned about string types and patterns and how they affect the playability of a racquet.

Let's discuss each of the four items more closely.

Weight

Weight, or mass, is a measurement of the overall weight of the racquet, measured without strings and recorded in grams. Some people still use ounces, but grams are more precise. To convert one to the other, use the following:

$$\text{Grams to ounces: grams} \times .035 = \text{ounces}$$

$$\text{Ounces to grams: ounces} \times 28.35 = \text{grams}$$

The tennis industry uses this general classification for the weight of racquets without strings (strings weigh 15 to 18 grams):

- Ultralight frames: less than 240 grams
- Lightweight frames: 240–280 grams
- Medium-weight frames: 280–320 grams
- Heavyweight frames: 320 or more grams

The current trend in the market is to make racquets lighter. Claims of "effortless power" and "easy to play with" are common. But the basic principles of physics apply to every racquet—no matter how light or heavy. The 12 commandments of racquet frames follow these principles, which we expand on here.

Remember that tennis balls always weigh about the same. A legally approved ball is 56.7 to 58.5 grams. So the lighter the racquet, the closer the weight of the racquet and ball. Thus, a light racquet will deliver less energy to the ball than a heavy racquet (when swung at the same speed). This simply means that for most people, a lighter racquet will produce less power!

Another important thing happens as the two weights become more alike—shock to the wrist, arm, and shoulder increases dramatically. To understand this, think about pounding a nail into a piece of wood. You can use either a lightweight cobbler's hammer that weighs five or six ounces or a construction sledgehammer that weighs five pounds. If you were to swing each hammer at the same speed, which would drive the nail with less effort, with less shock? This is the principle behind racquet weights. The point is that you should play with the heaviest racquet that doesn't affect your normal swing speed. That racquet will deliver the greatest impact on the tennis ball and have the least effect on your body.

Balance

The balance of a racquet depends on its longitudinal (tip to butt) weight distribution. The balance is the racquet's center of gravity. Balance is always read from the butt end of the frame and is usually measured in centimeters. Other common references are in inches and points (points are increments of one-eighth of an inch). Here is the conversion:

$$\text{Centimeters to inches: centimeters} \times .394 = \text{inches}$$

$$\text{Inches to centimeters: inches} \times 2.54 = \text{centimeters}$$

Racquet balance is classified as one of the following:

1. Head heavy (HH)—More of the weight is in the head of the racquet.

2. Head light (HL)—More of the weight is in the handle of the racquet.

3. Even balance (EB)—The weight is evenly proportioned along the entire frame.

Two racquets of identical weight with different balance will feel completely different. We will discuss this further in the section "Matching Frame Type to Playing Style." You first need to understand the characteristics of balance and its effect on your racquet.

Keep the following example in mind when discussing racquet balance. Let's take an ordinary 16-ounce carpenter's hammer. No matter how you pick it up, it will weigh 16 ounces. If you hold it as it was intended to be held, by the handle, it feels head heavy and somewhat difficult to swing. Now hold it by its metal head. It feels lighter, and it is head light. It is very easy to swing.

In both cases you are holding the same mass, or weight, but by holding the weight differently you have a different perception of its mass. This is how to describe racquet balance.

Stiffness

Stiffness, or flex, of a racquet is a measurement of how much deflection will occur on the frame when a given force is applied. This is a technical way of describing how much the racquet will give when you hit a tennis ball. We most often think of flex only in the longitudinal axis (from the head to the grip), but the ability of a racquet frame to withstand force placed on it from side to side in the hoop area (where the strings are) also plays a crucial role in its stiffness and in the way it plays. This stiffness of a racquet is known as *torsional stiffness.*

Without torsional stiffness, a racquet couldn't withstand any twisting or torque when a ball is hit off center. Generally, the stiffer a racquet frame is longitudinally, the stiffer it will be torsionally.

Racquet companies attempt to make racquets that deliver the best of all worlds. They attempt to make frames that are solid on off-center hits (with high torsional strength) yet are comfortable and controllable (with lower longitudinal stiffness). These frames, typically called wide-body frames, have different beam widths in different areas.

The longitudinal stiffness of a racquet provides power. The torsional stiffness gives control (less torque) and comfort on off-center shots. Both are important and work together to make up the feel of a racquet on impact.

To understand the issue of racquet stiffness, remember that the stiffer the frame, the less it will deflect on impact. Thus the string bed will have to do more work, and you will have to generate more power. This will cause greater shock to the arm and shoulder.

The less stiff the frame, the more feel you will have. Many players refer to this lack of power as control. A frame with less stiffness will cause less shock and vibration.

Racquets lose their stiffness over time. No matter how well you take care of it, you shouldn't expect a racquet to last forever. Racquets lose their stiffness for several reasons:

- Improper stringing techniques (wrong pattern, inconsistent tensioning, etc.)
- Excessively high tension
- Excessive stringing of the frame
- Hitting the ball hard
- Exposure to excessive heat (especially in vehicles)
- Court abuse (throwing, hitting the net cord, bouncing on the tip, etc.)

If you are buying a new frame and can have the stiffness checked, record the measurement and track it every time you restring the frame. When you have lost 5 to 10 percent of the original stiffness, replace the frame, no matter how good it looks. Always have this check done in the unstrung condition.

Inertia

Inertia (or swing weight) is how a racquet feels when you swing it. This is the most important way to understand just how the weight is distributed in the racquet. Many refer to inertia as a racquet's maneuverability. Try to understand the following example of inertia.

We have two racquets, identical in most respects. They both weight 300 grams and balance exactly in the middle. The first frame weighs 150 grams at the very top of the head of the racquet, and 150 grams at the extreme butt-end. The other racquet weighs 100 grams at the head, 100 grams at the butt, and 100 grams exactly in the middle. Both are 300 grams; both balance exactly in the middle. Which frame will feel heavier to swing? Why?

Obviously, the frame that weighs 50 grams more in the head will feel heavier when you swing it. This is how we explain inertia. Because the racquet that weighs 50 grams more in the head is less maneuverable, it will feel slower to swing than the other racquet. The frame that is heavier in the head will have more power and control but may be less maneuverable.

Remember the regular carpenter's hammer in the section on weight? You were not only feeling a difference in weight distribution and balance. When you tried to swing the hammer in the two different conditions, you felt a difference in inertia.

With knowledge of the basics, we can move on to matching a type of racquet to a style of play. These generalized examples are intended to steer players with certain styles to specific types of racquets. Again, remember that there are no bad racquets, only bad choices in racquets!

Matching Frame Type to Playing Style

Tennis players are of three basic styles—baseliner, serve and volley, and all-court. The three basic styles of racquets are head heavy (HH), head light (HL), and even balance (EB).

Let's look at the playing styles and how they differ. Baseliners typically feel more comfortable staying back behind the baseline and hitting ground strokes all day long. They tend to come to the net only to retrieve balls or shake hands! If this is you, the contact point (where you most often hit the ball on the strings) is probably toward the head of the racquet. Look for ball fuzz to determine this. Baseliners tend to hit most of their balls below the waist. Your contact point is farther away from your body and farther up the string bed of the racquet. Baseliners tend to prefer a head-heavy racquet because more of the weight is at the head of the racquet (this will also generally give it a higher inertia) and because the sweet spot of a racquet will be more toward where the most head weight is. The head-heavy racquet will have a higher sweet spot. Baseliners hit more balls near the head and usually need a little more power because they play farther from the net. If this is your game style, a head-heavy racquet will feel most comfortable to you.

Serve-and-volley players like to get to net quickly and force opponents into a defensive position. These players hit most balls above the waist and usually contact the ball closer to the bottom of the string bed, mainly because their hand-eye coordination finds it more comfortable to play the ball closer. The serve-and-volley player usually does not extend the arm as fully as a baseliner does. A head-light racquet is generally preferred here. With a head-light (HL) frame, the serve-and-volley player will have a more maneuverable racquet with a sweet spot that is lower on the string bed.

The final style is a blend of the other two. The all-court player will feel comfortable playing either serve and volley or baseline depending on each point or the opponent. Because this player feels comfortable playing a blend of styles, the racquet will tend to be balanced. An even-balance (EB) racquet offers the diversity needed to hit balls from all contact points. The all-court player will have a variety of contact points but tend to hit most balls near the middle of the frame. The sweet spot of an even-balance racquet will be toward the middle of the string bed, thus giving the all-courter a feel of an equal amount of power and control on contact.

Keep in mind that these are only examples of how to match a style of racquet to a style of player. To determine what style of racquet is best for you, try out a variety of frames to find which type best suits your needs.

Different Racquet Head Sizes

Unfortunately, manufacturers have not agreed on a standard classification of head sizes. One manufacturer may refer to a racquet with a head size of 98 square inches as a midsize, whereas another manufacturer would call the same frame a mid-plus. The following chart is helpful in classifying head sizes:

1. Traditional size (older wooden frames): 60–79 square inches
2. Midsize: 80–90 square inches
3. Mid-plus: 91–100 square inches
4. Oversize: 101–115 square inches
5. Super oversize: more than 115 square inches

If you are not sure of your racquet size, you can measure it by using the following calculation. Keep in mind that this will be close to the actual size, but not exact. You will need to measure the inside diameter of the string bed, both horizontally and longitudinally.

$$\text{Area (square inches)} = \frac{3.14 + L + H}{4}$$

where L is the measurement of the inside longitudinal length from the tip to throat area of the string bed and H is the measurement of the inside horizontal length of the middle of the string bed.

$$\frac{3.14 + 13.5 + 10.25}{4} = 108.7 \text{ square inches}$$

Deciding on the perfect head size is a complex subject. You need to use knowledge of the 12 commandments of frames to help answer the following head-size questions:

If I find that I	I should try
need more power	a larger head size
mis-hit many balls	a larger head size
have too much power	a smaller head size (if using a larger one)
feel that my racquet is too slow	a smaller head size (if using a larger one)

These are just a few examples. Remember that among racquets of various head sizes, every style of frame discussed earlier (head heavy, head light, and even balance) is available to meet your specific playing style.

Experimentation with different head sizes is crucial. Different head sizes of the same racquet model will play much differently from one another. A general guideline is that the more help (power) you need from the racquet, the larger the head size should be.

Most professional players today use racquets that would fall into the midsize or mid-plus categories, whereas most recreational players use oversize or super-oversize frames.

Deciding on what length of a racquet to use wasn't an issue until a few years ago. Extra-long, stretch, long body, and extended length are examples of the terminology manufacturers use to highlight racquets that exceed the standard length of 27 inches. The advantages and disadvantages of using a longer frame are listed here. Remember that these generalized statements may not apply to everyone. Your personal results are what matter. You should simply be aware that these differences can affect parts of your game. Note that we are assuming that weight, balance, inertia, and flex are equal and that your ability to swing each frame is the same.

	Regular length	Longer length
Power	Less	More
Control	More	Less
Maneuverability	More	Less
Spin on ball	Less	More
Power on the serve	Less	More
Shock to arm	Less	More
Hitting late	Less	More
Reach to ball	Less	More

The stiffness of the racquet frame relates directly to how much power it delivers as well as how much shock is created on impact with a tennis ball. If you have to string your racquet very tightly (over the highest tension recommended by the manufacturer) to gain the needed control, you probably have a frame that is too stiff for your style of play. On the other hand, if you need to string it very loosely (under the lowest tension recommended by the manufacturer), you should have a stiffer frame for your game. Examples of how stiffness affects your game are listed here. Again, we assume that weight, balance, inertia, and flex are equal and that your ability to swing each frame is the same.

	Flexible frame	Stiffer frame
Power	Less	More
Control	More	Less
Maneuverability	Same	Same
Spin on the ball	More	Less
Power on the serve	Less	More
Shock to arm	Less	More
Comfort	More	Less
Sweet spot	Less	More

When manufacturers discuss the stiffness of a frame, it is usually in terms of RA units. This standard numbering system is determined by placing a racquet (unstrung) on a piece of test equipment called an RA test. This device places a set amount of weight on a lever that makes the frame bend at its halfway point. The number read on the scale is the RA unit. The higher the number, the stiffer the frame. So a racquet with an RA of 80 RA units is much stiffer than a racquet with an RA of 60 RA units. Table 14.3 presents an unofficial classification chart that can help you understand stiffness.

These measurements are always recorded on an unstrung frame. Because of the added force placed on the frame at different tensions, the numbers will be lower when the racquet is strung. If you check the stiffness both ways, you should expect to see that the strung frame will be two to six units lower, depending on how the frame is strung and its construction. You should be aware of the stiffness of your frame so that you can determine if fatigue is becoming a factor. If it is, you should replace the frame.

Many string patterns are available. They fall into two broad categories—open patterns and tight patterns, which are distinguished by how many main strings (which run up and down) and cross strings (which run side to side) the racquet has.

The difference in string pattern can dramatically affect several elements of play. We assume here that you are using the same racquet, string, and string tension, varying only the string pattern.

	Tight pattern	**Open pattern**
Power	Less	More
Control	More	Less
Spin on the ball	Less	More
String durability	More	Less
String movement	Less	More
Shock to arm	More	Less

Table 14.3 Stiffness Classification

RA value	Type of frame
0–55	Very flexible
55–60	Flexible
61–65	Medium stiff
66–70	Stiff
70 or more	Very stiff

Don't be confused by some of the items listed. Because a dense string pattern will have smaller spaces between the strings, the string bed will play more firmly because the strings can't move as much as they can in an open pattern. Therefore, although the tension is the same, the feel will be that the denser pattern is strung tighter!

A racquet with a dense string pattern can be a real benefit to someone who has arm, elbow, or shoulder problems and can't control an open-pattern racquet. If the player strings the racquet at a lower tension, it feels better on the arm. By going to a frame with a denser pattern, the player can play with reduced string tension and still have the necessary control. This will help reduce the shock and strain that higher string tension places on the arm.

Be aware that if you change racquets, your trusty string tension may not stay the same. Even if you buy a racquet with the same head size, be sure to check for string-pattern differences. The basic classifications for string patterns are as follows:

Open patterns	Tight patterns
14 mains and 16 crosses	18 mains and 20 crosses
16 mains and 18 crosses	20 mains and 22 crosses
16 mains and 19 crosses	16 mains and 20 crosses

Remember that the main strings deliver the power and the cross strings give control. More mains mean less power and more control.

Buying Multiple Frames of the Same Model

It seems that the more you play, the more racquets you'll have. If you are serious about your game, your racquets must be the same in every detail:

- Same model (head size, grip size, and string pattern)
- Same string type, gauge, and color
- Same tension (unless you feel the need for a little more or less tension in one)
- Same weight
- Same balance
- Same stiffness
- Same inertia (or swing weight)

No problem, right? You just go to your favorite sports store and pick up as many racquets as you need of the exact model with the correct grip size. Have your stringer string them with the same string at the same tension. How can you go wrong?

The chances of your receiving frames that feel and play the same are slim! The only thing you can be sure of is that the color will be the same. Every manufacturer has tolerances for production as well as multiple factories that make the same racquets. None of this means that a specific racquet is bad; it only means that it may be different. You are trying to remove all variables to make your tennis game sounder. This is no exception.

If you are buying several new racquets of the same model, seek professional help to assure you that the frames in question are, in fact, the same or can be customized to be the same. Usually, the weight, balance, and inertia can be matched up. The only thing that can't be adjusted or altered is frame stiffness. Be sure that all racquets have similar stiffness.

This advice is especially important if you are buying a second (or third or more) frame sometime after your initial purchase. Take your old racquet along to have it tested against the one or several that you are looking to buy.

If you have an old racquet that you love and have finally decided to part with it but you have no idea what to look for in a new racquet, have your current frame analyzed by a professional racquet technician who has the necessary test equipment. The technician will be able to test current new frames against your old racquet and help you weed out some of the many racquets available today. Chances are that you will find a racquet similar to your old racquet. Remember to demo any racquet before you buy it.

Junior Racquets: Getting Your Child Started in Tennis

You probably have many questions about introducing your child to tennis—when to start, how to pick an instructor, whether to arrange private or group lessons, and so on. All too often the specialized equipment that kids need is either taken for granted or overlooked altogether. Most parents assume that because their child is just starting, any old racquet will do. They feel that when their child gets better, they will treat the youngster to a better racquet. This isn't good enough.

It isn't uncommon to see a child taking a first lesson using Mom or Dad's worn-out adult-size frame. The child is having a hard enough time just moving to the ball, let alone attempting to swing a racquet that is too long and too heavy and has too big a grip. This struggle will leave a lasting impression on the child: playing tennis is hard.

The racquet manufacturers do make frames called junior racquets that come in three different lengths, referred to as the graduated-length method (GLM) for juniors. These frames usually come with the following designations:

Length	Age
21 inches	4–6 years
23 inches	6–8 years
25 inches	8–10 years
26 inches	11 years and older

GLM is a wonderful idea!—shorter frames for smaller, weaker children. Unfortunately, the system doesn't work as well as it sounds. The biggest drawback isn't in the length; it is in the low quality of the frame and strings. These frames are produced with one goal in mind—to make the most inexpensive racquet possible. This isn't the fault of the manufacturers, the same people who produce the best racquets available today. The manufacturers are forced to make a price-point frame that will introduce tennis to as many people as possible. Parents are burdened with finding room in their budgets for all the other items that their children need. If these kids are participating in several sports, chances are they also need new ball gloves, soccer shoes, and so forth.

Parents must decide from the start whether tennis is something they want to introduce their child to properly or poorly! All the pieces of the puzzle (such as proper instruction) need equal attention. Your child can receive the best instruction money can buy, but if he or she can't hit a ball because the low-quality racquet twists in the hands or lacks the stiffness to provide power, tennis will not be any fun.

If you are a parent who wants to start your child playing tennis, chances are that you play tennis yourself. I encourage you to stop at the local mass-merchant chain store and buy the least expensive adult racquet you can find and *actually try to play with it.* The racquet will probably be made of aluminum, prestrung from the factory, and have a slippery low-quality grip. You will pay $20 or $30 for it, but you will learn why you shouldn't introduce your child to tennis with the same crummy racquet, only in a shorter length!

What are your options? Fortunately, you have many. If you are a tennis player, you probably have some old frames lying around. Gather them up and seek professional advice. A certified racquet technician can test them to see if any can be reduced in length, weight, and grip size. If so, they will need to be restrung for your child. If your child is just starting out, I suggest stringing the frame to half of the manufacturer's recommended tension. For example, if the old frame is rated to be strung between 60 and 70 pounds, have it strung to 30 or 35 pounds. The racquet will have the necessary power and the least shock possible, yet it will be easy to hit balls with.

The best option is to buy a new, good-quality adult frame that is considered very light in weight, preferably longer, and with a foam-pallet grip construction. Again, be sure to seek professional advice. This frame can probably be cut down to a shorter length, to 24 to 26 inches. Because it has a foam-construction pallet (handle), it can be shaved down to a small grip size for your child. The racquet will need to be strung and fitted with a good-quality grip.

Why does this work? Remembering all that we have learned in this chapter, we know that proper construction of a frame will lend more power with less effort and less twisting on off-center hits. We know that a longer frame is produced to be more head light to offset the extra length, so cutting this down will make the frame very head light and maneuverable for your child. And we know that proper string selection and tension are crucial for playing success.

Your child's introduction to the game of tennis is your responsibility. How you decide to implement that introduction will contribute directly to the success and fun your child has playing one of the true lifetime sports.

Adult Market Trends

With most items we buy, it seems that lighter, faster, stronger, and bigger are assumed to be better. Tennis racquets are no exception. The equipment available today is of better construction than the equipment of just a few years ago, but when is more power too much? When does lighter weight adversely affect your game? Remember that tennis has been around for a long time. Few changes have been made to court dimensions, ball specifications, or the way the game is played. If the size of a tennis court had increased along with racquet technology, we would be playing the game on a football field with a net at the 50-yard-line.

Use the knowledge in this chapter to fine-tune your game. Forget what you see your favorite professional tennis players using. They don't choose their racquets by watching you play; neither should you by watching them! I like to use the following example to explain the previous statement.

When watching professional car racing, say the Indy 500 or Daytona, we all marvel at the way drivers handle their cars at extreme speed. Not for an instant do we think we could do the same. Nor do we think that the Ford or Chevy we see on the track is available at the local dealer's lot.

Should we not think the same way when buying a tennis racquet? If manufacturers can make racquets that meet the specific needs of your favorite professional player, then be assured that they can make models suited to your needs.

Experimentation coupled with proper knowledge is the fastest way to success. By addressing your specific needs, you will have more fun playing tennis, stay healthier, and win more matches. As with anything important to you, seek professional advice.

Racquet Customization

This is the most complicated and critical section of this chapter. With all we have learned, we should realize that there is not a perfect racquet that will work for everyone.

Even if you understand all the information in this chapter, you will probably be unable to buy a new racquet that will be perfect for you. We all have unique equipment needs. These needs could be as simple as being left-handed and needing the grip wrapped correctly or as complex as needing a specialized grip mold that fits your hand exactly.

Whatever the case, we could all benefit by fine-tuning our equipment. This is where the factories leave us and the racquet technicians take over. The knowledge needed to apply customization to each player's specific requirements makes the work of the technician an art. These artisans can adjust your racquet, strings, and so on so that the equipment performs optimally and fits your needs perfectly.

In this section I will try to give you some knowledge about what happens when a racquet is customized. Why is lead tape added? How do you know where to add it? How much should be added? These are some of the basic questions answered in this section.

Let's start with understanding that every tennis racquet has three sweet spots: COP (center of percussion), node (nodal point), and COR (coefficient of restitution). Let's define the sweet spots and their locations more precisely.

1. COP, or center of percussion, is the point on the string bed where the impact of the ball gives your hand the least shock. This is also the point where a hit of the ball is described by players as feeling good. COP location will depend on weight distribution. Basically, COP will move toward the location of the greatest mass, or weight, in the frame. If you have a head-heavy racquet, COP will be higher up the string bed. A head-light racquet will have COP lower on the string bed. COP will be located approximately 17 to 20 inches from the butt end of a regular 27-inch racquet (depending on weight distribution), close to the middle of the string bed.

2. Node, or nodal point, is where the least amount of vibration occurs when hitting a ball. The actual location will always be slightly lower than COP. When you strike the ball with the node, you will feel as if you didn't hit the ball at all.

3. COR, or coefficient of restitution, is the point on the string bed that when struck delivers the greatest amount of power back to the ball. Its location is low in the string bed, close to the throat bridge of the frame. COR delivers the greatest power because it is located so close to the center of gravity of the racquet. The laws of physics apply to how an opposing force reacts on the mass and center of gravity of an object. Basically, the ball hits close to the halfway point (middle) of a racquet. Because almost the same amount of opposing force is applied to both halves of the racquet, the least amount of twisting occurs to the frame. Tennis players seldom strike this spot because it is so close to the hand. When a professional player is jammed on a volley, you may see that the player hits the ball much harder than the swing warranted. The player probably hit the ball on or very near COR.

As mentioned earlier, the three sweet spots exist in every racquet and will gravitate toward the most mass in the frame. Racquet manufacturers try to cheat the laws of physics by making very light, head-heavy racquets that move COP farther up the string bed where most recreational players hit the ball. Although this works in theory, we have learned (from the example of the carpenter's hammer) that you need a certain amount of mass to get the needed power and control and to absorb the shock and vibration produced from hitting a tennis ball.

These head-heavy racquets will be lighter overall, so one would assume that the arm would have less weight to move when swinging. Again, remember how light the carpenter's hammer felt when we held it backward. The mass was the same, but the feel was very different. The farther the weight is from the hand, the greater the weight will feel when we swing the racquet.

Many people may already have the correct racquet for their game but need a little fine-tuning to make it even better. The new lightweight racquets may be the perfect example.

The current trend for the average recreational player is to have a very light racquet that is head-heavy and has an oversized head. These racquets have great inertia (swing weight) from being so heavy in the head, but they lack the weight needed in the rest of the racquet to give the desired power. By adding weight in the handle or throat area, the player will perceive only slightly more weight but will gain substantial benefit. Try it! What do you have to lose, except maybe another match to the same person who beat you before you spent money on the latest, greatest, lightest racquet!

If you have started to experience arm problems that you never had before, don't say that it must be that you're getting older. Have your equipment checked. You may need some weight strategically placed in that new racquet. The placement of that weight will be determined by the following:

- Where does the racquet feel too light or too heavy to you?
- Do you need more power? More control?
- Does the frame feel as if it twists when you hit the ball?
- Where do you most often strike the ball? (Check the string bed for ball fuzz.)
- Do you hit flat or with topspin?
- What style of play—baseline, serve and volley, or all-court—do you prefer?
- Do you have arm, shoulder, or wrist problems?

The preceding questions are just a sample of those that you should be able to answer when seeking to have a racquet customized. Because every racquet is different, the application used may differ. The result, however, should be the same when custom fitting a racquet.

If you are going to experiment, start by asking if the racquet you are planning to customize is the correct style for your game. If you feel that it is but want to fine-tune it, start by looking at table 14.4, which gives some

Table 14.4	Guidelines for Lead Tape Application		
I need	**My racquet feels**	**Add lead-tape here**	**Test amount**
Power	Too head-light	At twelve o'clock	5–10 grams
Power	OK, but too light	In the throat area	10–20 grams
Power	Too unstable (twisting)	At three and nine o'clock	5–10 grams

examples about how to gain more power. We will refer to the racquet head as a clock face when recommending where to apply the lead tape.

These are only basic recommendations for you to try. Add lead tape until you feel the weight is too great. Then start removing it until you find the best condition for your needs. I highly recommended that you seek professional assistance about customizing your racquet.

CHAPTER 15

Tennis Clubs and Resorts

Today we try to convince people to choose tennis over all other recreational choices.

Much has changed since the tennis boom of the 1970s. The boom created many tennis enthusiasts and along with it an overbuilding of commercial tennis centers. Ultimately, a fallout occurred. The clubs still operating successfully have sound business plans and competent people who have adapted to a changing market.

In the 1970s we had to convince people that spending their discretionary dollars on recreation was worthwhile. Today we have to convince them to choose tennis over all the other recreational choices available. This chapter shows you some of the options available in tennis clubs today.

Program Time Options*

Tennis clubs have a variety of program options from which you can choose. Clubs divide court time into categories, each targeting a different time and day:

- Permanent time
- Leagues and play groups

---

*This section by Steve Contardi, Operating Partner, Club at Harper's Point, Cincinnati, Ohio.

- Teaching programs
- Tournaments
- Parties
- Special events

Programming is also broken down to serve various target groups:

- Daytime women
- Men
- Working women
- Juniors

Permanent Time

Permanent-time sales are still the backbone of clubs that offer upfront prepaid sales. Depending on the climate and market, permanent times are usually sold for a 33- to 38-week season, from mid-September through April or mid-May. Specifically, a group contracts and prepays to play at the same time each week for the entire indoor season.

Some clubs offer a discount, usually 10 percent or free balls, for this commitment, but busier clubs feel this is not necessary because the demand on court time provides enough incentive for members to secure a specific time for the season.

An active club will sell approximately 20 to 30 percent of its total weekly hours with permanent-time contracts, leaving a large portion unsold and up to the imagination and hustle of the club staff.

Leagues and Play Groups

Although tendencies vary from club to club, you usually find leagues and play groups programmed to the second most desirable times:

- 12 noon to 4 P.M. Monday through Friday for the ladies
- 12 noon to 4 P.M. Saturday for the men and career women

Activities should be available for players at all levels. A cardinal rule is to make certain that ability groupings are accurate. Clubs often do this with a club rating system (we suggest the NTRP) to make certain that everyone playing has the proper rating.

Leagues and playgroups can be categorized by degree of competition. Specific play activities, target groups, and suggested times include the following:

1. Interclub Competitive Leagues
   - Highly competitive league play with other clubs
   - Men, women, and mixed
   - All levels
   - Best play times: women—2 to 4 P.M. Monday through Thursday; men and career women—Saturday afternoon and Sunday afternoon; mixed doubles—Friday evening
   - Schedule: Involve all possible clubs in your area; 12- to 14-week schedules with play-offs

2. Interclub Recreational Leagues
   - League play within the club
   - Competitive
   - Men, women, and mixed
   - All levels
   - Best time plays: women—12 noon to 2 P.M. Monday through Friday; men—Saturday afternoon; career women and mixed doubles—Sunday evening
   - Schedule: six teams, two 12-week sessions

3. Round-Robin Leagues
   - Weekly league play directed at those not able to find their own game, new members
   - Socially competitive
   - Women's and men's mixed doubles
   - All levels
   - Best times to schedule: women—8:30 A.M. to 10 A.M. Monday through Friday, 11 A.M. to 1 P.M. Monday through Friday, 9 P.M. to 10:30 P.M. Monday through Thursday; men—9 P.M. to 10:30 P.M. Monday through Thursday; career women—9 P.M. to 10:30 P.M. Monday through Thursday; juniors—5 P.M. to 8 P.M. Saturday
   - Schedule: 8-week intervals

4. Men's Stag Night or Ladies Night
   - Organized doubles play
   - Socially competitive
   - Men (or women)
   - Carefully define abilities (suggest overlapping only two levels)

- Best time to schedule: a slow weekday evening, 8 P.M. to 10:30 P.M.
- Schedule: all year, weekly registration

5. Team Tennis

- Doubles play based on team format
- Competitive
- Adults or juniors
- Suggest two levels of ability, intermediate and advanced
- Format: adults—Sunday evenings; juniors—Sunday afternoons
- Best time to play: adults every other week; juniors weekly

Teaching Program

Although no single element or program is more important than another, the teaching program is certainly the most visible. It is essential that the professional staff of the club be well trained in every phase of teaching, organizing, and communicating.

The role of the teaching program changes somewhat throughout the life cycle of a club. Several basic functions are constant:

- Create new members
- Sell court time
- Serve the membership
- Serve the management

Typical instructional offerings include the following:

- Private lessons
- Instructional clinics
- Drill clinics
- Team practices
- Junior excellence program

Tournaments

Tournaments play an integral role in club programming. Too often, the word *tournament* implies a competition for only the best players. Make certain that your club schedules adult and junior tournaments at all levels.

Adult tournaments can be divided into three levels of competition:

- Club tournaments
- Area NTRP tournaments
- Sanctioned tournaments

Colony Beach and Tennis Resort*

All in the Family

What does it take to become the no. 1 tennis resort in the United States? At the Colony Beach and Tennis Resort, ideally situated on 18 tropical gulf-front acres on beautiful Longboat Key, the answer lies in the word *family.*

"This has been our family's life and business for 30 years," said Colony president Katie Klauber Moulton. "Our family and staff work to create every day a home away from home for our guests—a casual, secluded resort which people look forward to coming back to year after year."

Whether it's the tennis, the magnificent beach and warm waters of the Gulf of Mexico, the exceptional all-suite accommodations, or the other amenities that the Colony offers, it's easy to understand why *Tennis Magazine* has rated the Colony the nation's no. 1 tennis resort for four consecutive years.

Tennis Anyone?

The Colony's owner, Dr. Murray "Murf" Klauber, moved to Longboat Key from Buffalo, New York, in 1969. The reason? "Are you kidding?" he says. "This place is paradise. You won't find another setting as beautiful as this one."

When Murf packed up his family and moved to Sarasota, he took with him a love for tennis and a vision for the resort he wanted to create. "There was one court when we arrived," he remembers. "It wasn't much, but it was a start." In 1970, shortly after his arrival, Murf added five courts and hired his first tennis pro, Gene Nolan.

Murf's passion for the game guided, and still guides, every decision. "I knew if we did this right we could create a unique destination for young people and young families. Every decision I made came back to the question, 'Who's going to come?'"

One of those early decisions remains a hallmark of the Colony tennis program. "With four hours' notice, we will guarantee you a game of tennis at the Colony—the game of your choice. And, if we can't match you with a comparable player, one of the Colony's pros will play with you at no charge," said Murf. "We call it our match-making system, and it was a first among tennis resorts. Also, we have never charged for court time. That's completely against our policy."

Bollettieri at the Colony

The timing of Nick Bollettieri's arrival at the Colony in 1976 was fortuitous. Klauber was looking for someone new to head up his tennis program.

---

*This section by the staff of the Colony Beach and Tennis Resort, Longboat Key, Florida.

Colony Beach and Tennis Resort *(continued)*

"The publisher of *Tennis Magazine* called me and said that he knew I was going to interview Nick Bollettieri and that I should definitely not put Nick on the payroll. A tennis writer for the *Chicago Tribune* simply said, 'Don't hire him.' Then I sat in my office with Nick for one and a half hours, knew he would be my perfect match, and hired him on the spot," said Murf. "I never regretted it."

What qualities did Nick Bollettieri bring to the Colony? "He had tremendous enthusiasm, incredible charisma, impressive knowledge of and commitment to the game, and a staff that could immediately fulfill the needs of our guests," said Murf. "And like me, he never liked to finish second."

Nick's days at the Colony were filled with lessons and clinics for guests. In addition, he started a tennis camp for juniors. In just his third year, he had 30 to 40 youngsters taking part in the program. Among the early students were Jimmy Arias, Carling Bassett, Ril Baxter, Pam Casale, and many more. Though the academy soon outgrew the Colony, the relationship between the Klaubers and Bollettieri remains strong.

Indeed, today Bollettieri is a tennis consultant to the Colony and helps stage exhibitions and other special events, bringing an incredible array of tennis talent to the Colony, including Bobby Riggs, Billy Jean King, Chris Evert, Martina Navratilova, Ilie Nastase, Bjorn Borg, and Boris Becker. It was on the Colony's court no. 1 that Monica Seles played her first match after being stabbed in Germany. There is a lot of tennis history on the Colony courts.

Courtside

Tennis at the Colony is complimentary on all of the resort's 21 championship courts, including 10 soft Hydro courts. Whether you are a beginner or tournament player, the Colony offers a tennis program that matches your ability. Tennis at the Colony is as casual or high-powered as you want it to be.

A team of 10 certified teaching professionals makes instruction both meaningful and enjoyable in private lessons, fast-paced clinics, and training programs for juniors. The Colony offers a complimentary tiny tots program for children under six, introducing them to tennis in an enjoyable fashion.

Clinics and lessons offered at the Colony include private and semiprivate lessons seven days a week from 8:00 a.m. to 6:00 p.m.; personalized clinics; adult beginner clinics focusing on game basics including gripping techniques, stroke production, rules, strategies, and court etiquette; specialty and strategy clinics; junior masters and junior grand masters clinics; and video analysis.

The Colony offers many value packages as well as a variety of superb junior tennis programs to encourage the game's continued growth. These junior programs also offer the opportunity for families to build relationships while they vacation at the Colony.

The Resort

"A tennis resort—a truly superior resort—is more than just tennis," said Katie. "It starts with tennis, with the quality of the pros, and the teaching, but there is much, much more.

"In 1972 we made the decision to convert to an all-suite condominium resort, and I went out and personally sold every unit," said Murf. "We knew we didn't want it to be just another 'brass and glass' hotel. What we were creating was a small village—a home away from home."

The decision to transform the Colony stemmed largely from the family focus of the resort. "When you travel as a family, you need extra room," said Murf. "We want you to feel you're at home. There is no reason why parents and kids can't each have their own space. It's more fun for everybody."

Executives, couples, honeymooners, and families with children all find accommodations to suit their needs. Guests choose from 232 spacious villa suites. All feature comfortable contemporary furnishings, a living room, dining area, balcony, and as many as three bedrooms. Also standard are full kitchens and marble master baths with steam showers and whirlpool baths.

"The Colony guests usually have one of two priorities," said Katie. "Tennis and the amenities or the beach and the amenities. Fortunately, we can offer both."

When it comes to beaches, the Colony is unsurpassed, with 10 miles of sugary, powder-white sand, a balmy climate year-round, and the crystal-clear, warm turquoise waters of the Gulf of Mexico. If golf is your game, the Colony has memberships at eight of Sarasota's premier courses and can arrange a tee time at the course of your choice.

"You can't separate one part of the Colony's experience from the rest," said Katie. "It's a package—from the fabulous food, to the extraordinary fitness programs, to the world-class tennis, to the well-stocked shops, the naturally beautiful environment—it's a total experience and our attention to each of those details has made us no. 1 for four consecutive years."

Amenities

One resort amenity that has been a key to the Colony's success is the Colony Restaurant and its offshoots, the Bistro at the Colony, the Patio, the Monkey Room, and Tastebuds. "The Colony Restaurant is one of Sarasota's highly acclaimed fine dining establishments, having won the coveted Golden Spoon Award for five consecutive years as one of Florida's top 20 restaurants," said Katie. The Colony has also won the DiRoNa Award, is a member of the *Restaurant News* Dining Hall of Fame, and has won the Grand Award from *Wine Spectator* every year.

(continued)

Colony Beach and Tennis Resort *(continued)*

Guests may also enjoy the Colony Bistro for more casual beachside dining or the Patio for lunch and cocktails outdoors. In addition, the resort's gourmet market, Tastebuds, offers a tantalizing selection of gourmet take-out foods that guests can enjoy in the privacy of their suites or as a delectable picnic on the beach.

Another resort amenity is the Colony sports shop. "We have always offered state-of-the-art tennis equipment," says Murf. "We were one of the first pro shops in the country to carry the oversized lightweight racquet and have always been on the sport's cutting edge."

Although tennis is the game of choice at the Colony, the resort has an overall focus on fitness. Since 1972 the Colony has offered massage, steam, and whirlpool in its spa—making it one of the first resorts in the country to offer such amenities.

"Murf has always been into wellness," said Katie. "Our program at the Colony is very life-enhancing and is geared to helping people accomplish their own individual fitness goals. We offer complimentary state-of-the-art exercise equipment and have two to three staff members in the fitness center at all times to assist people. We offer a variety of fitness classes, including aerobics, modern yoga, step, cardio kickboxing, and body sculpting and will work with our guests to help them develop a lifelong healthy approach they can enjoy here and then take home with them."

Being a family, the Colony also puts great emphasis on their Kidding Around programs, designed specifically for kids. "We have always felt that a family vacation is only successful if every member of the family has fun," said Murf. "By placing our focus on the children as well as parents, we can make that happen."

The Colony currently has six full-time staff members to oversee children's programs. "All of our children's supervisors are CPR, water-safety, and first-aid trained. A lot of resorts charge up to $25 per half day; with availability dependent on having a minimum number of kids," said resort manager Jeremy Barker. "Not at the Colony. The children are our complimentary guests and, just like the parents, deserve our best efforts."

Game, Set, and Match

So, ultimately, what is it that sets the Colony apart? Why has *Tennis Magazine* so often honored the Colony as this nation's no. 1 tennis resort?

Many would say it goes back to Murf Klauber. "He can be extremely demanding," said Katie. "He's uncompromising about quality and about our guests." Murf added, "I've always felt everyone should experience first class. It doesn't cost that much more, but it's much more enjoyable."

"I think it boils down to our still being a family-run business, and our family puts its heart and soul into this resort," said Katie. "And by family I don't just mean our physical family. I also mean the members of our staff, who pour their energies year after year into making the Colony the finest resort in the country."

"Quality, service, and the price-value relationship are the cornerstones of the Colony's success," said Katie. "We always want to give people what they want and more. We are in the business of providing extraordinary memories for our guests."

"The reason the Colony is no. 1 is that we've never lost sight of the fact that this is all about having fun," said Murf. "This isn't a drill-sergeant type of tennis camp. We're not here to create players in the Colony image. If you come and have the best vacation you've ever had, we've done our job."

Junior tournaments can be divided into two levels of competition:

- Sanctioned junior tournaments
- Club junior tournaments

Tennis Parties

Historically, Friday and Saturday nights are the prime times to schedule parties at a club.

Many clubs host regularly scheduled club mixed-doubles parties. By combining organized play, rotation, breaks for refreshments, open play, and conversation, the evening can offer everything the club player wants. Clubs may also target the singles group. "Doubles for Singles" parties can be successful activities.

Special Events

Look for the availability of special events when choosing a club. A creative, well-planned special event will cause excitement throughout the membership and promote the growth of tennis.

Special events can take many forms. They may be used as charitable fund-raisers. Pro-ams are always fun and involve players and spectators. This event lends itself to sponsorship and charities.

Specialty clinics using prominent tennis authorities can make the club buzz. Some of the world's top tennis names are often available to make such appearances. I enjoy taking my staff as well as current and former students to clubs to share our knowledge and passion for the game.

Pro legends from the 1960s like Fred Stolle, Roy Emerson, Ken Rosewall, and Marty Riessen are appealing to most club memberships and are available.

Some clubs secure a sponsor and host a four- or eight-man (or woman) tournament using up-and-coming young pros or pros from yesteryear. They plan a two- or three-day event, secure sponsorship, and combine a pro-am, a clinic, and the competition.

Public Tennis Facilities

When we look at the history of sport, when games and sports were two different recreations consumed by two distinct populations, we realize the cultural, social, economic, and political importance of such pastimes in the evolution of society.

Today, more than ever, leisure plays a major role in our daily lives, made possible by such developments as flextime at work and greater discretionary income. By fulfilling its original role of education and social integration, leisure helps people discover themselves and become better human beings and better citizens.

What Is a Public Tennis Facility?*

To understand the role and function of a public tennis facility, we might ask why we need such a facility. Couldn't the private sector promote and develop tennis programs? Why should the taxpayer's money be invested in recreational amenities that benefit a small percentage of the population? Is the county or city in the business of promoting and developing recreational programs?

If we believe that recreational and sports activities contribute to the attainment of educational, health, and social goals and agree that those activities are part of the fabric of our daily life, then we have to say that sports and, in our case, tennis, is a public affair.

Consequently, developing a tennis facility is a question not only of affordability but also of political goals and public demand. Tennis becomes a reality in a community when forces such as local tennis associations, business organizations, and the public in general voice their opinions on the project.

The popularity of tennis and its social and educational effects provide our society a sense of order and stability. Few sports have the international dimension of tennis. Its players are welcomed anywhere in the world. For some people, local availability is a serious factor in making the decision about where to live. Availability has an effect on real estate in communities where tennis is exceptionally popular (Atlanta, Florida, Southern California).

The political machinery to promote and develop a public tennis facility responds to the needs of people to play, learn, and meet. Accessibility is a key. For instance, any good organization managing a public facility will provide

---

*This section by Ivo Barbic, North Fulton Tennis Center, Atlanta, Georgia.

open access to its tennis courts. In other words, courts will always be available for play without a reservation.

In general, the public is interested in promoting and developing the game beyond personal needs. It is motivated by social interest to educate others, to promote the health benefits of the sport, and to develop a stronger community through organized programs. A public tennis facility can be a neutral ground for public officials to meet and use tennis organizations, other associations, and the public in general. The facility is integrated among other businesses by its exterior aspects (building) and internal affairs (management programming). Serving the community with tennis programs and social interactions becomes the primary role of the facility. It is important for the operator of the facility and its landlord (county, city, or recreation department) to understand that the tennis business has the public in mind.

Social Fabric

Tennis as a whole is composed of many small groups or cliques. The clique or group chooses a place to gather, compete, and grow. Motives for joining a group include level of play, social status, and having a similar work place. Players may join a team for league play, because they have a desire to compete, or simply to be part of a tennis movement. When all those motives can be tied together in a convenient, secure, and friendly environment, a facility can become reality. It is then that people relate to a place ("I play at . . ."), but more important they relate to people, participating and sharing the tennis experience in an organized or casual way.

Because that place becomes an important tennis rendezvous within the community, it is important for the operator to meet the challenge of developing the facility as an appealing destination.

From the entrance all the way to the courts, the physical environment should please the eye and make patrons proud of the place. A sense of life through an ambiance of colors and shapes will grab patrons' attention and encourage others to become involved.

Every day the facility's heartbeat should show its strength. Tennis is not an obligation; it is a choice that people make. It is essential to show the breadth of the programs and to demonstrate effort to improve. The first concern should be to listen and to try to satisfy patrons' needs rationally and objectively. Organizing courts to suit different groups through scheduling and programming is essential to creating demand.

In general, people love the feeling of structured programs. For instance, through community tennis associations, players will build their own recreation program that the operator and staff can manage, guide, and promote. It is important that everybody involved feel comfortable and part of the overall tennis experience. Furthermore, because tennis is technical and emotional, the essence of the program should stress a nonjudgmental attitude and encourage universal participation.

Challenge of the Business

What makes a place successful? What makes people want to come and play? How can a tennis center maintain intensity and enthusiasm in its programs?

One of the most important ingredients of a successful place is the image created by the people who participate—its players, teachers, maintenance people, front-desk employees, and the people who come through the door. The perception of the place within the community should meet expectations in terms of facility and programs, but beyond that is something that cannot be measured or sold—the feeling of kindness, attention, and credibility. The operator must promote tennis as a way of life by spending endless hours on the courts, talking to people, participating in tennis events, and sharing the love of tennis with the management team. The challenge of making a business out of a game is met by taking care of people first. We, as operators, should know how to set the stage for players to perform to their best.

Other work places are becoming more anonymous, technical, functional, and, unfortunately, insecure. People are seeking a place where they can fulfill their creativity and discover themselves through emotion and experience. Tennis complements a person's life. It becomes a matter not of winning or losing but of learning to endure adversity, being content, reaching out, and sharing good moments.

With all that in mind, a public tennis facility can accomplish the task of delivering recreation and at the same time expanding people's horizons.

Conclusion

Instructional tennis programs, junior development, social events, and tournaments can develop an outstanding total tennis environment. But to meet the goal of having all participants reach their potential as tennis players, the operator must also consider emotions. The combination of enthusiasm, sensibility, and spirit of participation will ultimately determine the success of the program.

Epilogue:
The Future
of Tennis

If you want to be a top player in the future, you will have to love the grind and work extremely hard to develop physically and mentally.

With four and a half decades to look back on, what can I say about predicting the future of tennis? The boom of the 1970s and 1980s, when tennis came on the scene and its popularity peaked in the United States, it seemed there would be no end to continued growth. However, things change, and when you have endless options—from computers and video games to television and other activities—the interests of today's youth becomes fragmented in so many directions. Children can develop the habits of always following the "path of least resistance," steering away from the difficult challenges, like competing in tennis.

In the 70s and 80s, children were more inclined to play tennis, because their mothers would play at the club, and the children often sat watching. On the weekends, Dad would play with family and eventually the children would "catch the bug" and want to improve. Today with both parents working in many families, and fewer parents having the free time to spend playing tennis, the exposure of tennis to the children has lessened. "Out of sight, out of mind. . . ." The excitement and flair of skateboarding and activities like it has turned many children's heads.

Work ethic is much more difficult to instill today than it was years ago. Sure, there are still the special ones who have it all and are prepared to do what it takes to reach their potential, but they are fewer and farther between. This presents a major concern for me and it should for all families in America. How can we reverse the trend toward childhood obesity, lack of self-esteem, etc. and get the youth of America more involved again in sports? With fewer mandatory physical education courses left in schools, the children need to become more active after school and on weekends.

Research has shown that one of the most productive experiences for young children today is to be involved in early childhood development of motor skills programs. Serving as a basic introduction to both sport and life skills, these programs are confidence and self-esteem builders. Children from three to eight years old are challenged to compete against themselves in tasks that develop skills. They learn how to run, throw, kick a ball, and jump, and at the same time develop a positive outlook to accepting and confronting challenges. Progressing through the developmental levels of these programs, the children develop healthy habits of athletic skills and the desire to express themselves through sport. Tennis ranks up there with some of the most difficult sports to become proficient in. That is why I feel that a strong introduction is necessary to prepare children for the rigors of play. A child with a solid base of motor skill development prior to starting tennis will be much more inclined to stick with it. Years ago, I would not have hesitated to start a child into tennis at four or five years old. Today, I do not recommend it. I am working hard to promote early childhood development programs across the country, which I hope will lead to more growth in tennis.

Another area of concern for me is on the high school level. The USTA and I have just joined forces in the creation of a high school tennis team program to help the many inexperienced coaches in charge. Through a package of instructional materials and videos, we can help strengthen the effort of the coach and improve the development of each player on the team. We are hoping this initiative will build a better base of players in the United States and create more collegiate scholarship players, as well.

Brad Gilbert (Agassi's coach) and Paul Annacone (Sampras' coach) have both said to me many times that for any one player to make it through, you must have good players all around on a daily basis for the head-to-head competition. The strength is in the numbers, to create a top individual.

There is a definite trend that I am seeing in today's top players. These players are bigger and stronger athletes, with fewer weaknesses, if any. They are physically more conditioned and tough, which makes them more difficult to beat mentally. If you want to be a top player in the future, you are going to have to love the grind and work extremely hard to develop physically and mentally.

INDEX

ABOUT THE AUTHOR

Nick Bollettieri is the most well-known and successful tennis coach in the world today, and his training program is recognized as one of the best systems for developing top players. He has trained and coached some of the world's top players including Andre Agassi, Monica Seles, Anna Kournikova, Jim Courier, Tommy Haas, Mary Pierce, and Boris Becker.

Bollettieri has built one of the best training facilities in the world, the Nick Bollettieri Tennis Academy, which he founded in 1977. Today the Bollettieri Tennis Academy covers 190 acres and has grown into the most successful and diversified multi-sport training complex in the world. The success of his academy can be seen in the success of his students.

Bollettieri started out as a club tennis coach in the 1950s and once worked as a private coach for the Rockefeller family while serving as the director of tennis for all Rockefeller-owned hotels and resorts. He founded his first tennis academy, the Port Washington Tennis Academy on Long Island, New York, in 1969.

In 1999 the United States Tennis Association (USTA) named Nick Bollettieri the United States Olympic Committee (USOC) National Coach of the Year. In 1999 he also received the International Tennis Hall of Fame Tennis Education Merit Award. He is a regular contributor to *Tennis, Tennis Life,* and *Florida Tennis* magazines. Nick was listed as number 16 of the 50 most influential people in tennis by *Tennis Magazine*, and as number 19 of 25 people who have influenced tennis in the past century. Bollettieri resides in Bradenton, Florida.

The biggest player in tennis turns out to be a coach.

Congratulations,

Nick Bollettieri,

from your friends at Fila.

Continental Sports Group congratulates Nick Bollettieri on the publication of this work of art.

We have enjoyed our long relationship with Nick. We are proud to support you in fostering superior athletic talent in young adults and wish you continued good luck!

CONTINENTAL SPORTS GROUP

Swiss Army
Brands, Inc.
salutes
Nick Bollettieri
for his lifelong
contribution
and passionate
commitment to
the game of
tennis.

SWISS ARMY BRANDS